Applying Mortgage Knowledge to Exam Preparation

Mortgage Pre-Education Course [v1.2]

TrainingPro

NMLS-Approved Provider ID: 1400013
NMLS-Approved Course Title: 20 Hour_S.A.F.E. Comprehensive Applying Mortgage Knowledge to Exam Preparation
NMLS-Approved Course Number: 1053 (Webinar), 1054 (Live)

Course Content Date: July 24, 2014
Course Approval Date: September 18, 2014

Advanced Education Systems, LLC dba TrainingPro
11350 McCormick Road
Executive Plaza 2, Suite 1000
Hunt Valley, MD 21031

Applying Mortgage Knowledge to Exam Preparation

Page left intentionally blank.

Federal Mortgage-Related Laws

Page left intentionally blank.

FEDERAL MORTGAGE-RELATED LAWS

Learning Objectives

This chapter was created based on the Federal Mortgage-Related Laws section of the NMLS National Test Content Outline. The topics found in this chapter could likely appear on the NMLS national test in multiple choice question format. In this chapter, students will:

- Explore the requirements of the Real Estate Settlement Procedures Act (RESPA), including a look at the current Good Faith Estimate (GFE)

- Understand the history and purpose of the Equal Credit Opportunity Act (ECOA) and its regulations

- Review the current requirements of the Truth-in-Lending Act (TILA) and a brief overview of upcoming changes under the law

- Take a look at the Home Ownership and Equity Protection Act (HOEPA), including prohibited lending terms and practices under the law

- Review the special escrow account requirements and appraisal requirements for higher-priced mortgage loans

- Examine the requirements of the federal S.A.F.E. Act and how it affects mortgage professionals

- Review mortgage industry obligations of additional federal laws including:
  - The Homeowners Protection Act (HPA)
  - The Home Mortgage Disclosure Act (HMDA)
  - The Fair Credit Reporting Act (FCRA)
  - The Fair and Accurate Credit Transactions Act (FACTA)
  - The Federal Trade Commission (FTC) Red Flags Rule
  - The Dodd-Frank Wall Street Reform and Consumer Protection (Dodd-Frank) Act
  - The Mortgage Assistance Relief Services (MARS) Rule
  - The USA PATRIOT Act, including information related to the Bank Secrecy Act (BSA) and the Anti-Money Laundering (AML) Law
  - The Gramm-Leach-Bliley (GLB) Act
  - Privacy protection laws, including Do-Not-Call requirements
  - Mortgage fraud laws

Introduction

Since the early 1970s, the mortgage lending profession has been regulated by an increasing number of federal laws addressing consumer protection. When the mortgage market crashed in 2007, Congress adopted many laws to address perceived weaknesses in existing lending laws and regulations. Included in these legislative efforts was the 2010 Dodd-Frank Wall Street

Reform and Consumer Protection Act (Dodd-Frank Act). In addition to amending federal lending laws, the Dodd-Frank Act authorized the establishment of the Consumer Financial Protection Bureau (CFPB), which is focused first and foremost on protecting consumers in the financial marketplace. With the establishment of this agency, concerns regarding compliance with federal lending laws are greater than ever. There are many laws and rules regulating the business of mortgage professionals, and complying with them is critical to operating a successful business and avoiding the monetary fines and business losses that come with enforcement actions.

Until July 2011, mortgage professionals were subject to regulations issued by the Federal Reserve, the Department of Housing and Urban Development (HUD), and the Federal Trade Commission (FTC). With the exception of some regulatory authority retained by the FTC, the CFPB is now in charge of implementing and enforcing most of the provisions of federal lending laws that relate to protecting consumers while they are shopping for, securing, and paying off mortgages. The CFPB is proving its commitment to carrying out its statutory directives to monitor the compliance of all loan originators with the law, including those affiliated with both depository and non-depository institutions.

> *The Consumer Financial Protection Bureau (CFPB) is in charge of enforcing provisions of federal lending laws related to protecting consumers in the financial marketplace.*

Real Estate Settlement Procedures Act (RESPA/Regulation X – 12 U.S.C. §2601 *et seq.* and 12 C.F.R. §1024.1 *et seq.*)

RESPA Overview

Congress enacted RESPA in 1974 for two purposes:

- To allow consumers to obtain information on the costs of closing so that they can shop for settlement services. RESPA uses mandatory disclosure requirements to ensure that consumers obtain information on closing costs.
- To protect consumers from excessive settlement costs and unearned fees. RESPA establishes prohibited practices to protect consumers from unearned fees.

Regulatory Agency and Regulations

On July 21, 2011, the CFPB replaced the Department of Housing and Urban Development (HUD) as the federal regulatory agency that is responsible for enforcement of RESPA and for issuing implementing regulations. RESPA's regulations are known as **Regulation X** (12 C.F.R. §1024.1 *et seq.*). In January 2013, the CFPB completed rulemaking related to RESPA with the publication of final rules that became effective in January 2014. The CFPB made numerous changes to the existing regulations, including the addition of a new Subpart C to Regulation X. The regulations in this new Subpart address mortgage servicing. One of the most significant changes mandated by the Dodd-Frank Act is the creation of a new disclosure that will replace RESPA's Good Faith Estimate and the Truth-in-Lending Disclosure with new integrated disclosures. Effective August 1, 2015, lenders will be required to use the **Loan Estimate form** in place of the early Truth-in-Lending Statement and the Good Faith Estimate. Lenders will also be required to use the **Closing Disclosure**, to be given in place of the final Truth-in-Lending Disclosure Statement and the HUD-1 Settlement Statement. Until the 2015 effective date, mortgage professionals must use the existing forms.

Loans Covered by RESPA

RESPA applies to "federally-related mortgage loans," which are defined as loans secured by a first or subordinate lien on residential property which are:

- Made with funds insured by the federal government (e.g. FHA loans)

- Made with collateral insured by the federal government (e.g. flood insurance)

- Made with funds from a lender regulated by the federal government (e.g. FDIC or NCUA)

- Intended for sale to Fannie Mae or Freddie Mac

- Made by a creditor regulated under the Truth-in-Lending Act, or

- Transactions involving a federally-related mortgage loan, which includes most loans secured by a lien (first or subordinate position) on residential properties. This includes home purchase loans, refinances, lender-approved assumptions, property improvement loans, equity lines of credit, and reverse mortgages.

With such a broad definition of "federally-related mortgage loans," the requirements of RESPA apply to virtually every home loan secured by a mortgage.

Exempt Loans

RESPA does not apply to:

- Loans for 25 acres or more

- Loans for business, commercial, or agricultural purposes

- Temporary financing, such as bridge loans

- Loans secured by vacant land. A loan is secured by vacant or unimproved property when no proceeds of the loan will be used to construct a one-to-four-family residential structure. If the proceeds will be used to locate a manufactured home or construct a structure within two years from the settlement date, the loan is covered.

- Loan assumptions which are permissible without lender approval

- The sale of a loan into the secondary market

- Loan conversions, when a new note is not required and the provisions are consistent with those of the original mortgage

> *RESPA applies to federally-related mortgage loans. This includes virtually every home loan secured by a mortgage.*

Definition of Terms Related to RESPA

Most of HUD's enforcement actions result from violations of Section 8 of RESPA. There are a number of terms in RESPA that relate to the Section 8 prohibition against giving or receiving a fee, kickback, or "anything of value" pursuant to an "agreement or understanding" for the referral of settlement business. These terms are:

Settlement Services: Borrowers depend on a number of settlement service providers to prepare for closing. Third party services are provided by appraisers, inspectors, credit reporting agencies, title insurers, and loan processors. Settlement services include any service provided in connection with a real estate settlement including, but not limited to, the following: title searches, title examinations, the provision of title certificates, title insurance, services rendered by an attorney, the preparation of documents, property surveys, the rendering of credit reports or appraisals, pest and fungus inspections, services rendered by a real estate agent or broker, the origination of a federally related mortgage loan (including, but not limited to, the taking of loan applications, loan processing, and the underwriting and funding of loans), and the handling of the processing, and closing or settlement.

Things of Value: Includes, but is not limited to, any payment, advance, loan, or service including money, discounts, commissions, salaries, stock, opportunities to participate in a money-making program, special banking terms, tickets to theatre or sporting events, services at special rates, and trips at another's expense.

Agreement or Understanding: A written or verbal agreement or even an agreement established through a practice, pattern, or course of conduct, to offer things of value in exchange for the referral of settlement business.

Fee-Splitting and Kickbacks: The sharing of fees among settlement service providers. No person shall give or accept any split, or percentage of any charge other than for services actually performed.

Markups: A unilateral increase in the cost of a settlement service and retention of the additional fee by the party making the markup. Some federal courts have held that markups do not violate the RESPA rule against fee-splitting if they are not split or otherwise shared with the provider of the settlement service. Others have held that even unilateral markups are illegal. In a February 2012 Supreme Court Case, the Court confirmed that fee-splitting is prohibited only if the fee is actually split. As a result of this decision, a unilateral markup, which occurs when one settlement service provider marks up a fee and pockets the entire overage, is not a violation of RESPA.

Affiliated Business Arrangement: Many service providers have a business relationship and an ownership interest in other settlement service providers. For example, a mortgage company may have an ownership interest in a title company. Profit-sharing by these affiliated companies is permissible under RESPA. However, as discussed in the outline of RESPA disclosures, it is the ownership interest and the potential to realize some profit as a result of that interest which a party making a referral must communicate to a borrower through an "affiliated business arrangement disclosure."

Sham Affiliated Business Arrangement: A partnership or joint venture created between settlement service providers for the illegal purpose of splitting fees under the guise of a bona fide affiliated business arrangement. HUD's "Policy Statement on Sham Controlled Business Arrangements" outlines the factors that are considered in determining whether an affiliated business arrangement is legitimate, and this issue may be one that the CFPB will address in upcoming rulemaking proceedings. In a July 2011 notice in the Federal Register, it was noted that policy statements such as HUD's policy statements *"...will be applied by the CFPB pending further CFPB action"* [1]. Therefore, mortgage professionals should continue to rely on existing HUD policy statements to evaluate compliance with RESPA limitations on affiliated business arrangements.

Borrower Credit: Historically referred to as "yield spread premium" (YSP), the borrower credit is a fee paid to the borrower by the lender when a loan is originated at a higher interest rate than the lowest rate for which the borrower qualifies. The borrower credit is used to subsidize closing costs such as the origination or broker fee so that the loan results in a low- or no-fee transaction.

Closing Cost Disclosures Required by RESPA

There are several mandatory disclosures that are intended to provide consumers with the information that they need to shop for settlement services. These include the Good Faith Estimate, the Settlement Cost Information Booklet, the Mortgage Servicing Disclosure Statement, the Affiliated Business Arrangement Disclosure, and the HUD-1 Settlement Statement.

Good Faith Estimate (12 C.F.R. §1024.7)
Mortgage brokers and lenders must provide the Good Faith Estimate (GFE) at the time of application or mail it within **three business days** after receipt of a loan application. Under RESPA, business days do not include federal holidays, Saturdays, or Sundays (unless Saturday or Sunday is a regular business day). It is important to note that when a broker takes a loan application, regardless of whether a lender has been selected, the broker is responsible for providing the GFE.

In the case of a purchase transaction, the GFE does not have to be provided until a subject property is identified. In this situation, the loan application is considered a pre-qualification until there is a specific subject property.

The GFE includes an estimate of the charges that are due at the time of closing. The fees listed on the GFE include charges to the borrower for loan origination, property appraisal, credit reporting, title insurance, and recording the mortgage. The GFE also includes indirect fees, such as borrower credits, which are not paid directly by the borrower, but are received by mortgage brokers for the benefit of borrowers from lenders.

Fees found on the GFE can be consolidated into four key areas: lender and broker charges, title charges, government charges, and prepaid items and deposits.

Lender and Broker Charges: Lender and broker charges include fees for loan origination, appraisals, credit reports, inspections, mortgage broker services, underwriting, and processing.

Title Charges: Title charges include the costs of the title search, title insurance, and notary fees. Title insurance insurers extend coverage after researching land records to determine if a piece of real estate is free of encumbrances such as mortgages, liens, easements, or other claims.

Government Charges: Municipal and government charges vary between states and municipalities. Generally, they include the cost of recording the mortgage transaction in the public land records. If property is changing hands, the charges may also include a tax for the transfer of real estate from one person to another.

Prepaid Items and Deposits: Prepaid items are paid by the borrower at the time of closing, even though the payments are not due until a point in the future. Pro-rated real estate taxes, homeowner's and flood insurance, private mortgage insurance, and interim interest are among the most common prepaid items.

The key to understanding prepaid items is the idea that interest on a mortgage is always paid in arrears – after it has had a chance to accrue on the balance. This is why the first payment date on a mortgage is typically at least one month after the closing date.

> *Mandatory disclosures required by RESPA include the Good Faith Estimate, the Settlement Cost Information Booklet, the Mortgage Servicing Disclosure Statement, the Affiliated Business Arrangement Disclosure, and the HUD-1 Settlement Statement.*

The GFE

On November 17, 2008, HUD published revisions to Regulation X that were intended to make the GFE a document that consumers can rely on as an accurate estimate of settlement costs. Use of the revised GFE became mandatory on January 1, 2010. However, the CFPB has issued a rule in the Federal Register that includes new integrated disclosures, combining the information currently included in the GFE and the TIL Disclosure. Effective August 1, 2015, lenders will be required to use the **Loan Estimate** form in place of the early Truth-in-Lending Statement (discussed in a subsequent section of the course) and the Good Faith Estimate. A sample form may be found on the CFPB's website [2].

Until the 2015 effective date, lenders must use the existing GFE form. All charges listed on the GFE, other than the interest rate and fees tied to the interest rate, must be available for at least ten business days from the time that the GFE is provided. At the time of settlement, the following charges cannot exceed the charges listed on the GFE:

- The origination charge
- Charges for locking an interest rate, while the rate is locked
- The adjusted origination charge, while the interest rate is locked
- State/local property transfer taxes

At the time of settlement, the total of the following charges cannot exceed the estimated costs listed on the GFE by more than 10%:

- Lender-required settlement services when the lender chooses the settlement service provider
- Lender-required services, title services, and title insurance, when the borrower uses a provider identified by the loan originator
- Government recording charges

Other types of charges can exceed those listed on the GFE. If a loan originator charges a borrower an amount that wrongfully exceeds the amount listed on the GFE, he/she has 30 days after closing to cure the excess charge by reimbursing the excess amount to the borrower. Loan originators can offer a revised GFE, but they must document the reasons for any changes in the charges listed, and they must retain the information on the revisions for at least three years after settlement. Charges that can change on a GFE, requiring revisions, include required services that a borrower can shop for, title services and lender's title insurance, owner's title insurance, initial deposit for the borrower's escrow account, daily interest charges, and homeowner's insurance. These changes can be made at settlement.

Changed Circumstances: If "changed circumstances" lead to an increase in the cost of settlement services or a change in the eligibility of the borrower for the loan terms stated in the GFE, the loan originator may provide a revised GFE to the borrower. Regulations X defines "changed circumstances" to include:

- *Acts of God, war, disaster, or other emergency*
- *Information particular to the borrower or transaction that was relied on in providing the GFE and that changes or is found to be inaccurate after the GFE has been provided. This may include information about the credit quality of the borrower, the amount of the loan, the estimated value of the property, or any other information that was used in providing the GFE*
- *New information particular to the borrower or transaction that was not relied on in providing the GFE; or*
- *Other circumstances that are particular to the borrower or transaction, including boundary disputes, the need for flood insurance, or environmental problems*

(12 C.F.R. §1024.2(b))

If a revised GFE is provided, it must be issued within three business days of the loan originator becoming aware of information that constitutes changed circumstances.

With the GFE due no later than three business days after receipt of a completed loan application, it is important to understand how "loan application" is defined. A loan application has been made when the loan originator has received six pieces of information. The six pieces of information are:

- The borrower's name
- The borrower's monthly income
- The borrower's Social Security number

- The property address
- The estimated value of the property
- The amount of the mortgage loan sought by the borrower

(12 C.F.R. §1024.2(b))

Settlement Cost Booklet or Information Booklet (12 C.F.R. §1024.6)

The Settlement Cost Booklet is due **three business days** after completion of a loan application for a purchase transaction. Loan originators can use their own booklet, or use the CFPB booklet, which:

- Explains the settlement process
- Tells borrowers that they have the right to negotiate the terms of a loan
- Reviews the protections that RESPA creates for borrowers
- Warns borrowers that their use of false information on a loan application can lead to loss of their home, a poor credit rating, and even criminal prosecution for fraud

There is some flexibility in providing the Settlement Cost Booklet. If there are multiple borrowers, such as a husband and wife, only one disclosure is necessary, and it may be provided to any one of the borrowers. The booklet may also be reproduced in any form, stamped with a mortgage professional's contact information and translated into any language. However, it cannot be combined into a larger document with other disclosures.

The CFPB's version of the booklet is available online [3]. The Dodd-Frank Act requires the CFPB to revise the booklet at least once every five years and to draft multiple versions *"...in various languages and cultural styles... so that the booklet is understandable and accessible to homebuyers of different ethnic and cultural backgrounds"* (12 U.S.C. §2604(a)).

There is a difference between booklets offered in home purchase transactions and those offered in transactions for a home equity line of credit (HELOC). The Settlement Cost Booklet is for home purchase transactions. Consumers who are shopping for an open-ended loan, such as a home equity line of credit, must receive an information brochure entitled, "What You Should Know About Home Equity Lines of Credit." This booklet, which was written by the Federal Reserve Board, is also available online [4].

> *The Settlement Cost Information Booklet is due three business days after completion of a loan application for a purchase transaction.*

Mortgage Servicing Disclosure Statement (12 C.F.R. §1024.33(a))

This disclosure requirement applies only to first-lien mortgages. The Mortgage Servicing Disclosure Statement is due **three business days** after completion of the loan application.

The disclosure must be provided by:

- A lender
- A mortgage broker that is table-funding the loan, or
- A dealer in a first-lien loan for the purchase of a manufactured home

The disclosure must state whether the loan servicing can be sold, assigned, or transferred during the life of the loan. Model language for the Servicing Disclosure Statement is available in Appendix MS-1 to Part 1024 of Regulation X.

Servicing rights are bought and sold regularly. A borrower may see the servicing sold several times over the life of a loan. Servicing transfer statements, which are discussed below, ensure that borrowers know that a new loan servicer has their loan.

Affiliated Business Arrangement Disclosure (12 C.F.R. §1024.15(b)(1))
If a settlement service provider refers a loan applicant to an affiliated business for settlement services, he or she must disclose the affiliated business arrangement **at the time of making the referral**. For example, if a loan originator refers a client to a title insurance company in which the loan originator has an ownership interest, disclosure of the ownership interest is required at the same time as the referral. When referrals are made by telephone, borrowers must receive written disclosures within three business days after the call. If the lender requires use of a particular settlement service provider, the disclosure is due at the time of the loan application.

The disclosure must:

- Describe the business arrangement, including the percentage of ownership of the interest of the referring party and service provider
- Indicate that the referral may result in a financial benefit for the referring party
- Estimate the costs that will be charged by the provider to whom the loan applicant is referred
- Advise the borrower that he/she is not required to use the service provider to whom he/she was referred and that other providers are available (Note, however, that lenders can require the use of a particular attorney, appraiser, and credit reporting agency)

Appendix D to Regulation X includes a recommended format for use in disclosing an affiliated business arrangement.

HUD-1 Settlement Statement (HUD-1) (12 C.F.R. §1024.8)
The HUD-1 Settlement Statement is the form used for the itemization of actual costs in a transaction that involves a borrower and a seller. The HUD-1A Settlement Statement discloses the costs of settlement in lending transactions, such as refinancing or closings on second mortgages, which do not involve a seller. Both are subject to the same rules for proper disclosure.

While the GFE provides an estimate of the closing costs, the HUD-1 must show the actual, final dollar amounts for the costs associated with settlement. Both forms have corresponding numbered fields so that a borrower can compare the costs between the two documents.

The HUD-1 or the HUD-1A Settlement Statement is due at the time of closing, but the borrower may request a copy **one business day** prior to settlement. If the borrower or his/her agent is not at the closing, the settlement statement **must be mailed** as soon as practicable after closing.

In addition to the aforementioned Loan Estimate form, the CFPB has also created a new **Closing Disclosure**, which will replace the final Truth-in-Lending Disclosure Statement (discussed in a subsequent section of the course) and the HUD-1 Settlement Statement. A sample form may be found on the CFPB's website [5]. As with the Loan Estimate form, lenders will not begin using the Closing Disclosure until August 1, 2015.

Often, borrowers do not see the HUD-1 Settlement Statement until they arrive at the closing and discover that they must pay more than anticipated for settlement services. Confused by discrepancies between closing costs listed on the GFE and the HUD-1 Settlement Statement, and too frustrated to do anything other than assume the unanticipated costs, few consumers are willing to back away from the closing table to shop for better fees. Reforms to the disclosures by the CFPB are intended to address these concerns.

List of Homeownership Counseling Organizations (12 C.F.R. §1024.20)

Not later than three business days after receipt of a loan application, lenders must provide loan applicants with a written list of counseling organizations that provide counseling services in the loan applicant's area. The list provided must be obtained from the CFPB website or from data that the CFPB or HUD provides for lenders' use in complying with this disclosure requirement. The CFPB and HUD regularly update these lists, and the lists provided to loan applicants may not be more than 30 days old. Mortgage brokers are also allowed to provide this information, but lenders are required to ensure that loan applicants receive the list. There are two exemptions from this disclosure requirement, and they are for transactions involving reverse mortgages and timeshare plans. This is a new disclosure requirement that was created under the Dodd-Frank Act.

Consumer Protections Provided by RESPA after Closing (12 U.S.C. §2605)

RESPA continues to protect consumers after the closings on their mortgage loans take place. The law protects consumers by attempting to ensure that:

- Borrowers know the amount of funds deposited in escrow and by preventing lenders from overcharging borrowers for escrow deposits (12 C.F.R. §1024.17)
- Borrowers know who is servicing their loans (12 C.F.R. §1024.33)

Mandatory Disclosures

The mandatory disclosures that are related to escrow accounts include the Initial Escrow Statement and the Annual Escrow Statement. The **Initial Escrow Statement** is typically given at settlement, however, the lender has **45 days** from settlement to deliver it. Regulation X also prevents loan servicers from overcharging for escrow payments by:

- Requiring escrow account analysis annually
- Limiting the cushion a borrower must maintain to cover escrow disbursements to 1/6 of the estimated total annual disbursements

- Generally, requiring the refund of any surpluses over $50 within 30 days after the completion of the escrow account analysis that reveals a surplus

Since servicing rights for home loans are often sold, Regulation X includes a disclosure requirement that is effective during the full term of a loan that is intended to ensure that borrowers have adequate notice when their loan servicing is transferred to another institution. The disclosure required by this section is the **Notice of Transfer of Servicing Rights**. A model form for this disclosure is found in Appendix MS-2 of Regulation X. The lender or servicer who is transferring the servicing must provide the Notice of Transfer of Servicing Rights at least **15 days** prior to the transfer. The new loan servicer must also provide notice within 15 days after the transfer has occurred and may not assess late fees to a borrower who has made timely payment to the wrong servicer for a period of **60 days** after the transfer. The regulations allow the transferor of the servicing rights and the transferee to send a combined notice that is due 15 days before the effective date of the transfer.

There are three exceptions to the requirement to provide this notice. The notice is not required when the transfer is:

- Between affiliates
- The result of a merger or acquisition, or
- The transfer occurs between master servicers without changing the subservicer

> *Regulation X works to protect consumers by ensuring that borrowers know the amount of funds deposited in escrow accounts, preventing lenders from overcharging borrowers for escrow deposits, and requiring a disclosure when servicing rights are transferred.*

Mortgage Servicing Regulations (12 C.F.R. §1024.30 *et seq.*)

The foreclosure crisis that followed the 2007-2008 collapse of the mortgage market brought attention to some of the problems that consumers experienced with the servicing of their mortgages. The CFPB adopted new regulations in response to findings that many foreclosures may have been avoided had it not been for the inaccurate application of mortgage payments, the difficulties that borrowers had in identifying their loan servicers, and the inability of servicers to complete loan modifications.

The rules apply to all federally-related mortgages, other than open-end home equity plans. As these requirements do not apply directly to loan originators, this course will not review them in detail. However, if a loan originator receives inquiries about loan modifications or refinances from a borrower who is struggling with mortgage payments, the originator should advise the borrower that rules are in place to facilitate negotiations with the servicer that is currently servicing the loan. These new provisions, found in Subpart C of Regulation X, are intended to:

- Ensure timely application of payments received from a borrower
- Facilitate prompt resolution of errors made during the servicing of home loans

- Create strict deadlines that servicers must adhere to in responding to borrowers' requests for information about their loans

- Establish requirements that servicers must meet prior to charging borrowers for force-placed insurance

- Encourage loss mitigation options and early intervention when a delinquency occurs, and

- Facilitate continuity of contact between servicers and borrowers

Record Retention Requirements for RESPA Disclosures

RESPA imposes a five-year record retention requirement on lenders for the following disclosures:

- Mortgage Servicing Disclosure Statement
- HUD-1 or HUD-1A Settlement Statement
- Affiliated Business Arrangement Disclosures

Regulation X states that when selling a loan or transferring the servicing, lenders must include the HUD-1 or HUD-1A Settlement Statement in the loan file. The new owner or servicer must retain the Settlement Statement for a period of five years or until the loan is sold, paid off or its servicing is transferred again.

Lending Practices Prohibited by RESPA

Borrowers depend on a number of settlement service providers to prepare for closing. Mortgage brokers, real estate brokers, attorneys, appraisers, inspectors, credit reporting agencies, notaries, and title insurers are examples of professionals who offer settlement services. As industry partners, it is natural for these settlement service providers to exchange referrals. In fact, consumers rely on those who are in the lending industry to help them find the professionals they need to close a loan.

Section 8(a) of RESPA prohibits anyone from giving or accepting referral fees, kickbacks, or "things of value" unless a commensurate amount of work is performed to earn the fee. Section 8(b) prohibits the splitting of fees in situations in which fees are received for services not actually performed.

Violations of Section 8(a) and Section 8(b) can result in the payment of significant fines and even imprisonment. Therefore, it is important to understand how HUD applies the law to particular facts.

When investigating the practices of settlement service providers, HUD looks for:

- **Exchange of "things of value" for business referrals**: The term includes, but is not limited to, any payment, advance, loan, or service including money, discounts, commissions, salaries, stock, opportunities to participate in a money-making program, special banking terms, tickets to theatre or sporting events, services at special rates, and trips at another's expense

- **Fee-splitting**: Sharing of fees among settlement service providers even though one or both parties fail to perform enough work to earn the fee

- **Unreasonable charges**: Excessive charges (such as double-billing) even when services are performed to earn a fee. RESPA also prohibits charging any fees (other than a credit reporting fee) until the loan applicant has received the GFE.

- **Illegal "agreement or understanding"**: Two parties share a written or verbal agreement or even an agreement established through a practice, pattern, or course of conduct, to offer things of value in exchange for referrals

HUD has tried to facilitate an understanding of its interpretation and enforcement of the law by offering descriptions of factual situations that demonstrate RESPA compliance failures. These descriptions may be found in Appendix B of Regulation X.

> *Violations of Sections 8(a) and 8(b) can result in the payment of significant fines and even imprisonment.*

Sham Affiliated Business Arrangements

In 1996, HUD reported receipt of numerous complaints about the creation of sham affiliated business arrangements. HUD's response was the publication of its "Policy Statement on Sham Controlled Business Arrangements." In its Policy Statement, HUD explained its method of determining whether the party receiving referrals is a "bona fide provider of settlement services" or if the arrangement is a sham. The CFPB has indicated that it intends to continue to enforce HUD's policy statements, so despite the transfer of implementation and enforcement authority from HUD to the CFPB, this policy statement remains relevant.

The ten factors HUD considered, and that the CFPB will now consider, when assessing an affiliated business arrangement for legitimacy, include:

1. Sufficient capital to operate
2. Its own employees
3. Control of its own business affairs
4. A separate office
5. Assumption of the risks and rewards of a comparable enterprise
6. Performance of the services it purports to offer, instead of contracting out the work
7. Agreements to contract out work to an independent third party
8. Proof that it pays an amount that reflects the reasonable value of services performed by a third party
9. Evidence that it competes in the market for business
10. Business interaction with members of the lending industry other than its affiliate

In order to determine whether affiliated businesses are properly limiting their financial gains to the "return of an ownership interest," the CFPB will consider the following factors deemed relevant by HUD, including whether:

- Each owner in the new entity has made an investment of his/her own capital
- Each owner's interest in the business is based on the amount he/she/it invested
- The owners receive financial awards from the new entity based on the amount they invested or based on the number of business referrals
- Ownership interest is adjusted, based on the number of business referrals [6]

Markups and Borrower Credit

Sham affiliated business arrangements have been a focus of RESPA enforcement actions. However, there are two additional practices that have resulted in years of legal challenge and unresolved controversy.

These practices are:

- Earning compensation from **markups**
- Earning compensation from borrower credit

Both practices have been subject to the challenge that they violate Section 8 prohibitions of RESPA and result in unearned compensation.

Earning Compensation from Markups

The issue of markups has led to extensive litigation and to disagreement among courts in different jurisdictions. A "markup" is a unilateral increase by a settlement service provider of a charge for a service that was completed by another provider. The markup of the charge is made for the purpose of collecting and retaining an additional fee. For example, in one case disputing the legality of a markup, a mortgage banker marked up the fees charged by a courier and retained the difference between the actual cost of the courier's service and the markup.

Some federal courts have held that markups do not violate the RESPA rule against fee-splitting because they do not involve the actual splitting or sharing of a fee between settlement service providers. Other courts have deferred to HUD's interpretation of markups as a violation of Section 8 of RESPA. As noted in the section of this course that defined the term "markup," in a February 2012 Supreme Court Case, the Court confirmed that fee-splitting is prohibited only if the fee is actually split. It is important to note, however, that some states maintain a strict prohibition on markups.

The Controversy over Borrower Credit

The topic of borrower credit is an important consideration when generating the Good Faith Estimate and effectively communicating costs and fees associated with a loan to a borrower. The borrower credit has historically been known by the industry term "yield spread premium," or YSP. The fee is calculated by determining the difference between the best rate for which a borrower qualifies and the interest rate the borrower accepts. The fee was controversial because some mortgage brokers placed borrowers in loans with rates higher than which they qualified in order to pocket larger commissions from the lenders that funded the loans. As a result of rules adopted by the Federal Reserve in 2010, this practice is illegal, and YSPs may only be used to help borrowers cover settlement costs. Now, borrowers can finance closing costs and reduce the out-of-pocket cash needed at closing.

Page two of the GFE includes a block of information called "Your Adjusted Settlement Charges" and includes three options for disclosing the interest rate and coverage of settlement costs. When a borrower credit fee is involved in a transaction, mortgage brokers must disclose to the borrower that he/she will *"...receive a credit of $_____ for this interest rate of _____%"* and that this credit *"...**reduces** your [out of pocket] settlement charges."* This disclosure is intended to ensure that borrowers receive a benefit from accepting a loan at a higher rate of interest than a lower rate for which they may qualify.

Understanding your estimated settlement charges

Your Adjusted Origination Charges		
1. **Our origination charge** This charge is for getting this loan for you.		
2. **Your credit or charge (points) for the specific interest rate chosen** ☐ The credit or charge for the interest rate of [____] % is included in "Our origination charge." (See item 1 above.) ☐ You receive a credit of $ [____] for this interest rate of [____] %. This credit **reduces** your settlement charges. ☐ You pay a charge of $ [____] for this interest rate of [____] %. This charge (points) **increases** your total settlement charges. The tradeoff table on page 3 shows that you can change your total settlement charges by choosing a different interest rate for this loan.		
A Your Adjusted Origination Charges		$

> The borrower credit, known as the *"yield spread premium,"* or *YSP, is used to help borrowers cover settlement costs and reduce out-of-pocket cash needed at closing.*

Penalties for Violations of RESPA and Regulation X

Violations of Section 8, which prohibits kickbacks, referrals, and fee-splitting, are subject to RESPA's most severe penalties including fines of up to $10,000 and one year in prison.

Section 6 of RESPA addresses loan servicing and allows consumers to file individual or class actions against loan servicers for RESPA violations. In individual actions, loan servicers may be liable for damages. If a pattern or practice of noncompliance with the servicing requirements of RESPA exists, the loan servicer can be liable for additional penalties of up to $1,000. In class actions, damages may not exceed $1,000 for each member of the class, and total damages may not exceed $500,000 or 1% of the net worth of the servicer.

Failure to submit an initial or annual escrow statement in compliance with Section 10 of Regulation X can result in a civil penalty of $75, with a limitation of $130,000 on the penalty imposed on one servicer for violations occurring within a consecutive 12-month period. However, if a loan servicer intentionally disregards the requirements of Section 10, penalties are $110 for each violation, with no limit on the total amount of the penalty.

RESPA Reform

The primary goals of RESPA are to provide consumers with adequate information to shop effectively for settlement services and to protect consumers from excessive settlement costs. In spite of these goals, settlement costs have increased steadily since the 1974 enactment of the law. With Americans paying more than $55 billion to complete real estate closings each year, many critics argue that RESPA has failed to control these costs.

For close to a decade, regulators, mortgage professionals, consumer interest groups, and legislators have dedicated countless hours to reforming RESPA to ensure that it provides consumers with the protections that it was intended to give to them in mortgage lending transactions.

Reforms Made by HUD

In November 2008, HUD published a rule that included a new GFE and a revised HUD-1 Settlement Statement. Use of the forms that resulted from this rulemaking effort began on January 1, 2010.

Following is a summary of the information found on these forms:

- The GFE is a three-page document that features an instructional page aimed at helping borrowers understand their loan offer. Information that should be apparent to borrowers includes:

  ◦ What is the term of the loan?

  ◦ Is the interest rate fixed?

  ◦ Is there a prepayment penalty?

  ◦ Is there a balloon payment?

  ◦ What are the closing costs?

- A page on the HUD-1 Settlement Statement which corresponds with the GFE

- Yield spread premiums must be clearly disclosed as a credit to the borrower. The GFE and HUD-1 include an area for disclosure if a premium is earned by the broker in conjunction with the loan transaction.

- Verification of information on the loan application cannot proceed until the applicant has given the loan originator the go-ahead. This is intended to ensure the consumer has had time to shop, following receipt of the GFE.

- Lenders and settlement service providers have 30 days from the date of closing to correct any errors or violations of RESPA's disclosure and tolerance requirements. This includes repayment of any overcharges to consumers.

The CFPB carried on the work done by HUD and began working on additional improvements to the GFE and the HUD-1, even before the CFPB was officially open for business. The CFPB's primary goals related to these rulemaking efforts were to eliminate the "overlapping information" found in separate RESPA and TILA disclosures, to make the disclosure more understandable, and to fulfill the mandate, issued by Congress through the Dodd-Frank Act, to *"...publish a single, integrated disclosure for mortgage loan transactions (including real estate settlement costs)..."* (15 U.S.C. §1604(b)). This rulemaking, which included industry input and consumer testing of model forms, culminated in the CFPB's publication of a new Loan Estimate Disclosure and a new Closing Disclosure in November 2013. Use of these forms will become mandatory in August 2015.

Along with the new disclosure forms, the CFPB published a new set of regulations for completing the forms. These new regulations are referred to in the Preamble to the rule as the "Title XIV Disclosures" since they are mandated in Title XIV of the Dodd-Frank Act. These new disclosure rules impose requirements for:

- A warning regarding the presence of negative amortization features
- Disclosure of state law anti-deficiency protections
- A description of the creditor's partial payment policy
- Disclosure of mandatory escrow or impound accounts
- Disclosure, before a loan is consummated, regarding waiver of escrow in connection with the transaction
- Disclosure regarding cancellation of escrow after consummation
- Monthly payment disclosure for ARMs, including escrow, at both the introductory and fully-indexed rates
- Repayment analysis disclosure showing the amount escrowed for taxes and insurance
- Disclosure of the aggregate amount of settlement charges, including:
  - The amount of charges included in the loan
  - The amount the consumer must pay at closing
  - The approximate amount of the wholesale rate of funds
  - The aggregate amount of other fees related to the loan
- Disclosure of the aggregate of mortgage loan originator fees, showing amounts paid by the consumer and the creditor
- Disclosure of total interest as a percentage of the principal
- Optional disclosure of appraisal management company fees
- Disclosure regarding notice of the reset of a hybrid adjustable-rate mortgage
- The loan originator identifier requirement
- Consumer notification regarding appraisals for higher-risk mortgages, and
- Consumer notification regarding the right to receive a copy of the appraisal

Neither these new rules nor the new model forms for the Loan Estimate Disclosure and the Closing Disclosure are located in Regulation X. With the integration of these RESPA and TILA disclosure requirements, the new rules are located in TILA's Regulation Z, under sections 1026.19, 1026.37, and 1026.38.

> *Use of the new Loan Estimate and Closing Disclosure forms will be mandatory in August 2015.*

Equal Credit Opportunity Act (ECOA/Regulation B – 15 U.S.C. §1691 *et seq.* and 12 C.F.R. §1002.1 *et seq.*)

ECOA Overview

In 1974, Congress enacted the Equal Credit Opportunity Act (ECOA) to eliminate discriminatory treatment of credit applicants. The primary reason for the enactment of ECOA was anecdotal evidence that women were not treated on an equal basis with men when applying for credit, including their applications for mortgages.

ECOA and its regulations are intended to promote the availability of credit to all creditworthy applicants regardless of race, color, religion, national origin, sex, marital status, or age. The law also prohibits credit decisions being based on the fact that the applicant has income from a public assistance program, or that the applicant has exercised his or her rights under the Consumer Credit Protection Act (e.g. participation in a consumer credit counseling program).

ECOA addresses specific discriminatory practices such as **"redlining,"** which occurs when creditors refuse to make loans in certain neighborhoods due to the personal characteristics of the residents, and the more recent practice of **"reverse redlining,"** which first occurred during the lending boom when predatory lenders targeted neighborhoods with elderly, immigrant, and minority populations to make risky loans that included oppressive lending terms.

Regulatory Agency and Regulations
Before the creation of the CFPB, the Board of Governors of the Federal Reserve was the agency that issued regulations for the implementation of ECOA. These regulations are known as **Regulation B** (12 C.F.R. §1002.1 *et seq*). Until July 2011, the enforcement of ECOA was shared by the federal banking agencies, but the CFPB is now the agency that has authority to enforce the law and regulations. As directed by the Dodd-Frank Act, the CFPB has established an Office of Fair Lending and Equal Opportunity that is directly responsible for enforcing ECOA and the Fair Housing Act. Although the CFPB is the agency that is primarily responsible for implementing and enforcing ECOA, the FTC retains some of the authority that it historically held for enforcing the compliance of non-depository lenders, mortgage brokers, and mortgage loan originators with ECOA.

Loans Covered by ECOA

ECOA applies to transactions for the extension of credit by any person who regularly extends, renews or continues credit. The law also applies to a person who *"...regularly refers applicants to creditors, or selects or offers to select creditors to whom requests for credit can be made."*

Mortgage brokers serve primarily as a liaison between borrowers and lenders by referring applicants to select lenders or by offering borrowers a variety of loan products from a number of lending institutions. Therefore, the definition of creditor applies to mortgage brokers, and is not limited to lenders or mortgage bankers who actually extend credit.

Unlike RESPA and TILA, ECOA applies to extensions of credit for business, commercial, and agricultural use.

> *ECOA and its regulations are intended to promote the availability of credit to all creditworthy applicants regardless of race, color, religion, national origin, sex, marital status, or age.*

Definition of Terms Related to ECOA (12 C.F.R. §1002.2)

Adverse Action: (i) A refusal to grant credit in substantially the amount or on substantially the terms requested in an application unless the creditor makes a counteroffer (to grant credit in a different amount or on other terms) and the applicant uses or expressly accepts the credit offered; (ii) A termination of an account or an unfavorable change in the terms of an account that does not affect all or substantially all of a class of the creditor's accounts; or (iii) A refusal to increase the amount of credit available to an applicant who has made an application for an increase.

Discriminate: To treat an applicant less favorably than other applicants.

Discouragement: An oral or written statement, communicated to applicants in advertising or by any other means that discourages an applicant from applying for credit on a prohibited basis.

Prohibited Basis: Prohibited basis means race, color, religion, national origin, sex, marital status, or age (provided that the applicant has the capacity to enter into a binding contract); the fact that all or part of the applicant's income derives from any public assistance program; or the fact that the applicant has in good faith exercised any right under the Consumer Credit Protection Act or any state law upon which an exemption has been granted by the CFPB.

Self-Testing: Any program or study conducted by a creditor that is designed to evaluate the creditor's compliance with ECOA and Regulation B.

Tester: An individual who poses as a loan applicant to test a creditor's fair lending policies and practices.

Corrective Action: Action that a creditor must take if a self-test shows that "it is more likely than not" that a violation of ECOA has occurred. The action must include identification of the policies and practices that led to the violation, and an assessment of the scope of the violation. If corrective action is adequate to remedy possible violations, the information and data obtained during the self-test is privileged. Taking corrective action is not an admission that a violation occurred.

Disclosures and Notifications Required by ECOA

Notice of Action Taken: Within **30 days** of receipt of a loan or credit application, lenders must notify consumers in writing of action taken. If the creditor takes *adverse action* on the application, the notice must provide a statement of the reasons for the unfavorable decision, and must include a statement that ECOA prohibits discrimination against credit applicants. This notice must also include the name and address of the creditor and the name of the agency that enforces the lender's compliance with the law. A description of the credit is also provided on the notice and, if the adverse action was based on data from a consumer credit report, information on the credit reporting agency must also be included (12 C.F.R. §1002.9(a)).

Notice of Incomplete Application: Within **30 days** of receipt of an application that lacks information that the applicant can provide, the creditor must provide a Notice of Action or a Notice of Incompleteness. A Notice of Incompleteness must state the information needed, set a reasonable time for submission of the information, and advise the applicant that failure to provide the information will result in no further consideration of the application (12 C.F.R. §1002.9(c)).

Valuation Disclosures: Effective January 18, 2014, creditors are required to give loan applicants a copy of all appraisals and other written valuations developed in connection with an application for credit that is to be secured by a first lien on a dwelling. The appraisal or other valuation must be provided promptly upon completion or three business days prior to consummation, whichever is earlier.

The regulations allow applicants to waive the timing requirement and to agree, instead, to receive a copy of the appraisal before consummation. However, when applicants exercise their right to waive the timing requirement, they must obtain the waiver at least three business days prior to consummation (12 C.F.R. §1002.14(a)).

Disclosures Regarding Monitoring Programs: While ECOA establishes prohibited bases that may not be considered when granting credit, the law does make an exception for demographic information gathered for government monitoring programs. The Home Mortgage Disclosure Act is one law which requires compliance with government monitoring. Providing information about a prohibited category such as race or sex is voluntary on the part of a loan applicant.

When obtaining information on race, ethnicity, sex, marital status, and age for monitoring purposes, creditors must advise applicants that the information is requested by the federal government for monitoring purposes and that the creditor must provide information on ethnicity, race, and sex, and will provide the information to the government based on visual observation if the applicant refuses to provide it (12 C.F.R. §1002.12(c)).

> *Notices and disclosures required by ECOA include Notice of Action Taken, Notice of Incomplete Application, copies of all appraisals and valuations, and disclosures regarding monitoring programs.*

Lending Practices Prohibited by ECOA

In order to prevent discrimination in the extension of credit, ECOA prohibits lenders from discriminating against an applicant on a prohibited basis regarding any aspect of a credit transaction.

In relation to information relied on in making a credit decision, lenders may not ask questions regarding:

- Marital status (permissible inquiries for government monitoring may only use the categories "married," "unmarried," or "separated")
- Sex of the applicant
- Bearing and rearing of children
- Race or color
- Religion
- National origin
- Age (unless the loan applicant is too young to enter into a contract)
- The exercise of rights under the Consumer Credit Protection Act
- Receipt of income from a public assistance program, although creditors may inquire about public assistance income in order to determine *"...the amount and probable continuance of income levels, credit history, or other pertinent element of creditworthiness..."* (15 U.S.C. §1691(b)(2))

Federal legislation has been introduced to make it unlawful to discriminate on the basis of sexual orientation and gender identity, but has not yet passed. Numerous states have enacted laws that extend protection on this basis, and creditors must ensure that they comply with such laws.

Lenders may not make oral or written statements that would discourage prospective credit applicants from applying for a loan. This prohibition also applies to advertisements using statements and images that are intended to discourage members of a protected class from applying for credit while encouraging others to do so (12 C.F.R. §1002.4(b)).

In addition, lenders may not:

- Refuse to consider public assistance as income
- Assume a woman of childbearing age will stop work to raise children

- Refuse to consider income from a pension, annuity, or retirement benefit
- Refuse to consider regular alimony or child support (although borrowers are not required to disclose alimony and child support unless it is used as qualifying income)

(12 C.F.R. §1002.6(b))

The CFPB began formally accepting complaints from consumers about mortgage transactions in December 2011. The online complaint form includes an optional question: "Do you believe the issue involves discrimination?" With a special department in place to address fair lending matters, the CFPB is equipped to address claims involving allegations of discrimination.

Exceptions

There are very few exceptions to ECOA's prohibitions against unlawful inquiries concerning the personal characteristics of credit applicants. Two notable exceptions include:

- Inquiries regarding race, ethnicity, sex, marital status, and age are required for purposes of federal programs that monitor compliance with fair lending laws, such as the Home Mortgage Disclosure Act (HMDA) (12 C.F.R. §1002.13)
- Creditors may obtain information about an applicant's protected characteristics in order to determine the applicant's eligibility for special-purpose credit such as a credit assistance program offered by a non-profit organization or for a federal or state program to assist the economically disadvantaged (12 C.F.R. §1002.8(c))

Loan originators may inquire if the borrower wishes to voluntarily provide information on personal characteristics for purposes of completing HMDA forms or for determining the borrower's eligibility for credit assistance. If the borrower does not want to provide such information, the loan originator must use his/her best judgment to guess.

Penalties for Violations of ECOA

Violations can result in civil penalties of $5,000 per day for violations of ECOA or Regulation B. Where a pattern of misconduct exists, penalties of $25,000 are permitted. Violations of ECOA can also lead to punitive damages for non-governmental entities.

Punitive damages are limited to $10,000 in individual actions and to the lesser of $500,000 or 1% of the creditor's net worth in class actions. Costs and attorney's fees may also be awarded (12 C.F.R. §1002.16(b)). The statute of limitations for a civil action for an ECOA violation is **five years**, and the five-year period is measured from the date the violation occurred (12 C.F.R. §1002.16(b)(2)). However, if the Attorney General or an agency such as the CFPB or FTC brings an action for an ECOA violation, an applicant who has suffered discrimination must bring his/her action no later than one year after the commencement of the Attorney General or agency action (15 U.S.C. §1691e(f)((2)).

Discussion Scenario: Equal Credit Opportunity Act and Redlining

The United States Department of Justice (DOJ) entered into a consent decree with Big Bux Mortgage Lender after charging Big Bux with multiple violations of the Equal Credit Opportunity Act.

Big Bux Mortgage Lender is a mortgage lender headquartered in a large metropolitan area of a mid-west state. Big Bux is primarily a residential real estate and small business lender, and has been one of the area's largest volume lenders in each category for many years.

DOJ claimed that Big Bux avoided doing business in a large number of minority census tracts in the area that it served. The complaint alleged that the lender's policies and practices denied minority residents an equal opportunity to obtain financing because of their race and ethnicity. As a result, hundreds of potential African American and Hispanic borrowers were denied loans.

The case also alleged:

- In operating and extending its business, Big Bux acted to meet the credit needs of predominantly white residential areas while avoiding the majority minority neighborhoods.
- Big Bux had a pattern of acquiring branch offices outside of African American and Hispanic communities. In one particular year, Big Bux opened 20 branch offices throughout the metropolitan area, but none in a majority minority census tract.
- None of the branches in the minority census tracts offered the full range of lending services available at Big Bux's full-service branches located in white suburban communities.
- Big Bux unlawfully considered race and national origin in its business practices by marketing and advertising only to a general audience, despite the existence of minority format radio and newspaper.
- During a four-year period, only 4.8% of the residential loan applications Big Bux generated were secured by property located in majority minority census tracts – in an area in which 38% of the census tracts are majority minority tracts.

Big Bux Mortgage Lender denied the DOJ's allegations and claimed it never deliberately discriminated against any individuals, groups, or areas based on race or national origin. However, it freely entered into a consent decree with the United States. The decree included a number of provisions including a nondiscrimination injunction prohibiting Big Bux and its agents from engaging in discriminatory acts. The decree forced Big Bux to take reasonable steps to ensure that all credit offers are made available and marketed in the minority census tracts throughout the metropolitan area.

The decree also required Big Bux to open additional full-service branch offices located in the designated areas that provide the same range of services typically offered at its full-service branches in suburban areas. Finally, Big Bux was required to train employees regarding ECOA statutes and the Fair Housing Act.

Discussion Questions

- *What are some steps mortgage loan originators can take to ensure they are not engaging in discriminatory practices?*
- *What should a mortgage loan originator do if he/she feels that a potential loan applicant has no way of qualifying for a loan? Is it ever ok to refuse an application?*

Discussion Feedback

ECOA prohibits creditors from discriminating in any aspect of a credit transaction on the basis of race, color, religion, national origin, sex, marital status, age, because the credit applicant receives income from a public assistance program, or because the credit applicant has exercised rights under the Consumer Credit Protection Act.

The provisions in the consent decree illustrate the DOJ's commitment to enforcing fair lending practices and protecting borrowers' rights. Through this and similar lawsuits, the DOJ enforces the idea that all Americans have the right to purchase homes and to borrow that money free of illegal discrimination.

Mortgage professionals can ensure their origination and lending practices are compliant by:

- Putting business policies and procedures in place which ensure discrimination does not occur during the loan origination or underwriting processes
- Ensuring their advertising campaigns are inclusive of their service area and appropriately communicate a commitment to non-discriminatory practices
- Accepting applications from potential borrowers without regard to any of the protected categories and only discussing with a borrower the factors that have relevance to creditworthiness (i.e. income, assets, credit history, etc.). Remember that it's the lender's determination to extend or deny credit; loan originators cannot refuse to accept a loan application.

Truth-in-Lending Act (TILA/Regulation Z – 15 U.S.C. §1601 *et seq.* and 12 C.F.R. §1026.1 *et seq.*)

TILA Overview

Congress enacted the Truth-in-Lending Act (TILA) in 1968 as Title I of the Consumer Credit Protection Act (CCPA). The ultimate goal of the CCPA was to promote the informed use of credit by consumers. TILA was the first law in which the federal government adopted disclosure requirements as a means of protecting consumers from unfair treatment by creditors. The primary goals of TILA are to:

- Protect consumers by disclosing the costs and terms of credit
- Create uniform standards for stating the cost of credit, thereby encouraging consumers to compare the costs of loans offered by different creditors
- Ensure that advertising for credit is truthful and not misleading
- Provide borrowers with the right to rescind certain types of mortgage transaction

TILA has been amended many times since its enactment. TILA's most recent amendments were made when Congress adopted the Dodd-Frank Act. Title XIV of the Dodd-Frank Act, referred to in the law as the "Mortgage Reform and Anti-Predatory Lending Act," creates many new provisions under TILA, and the effective date for most of these provisions was January 2014. The last amendments to become effective are those that relate to disclosures made at the beginning of a mortgage transaction and those made at the time of closing, and the regulations that implement these changes have an effective date of August 1, 2015.

> *The Truth-in-Lending Act (TILA) was enacted as part of the Consumer Credit Protection Act (CCPA) to promote the informed use of credit by borrowers.*

Regulatory Agencies and Regulations

The regulations issued pursuant to TILA are known as **Regulation Z** (12 C.F.R. §1026.1 *et seq.*). Before the creation of the CFPB, the Board of Governors of the Federal Reserve (the Board) was responsible for writing TILA's implementing regulations, and the Board and the federal bank regulatory agencies enforced them. Now, the CFPB is primarily responsible for implementing and enforcing TILA and Regulation Z.

When the transfer of authority to the CFPB occurred in July 2011, the CFPB immediately began formal rulemaking proceedings to implement the changes to TILA that were dictated by the Dodd-Frank Act. Although the Federal Trade Commission (FTC) and the federal bank regulatory agencies do retain some supervisory and enforcement authority, these agencies and the CFPB have entered Memoranda of Understanding to address the allocation of supervisory authority.

Loans Covered by TILA (12 C.F.R. §§1026.2(c), 1026.3)

TILA applies to all credit transactions which meet the following four conditions:

- The credit is offered to consumers
- The offer or extension of credit is made regularly
- The credit includes a finance charge or a written agreement stating that the loan may be repaid in more than four installments
- The credit is primarily for personal, family, or household purposes

TILA does not apply to the following types of credit transactions:

- Transactions for business, agricultural, or organizational credit
- Credit in excess of a threshold amount that is adjusted annually. These amounts have ranged from $25,000 in 2011 to $53,000, which was the threshold amount from January 1, 2013 through December 31, 2013. The threshold does not apply in transactions that are secured by real property or a dwelling, but if the creditor later uses the borrower's dwelling to secure the loan, it becomes necessary to comply with TILA.
- Public utility credit
- Credit extended by a broker registered with the Securities and Exchange Commission or the Commodity Futures Trading Commission

- Home fuel budget plans
- Student loans, or
- Employment-sponsored retirement plans

The loans that are covered by TILA are subject to two sets of rules: those for open-end credit and those for closed-end credit.

While differences in Regulation Z's rules for closed-end and open-end credit may be minor at times, it is important to note the distinction in order to fully comply with the law:

- **Closed-end loans**: In a closed-end transaction, a lender disburses all of the funds at closing and demands repayment within a specified period of time. During the repayment period, borrowers may not receive an increase in the principal amount of the loan. A loan to purchase a home and a mortgage refinancing to secure a lower interest rate are examples of closed-end loans that are subject to the provisions of TILA and Regulation Z.

- **Open-end loans**: The primary characteristic of an open-end loan is that both the borrower and the lender anticipate repeat transactions. In an open-end transaction, a lender gives the borrower a limit on the amount of funds that he/she can withdraw, and the borrower can request a cash advance in any amount. The borrower may have the option of requesting an increase in the credit amount. Payments depend on the interest due on the amount withdrawn.

Creditors Regulated by TILA (12 C.F.R. §1026.2(a))

TILA regulates "creditors," defining them as natural persons or business and financial organizations that do all of the following:

- Regularly extend consumer credit
- Make the credit subject to a finance charge or make the credit payable under the terms of a written agreement that requires repayment in more than four installments
- Receive the initial payments on the debt that the borrower assumes in the lending transaction

A person **"regularly extends consumer credit"** if:

- The credit is secured by a dwelling and is extended more than five times in the preceding calendar year
- The credit is secured by a dwelling and, in any 12-month period, the creditor originates more than one credit extension that is a high-cost mortgage regulated under HOEPA, or
- The credit is secured by a dwelling and, in any 12-month period, the creditor originates one or more high-cost mortgages regulated under HOEPA through a mortgage broker

(12 C.F.R. §1026.2(a)(17)(v))

Definitions Relating to TILA

The Truth-in-Lending Act has a vocabulary of its own, and knowing these terns is essential to understanding the law's requirements. Following are concise definitions of some of the terms most frequently used in TILA and its implementing regulations.

These terms will be addressed in greater detail throughout the course.

- **Finance charge**: The cost of credit expressed as a dollar amount
- **Prepaid finance charge**: Any finance charge paid before or at the time of consummation
- **Annual percentage rate (APR)**: The cost of credit expressed as a percentage
- **Closed-end credit**: Credit that is extended in a lump sum at one time, such as a traditional mortgage loan for a home purchase
- **Open-end credit**: Credit that may be accessed in a revolving manner, such as a credit card. Home Equity Lines of Credit (HELOCs) are a common example in the mortgage industry.
- **Creditor**: An individual or entity, such as a depository lender, that extends closed-end or open-end credit and imposes a finance charge
- **Truth-in-Lending (TIL) Disclosure Statement**: The primary disclosure required by TILA
- **Customer Handbook on Adjustable-Rate Mortgages (CHARM) Booklet**: A disclosure booklet used to educate consumers on the risks associated with adjustable-rate mortgages
- **Trigger terms**: Terms used in advertising that trigger an obligation to provide specific information regarding the cost and terms of a loan product

TILA defines "creditors" as individuals or entities that regularly extend closed-end or open-end credit and impose finance charges.

Stating the Cost of Credit

One of the primary goals of TILA is the establishment of uniform standards for stating the cost of credit. Use of the same standard is intended to help consumers to compare the costs of loans offered by competing creditors. The two uniform standards created by TILA are:

- **The finance charge**: Regulation Z defines **"finance charge"** as the cost of credit as a dollar amount (12 C.F.R. §1026.4(a)). The calculation of a loan's finance charge is a process that involves determining which of the many fees associated with a loan's origination and closing are included in the charge.
- **The annual percentage rate**: The CFPB describes the APR as *"...a measure of the cost of credit, expressed as a nominal yearly rate. It relates the amount and timing of value received by the consumer to the amount and timing of payments made"* [7].

Both of these standards include not only the interest charged for a loan, but the additional costs of completing a lending transaction. It should be noted that loan originators cannot charge any fees, other than a reasonable cost for obtaining a credit report, prior to providing these disclosures to a potential borrower. The calculation of the finance charge and APR for home loans is discussed below.

Determining Finance Charges (12 C.F.R. §1026.4)

The primary challenge in calculating the finance charge is determining which fees are included and which are not. There are two basic rules for determining whether a fee is included in the calculation of the finance charge:

- **The finance charge does not include**: Any fees of the type that are payable in a comparable cash transaction, such as taxes.

- **The finance charge does include**: Fees paid to third parties if the creditor requires the use of a particular third party or retains a portion of the third party charge. This is particularly important in mortgage transactions because third party settlement service providers generate many of the fees.

Regulation Z also creates two additional rules related to the calculation of finance charges, referring to each as a "*Special Rule.*" These include the following rules related to closing agent and mortgage broker fees:

- **Closing agent charges**: Fees charged by the closing agent are included in the finance charge if the creditor requires these services, requires a charge for these services, or retains a portion of the charge. If the creditor retains a potion of the charges, the finance charge should reflect only the portion of the fee that the creditor keeps (12 C.F.R. §1026.4(a)(2)).

- **Mortgage broker fees**: A mortgage broker's fees are always included in the finance charge, even if the lender does not require the use of the broker's services and does not retain a portion of the charge (12 C.F.R. §1026.4(a)(3)).

The CFPB website contains a chart that is helpful in identifying charges that are included and those that are excluded from the finance charge [8]. A copy of this chart may be found below. The columns that list conditional charges show that, generally, optional charges such as charges for insurance policies and debt cancellation plans are excluded if the consumer voluntarily purchases and pays monthly premiums for these products after receiving the disclosures that are related to their purchase. If the choice of these products is not voluntary, or if the creditor fails to provide the proper disclosures or to obtain the borrower's agreement to purchase them, the related fees are included in the finance charge.

Finance Charge Chart

FINANCE CHARGE = DOLLAR COST OF CONSUMER CREDIT: It includes any charge payable directly or indirectly by the consumer and imposed directly or indirectly by the creditor as a condition of or incident to the extension of credit.

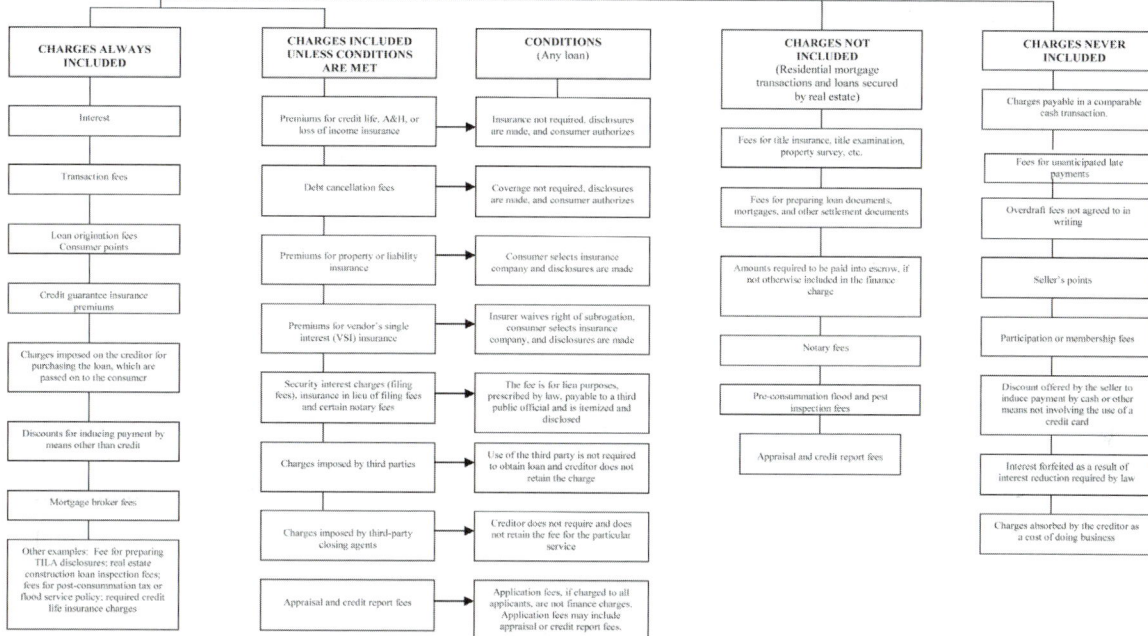

CHARGES ALWAYS INCLUDED	CHARGES INCLUDED UNLESS CONDITIONS ARE MET	CONDITIONS (Any loan)	CHARGES NOT INCLUDED (Residential mortgage transactions and loans secured by real estate)	CHARGES NEVER INCLUDED
Interest	Premiums for credit life, A&H, or loss of income insurance	Insurance not required, disclosures are made, and consumer authorizes	Fees for title insurance, title examination, property survey, etc.	Charges payable in a comparable cash transaction.
Transaction fees	Debt cancellation fees	Coverage not required, disclosures are made, and consumer authorizes	Fees for preparing loan documents, mortgages, and other settlement documents	Fees for unanticipated late payments
Loan origination fees Consumer points	Premiums for property or liability insurance	Consumer selects insurance company and disclosures are made	Amounts required to be paid into escrow, if not otherwise included in the finance charge	Overdraft fees not agreed to in writing
Credit guarantee insurance premiums	Premiums for vendor's single interest (VSI) insurance	Insurer waives right of subrogation, consumer selects insurance company, and disclosures are made	Notary fees	Seller's points
Charges imposed on the creditor for purchasing the loan, which are passed on to the consumer	Security interest charges (filing fees), insurance in lieu of filing fees and certain notary fees	The fee is for lien purposes, prescribed by law, payable to a third public official and is itemized and disclosed	Pre-consummation flood and pest inspection fees	Participation or membership fees
Discounts for inducing payment by means other than credit	Charges imposed by third parties	Use of the third party is not required to obtain loan and creditor does not retain the charge	Appraisal and credit report fees	Discount offered by the seller to induce payment by cash or other means not involving the use of a credit card
Mortgage broker fees	Charges imposed by third-party closing agents	Creditor does not require and does not retain the fee for the particular service		Interest forfeited as a result of interest reduction required by law
Other examples: Fee for preparing TILA disclosures; real estate construction loan inspection fees; fees for post-consummation tax or flood service policy; required credit life insurance charges	Appraisal and credit report fees	Application fees, if charged to all applicants, are not finance charges. Application fees may include appraisal or credit report fees.		Charges absorbed by the creditor as a cost of doing business

Accuracy Tolerances for Finance Charges (12 C.F.R. §1026.18(d)(1))

Regulation Z does not establish tolerances for errors in the calculation of the finance charge for open-end loans. For closed-end transactions, disclosure of the finance charge is regarded as accurate if:

- The charge is not understated by more than $100, or
- The amount stated is greater than the amount required to be disclosed

The accuracy of the finance charge impacts other disclosures, including the "amount financed" and the "annual percentage rate" because the finance charge is used in calculating these numbers. The regulations state that if the finance charge meets the accuracy tolerances, then *"...the disclosures affected by the disclosed finance charge (including the amount financed and the annual percentage rate) shall be treated as accurate..."* (12 C.F.R. §1026.18(d)(1)). If the disclosures are not accurate within the tolerances that the regulations establish, and the APR is based on an inaccurate finance charge, the creditor will need to re-disclose these amounts.

Another set of tolerances for the accuracy of finance charges is established in the provisions of Regulation Z that address rescission. As the course section on rescission explains, inaccurate disclosures of the finance charge or the annual percentage rate give consumers a basis for exercising the right to rescind a loan up to three years after consummation.

> *Regulation Z does not establish tolerances for errors in calculating finance charges for open-end loans.*

Determining the APR (12 C.F.R. §§1026.14, 1026.22)

Regulation Z defines "annual percentage rate" as a measure of the cost of credit, expressed as a yearly rate (12 C.F.R. §§1026.14(a), 1026.22(a)). Determining the APR for a home loan is a calculation that involves several steps and the use of complex mathematical formulas. Therefore, the calculation of the APR is typically completed with the use of an APR calculator. Although intended to facilitate loan shopping, the APR is the cause of much confusion for consumers who do not understand why the APR is higher than the interest rate that is quoted for a loan.

When mortgage professionals are asked to explain what appears as a discrepancy, they should explain to consumers that if there were no fees associated with the origination of a mortgage, and if the interest rate for the mortgage was fixed, there would be no difference between the APR and the interest rate. Consumers need to understand that the APR, like the finance charge, shows the loan costs that they pay in addition to the interest rate on a loan.

The fees that are included in the calculation of the APR include many of the fees that are included in the calculation of the finance charge, such as:

- Private Mortgage Insurance (PMI) or Mortgage Insurance Premium (MIP)
- Discount points and mortgage borrower fees
- Origination fees
- Processing fees, and
- Underwriting fees

When calculating the APR, the following fees are generally excluded, just as they are in the calculation of the finance charge:

- Title fees
- Escrow fees
- Notary fees
- Appraisal and credit report fees, and
- Document preparation fees

The APR is a more reliable estimation of the cost of a loan in some types of mortgage transactions than in others. The APR is useful for borrowers shopping for an adjustable-rate mortgage, who expect to hold the mortgage a long time, and who are not doing a cash-out refinance, a low or non-cost mortgage, or a HELOC. This is particularly true in the case of a homebuyer who intends to stay in the home for many years.

The usefulness of the APR in these transactions is due to the fact that the APR calculation for an ARM takes into account changes in the interest rate that will occur over the loan term.

The calculation of the APR differs for closed-end and open-end credit. For closed-end transactions, the APR is defined as, *"...a measure of the cost of credit, expressed as a yearly rate, that relates to the amount and timing of value received by the consumer to the amount and timing of payments made"* (12 C.F.R. §1026.22(a)). The finance charge, amount financed, and total payments are all factors that go into the computation of the APR for a closed-end loan. Course participants who want to examine the computations involved in determining the APR for a closed-end loan should turn to Appendix J in Regulation Z. This Appendix provides an explanation of the actuarial method that is used to determine the APR for closed-end transactions and shows the equations used in the computation. Regulation Z requires the APR calculation to be made using the actuarial method *"...or the United States Rule method"* (12 C.F.R. §1026.22(a)).

For initial disclosures and advertising purposes, the APR for open-end mortgages, such as home equity plans, *"...shall be computed by multiplying each periodic rate by the number of periods in a year"* (12 C.F.R. §1026.14(b)). In addition to this formula, the regulations create an optional method for creditors to compute the APR for open-end credit plans secured by a consumer's dwelling. The regulations provide that if the finance charge is determined solely by applying one or more periodic rates, the creditor may compute the effective APR:

- *By multiplying each periodic rate by the number of periods in a year; or*
- *By dividing the total finance charge for the billing cycle by the sum of the balances to which the periodic rates were applied and multiplying the quotient (expressed as a percentage) by the number of billing cycles in a year.*

(12 C.F.R. §1026.14(c)(1))

The use of this particular method for determining the APR for open-end mortgages is reviewed in Appendix F of Regulation Z.

There may be some circumstances in which a consumer who is shopping for mortgages may consider an open-end or closed-end loan. Comparing the APRs of open-end and closed-end loans would not be very helpful since the calculations are based on different factors.

Accuracy Tolerances for the APR for Closed-End Mortgages (12 C.F.R. §1026.22(a))
Regulation Z creates accuracy tolerances which provide that an APR is accurate if it is not more than 1/8 of one percentage point above or below the APR when the APR is calculated using the actuarial method (12 C.F.R. §1026.22(a)(2)).

If the loan is an "irregular loan," or one that allows for multiple advances or irregular payment periods or amounts, the APR is regarded as accurate if it is not more than 1/4 of one percentage point above or below the APR when the APR is calculated using the actuarial method (12 C.F.R. §1026.22(a)(3)).

The rules on accuracy tolerances create incentives to establish and maintain a compliance program that includes internal audits for accurate calculations of values such as the APR and finance charge.

The rules provide that an error in the disclosure of the APR is not a violation of Regulation Z if:

- *The error resulted from a corresponding error in a calculation tool used in good faith by the creditor; and*

- *Upon discovery of the error, the creditor promptly discontinues use of that calculation tool for disclosure purposes and notifies the Bureau in writing of the error in the calculation tool.*

(12 C.F.R. §1026.22(a)(1))

Disclosures Required by TILA

TILA is a law that depends on the use of disclosures for the achievement of its goals of protecting consumers in the financial marketplace and providing them with the information needed to make informed choices about consumer financial products. There is no uniform set of disclosures for every mortgage lending transaction. The content of the disclosures differs, based on the nature of the underlying transactions. For example, disclosures differ for:

- Closed-end credit

- Open-end credit

- Adjustable-rate mortgages, and

- High-cost mortgages

One of the most important compliance concerns related to TILA disclosures is meeting the time limitations for providing mandatory disclosures. An important definition to know in order to comply with the time limitations is the definition of **"business day,"** which Regulation Z defines as, *"...a day on which the creditor's offices are open to the public for carrying on substantially all of its business functions"* (12 C.F.R. §1026.2(a)(6)). Generally, business days include calendar days except for Sundays and public holidays including New Year's Day, Martin Luther King Day, Washington's Birthday, Memorial Day, Independence Day, Labor Day, Veterans Day, Thanksgiving, and Christmas.

The timing of disclosures was addressed in the 2008 Mortgage Disclosure Improvement Act, which requires creditors to give consumers "early disclosures" of good faith estimates of mortgage loans costs within three business days of receipt of a complete loan application. Specific disclosure requirements and timelines for providing them are described in the following course sections.

Closed-End Loans - The TIL Disclosure Statement (12 C.F.R. §1026.18)
TILA requires numerous disclosures, but it is the initial disclosure, known as the Truth-in-Lending (TIL) Disclosure Statement, that is intended to help consumers compare costs and to shop competitively for closed-end credit plans and mortgages.

Regulation Z does not prescribe a particular format for the Truth-in-Lending Disclosure Statement, but it requires that the words "finance charge" and "annual percentage rate" are made more conspicuous than any other terms on the disclosure (12 C.F.R. §1026.17(a)(2)).

In its Staff Commentary, the Federal Reserve suggests several methods of making the terms conspicuous such as segregating them and *"outlining them in a box"* [9]. This suggestion led to the standard industry use of the Truth-in-Lending Disclosure Statement which includes the four prominent boxes for:

- APR
- Finance Charge
- Amount Financed
- Total of Payments

These disclosures, as well as the other information required on the TIL Disclosure, provide consumers who are shopping for a closed-end mortgage with the following information:

- **APR**: The creditor must describe this disclosure as *"...the cost of your credit as a yearly rate"* (12 C.F.R. §1026.18(e)).

- **The finance charge**: This shows the *"...dollar amount the credit will cost you..."* (12 C.F.R. §1026.18(d)). For mortgage loans, the amount disclosed as the finance charge is accurate if it is:

  ◦ Understated by no more than $100, or

  ◦ Is greater than the amount required to be disclosed

- **Amount financed**: This amount is calculated by determining the principal loan amount (minus the down payment), adding other amounts financed by the consumer that are not a part of the finance charge or the principal, and subtracting charges that are part of the finance charge that the consumer will pay before or at consummation (i.e. prepaid finance charges). [10] TILA simply and accurately defines "amount financed" as *"...the amount of credit of which the consumer has actual use"* (15 U.S.C. §1638(a)(2)).

- **Payment schedule**: This shows *"...the number, amounts, and timing of the payments scheduled to repay the obligation"* (12 C.F.R. §1026.18(g)).

- **Total of payments**: This refers to the total amount that a consumer will have paid after making all scheduled payments.

- **Total sale price**: For a credit sale, this amount includes the cash price, including any down payment, plus any amounts financed by the creditor that are not part of the finance charge and the finance charge.

- **Prepayment**: The fact that there will be a penalty for prepaying the loan must be disclosed. With so many new restrictions on prepayment penalties, this disclosure should only be found in transactions involving fixed-rate qualified mortgages. Prepayment penalties are prohibited in transactions for ARMs, higher-priced mortgage loans, and high-cost mortgages.

- **Late payment**: Any dollar amount or percentage of a payment amount that the creditor will charge for late payments must be disclosed. If a grace period is permitted during which a late charge will not be assessed, this fact may also be disclosed.

- **Security interest**: This disclosure reminds borrowers that the creditor will have a security interest in the property purchased.

- **Insurance and debt cancellation**: If the creditor wants to exclude premiums and fees for certain types of insurance or debt cancellation policies from the finance charge, it must disclose:
  - The fact that the insurance coverage such as credit life, accident, health or employment, or loss-of-income insurance is not required by the creditor
  - The amount of the premium
  - The fact that the insurance coverage may not last for the duration of the loan term (this disclosure is only required when this is the case), and
  - The consumer must sign affirmative statements on the TIL disclosure, stating that he/she wants to purchase the insurance

- **Contract reference**: The TIL disclosure must include a reference to the contract with the creditor with specific information regarding issues such as the consequences of nonpayment, the consumer's default, the right to accelerate the debt, and information on prepayment penalties and rebates. This is an important disclosure since it reminds consumers that while the TIL disclosure provides an overview of important facts about the mortgage that they hope to purchase, there are other important details that may only be found in the lending agreement.

A copy of the Truth-in-Lending Disclosure Statement may be found below.

TRUTH IN LENDING DISCLOSURE STATEMENT
(THIS IS NEITHER A CONTRACT NOR A COMMITMENT TO LEND)

LENDER: ☐ Preliminary   ☒ Final   LOAN #:
                                                          DATE
BORROWERS: NEW TIL TEST   LOAN
                                                          CASE NO.

ADDRESS   TEST
CITY/STATE/ZIP TESTINGTON, FL 92300
PROPERTY   111 TEST, TESTINGTON, FL 92300

ANNUAL PERCENTAGE RATE	FINANCE CHARGE	Amount Financed	Total of Payments
The cost of your credit as a yearly rate.	The dollar amount the credit will cost you.	The amount of credit provided to you or on your behalf.	The amount you will have paid after you have made all payments as scheduled.
2.937 %	$ 106,599.79	$ 209,222.62	$ 315,822.41

INTEREST RATE AND PAYMENT SUMMARY:

	INTRODUCTORY Rate & Monthly Payment (for first 60 months)	MAXIMUM during FIRST FIVE YEARS (2/1/2011)	MAXIMUM EVER (as early as 2/1/2016)
Interest Rate	2.750%	2.750%	7.750%
Principal + Interest Payment	$857.31	$857.31	$1,403.71
Est. Taxes + Insurance (Escrow)	$75.01	$75.01	$75.01
Total Est. Monthly Payment	$932.32	$932.32	$1,478.72

There is no guarantee that you will be able to refinance to lower your rate and payments.

DEMAND FEATURE: ☒ This loan does not have a Demand Feature.   ☐ This loan has a Demand Feature as follows:

VARIABLE RATE FEATURE:
☒ This loan has a Variable Rate Feature. Variable Rate Disclosures have been provided to you earlier.

SECURITY: You are giving a security interest in the property located at:
111 TEST, TESTINGTON, FL 92300

ASSUMPTION: Someone buying this property   ☐ cannot assume the remaining balance due under original mortgage terms
☒ may assume, subject to lender's conditions, the remaining balance due under original mortgage terms.

PROPERTY INSURANCE: Hazard insurance, including flood insurance if the property is in a Special Flood Hazard Area, is required as a condition of this loan. You may obtain the insurance coverage from any insurance company acceptable to the lender. Complete details concerning insurance requirements will be provided prior to loan closing.

LATE CHARGES: If your payment is more than 15   days late, you will be charged a late charge of   5.000%
of the overdue payment.

PREPAYMENT: If you pay off your loan early, you
☐ may   ☒ will not   be entitled to a refund of part of the finance charge.
☐ may   ☒ will not   have to pay a penalty.

See your contract documents for any additional information regarding non-payment, default, required repayment in full before scheduled date, and prepayment refunds and penalties.

"e" means an estimate
I/We hereby acknowledge reading and receiving a complete copy of this disclosure.

BORROWER NEW TIL TEST	DATE
BORROWER	DATE
BORROWER	DATE
BORROWER	DATE

Truth in Lending Disclosure Statement

Timing for the TIL Disclosure and Effects of Re-Disclosure (12 C.F.R. §1026.19)

Disclosures that are due the **third business day** after the creditor receives the consumer's written credit application include:

- The TIL disclosure of the amount financed, finance charge, APR, total of payments, and payment schedule, etc.

- A notice that *"You are not required to complete this agreement merely because you have received these disclosures or signed a loan application"* (12 C.F.R. §1026.19(a)(4))

TILA mandates that the TIL Disclosure Statement must be re-disclosed if the APR on a regular loan varies by more than 1/8 of 1% (0.125%) at any time prior to closing (12 C.F.R. §1026.22(a)(2)). This re-disclosure is required at least three business days prior to the settlement, whether the variance increases or decreases the APR. In other words, if there is a change in APR prior to settlement that is above or below 0.125%, the borrower must be provided with a new disclosure as soon as the variance is known. There must be at least a three-business-day waiting period prior to closing if an inaccurate APR must be re-disclosed. This is assuming the APR inaccuracy occurs after the seven-business-day disclosure, discussed below (12 C.F.R. §1026.19(a)(2)).

A creditor meets the three-business-day deadline if it delivers the disclosure or places it in the mail no later than the third day after receipt of the loan application. The TIL Disclosure Statement is presented along with the Good Faith Estimate (required by the Real Estate Settlement Procedures Act) and provides the cost of credit.

In a mortgage transaction subject to the Real Estate Settlement Procedures Act, the requirements for the timing of the Good Faith Estimate do not apply to:

- Home equity lines of credit regulated under 12 C.F.R. §1026.40, and

- Transactions secured by a consumer's interest in a timeshare plan

(12 C.F.R. §1026.19(a))

In addition to the three-day deadline for an early TIL Disclosure Statement, the law also requires delivery of the disclosure no less than **seven business days** prior to consummation of a loan transaction. If a mortgage professional is properly providing the early TIL Statement (within three business days after application) and there are no changes to the information on the TIL Statement, settlement can be scheduled as early as seven business days following the initial disclosure (12 C.F.R. §1026.19(a)(2)).

The borrower may waive this seven-business-day waiting period if he/she has a bona fide emergency and the initial disclosure is still accurate. However, if the consumer waives the waiting period and a change occurs to make the APR inaccurate, the waiver is no longer effective and a new disclosure must be provided. The new disclosure must be provided no less than three business days prior to settlement, although the consumer can provide a new waiver. The three-business-day waiting period would not apply if the consumer provides a waiver after corrected disclosures are made.

In order to waive a waiting period, the consumer must provide a written and dated statement. Mortgage professionals may not provide a pre-printed form for the purposes of submitting a waiver. The statement providing the waiver must be signed by each party to the loan who is entitled to receive Truth-in-Lending disclosures. The requirements for a bona fide emergency and the waiver of a waiting period are substantially similar to those for the waiver of the rescission period or waiver of the waiting period for consummation of a Section 32 (HOEPA) loan (12 C.F.R. §1026.19(a)(3)).

As previously mentioned, both the initial and final Truth-in-Lending disclosures will be replaced once the Loan Estimate and Closing Disclosure forms are effective in 2015.

> *A TIL Disclosure must be given to the borrower no more than three business days after application and at least seven business days prior to consummation.*

Additional Disclosures for Closed-End Transactions

When a creditor gives a consumer the information found in the TIL Disclosure Statement, it may also provide the following disclosures, although the only deadline for these disclosures is that the creditor must make them prior to consummation of the transaction (12 C.F.R. §1026.17(b)):

- **Assumption Policy**: The creditor must let the consumer know *"...whether or not a subsequent purchaser of the dwelling from the consumer may be permitted to assume the remaining obligation on its original terms"* (12 C.F.R. §1026.18(q)). Appendix H-6 provides the following model language for this disclosure: **"Assumption: Someone buying your house [may, subject to conditions be allowed to] [cannot] assume the remainder of the mortgage on the original terms"** [11].

- **Balloon Payments**: If a closed-end transaction includes a provision for a balloon payment, it must be disclosed separately from other periodic payments (12 C.F.R. §1026.18(s)(5)).

- **No Guarantee to Refinance**: Closed-end transactions secured by real estate or a dwelling (except for timeshare transactions) must include a statement that says the following: **"There is no guarantee that you will be able to refinance to lower your rate and payments"** [12].

- **Interest Rate and Payment Summary**: All closed-end transactions secured by real estate or a dwelling (except for timeshare transactions) must include, in the form of a table, information on the interest rate and payments for the loan.

There are other special disclosure requirements related to the interest rates and payments for negative amortization and interest-only loans, but with these types of loans so seldom made today, this course will not review these requirements.

Disclosures for Closed-End ARMs (12 C.F.R. §1026.19(b))

TILA functions not only as a law that helps consumers to understand the cost of credit, but also as one that discloses the risks associated with particular types of transactions. These disclosures include those that warn consumers of the risks associated with mortgages that have adjustable or variable rates. If a borrower obtains an ARM, creditors must provide additional disclosures at the time an application form is provided or before the borrower pays a nonrefundable fee, whichever is earlier.

This requirement is specific to ARMs, which are secured by the borrower's principal dwelling and have a term of more than one year. As with other disclosures mandated by TILA, if the borrower makes the application by phone, the creditor must deliver the disclosures within three business days following receipt of the completed loan application.

The special disclosures for closed-end ARMs include the Consumer Handbook on Adjustable-Rate Mortgages and loan program disclosures.

The Consumer Handbook on Adjustable-Rate Mortgages (CHARM) Booklet: This booklet was originally created in 1987 to educate consumers on the risks associated with ARMs. In 2006, the Federal Reserve Board revised the booklet to address the risks associated with nontraditional mortgage products, such as interest-only ARMs and payment-option ARMs. The booklet is available online [13].

Loan Program Disclosures: The lender must provide a loan program disclosure for each variable-rate mortgage product in which the applicant has expressed an interest.

Each disclosure must include:

- A statement that the interest rate, payment, or loan term can change
- Identification of the index or formula used to make adjustments
- An explanation of how the interest rate and payment will be determined
- A recommendation that the borrower ask about the current margin value and current interest rate
- A notation that the interest rate will be discounted and a recommendation that the loan applicant ask about the amount of the discount
- The frequency of interest rate and payment changes
- The rules relating to index, interest rate, and payment amount, such as the use of rate and payment caps
- A statement, when applicable, of the fact that negative amortization can occur
- An explanation of how to calculate payments for the loan amount
- A reminder that the loan contains a demand feature
- A statement of the type of information that will be provided in notices of interest rate adjustments and an indication of when these notices will arrive
- An indication that disclosure forms are available for other variable-rate loan programs
- At the option of the creditor, an example based on a $10,000 loan:
  - A historical example that shows how payments and loan balances are impacted by interest rates, based on the most recent 15 years of index values, or
  - The maximum interest rate and payment for a $10,000 loan at the initial interest rate, based on the index and volume, and *"...in effect as of an identified month and year for the loan program disclosure assuming maximum periodic increases in rates and payments under the program..."*

(12 C.F.R. §1026.19(b)(2))

Regulation Z includes a model disclosure form for variable-rate mortgages in Appendix H-14 of the regulations. This model form includes an example of how monthly payments can change.

TILA was originally enacted to enable consumers to make informed choices about loans and credit. TILA functions as a risk disclosure law with regard to adjustable-rate loans (ARMs).

Disclosing the Cost of Credit for Home Equity Plans (12 C.F.R. §1026.40)

The sections of Regulation Z that apply to open-end loans secured by a consumer's dwelling are called "Requirements for Home Equity Plans." A home equity plan is a form of revolving credit that is secured by a mortgage on the borrower's home. Disclosures for home equity plans are due at the time an application is provided to a consumer (12 C.F.R. §1026.40(b)). However, just like the TIL Disclosure Statement, if the consumer applies via phone or Internet, the disclosures must be delivered within three business days. The consumer may not be required to pay any nonrefundable fees in connection with an application for a home equity plan unless he/she has received the disclosures and the brochure titled *"What You Should Know About Home Equity Lines of Credit."* This brochure is available on the CFPB website [14].

The statement of the APR and finance charge in closed-end transactions must be more conspicuous than the other disclosures. The disclosure for a home equity plan must also include clear and conspicuous disclosure of this information; however, other disclosures take precedence over information on loan costs. Regulation Z lists four topics that must precede the other required disclosures (12 C.F.R. §1026.40(a)(2)).

Disclosures provided to consumers who are applying for home equity loans must include the following four pieces of information:

- **Retention of disclosure**: The disclosure must include a statement advising the consumer to retain a copy of the disclosure.

- **Availability of disclosed terms**: The disclosure must explain that the lending terms described are subject to change and that a loan applicant must submit an application to obtain specific terms disclosed. The disclosure should also note the terms that are subject to change and that if a disclosed term changes (other than changes related to the fluctuating index for an ARM), the consumer may elect not to open the plan and receive a refund of fees paid for the loan application.

- **Risk of losing the home**: The disclosure must state that the creditor will have a security interest in the borrower's home and that payment defaults could result in the loss of the home.

- **Possibility of unfavorable actions by the creditor**: The disclosure must advise consumers that in certain conditions, the creditor can take adverse actions, such as demanding payment of the outstanding balance in a single payment, reducing the credit limit, or prohibiting additional extensions of credit.

After these disclosures are made, the disclosure statement must provide information on:

- Payment terms
- APR
- Fees associated with use of the plan
- Fees imposed by third parties to open a plan
- Negative amortization
- Transaction requirements, and
- Tax implications

Special Disclosures for Home Equity Plans with Adjustable Rates (12 C.F.R. §1026.40(d)(12))

If the home equity plan has an adjustable rate, the disclosure must also include the following information:

- The fact that the APR may change
- A statement that the APR does not include costs other than interest (this is only true for open-end loans)
- The index used for rate adjustments and the offer of a source of information on the index
- A description of how the APR will be determined
- A statement that the consumer should ask for information about the current index, margin, and APR
- An indication of how long the initial rate will be effective
- The frequency of changes in the APR
- Explanations regarding payment limitations and rate carryovers
- A statement of the maximum APR that may be imposed under each payment option
- The minimum periodic payment required when the maximum APR for each payment option is in effect for a $10,000 outstanding balance, and a statement of the earliest date or time the maximum rate may be imposed
- A historical example that shows how payments and loan balances are impacted by index value changes, based on the most recent 15 years of index values, reflecting plain terms and rate and payment limitations, and
- A statement that rate information will be available on every periodic statement

In addition to these disclosure requirements, Regulation Z states that the creditor must provide loan applicants with a copy of its brochure on home equity plans or a "suitable substitute." The brochure written by the Federal Reserve, entitled *What You Should Know about Home Equity Lines of Credit*, is a good option (12 C.F.R. §1026.40(e)). This brochure is available online [15].

Also useful are the model forms for the disclosures required for home equity plans that are available in the Appendix to Regulation Z under Sections G-14 and G-15.

Limitations and Prohibitions Related to Home Equity Plans (12 C.F.R. §1026.40(f))

- Creditors may not take any of the following actions:
- Change the APR unless the change is based on an index that the creditor does not control
- Terminate a plan and demand payment of the entire balance in advance of the original loan term unless the consumer has:
    - Committed fraud
    - Defaulted on the loan, or
    - Taken any action or failed to take action that might adversely impact the security for the loan
- Change any term, unless the creditor indicated in the initial agreement that it may prohibit extensions of credit or reduce the credit limit during any period in which the maximum APR is reached, and
- Change the index and margin unless the index is no longer available, in which case the creditor may select an index that it has proven to have historical movement similar to the index replaced

Changes that a creditor is allowed to make include:

- Making a change that the consumer agrees to in writing
- Making a change that will clearly benefit the consumer throughout the remainder of the plan
- Making an insignificant change to the terms
- Prohibiting additional extensions of credit or reducing the credit limit during any period when:
    - The value of the dwelling securing the loan decreases significantly below the dwelling's appraised value for purposes of the plan
    - Based on a material change in the consumer's finances, the creditor does not believe that the consumer can repay the loan
    - The consumer is in default
    - Government action precludes the creditor from imposing the APR provided for in the agreement
    - Government action has adversely affected the priority of the creditor's security interest to the extent that the value of the security is less than 120% of the credit line, and
    - A regulatory agency has notified the creditor that continued advances are an unsafe and unsound practice

There are other special disclosure requirements related to the interest rates and payments for negative amortization and interest-only loans, but with these types of loans so seldom made today, this course will not review these requirements.

> *Disclosures for home equity plans are due at the time an application is provided to a consumer. If the consumer applies via phone or Internet, disclosures must be delivered within three business days.*

Disclosing Interest Rate Changes after Consummation (12 C.F.R. §1026.20(c), (d))

There are two disclosures that Regulation Z refers to as *"Disclosure requirements regarding Post-Consummation Events."* The post-consummation events that these disclosures address are interest rate changes in ARMs. These disclosures are intended to ensure that consumers receive advance notice of upcoming changes in their interest rates and monthly payments. The disclosure requirements under 12 C.F.R. §1026.20(c) apply to recurring interest rate changes that result in a payment change. The course will refer to this disclosure as the **rate/payment change disclosure**. The requirements under subsection (d) apply only to the initial rate adjustment. The course will refer to the subsection (d) disclosure as the **initial rate adjustment disclosure.**

Both of these disclosures apply only to ARMs that are:

- Closed-end loans, and
- Secured by the borrower's principal residence

These disclosure requirements apply not only to creditors, but also to assignees and servicers of ARMs. In its Official Interpretations of Regulation Z, the CFPB notes that creditors, assignees, and servicers *"...may decide among themselves which of them will provide the required disclosures"* [16].

There are some significant differences between the post-consummation disclosure rules that became effective on January 10, 2014 and the previous rules. For example, the revised rules eliminate the requirement for an annual notice for rate adjustments that do not lead to payment changes due to payment caps. The new rules also create new model disclosure forms for rate changes and require earlier delivery of these disclosures in order to give consumers *"...enough time to budget for any increase or to take appropriate action, such as pursuing refinancing or options offered by servicers relating to individual hardship"* [17].

Exemptions from the Rate/Payment Change Disclosure (12 C.F.R. §1026.20(c)(1)(ii))

There are two exemptions to the subsection (c) requirement for providing rate/payment change disclosures:

- A disclosure is not required when the transaction involves an ARM with a term of one year or less, and
- A disclosure is not required for an ARM's first interest rate adjustment if:
  - The first adjusted payment is due within 210 days after consummation, and
  - The initial rate adjustment that was disclosed at consummation was not an estimate

The exemption for loans of a year or less generally includes construction loans, bridge loans, and home improvement loans. The exemption for loans that adjust within 210 days of consummation is intended to eliminate duplicative disclosures. Consumers who have loans with rate changes that occur this early in the loan term will typically receive a disclosure at the time of closing that addresses the first rate adjustment.

Content of Rate/Payment Change Disclosures (12 C.F.R. §1026.20(c)(2))

The rule provides numerous requirements for the content of rate/payment change disclosures. These disclosures must provide:

- An explanation that the effective period for the current interest rate is ending and that the interest rate and payment amounts are going to change

- The effective date of the upcoming interest rate adjustment and a statement of when future interest rate adjustments will occur, and

- A description of other changes to the loan that will occur on the date that the interest rate changes, such as the expiration of interest-only or payment-option features

This disclosure must include a table that shows:

- Current and new interest rates

- Current and new payments and the date that the first new payment is due, and

- How much of the payment for interest-only and negative amortization loans will be allocated for principal, interest, taxes, and insurance (with numerous prohibitions against negative amortization and interest-only loans, the need to make these disclosures should not arise in many transactions)

The disclosure must also include:

- **An explanation of how the interest rate is determined**: This explanation must reference the index used and reference information that the consumer can access regarding the index used for the loan. It must also identify the margin and explain how the margin is used to calculate the new rate.

- **A description of any limits on the interest rate increase**: If the ARM has interest rate caps, the disclosure must describe the periodic rate adjustment caps or lifetime caps and show how they may limit increases in the interest rate and payments.

- **An explanation of how the new payment is determined**: This explanation will state the index and margin used, the loan balance expected on the date of the interest rate/payment adjustment, the length of the remaining loan term, and any change in the term of the loan caused by the adjustment.

- **Information on negative amortization and prepayment penalties**: If the new payment will not be allocated to pay the principal, will not reduce the loan balance, or may increase the loan balance, these facts must be noted. If the loan is one of the few in which prepayment penalties are allowed, the disclosure must state the circumstances that may trigger a prepayment penalty, such as a refinancing, or selling the home securing the loan.

When providing consumers with a table containing this information, creditors must use a model form or a disclosure including a table and formatting that is substantially similar to that displayed in the model form.

Timing for the Rate/Payment Change Disclosure (12 C.F.R. §1026.20(c)(2))

When the CFPB made revisions to the timing for rate/payment change disclosures, its general objective was to give consumers more time to either prepare to make higher monthly mortgage payments, or to refinance or take other loss mitigating actions. In the rule that existed prior to 2014, the minimum time for providing a rate/payment change disclosure was 25 days. The CFPB determined that such short notice regarding a rate change does not give consumers sufficient time to prepare to meet the challenges of more expensive monthly mortgage payments. The CFPB's final rule creates a general requirement for rate/payment change disclosures to be provided at least 60 days, and no more than 120 days, prior to the rate change. There are three exceptions to this rule. The general rule and the exceptions are outlined below.

In order to understand the reasoning behind the general rule and its exceptions, it is necessary to know that the timing requirements for rate change disclosures are based on the **"look-back period,"** which the CFPB defines as *"...the number of days prior to the change date on which the index value would be selected which would serve as the basis for the new interest rate and payment"* [18]. Look-back periods may range between 15 and 60 days.

The CFPB found that most loans have a 45-day look-back period *"...with an approximately 30-day billing cycle between the change date and the date the first payment at the new level would be due..."* [19]. With creditors and servicers having a 45-day look-back period and another 30 to prepare a new billing statement based on the adjusted rate, the CFPB concluded that a requirement to provide disclosure of a rate and payment change 60 days in advance is reasonable. Some consumer groups suggested a notice of at least 70 to 90 days in advance, but the CFPB determined that a 60-day period balances industry and consumer interests [20].

The general rule requiring at least a 60-day advance notice and its exceptions are outlined below:

60- to 120-Day Advance Notice: Creditors, assignees, or servicers must provide consumers with a rate/payment change disclosure *"...at least 60, but no more than 120, days before the first payment at the adjusted level is due"* (12 C.F.R. §1026.20(c)(2)). Sixty days was chosen as the minimum period for prior notice since the CFPB confirmed, during rulemaking, that *"...most servicers would know the index value approximately 75 days before the due date of the first new payment..."* [21]. They should, therefore, know what the new rate and payment will be in time to provide a 60-day notice. This 60- to 120-day timeframe for rate/payment change disclosures is the one that will apply to most ARMs.

25- to 120-Day Advance Notice for Grandfathered ARMs: This shorter period for an advance notice is intended as a grandfather provision to accommodate existing ARMs that have look-back periods that are shorter than 45 days. Examples of mortgages with shorter look-back periods include FHA and VA loans. This grandfather provision is intended to relieve creditors of the burden of *"...altering existing contractual agreements regarding the look-*

back period" [22]. It applies to those ARMs originated prior to **January 10, 2015** with lending agreements that require the rate and payment adjustment to be based on an index that is available less than 45 days prior to the date for rate adjustments.

25- to 120-Day Advance Notice for ARMs with Frequent Rate Adjustments: The shorter period for advance notices is permanently extended to frequently adjusting ARMs *"...with a uniform schedule of interest rate adjustments occurring every 60 days or less..."* [23]. These types of loans are not sought by many consumers, but *"...are in demand in certain sectors of the marketplace and offer benefits to those consumers"* [24]. If the rules did not make accommodations for these loans that typically adjust monthly, creditors would no longer be able to offer them since they would be unable to provide a notice 60 days in advance of a loan rate that changes every 30 days. The CFPB justifies this exception stating that *"Consumers whose interest rates adjust monthly run little risk of surprise at a changed payment compared to consumers whose ARM interest rates have not adjusted for one, three, five, or seven years before the payment change"* [25].

25- to 120-Day Advance Notice for ARMS Adjusting 60 Days after Consummation: The 25- to 120-day deadline also applies to transactions in which the rate adjusts for the first time within 60 days of consummation, if the new rate disclosed at consummation was an estimate and was not the actual rate that would be effective at the time of the rate adjustment.

Initial Rate Adjustment Disclosures (12 C.F.R. §1026.20(d))
The other post-consummation disclosure for closed-end ARMs secured by a borrower's principal dwelling is the initial interest rate adjustment disclosure. There is an exemption from this disclosure requirement for ARMs with loan terms of one year or less (12 C.F.R. §1026.20(d)(1) (ii)).

The timing requirements for initial rate adjustment disclosures are far less complicated than are those for rate/payment change disclosures. The rules simply provide that the disclosures must be provided to consumers *"...at least 210, but no more than 240, days before the first payment at the adjusted level is due. If the first payment at the adjusted level is due within the first 210 days after consummation, the disclosures shall be provided at consummation"* (12 C.F.R. §1026.20(d)).

The initial rate adjustment disclosure provides much of the same information that is found in a rate/payment change disclosure. However, there are some differences, and one of the first differences between the two types of disclosures is that there may be circumstances in which an initial disclosure may provide an estimated adjustment instead of an actual rate adjustment.

If the disclosure of the initial rate adjustment provides an estimated adjustment instead of an actual interest rate adjustment, the disclosure should be labeled as an estimate. The estimated interest rate and payment change must be calculated **15 business days prior** to the date of the disclosure, and must be based on the index that is to be used for the loan's adjustments.

Like the notice required for rate/payment change disclosures, the initial rate adjustment disclosure must include:

- An explanation that the effective period for the current interest rate is ending and that the interest rate and payment amounts are going to change
- The effective date of the upcoming interest rate adjustment and a statement of when future interest rate adjustments will occur, and
- A description of other changes to the loan that will occur on the date that the interest rate changes, *such as the expiration of interest-only or payment-option features*

(12 C.F.R. §1026.20(d)(2)(ii))

Like the rate/payment disclosure, the disclosure for initial rate adjustments must include a table that shows the current and new interest rates, the date that the first new payment is due, and payment allocation information for interest-only and negative amortization loans. The disclosure must also provide an explanation of how the rate is calculated, disclose the index and margin used to make this calculation, and identify any caps that will limit the increase in the rate. The disclosure must provide information on calculating new payments, the loan balance expected on the date that the rate adjusts, the loan term remaining, and any change in the loan term caused by the adjustment.

Since an initial rate adjustment disclosure may provide an estimated rate adjustment, this disclosure must state that *"...another disclosure containing the actual new interest rate and new payment will be provided to the consumer between two and four months before the first payment at the adjusted level is due..."* (12 C.F.R. §1026.20(d)(2)(vi)(E)).

Like rate/payment change disclosures, the initial rate adjustment disclosure must also address, if applicable, whether the new payment might result in negative amortization and indicate any circumstances in which the borrower might have to pay a prepayment penalty. Unlike the rate/payment change disclosures, initial rate adjustment disclosures must provide the following additional information:

- A telephone number that the consumer can use to reach the creditor, assignee, or servicer if the consumer does not anticipate that he/she can make the new payments
- A list that includes the following alternatives to making mortgage payments at the new adjusted rate, with a simple explanation of each alternative:
  - Refinancing the loan
  - Selling the home securing the loan and paying off the loan
  - Modifying the terms of the lending agreement, and
  - Arranging a payment forbearance
- Phone numbers and websites where the consumer can obtain information from the CFPB and HUD about loan counselors and about state housing finance authorities

The regulations are very particular about the format used to provide the required information. The CFPB has created model forms for use in making the initial rate adjustment disclosures and in order to ensure compliance with the regulations, use of the CFPB's forms may be the safest practice.

> *The initial interest rate adjustment disclosure is not required for ARMs with loan terms of one year or less.*

Right of Rescission under TILA (15 U.S.C. §1635)

Rescission is a legal remedy that voids a contract between two parties, restoring each to the position held prior to the transaction. TILA includes two provisions that address the right to rescind certain types of mortgage loans:

- **Three-Business-Day Rescission Period**: The three-business-day rescission period creates a cooling-off interval after closing on a loan. This interval is intended to give a borrower the opportunity to reconsider whether he/she wants the loan, and the ability to cancel the loan by simply providing the lender with timely notice of the cancellation.

- **Three-Year Rescission Period**: The three-year rescission period is available to a borrower who did not receive a notice of the right to rescind or accurate Truth-in-Lending disclosures at the time that he/she entered an agreement for a mortgage loan.

Loans Subject to the Right of Rescission (12 C.F.R. §§1026.15(f), 1026.23(f))

The right to rescind applies to loans for open-end and closed-end credit. Therefore, citations are provided for the provisions in Section 1026.15 that establish the rescission rules for open-end transactions, and for the provisions under 1026.23 that establish the rescission rules for closed-end transactions. The provisions for open-end and closed end loans are almost identical, and the course will note sections of the two sets of rules that are different.

There are important limitations to the right to rescind. The right of rescission is only available for loans that are secured by the consumer's **principal dwelling**, and generally, no right to rescind exists for:

- A **"residential mortgage transaction,"** which is defined in Regulation Z as a mortgage or other security interest that is created to finance the purchase or construction of a dwelling

- A refinancing or consolidation of credit already secured by the consumer's principal dwelling with the same creditor that made the first loan. Note, however, that the right to rescind may apply *"...to the extent the new amount financed exceeds the unpaid principal balance, any earned unpaid finance charge on the existing debt, and amounts attributed solely to the costs of the refinancing or consolidation."*

- A lending transaction with a state agency

- An advance (except for the initial advance) in a series of advances, such as those made in a multiple-advance loan for the construction of a dwelling, and

- A renewal of optional insurance products

Home equity lines of credit, refinances, and home improvement loans secured by the consumer's principal dwelling are examples of the types of loans that are subject to a right of rescission.

Recipients of the Right to Rescind Notice (12 C.F.R. §§1026.15(a), 1026.23(a))
The consumer who signs a lending agreement is not the only party who must receive notice of the right to rescind. Creditors must also provide two copies of the notice to each party with an ownership interest in the principal dwelling that serves as security for the loan. If the notice of the right to rescind is provided electronically, and the creditor is providing electronic notices in compliance with the E-Sign Act, only one copy is necessary for each party with an ownership interest in the property (12 C.F.R. §§1026.15(b), 1026.23(b)).

Format and Content of the Right to Rescind Notice (12 C.F.R. §§1026.15(b), 1026.23(b))
The notice of the right to rescind must consist of a document that is separate from other TILA disclosures, and it must clearly and conspicuously disclose the following:

- The creditor's retention or acquisition of a security interest in the consumer's principal dwelling
- The consumer's right to rescind
- Instructions on how to exercise the right to rescind, including a form the consumer has the option of using, stating the lender's business address
- The date that the right of rescission expires, and
- A description of the effects of rescission for the consumer

For closed-end transactions, creditors must use one of the model forms for rescission found in Appendix H of Regulation Z or a substantially similar notice (12 C.F.R. §1026.23(b)(2)). The course Appendix provides a copy of the general rescission form and a rescission form for a refinance with the original creditor, when the refinance involves an increase in the original amount of credit provided.

Creditors should be careful to use the form that is appropriate for the transaction, because there is case law which holds that failing to give the borrower the correct form constitutes a failure to provide notice of the right to rescind. For example, a lender would risk violating the law by giving a general rescission form to a borrower who is engaged in a transaction to refinance a loan to increase his/her credit limit.

Three-Business-Day Right to Rescind (12 C.F.R. §§1026.15(a)(3), 1026.23(a)(3))
In order to rescind a loan during the three-business-day cooling-off period, a consumer must comply with the deadlines for exercising the right to rescind.

If the loan is for closed-end credit, any party with an ownership interest in the property can exercise his/her right to rescind the transaction until midnight on the third business day after the last of the following events occurs:

- Consummation of the loan
- Delivery of the notice of the right to rescind, or

- Delivery of all **"material disclosures,"** which are the disclosures of the APR, finance charge, total of payments, payment schedule, and the special HOEPA disclosures required for high-cost mortgages

(12 C.F.R. §1026.23(a)(3))

In open-end transactions, the deadline for the right to rescind is three business days after the last of the following events occurs:

- A credit plan is opened
- A security interest is added or increased to secure an existing plan
- A credit limit on a credit plan is increased
- Delivery of the notice of the right to rescind, or
- Delivery of all material disclosures, and for open-end transactions, these include information on computation of finance charges and payment terms that may apply during the draw and repayment periods

(12 C.F.R. §1026.15(a)(3))

In calculating the time limitations for exercising the right to rescind, recall that business days include Saturdays, but do not include Sundays and federal public holidays.

During the three-day rescission period, *"...no money shall be disbursed other than in escrow, no services shall be performed and no materials delivered until the rescission period has expired and the creditor is reasonably satisfied that the consumer has not rescinded"* (12 C.F.R. §§1026.15(c), 1026.23(c)). The Official Interpretations of Regulation Z clarify that in order to be "reasonably satisfied" that a consumer is not exercising the right to rescind, a creditor should allow enough time to receive a notice of rescission that the consumer may have sent by mail. Reasonable satisfaction that the consumer will not cancel the loan may be based on receipt of a written notice from the consumer that he/she does not intend to exercise the right to rescind [26].

Although creditors must delay performance under loan agreements that are subject to a right to rescind, there are some steps toward performance that they can take during the rescission period. For example, in a closed-end transaction, creditors may prepare the loan check, prepare to assign the loan to a third party, and may accrue finance charges. A creditor in an open-end transaction may prepare the cash advance check and accrue finance charges.

Exercising the Right to Rescind (12 C.F.R. §§1026.15(a)(2), 1026.23(a)(2))
If a consumer decides to exercise the right to rescind, he/she must provide written notice within the three-business-day rescission period. When multiple parties have rescission rights in a particular transaction, any one of them may exercise the right to terminate the transaction. The regulations provide that *"Notice is considered given when mailed, or when filed for telegraphic transmission, or, if sent by other means, when delivered to the creditor's designated place of business"* (12 C.F.R. §§1026.15(a)(2), 1026.23(a)(2)).

Consequences of Rescission (12 C.F.R. §§1026.15(d), 1026.23(d))

A consumer's decision to rescind a transaction has the following consequences:

- The creditor no longer has a security interest in the consumer's principal dwelling

- The creditor has 20 calendar days to return any money or property paid by the consumer in connection with the transaction. This would include closing costs and interest that the borrower has paid on the loan. If the loan is secured through a mortgage, the creditor must release the mortgage and ensure that the land records show that it no longer has a lien on the property.

- After the creditor has completed the requirements of terminating its security in the consumer's home and returning money or property to the consumer, the consumer must return any funds received to the lender

When multiple parties have rescission rights in a particular transaction, any one of them may exercise the right to terminate the transaction.

> *Rescission is a legal remedy that voids a contract between two parties, restoring each to the position held prior to the transaction.*

Waiver of the Right to Rescind (12 C.F.R. §§1026.15(e), 1026.23(e))

A consumer can request that the lender waive the right to rescind in situations in which credit is needed to meet a bona fide financial emergency. The waiver must be in writing and include:

- A description of the emergency, and
- Signatures of all parties that have a right to rescind a particular transaction

As with the waiver of the waiting period related to the TIL Disclosure, waiver of the right to rescind must be made by the consumer in a dated, written statement. Mortgage professionals are prohibited from providing any type of pre-printed form for the purposes of rescission.

Three-Year Right to Rescind (12 C.F.R. §§1026.15(a)(3), 1026.23(a)(3))

For both closed- and open-end lending transactions, a three-year right to rescind exists for the following violations by the creditor:

- Failure to provide a notice of the right to rescind that complies with Regulation Z, and

- Failure to provide **material disclosures**, such as the annual percentage rate, the finance charge, the amount financed, the total number of payments, and the payment schedule. If the loan is a high-cost or higher-priced loan, the lender must include disclosures related to HOEPA. If the loan is an open-end transaction, the material disclosures include account-opening disclosures, such as information regarding the calculation of finance charges.

The three-year rescission period is measured from the date of the consummation of the lending transaction. However, the right to rescind may expire in less than three years *"...upon transfer of all of the consumer's interest in the property, or upon sale of the property, whichever occurs first."*

Tolerances for Accuracy of Disclosures (12 C.F.R. §1026.23(g))

A primary concern for creditors during the three-year rescission period is whether the "material disclosures" that they have provided to consumers are accurate. In an article by an examiner for the Federal Reserve Bank of New York, creditors are cautioned that they *"...should be especially careful with disclosures for APR, the finance charge, and the payment schedule, because violations of these most frequently trigger the three-year rescission period"* [27]. For some of these disclosures, Regulation Z created accuracy tolerances; for others, it does not.

With regard to accuracy tolerances, the bank examiner's article cites the example of a lender that provided a borrower with a disclosure stating the payment amount and the number of payments, but failed to disclose that the payments were due monthly. A seventh circuit federal court held that the disclosure violated TILA, and *"As a result, the consumer was granted three years to exercise the right to rescind"* [28].

The lender's mistake was an easy one to make because there are no accuracy tolerances for payment schedule disclosures. Therefore, any mistake can lead to a violation of disclosure requirements and trigger the three-year rescission period.

Regulation Z does create accuracy tolerances in closed-end transactions for the finance charge and other disclosures affected by the finance charge (such as the amount financed and the annual percentage rate). These accuracy tolerances provide that the disclosed finance charge is regarded as accurate if it is:

- Understated by no more than 1/2 of 1% of the face amount of the note or $100, whichever is greater, or
- Greater than the amount required to be disclosed

(12 C.F.R. §1026.23(g)(1))

There is another accuracy tolerance for refinancings with a new creditor as long as the transaction does not involve a HOEPA high-cost mortgage. If the refinancing does not involve a new advance or consolidation of an existing loan, the disclosed finance charge and the other disclosures that it affects are accurate if they are:

- Understated by no more than 1% of the face amount of the note or $100, whichever is greater, or
- Greater than the amount required to be disclosed

(12 C.F.R. §1026.23(g)(2))

Section 1025.15 does not include accuracy tolerances for open-end transactions. Creditors should, therefore, take great care to make an accurate disclosure of finance charges and payment terms for open-end mortgages.

Special Rules for Foreclosures (12 C.F.R. §1026.23(h))

A consumer may exercise the right to rescind after foreclosure proceedings have been brought against his/her principal dwelling if:

- The loan was originated through a mortgage broker and the creditor failed to include the mortgage broker fee in the finance charge, or
- The creditor failed to use a model H form or a substantially similar form for the rescission notice

When a foreclosure proceeding against the consumer's principal dwelling has been initiated, the accuracy tolerances for the finance charge and for other disclosures affected by the finance charge are regarded as accurate if the disclosed finance charge is:

- Understated by no more than $35, or
- Greater than the amount required to be disclosed

(12 C.F.R. §1026.23(h)(2))

Since defaults on subprime loans have led to a record number of foreclosures, many consumers have sought to save their homes by exercising their right to rescind a loan. If they review their loan documents and find that the finance charge was understated by $36, they may exercise their right to rescind the loan.

A lot of litigation has arisen as a result of these actions, and examples of some of the points litigated have focused on questions such as:

- Is an understatement of the finance charge by only $1 a *de minimis* violation of the law or a material violation of the law?
- Are borrowers required to provide a notice of rescission to the loan servicer as well as the creditor?
- Are borrowers required not only to exercise their right of rescission, but also to sue their creditors to resolve disputes about the rescission before the three-year rescission period expires?

The CFPB weighed in on the third question, filing an amicus brief with the Third Circuit Court of Appeals in which it argued:

> *"To rescind a mortgage loan under TILA and Regulation Z, consumers must notify their lenders within three years of obtaining the loan, but are not also required to sue their lenders within that same timeframe if the lenders contest the rescission"* [29].

Since the right of rescission was rarely exercised in the past, most of the cases resolving issues about rescission are new. As consumers continue to rely on rescission as a tool to challenge foreclosure actions, the number of decisions that attempt to resolve these issues will continue to grow.

Advertising

Regulation Z creates two sets of advertising rules, with one set applying to open-end transactions and the other applying to transactions for closed-end loans. However, both share a fundamental rule that relates to the advertisement of mortgage loans.

This rule states:

> *"If an advertisement for credit states specific credit terms, it shall state only those terms that actually are or will be arranged or offered by the creditor"* (12 C.F.R. §§1026.16(a), 1026.24(a)).

Both sets of rules also require creditors to make additional disclosures in advertisements, and to make them "clearly and conspicuously." The clear and conspicuous standards are discussed at length in the Official Interpretations of the advertising rules for open-end and closed-end loans. With the exception of the advertisement of specific interest rates and payments, Regulation Z does not outline specific rules for the format of the required disclosures [30]. When a creditor advertises rates and payments, it must:

- Make the required disclosures *"...with equal prominence and in close proximity to the promotional rate or payment..."* that it advertises for open-end credit [31]
- Make the required disclosures *"...with equal prominence and in close proximity to the advertised rates or payments..."* for closed-end credit [32]

The official comments also address the clear and conspicuous standards for advertisements that are not printed. For example, when advertisements for home equity loans or other loans secured by a dwelling are on the Internet, the disclosures cannot be obscured by graphical displays, shading, or coloring. When advertising on television, creditors must make disclosures in a way that allows consumers to read them and cannot be presented in fine print that is not readable. Disclosures provided during radio advertisements must be made at a speed and volume that consumers can follow.

> *TILA and Regulation Z prohibit the advertisement of lending terms that a lender or creditor is not actually prepared to offer.*

Advertising Rules for Open-End Credit (12 C.F.R. §1026.16)

Many of the requirements for advertising both open-end and closed-end credit are "triggered" by the use of particular terms that necessitate the use of additional disclosures, which are intended to ensure that consumers are aware, not only of the benefits of certain mortgage products that are advertised, but of particular detriments as well.

Trigger terms for open-end mortgages, such as home equity plans include references to any of the following:

- Finance charge
- Other charges, such as late payment charges, title, appraisal, and credit report fees [33]
- Taxes imposed on the credit transaction, and
- Payment terms of the home equity plan

The use in an advertisement of any of the terms listed above triggers the requirement to clearly and conspicuously include the following additional information:

- Any loan fee that is a percentage of the credit limit
- An estimate, stated as a dollar amount, of any fee to open the plan
- Any periodic rate used to compute the finance charge, and
- The maximum annual percentage rate that may be imposed under a variable-rate plan

Advertisements for home equity plans often promote features such as a low APR, minimum periodic payments, and tax advantages. As discussed in the following sections, the advertisement of these terms triggers requirements to provide additional information (12 C.F.R. §1026.16(d)).

Advertising Discounted and Premium Rates (12 C.F.R. §1026.16(d)(2))
A discounted or premium rate is an initial APR that is not based on the index and margin used to make rate adjustments for adjustable-rate home equity plans. Advertising a discounted or premium rate triggers the requirement to include the following additional information:

- The period of time that the discount or premium rate will be in effect
- A reasonably current APR for the loan, if it is fully indexed, and the presentation of this information with equal prominence to the discount rate, and
- The fully indexed rate in close proximity to the discount rate

The Federal Trade Commission offers the following example of an advertisement with balanced information on the initial discounted APR and the APR in effect after the first few months of the loan term:

> *7.5% APR FOR THE FIRST SIX MONTHS! After first six months, APR is 10.5% (as of November 1), subject to increase based on market conditions.*

Advertising Minimum Periodic Payments (12 C.F.R. §1026.16(d)(3))
Advertising a minimum periodic payment triggers the requirement to include a statement, if applicable, that a balloon payment may result. For example:

- Even if a balloon payment is uncertain or unlikely, the advertisement of a minimum periodic payment must include, with equal prominence and in close proximity, a statement that a balloon payment may result when borrowers make only the minimum periodic payments required

- If a balloon payment will occur when the borrower makes only the minimal and non-amortizing payments under the plan, advertisement of a minimum periodic payment must include, with equal prominence and in close proximity to the statement about minimum payments, another statement that:
  - A balloon payment will result, and
  - The amount of the balloon payment that the borrower will have to pay if he/she makes minimum periodic payments for the maximum period that minimum payments are allowed

Advertising Tax Deductible Interest (12 C.F.R. §1026.16(d)(4))

Home equity plans have been popular since the Tax Reform Act of 1986 was enacted. This law included a provision that prohibited consumers from deducting the interest paid on unsecured loans from their income taxes. Since 1986, countless consumers have obtained home equity loans to pay off unsecured debt, such as credit card debt and automobile loans, and have deducted the interest they pay on their secured home equity loans.

Lenders often advertise the tax benefits of home equity loans. Regulation Z specifically prohibits the use of advertisements that include any misleading statements regarding the tax benefits of a home equity plan. These advertisements must "clearly and conspicuously" state that:

- If home equity loans exceed the value of the home used to secure the loan, the interest on the portion of the credit extension that is greater than the market value of the property is not deductible, and
- The consumer should consult a tax adviser regarding the amounts that may be deductible

During the lending boom when loan-to-value ratios were often ignored, consumers accepted loans, such as 125% home equity plans, under the misconception that all interest is deductible. These disclosures were intended to discourage this type of borrowing.

Prohibition against Misleading Terms (12 C.F.R. §§1026.16(d)(5), 1026.16(f))

The regulations prohibit the use of misleading terms and phrases in an advertisement for home equity plans such as "Free Money." They also prohibit any reference to an APR as "fixed" unless the advertisement specifies the period of time that the rate will be fixed.

Advertising Promotional Rates and Payments (12 C.F.R. §1026.16(d)(6))

Under Regulation Z, any reference to promotional rates and payments triggers a requirement to provide additional information in a clear and conspicuous manner, with equal prominence and in close proximity to each listing of the promotional rate or payment.

The additional information required by the advertisement of promotional rates and payments includes:

- The time period that the promotional rate or payment will apply
- Any APR that will apply under the home equity plan, and
- Amounts and time periods of any payments that will apply under the home equity plan

These requirements apply to advertisements even if there is no use of the term "promotional rate" or "promotional payments." The point of this requirement is to ensure borrowers have a clear understanding that promotional rates and payments are not the same as fully indexed rates and payments.

The rules also provide that when there is a reference in an advertisement for home equity plans to finance charges, other charges, or payments, the advertisement must "clearly and conspicuously" provide the following additional information:

- A statement, as a single dollar amount, of any loan fee that is a percentage of the credit limit under the plan, and an estimate of other fees for opening the plan

- A statement of the periodic rate used to compute the finance charge, expressed as an APR, and

- The maximum annual percentage rate that can be imposed in a variable-rate plan

Advertising Rules for Closed-End Credit (12 C.F.R. §1026.24)

The need to make particular disclosures when advertising closed-end mortgages is "triggered" by the use of particular terms. The disclosures for closed-end loans, like those for open-end loans, are intended to make consumers aware of the detriments, as well as the benefits, of certain mortgage products.

Trigger Terms for Closed-End Loans (12 C.F.R. §1026.16(d))
The "triggering terms" for closed-end loans are:

- Amount or percentage of any down payment

- Number of payments or the period of repayment

- Payment amounts, and

- The finance charge

The use in an advertisement of any of the terms listed above triggers the requirement to clearly and conspicuously include the following additional information:

- The amount or percentage of the down payment

- The terms of repayment over the full term of the loan, and

- The APR and whether the rate may increase after consummation

> *Regulation Z creates a list of trigger terms for closed-end loans. Related information may also trigger the need for additional disclosures.*

Disclosure of Interest Rates and Payments (12 C.F.R. §1026.24(f))
If an advertisement for a mortgage states a simple rate of interest, and more than one APR will apply over the loan term, the advertisement must disclose the following information *"...with equal prominence and in close proximity to any advertised rate that triggered the required disclosures..."*

(12 C.F.R. §1026.24(f)(2)(ii)). This is the highest standard for a clear and conspicuous disclosure. The disclosures include:

- Each simple interest rate that will apply. For ARMs, the advertisement must state the rate as determined by adding a current index and a margin.
- The period of time that each simple annual rate of interest will apply, and
- The APR for the loan

If an advertisement for a mortgage product states the amount of any payment, the advertisement must clearly and conspicuously disclose the following information with prominence and close proximity to advertised terms:

- The amount of any payment that will apply during the loan term, and payments for ARMs must be based on a current index plus a margin
- The period of time that each payment will apply, and
- The fact that payments do not include taxes and insurance (this requirement applies only to transactions for first-lien mortgages)

Tax Implications (12 C.F.R. §1026.24(h))
If an advertisement states that a loan may exceed the fair market value of the dwelling used to secure it, the advertisement must clearly and conspicuously state:

- That the interest on the portion of the credit extension greater than the market value of the property is not deductible, and
- The consumer should consult a tax adviser regarding the amounts that may be deductible

Home loans that exceed the value of the homes that secure them are very rare in this era of lending that is characterized by more traditional and conservative lending standards. These standards include caps on loan-to-value ratios.

Advertising Prohibitions for Closed-End Credit (12 C.F.R. §1026.24(i))
Regulation Z includes a list of seven prohibited practices when advertising closed-end credit secured by a dwelling. These prohibitions were adopted when the Federal Reserve Board revised Regulation Z in 2008, and were based on studies of advertising copy that allowed the Federal Reserve to identify misleading and deceptive practices in the advertisement of mortgage loans.

Following are the seven practices that are prohibited in closed-end mortgage loans and some of the examples that the Federal Reserve offers, in its Staff Commentary, of prohibited advertisements:

- **Misleading advertising of "fixed" rates and payments**: Today, mortgage products are complex, and there are many that combine fixed and variable rates, such as a stepped-rate mortgage with an initial lower rate that is subject to an increased fixed rate. The use of the word "fixed" in advertisements for these types of loans is prohibited unless there is conspicuous and equally prominent information about variable rates and increasing payments.

- **Misleading comparisons in advertisements**: Comparisons between an advertised mortgage and a hypothetical loan that a consumer may have are prohibited unless the ad includes the requisite disclosures regarding APRs and payments. An advertisement to *"save $300 per month on a $300,000 loan"* is an implied and prohibited comparison between the payment due on the advertised loan and a consumer's current loan payments.

- **Misrepresentations about government endorsement**: Statements that lead consumers to the incorrect assumption that a mortgage product is endorsed by the government are illegal.

- **Misleading use of the current lender's name**: Some lenders and mortgage brokers have made direct solicitations that lead consumers to the incorrect assumption that their own lender is contacting them with information on mortgage products.

- **Misleading claims of debt elimination**: claiming debt elimination when one debt merely replaces another debt.

- **Misleading use of the term counselor**: An advertisement cannot refer to a for-profit lender, mortgage broker, or its employees as a "counselor."

- **Misleading foreign-language advertisements**: Some advertisements target immigrants who lack fluency in English by advertising favorable lending terms in their first language, while providing information on the additional and less favorable lending terms in English.

Regulation Z prohibits the use of misleading terms in advertisements for home equity loans. "Free Money!" is an example that the regulations give of a misleading and, therefore, prohibited term. As stated above, Regulation Z also prohibits misleading statements regarding tax deductions for interest paid on home equity loans.

Liability and Penalties for Violations of TILA (15 U.S.C. §§1611, 1640)

Violations of TILA may lead to criminal liability and penalties, which are addressed in Section 1611 of the law, and to civil liability and penalties, which are addressed in Section 1640 of the law.

Criminal Liability
Criminal liability may arise from willful and knowing violations of the law. The law specifically states that liability may arise as a result of:

- Giving false or inaccurate information

- Failing to provide information that the law or the regulations require to be disclosed, or

- Using any charts or tables that the CFPB has authorized for use in determining and disclosing the APR *"...in a manner as to consistently understate the annual percentage rate..."*

(15 U.S.C. §1611(2))

In addition to these specific violations that may result in criminal liability, TILA includes a broad statement creating criminal liability for other willing and knowing actions that violate the law (15 U.S.C. §1611(3)). Penalties for criminal liability may include a fine of up to $5,000, imprisonment for up to one year, or both a fine and imprisonment.

Civil Liability

TILA contains numerous provisions that relate to civil liability. Individual actions for violations of TILA and Regulation Z may lead to:

- Actual damages, which are the losses that a consumer can show that he/she actually suffered as a result of the violation(s)
- Twice the amount of any finance charge
- Monetary penalties, and
- The costs of bringing the action and attorney's fees

These provisions do not address penalty amounts for open-end credit secured by a dwelling, but for closed-end loans secured by a dwelling, the penalty for violating the law is no less than $400, and no more than $4,000.

Creditors may face a penalty of *"...an amount equal to the sum of all finance charges and fees paid by the consumer..."* for violations of:

- HOEPA
- Prohibitions against incentives for loan originators to steer consumers towards particular loan products, and
- The prohibition against making a residential mortgage loan without determining the borrower's ability to repay the loan

(15 U.S.C. §1640(a)(4))

In class actions, the amount of recovery possible is limited to $1,000,000 or 1% of the creditor's net worth, whichever is less.

TILA states that factors that courts must consider in awarding damages to consumers in class action lawsuits include:

- The amount of actual damages awarded
- The frequency and persistence of the creditor's compliance failures
- The creditor's resources
- The number of consumers affected, and
- The extent to which the compliance failures were intentional

The liability provisions of TILA give creditors the incentive to maintain a compliance program. For example, there is no liability for unintentional violations of the law that result from bona fide errors, if these errors occur *"...notwithstanding the maintenance of procedures reasonably adapted to avoid any such error"* (15 U.S.C. §1640(c)). Examples of "bona fide errors" include *"...clerical, calculation, computer malfunction and programming, and printing errors, except that an error of legal judgment with respect to a person's obligations under this subchapter [TILA] is not a bona fide error"* [34].

In addition to limitations to liability for bona fide errors, there is a provision that limits liability if an act is *"…done or omitted in good faith in conformity with any rule, regulation, or interpretation thereof by the Bureau…"* (15 U.S.C. §1640(f)). These provisions that limit TILA liability are an acknowledgment of the challenges of complying with this very complex law and with the related maze of regulatory provisions.

> *Liability provisions under TILA are meant to give creditors the incentive to maintain compliance programs.*

Discussion Scenario: Disclosure Requirements

Golden Doubloon Finance was just licensed as a mortgage banker in several new states and immediately began a massive advertising campaign. Because of low interest rates, customers flocked in and business was booming. Davey Jones, the managing principal of Golden Doubloon, quickly hired a huge team of new loan originators and got them licensed in record time.

Over the next nine months, business was steady, and there was some loan originator staff turnover. Jones and his management staff were careful to ensure only licensed individuals handled origination tasks, but often the team was new and inexperienced. More often than not, the administrative staff had to rush to advise borrowers of adjustments caused by miscommunications in fees a day or less prior to settlement.

Amidst the chaos of prosperous business, Jones acquired a share in a title company, Ahoy Title. Frequent business referrals from Golden Doubloon allowed Ahoy to share in the success.

It soon came time for several of the state regulators to conduct routine business office examinations of Golden Doubloon. Without exception, all of the regulators came back with the same findings – consumer disclosures were not in order.

Discussion Questions

- *Based on the facts in the scenario, what are some disclosure requirements that might not have been met?*
- *At a minimum, what are the disclosures that should have been issued to borrowers?*
- *How can mortgage professionals ensure they are meeting disclosure requirements?*

Discussion Feedback

Based on the information presented in the scenario, Golden Doubloon's high turnover may have had a significant impact on proper disclosure. It is important to note that licensing requirements were met, meaning the loan originators were likely educated on disclosure requirements. However, the company either did not have policies and procedures in place to ensure disclosures were made, or the policies/procedures were not enforced.

Some of the primary disclosures that could have been missing include:

- Good Faith Estimate – provided within three business days of application
- Affiliated business arrangement disclosure – provided at the time a referral is made
- TIL Disclosure Statement – provided within three business days of application (and no less than seven business days prior to settlement)
- TIL Re-disclosure – provided no less than three business days prior to settlement if the APR/finance charges are inaccurate

Mortgage professionals can ensure they meet disclosure requirements by:

- Establishing and following procedures to ensure disclosures are made pursuant to state and federal laws for all loan applicants without exception
- Ensuring re-disclosure requirements are met if re-disclosure is necessary

The Home Ownership and Equity Protection Act (HOEPA/Regulation Z – 15 U.S.C. §1639 *et seq.* and 12 C.F.R. §§1026.31, .32, and .34)

HOEPA Overview

The federal government addressed predatory lending for the first time in 1994 with the adoption of the Home Ownership and Equity Protection Act (HOEPA). HOEPA creates certain protections under the Truth-in-Lending Act for loans with high interest rates and high fees, and it refers to these loans as **"high-cost mortgages."**

Regulatory Agencies and Regulations

The Board of Governors for the Federal Reserve was the federal agency responsible for issuing implementing regulations for HOEPA. The regulations for HOEPA are set forth in Section 32 of Subpart E of Regulation Z and are sometimes referred to as Section 32 loans. The Dodd-Frank Act greatly expanded the scope of HOEPA, and in 2013, the CFPB issued regulations to implement the amendments that the Dodd-Frank Act made to HOEPA.

Enforcement authority for HOEPA is the same as it is for other provisions of TILA, with the Federal Trade Commission sharing some enforcement authority with the CFPB.

Loans Regulated by HOEPA

The Dodd-Frank Act made many changes to HOEPA that have broadened the scope of the law. Now, there are more loans and types of transactions that are subject to HOEPA. Pursuant to the changes made to HOEPA by the Dodd-Frank Act, the law now defines a **"high-cost mortgage"** as a mortgage loan, other than a reverse mortgage, that:

- Is secured by the borrower's principal dwelling, and
- Meets at least one of the following thresholds:
  - An APR threshold, which differs for first-lien and subordinate-lien mortgages

- ◦ A points and fees threshold, or
- ◦ A prepayment penalty threshold

(15 U.S.C. §1602(aa))

The APR thresholds for first-lien and subordinate-lien high-cost mortgages are:

- **First-lien mortgages**: a first-lien home loan is a high-cost mortgage if its APR is **6.5 percentage points** above the average prime offer rate for a comparable transaction.
- **Subordinate-lien mortgages**: a subordinate-lien home loan is a high-cost mortgage if its APR is **8.5 percentage points** above the average prime offer rate for a comparable transaction.

(12 C.F.R. §1026.32(a)(1)(i))

The points and fees threshold varies based on the amount of the loan, according to a dollar amount that is adjusted annually (12 C.F.R. §1026.32(a)(1)(ii)(A)). Effective January 1, 2015, the threshold is triggered if points and fees exceed the following amounts for a transaction:

- **Threshold for loans of $20,391 or more**: The threshold is triggered if the points and fees exceed 5% of the total loan amount.
- **Threshold for loans of less than $20,391**: The threshold is triggered if the points and fees exceed the lesser of 8% of the total loan amount or $1,020.

A home loan may also be a high-cost mortgage if it includes:

- A prepayment penalty provision that is in force for more than 36 months after consummation, or
- Prepayment penalties that can exceed more than 2% of the amount prepaid

(12 C.F.R. §1026.32(a)(1)(iii))

The Dodd-Frank Act amendments to HOEPA were not limited to lowering the thresholds that define which loans are high-cost mortgages. The scope of the law was expanded to include open-end home equity lines of credit as well as closed-end home equity loans. It was also expanded to include mortgages for the purchase and construction of a borrower's principal dwelling. Refinances continue to be subject to HOEPA. Today's version of HOEPA is therefore applicable to most transactions involving loans that are secured by a consumer's principal dwelling, except for reverse mortgages.

> *The Home Ownership and Equity Protection Act (HOEPA) creates certain protections under the Truth-in-Lending Act (TILA) for loans that cross APR, points and fees, or prepayment penalty thresholds.*

Disclosures and Notifications Required by HOEPA

Loans that fall within the scope of HOEPA are subject to the TILA disclosure requirements for closed-end loans.

These include the following disclosures:

- A Truth-in-Lending Disclosure Statement that includes the APR, finance charge, amount financed, and total of payments

- For adjustable-rate mortgages (ARMs), disclosure requirements include (but are not limited to) a statement that the rate may increase, the index and margin used to adjust the APR, the frequency of adjustments, limitations on increases, and the Customer Handbook on Adjustable-Rate Mortgages (CHARM) booklet

- Notices of the right to rescind, provided to all those with an ownership interest in the mortgaged property

The first two disclosures are due within three business days after the completion of a loan application. The notice of the right to rescind is due at closing.

HOEPA loans are also subject to additional disclosure requirements. Regulation Z requires the presentation of each of these disclosures in "conspicuous type size." The additional disclosures for HOEPA loans include the following.

Special HOEPA Disclosure: HOEPA loans must include a special disclosure that states:

> **You are not required to complete this agreement merely because you have received these disclosures or have signed a loan application. If you obtain this loan, the lender will have a mortgage on your home. You could lose your home, and any money you have put into it, if you do not meet your obligations under the loan.**

Many subprime borrowers are first-time borrowers and do not qualify for a prime loan because they have not had the opportunity to establish their creditworthiness. Having no experience in lending transactions, some do not understand that the completion of a loan application does not obligate them to accept a loan. The special notice is intended to alert subprime borrowers who are pressured by predatory lenders into completing detrimental lending transactions.

Notice of Balloon Payment: When balloon payments are not prohibited, as discussed in the following section, the lending agreement must state the existence of a balloon payment.

HOEPA includes special requirements for the disclosure of balloon payments because many victims of predatory loans do not realize that their repayment agreement includes a balloon payment until it is due. If unable to make a balloon payment, a borrower's only options are to refinance the loan or to default on it.

Amount Borrowed: In a mortgage refinancing, there must be a statement of the total amount borrowed, as shown on the face amount on the promissory note. This disclosure is accurate if it is not more than $100 above or below the amount that must be disclosed.

Notice of the Inclusion of Insurance Premiums: If the "amount borrowed" includes premiums for optional insurance products or debt cancellation coverage, a statement that these premiums are included must accompany the disclosure of the amount borrowed.

The statements of the amount borrowed with an accompanying statement of the amount of any insurance premiums are intended to deter the covert packing of unnecessary insurance products into a loan.

Variable-Rate Disclosure: If the mortgage has an adjustable rate, the disclosure must include a statement that the monthly payment may increase, showing the maximum monthly payment amount based on the information on rate increases provided in the Truth-in-Lending Statement.

The recent rash of foreclosures has coincided with scheduled rate increases in adjustable-rate mortgages. The disclosure of the maximum monthly payment is intended to alert borrowers to the payment shock that they will face when interest rates reset.

Recipients of the Disclosures

The recipients of HOEPA disclosures include:

- Any consumer who is primarily liable on the obligation
- Those with a right to rescind the transaction (each person with an ownership interest in the property used to secure the loan)

Deadline for HOEPA Disclosures (12 C.F.R. §1026.31(c))

The disclosures for HOEPA loans are due at least three business days (all days other than Sunday and federal holidays) prior to the consummation of the mortgage. The disclosures are made prior to the time of closing so that the loan applicant will have at least a three-business-day waiting period to consider whether it is best to proceed with the transaction.

Right to Waive the Waiting Period (12 C.F.R. §1026.31(c)(iii))

HOEPA allows for the waiver of the three-business-day waiting period if the funds to be obtained from a loan are needed to meet a "bona fide personal emergency." In order to waive the three business day waiting period and to proceed directly to closing, the borrower must:

- Give the lender a dated and written statement that describes the emergency (the use of printed forms is not allowed)
- Signatures from all parties who are entitled to the waiting period (the recipients of the disclosures)

Loans that fall within the scope of HOEPA are subject to the TILA disclosure requirements for closed-end loans.

Affirmative Requirements for HOEPA Transactions

Three specific requirements that HOEPA imposes on transactions for high-cost mortgages include evaluating the ability of borrowers to repay their loans, ensuring that borrowers of high-cost mortgages receive counseling, and notifying assignees when a loan they are assuming is a high-cost mortgage. These specific requirements are discussed below.

Evaluation of Borrower Repayment Ability (12 C.F.R. §1026.34(a)(4))

During the mortgage lending boom, countless loans were made without analyzing the ability of borrowers to repay their loans. This practice occurred in the subprime market despite the fact that revised HOEPA regulations required creditors to evaluate repayment ability. Now that HOEPA applies to both open- and closed-end transactions, the regulations have been revised to address ability-to-repay evaluations for both types of transactions, as follows.

Evaluating Repayment Ability in Closed-End Transactions: For closed-end high-cost mortgages, creditors are required to comply with the repayment ability requirements set forth in 12 C.F.R. §1026.43. To summarize, these rules require creditors to base lending decisions on a reasonable, good faith determination, at or prior to consummation, that the consumer has a reasonable ability to repay the loan according to its terms (12 C.F.R. §1026.43(c)).

This determination of repayment ability must be based on the consumer's:

- Income or assets, other than the home used to secure the loan
- Current employment status
- Monthly mortgage payments, calculated at the fully-indexed rate
- Payments on any simultaneous loans
- Monthly mortgage-related obligations, such as taxes and insurance
- Current debt obligations
- Monthly debt-to-income ratio, and
- Credit history

Section 43 also requires creditors to verify the information used to assess repayment ability using reasonably reliable third-party records (12 C.F.R. §1026.43(c)(3)). Verification of income and assets must be made with records such as tax returns, payroll statements, and financial institution records.

Evaluating Repayment Ability in Open-End Transactions: For open-end high-cost mortgages, creditors must base an assessment of repayment ability on the verification of income, assets, and current obligations using:

- IRS W-2 forms, tax returns, payroll receipts, financial institution records, or other reasonably reliable third-party documents, and

- Evidence of current obligations, including those related to other mortgages secured by the same dwelling that will secure the high-cost mortgage. Current obligations include property taxes, insurance, and homeowners' association fees.

(12 C.F.R. §1026.34(a)(4))

The regulations create a **"presumption of compliance"** for open-end transactions. It is presumed that a creditor has complied with the requirement to assess a borrower's ability to repay an open-end high-cost mortgage if the creditor:

- Evaluates a consumer's repayment ability by verifying income and assets using the required documentation and verifies current obligations, including obligations to pay other mortgages

- Determines repayment ability using the largest required minimum periodic payment, which must be based on the following assumptions:
  - The consumer borrows the full credit line when opening the account, with no additional extensions of credit
  - The consumer makes only the minimum periodic payments during the draw period and any repayment period, and
  - The maximum APR that the contract provides for applies to the plan at the time the account is opened, and will apply during the draw period and any repayment period

- Evaluates repayment ability after taking at least one of the following factors into account:
  - The ratio of current obligations to income, or
  - The income that the borrower will have after paying current obligations

The only transactions that are exempt from the ability-to-repay analysis are temporary or bridge loans with terms of 12 months or less (12 C.F.R. §1026.34(a)(4)).

Counseling Requirements (12 C.F.R. §1026.34(a)(5))
Before creditors offer a high-cost mortgage to a borrower, they must make certain that the borrower has completed counseling with a HUD-approved counselor by reviewing the borrower's certification of counseling.

This certification must include:
- Names of the consumers who completed counseling
- Dates of the counseling
- Name and address of the counselor
- A statement that the consumer received counseling that addressed the advisability of a high-cost mortgage, and that the counseling was based on the terms presented in the Good Faith Estimate or in the disclosures required for home equity loans, and
- Verification that the consumers received the disclosures required under HOEPA and RESPA

The regulations allow creditors to pay counseling fees, but prohibit them from:

- Allowing consumers to receive counseling from a counselor that is employed by or affiliated with the creditor

- Conditioning the payment of counseling fees on consummating a loan or opening a credit plan, and

- Steering a consumer to select a particular counselor or counseling organization

Required Notice to Assignees and Purchasers (12 C.F.R. §1026.34(a)(2))

Many loans are assigned or sold shortly after closing. Assignments occur when a non-depository mortgage banker closes a loan in its name using a line of credit and immediately assigns the loan to the creditor that provided the loan funds. Many lenders sell home loans in the secondary mortgage market instead of holding them in their portfolios, so that they can secure funds to make more loans.

When the sell or assignment of a loan occurs, legal questions arise regarding the liability of the assignee or purchaser for claims that the borrower could raise against the creditor. Because claims for violations of lending laws are more common in the subprime market, assignees and purchasers of high-cost mortgages may have concerns regarding potential liability for violations of HOEPA. New provisions in Regulation Z require originators of high-cost mortgages to provide assignees and purchasers with notice of the fact that these loans are subject to HOEPA.

This notice states:

> *"Notice: This is a mortgage subject to special rules under the federal Truth in Lending Act. Purchasers or assignees of this mortgage could be liable for all claims and defenses with respect to the mortgage that the consumer could assert against the creditor."*

> *Three specific requirements that HOEPA imposes on high-cost mortgage transactions include evaluating borrower repayment ability, ensuring that borrowers receive counseling, and notifying assignees when they assume a high-cost mortgage.*

Prohibited Lending Terms (12 C.F.R. §1026.32(d))

The following lending terms are often found in predatory home loans. HOEPA prohibits the use of these terms in high-cost mortgages:

Balloon payments: balloon payments are not allowed in high-cost mortgages. There are exceptions for:

- Loans that use a payment schedule adjusted according to the consumer's seasonal or irregular employment

- Loans with terms of 12 months or less, if the loan is a bridge loan related to the purchase or construction of a home that will be the borrower's principal dwelling, and

- A balloon payment qualified mortgage or a temporary balloon payment qualified mortgage, which small creditors are allowed to make until January 10, 2016

Negative amortization: loans that meet the HOEPA interest rate or fee triggers cannot include a payment schedule that results in negative amortization.

Advanced payments: HOEPA prohibits the consolidation of more than two periodic payments and payment of this amount, in advance, from the proceeds of a loan.

Increased interest rate after default: high-cost mortgages cannot include terms that allow interest rates to increase after the borrower defaults on a payment.

Improperly calculated rebates: when calculating a rebate of interest that results from loan acceleration due to default, creditors are prohibited from using any method that is less favorable than the actuarial method.

Prepayment penalties: prepayment penalties are not allowed for HOEPA loans under any circumstances.

Acceleration of debt: high-cost mortgages cannot include a term that allows the creditor to accelerate the debt and to demand payment of the entire loan balance, except under the following circumstances:

- Fraud or misrepresentation on the part of the borrower
- Consumer's failure to meet the repayment terms of the lending agreement, or
- Any action or inaction of the borrower that affects the creditor's security for the loan or the creditor's rights related to the security

Prohibited Lending Practices (12 C.F.R. §1026.34)

HOEPA prohibits the use of the following lending practices when originating a high-cost mortgage:

Direct payments to home improvement contractors: some of the most outrageous accounts of predatory lending involve fraudulent schemes in which unethical mortgage brokers and home improvement contractors coordinate efforts to fleece unsuspecting homeowners with aggressive door-to-door sales tactics. After persuading these homeowners to allow them to complete repairs, fraudulent contractors bring in a mortgage broker to manage the financing. After the closing, with the loan funds secured, the broker pays the home improvement contractor. The contractor then performs little or no work, and the homeowner realizes too late that he/she is the victim of fraud. HOEPA prohibits direct payments to home improvement contractors, unless payment is a joint payment to the borrower and the contractor, or is made to a third-party escrow agent pursuant to a written agreement between the lender, borrower, and contractor.

Loan flipping: "loan flipping" is the repeated refinancing of a loan within a short period of time. No high-cost mortgage can be refinanced within 12 months of the initial extension of credit, unless the refinancing is in the borrower's interest. This prohibition applies not only to the creditor funding the loan, but also to loan servicers and assignees. A pattern or practice of using affiliates or nonaffiliated lenders to refinance a high-cost mortgage within the first year of the loan term is also prohibited.

Financing points and fees: another provision that is intended to prevent loan flipping is the prohibition against financing charges that must be included in the calculation of points and fees. When funds for subprime loans were readily available, many borrowers tried to get out of expensive ARMs by refinancing. With lenders offering to finance the fees related to the transaction, many borrowers rushed into a refinance, taking on even more debt than they already owed.

Lending without regard to repayment ability: HOEPA prohibits lending based on the amount of equity in a borrower's home without also considering the borrower's ability to repay.

Lending without pre-loan counseling: HOEPA prohibits the making of a high-cost mortgage unless the creditor receives written certification of completion of counseling from a HUD-approved counselor.

Recommending default: HOEPA prohibits creditors and mortgage brokers from recommending or encouraging a consumer's default on an existing loan or other debt in connection with a high-cost mortgage that will refinance all or part of the existing loan or debt. This is another provision intended to discourage loan flipping.

Charging loan modification or deferral fees: HOEPA prohibits creditors, assignees, and agents of these parties from charging any fee to modify, renew, extend, or amend a high-cost home loan, and from charging a fee for payment deferrals.

Charging late fees: late charges may not be imposed unless the contract for the high-cost mortgage permits them. Late charges may not exceed 4% of the amount of the payment past due, and a charge may not be imposed more than once for the same late payment. Late payments may not be charged unless a payment is late by at least 15 days.

Charging fees for payoff statements: while there are some exceptions, HOEPA generally prohibits a creditor or servicer from charging a consumer a fee for a statement of the amount due to pay off a high-cost mortgage. Creditors or servicers may charge a fee to fax a payoff statement or to send a statement by courier, if these fees are comparable to those charged in lending transactions that do not involve high-cost mortgages. However, before providing a payoff statement via fax or courier, the creditor or servicer must advise the consumer that the statement is available by other methods without any charge.

If a creditor or servicer has already provided a payoff statement four times within one calendar year, it may charge a "reasonable fee" for providing subsequent statements during that year. Payoff statements are due within **five business days** of receipt of a request for the statement.

Evading HOEPA: it is a violation of HOEPA to structure a loan to avoid application of the law, including by dividing any loan transaction into separate parts.

Penalties for HOEPA Violations

Congress enacted HOEPA as an amendment to the Truth-in-Lending Act (TILA). Therefore, penalties for violations of HOEPA are the same as those imposed under TILA.

Prohibitions for Loans Secured by a Principal Dwelling

The prohibitions that are reviewed in the previous section are limited to loans that meet the interest rate and fee triggers under HOEPA. In amendments that it made to Regulation Z in 2008, the Federal Reserve created new prohibitions that relate to all loans secured by a borrower's principal dwelling. These regulations relate to two issues: The appraisal of a principal dwelling that secures a loan and the servicing of mortgages on principal dwellings. These regulations were effective on October 1, 2009.

Prohibited Appraisal Practices

The regulations provide that no lender, mortgage broker, or their affiliates can directly or indirectly influence the judgment of an appraiser who is assessing the value of a principal dwelling. Illegal influence includes encouraging an appraiser to misstate or misrepresent the value of the principal dwelling used to secure a loan. The regulations provide the following examples of actions that violate this prohibition:

- Implying to an appraiser that current or future retention of the appraiser depends on the amount at which the appraiser values a consumer's principal dwelling
- Excluding an appraiser from consideration for future engagement because the appraiser reports a value of a consumer's principal dwelling that does not meet or exceed a minimum threshold
- Telling an appraiser a minimum reported value of a consumer's principal dwelling that is needed to approve the loan
- Failing to compensate an appraiser because the appraiser does not value a consumer's principal dwelling at or above a certain amount
- Conditioning an appraiser's compensation on loan consummation

(12 C.F.R. §1026.42(c))

The regulations also include examples of actions that a lender or mortgage broker can take without violating the prohibition against influencing the opinion of an appraiser:

- Asking an appraiser to consider additional information about a consumer's principal dwelling or about comparable properties
- Requesting that an appraiser provide additional information about the basis for a valuation
- Requesting that an appraiser correct factual errors in a valuation

- Obtaining multiple appraisals of a consumer's principal dwelling, so long as the creditor adheres to a policy of selecting the most reliable appraisal, rather than the appraisal that states the highest value

- Withholding compensation from an appraiser for breach of contract or substandard performance of services as provided by contract

- Taking action permitted or required by applicable federal or state statute, regulation, or agency guidance

Prohibited Servicing Practices

When servicing a loan that is secured by a borrower's principal dwelling, loan servicers cannot:

- Fail to credit a payment on the day of its receipt

- Impose a late fee or delinquency charge for any payment other than the payment that is actually late

- Fail to provide an accurate statement of the payoff amount within a reasonable time after requested

(12 C.F.R. §1026.36(c))

> *No lender, mortgage broker, or their affiliates may directly or indirectly influence the judgment of an appraiser who is assessing the value of a principal dwelling.*

Regulations for Higher-Priced Mortgages

While the subprime market was strong, the effectiveness of HOEPA in eliminating the use of predatory lending terms and practices was impaired by thresholds that were set so high that only the most expensive subprime loans were subject to its provisions. In 2008, the Federal Reserve Board attempted to make protections available to more borrowers in the subprime market by writing a new set of regulations that apply to **"higher-priced mortgage loans"** (HPMLs). These regulations are found in Section 35 of Regulation Z.

After the CFPB inherited implementation and enforcement authority from the Federal Reserve, it made numerous revisions to Section 35. These revisions include those that address appraisals for HPMLs, as discussed below.

Loans Protected by the Higher-Priced Mortgage Regulations (12 C.F.R. §1026.35(a))

Section 35 of Regulation Z applies to closed-end loans that are secured by the borrower's principal dwelling and surpass a given threshold. A loan of this type will be considered a higher-priced mortgage loan if the annual percentage rate for the loan exceeds the average prime offer rate for a comparable transaction by:

- **1.5 percentage points** for first-lien loans with a principal amount that does not exceed the maximum principal obligation eligible for purchase by Freddie Mac (i.e., non-jumbo loans or loans that meet the conforming loan limits of $417,000, or up to $625,500 in high-cost areas)

- **2.5 percentage points** for first-lien loans with a principal amount that exceeds the maximum principal obligation eligible for purchase by Freddie Mac (i.e., jumbo loans or loans that exceed the conforming loan limit)
- **3.5 percentage points** or more for loans secured by a subordinate lien

(12 C.F.R. §1026.35(a)(1))

The average prime offer rate that is used for determining whether a transaction triggers the HPML thresholds is the rate for a comparable transaction as of the date the interest rate is set (12 C.F.R. §1026.35(a)(1)). The Federal Financial Institutions Examination Council (FFIEC) publishes average prime offer rates on the Internet. They represent the average of interest rates, indexes, margins, points, and other information relevant to loan pricing for prime rate loans [35].

Requirements for Higher-Priced Mortgage Loans

The 2008 regulations for HPMLs included:

- A rule requiring creditors to assess borrower repayment ability
- A rule restricting prepayment penalties in HPMLs, and
- A rule requiring creditors to establish escrow accounts for the payment of taxes and insurance

As a result of amendments to the regulations that were made by the CFPB, the only one of these rules that remains in Section 35 is the requirement for creditors to establish escrow accounts.

The removal of rules related to the assessment of repayment ability and prepayment penalty restrictions does not mean that these requirements and restrictions no longer apply to HPMLs. When it issued the revised version of Section 35, the CFPB explained that *"...the subsections on repayment ability (existing §1026.35(b)(1)) and prepayment penalties (existing §1026.35(b)(2)) will be deleted because the Dodd-Frank Act addressed these matters in other ways"* [36]. The "other ways" that these matters are addressed include:

- Provisions under the Ability to Repay Rule (ATR Rule) that require an assessment of repayment ability in most mortgage lending transactions, including closed-end HPMLs, and
- Provisions under the Qualified Mortgage Rule (QM Rule) that prohibit prepayment penalties in transactions involving HPMLs.

As a result of these changes in regulations, the primary requirements for HPMLs are those that relate to the establishment of escrow accounts and those that relate to appraisals.

2008 revisions to Regulation Z included a new set of rules that apply to "higher-priced mortgages," to ensure that protections exist for subprime loans that do not meet the interest rate or fee triggers of HOEPA.

Establishment of an Escrow Account for Taxes and Insurance (12 C.F.R. §1026.35(b))

An **escrow account** is any account established or controlled by a servicer on behalf of a borrower to pay taxes, insurance premiums, or other charges related to a mortgage loan, including charges to which the borrower and servicer have voluntarily agreed.

Creditors may not extend a higher-priced mortgage loan secured by a first lien on a consumer's principal dwelling without establishing, prior to consummation, an escrow account for the payment of property taxes and mortgage-related insurance premiums.

Escrow accounts for higher-priced mortgage loans must be established and maintained for a minimum of **five years.** Note that this is a significant expansion on the previous one-year requirement. After this five-year period has expired, the consumer may request cancellation of the escrow account; however, this may only occur if the loan's unpaid principal balance is less than 80% of the original value of the property securing the debt. In addition, the consumer may not be delinquent or in default on the loan.

An escrow account is not required for:

- A transaction secured by shares in a cooperative
- A transaction to finance the initial construction of a dwelling
- A temporary or bridge loan with a term of 12 months or less
- A reverse mortgage
- Open-end credit (such as HELOCs), or
- Insurance premiums purchased by the consumer and not required by the creditor

Insurance premiums do not need to be included in escrow accounts for loans securing dwellings in condominiums, planned unit developments, or other common interest communities in which there is required participation or membership in a governing association, where that association has an obligation to the dwelling owners to maintain a master policy insuring all homes (12 C.F.R. §1026.35(b)(2)).

An exemption from escrow requirements also exists for small creditors. This exemption will be discussed in further detail in the following section.

Small Creditor Exemption (12 C.F.R. §1026.35(b)(2)(iii))

The regulations include an exemption from the escrow requirements for small creditors. The reasoning behind this exemption is that when small creditors hold the home loans that they make in their portfolios, they have the incentive to evaluate the ability of borrowers to make regular and timely payments of principal, interest, taxes, and insurance.

The small creditor exemption is applicable to creditors in rural and underserved areas. Rural counties are identified based on U.S. Department of Agriculture (USDA) data, and the identification of underserved areas is based on data collected through the Home Mortgage

Disclosure Act (HMDA). In order to determine if their loans are secured by properties in rural or underserved areas, small creditors can refer to the CFPB's *Final List of Rural and Underserved Counties for Use in 2014*, found on the CFPB's website [37]. The regulations provide that when a creditor is trying to determine if a county is rural or underserved, it may rely as a safe harbor on the list of counties published by the CFPB (12 C.F.R. §1026.35(b)(iv)(A), (B)).

The status of lenders as small creditors also depends on the number of "covered transactions" originated during the preceding calendar year. Covered transactions are consumer credit transactions secured by a dwelling other than an open-end home equity line of credit, a mortgage related to a timeshare plan, a reverse mortgage, or a bridge loan of 12 months or less. [1]

A creditor is able to qualify for the small creditor exemption if:

- During any of the three preceding years, the creditor extended **more than 50%** of covered transactions secured by a first lien on residential real property in counties qualified as "rural" or "underserved"

- The combined first-lien originations of the creditor and its affiliates did not exceed **500 loans** during the preceding calendar year

- At the end of the preceding calendar year, the creditor had assets worth less than **$2 billion** (this amount will be adjusted annually), and

- Neither the creditor nor its affiliates maintain an escrow account for any extension of consumer credit secured by real property or a dwelling that the creditor or its affiliate currently services

(12 C.F.R. §1026.35(b)(2)(iii))

The exemption from the requirement to establish an escrow account does not apply if a first-lien HPML will be purchased by an investor that does not qualify as a small creditor. In cases in which a first-lien HPML is subject to a commitment at consummation to be acquired by a creditor that is not a small creditor, an escrow account must be established (12 C.F.R. §1026.35(b)(2)(v)).

> *The small creditor exemption is determined based on the number of "covered transactions" originated in the preceding calendar year.*

Appraisal Requirements for HPMLs (12 C.F.R. §1026.35(c))

The Dodd-Frank Act addressed numerous issues that contributed to the collapse of the mortgage market. One of these issues, particularly in the subprime market, was the widespread use of unethical appraisal practices. A solution to this problem that is outlined in the law and implemented in Section 35 of Regulation Z is the creation of special appraisal requirements for HPMLs. The general rule created by these regulations is that a creditor may not offer an HPML

---

1   Section 35 incorporates the definition of "covered transaction" found in 12 C.F.R. §1026.43(b)(1).

to a consumer without obtaining, before consummation, a written appraisal of the property to be mortgaged (12 C.F.R. §1026.35(c)(3)(i)).

Appraisals for HPMLs are required to:

- Be conducted by an appraiser, who is certified or licensed in the state where the property securing the loan is located. This person must conduct the appraisal in conformity with Uniform Standards of Professional Appraisal Practice and requirements applicable under the Financial Institutions Reform, Recovery, and Enforcement Act (12 C.F.R. §1026.35(c)(1)(i)).
- Make a physical visit to the interior of the property securing the transaction (12 C.F.R. §1026.35(c)(3)(i)).

The regulations create a **"safe harbor"** to reduce creditors' exposure to liability by providing that an appraisal is deemed to meet the requisite standards if the creditor:

- Orders the appraiser to perform the appraisal in compliance with USPAP and FIRREA
- Uses the National Registry to verify that the appraiser is certified or licensed in the state where the appraised property that is securing the loan is located
- Confirms that the written appraisal meets each of the requirements of Appendix N, described below, and
- Has no knowledge contrary to the facts or certifications contained in the appraisal

(12 C.F.R. §1026.35(c)(3)(ii)(D))

No later than the third business day after a creditor receives a consumer's application for an HPML, the creditor must provide the loan applicant with a written disclosure that states:

> *"We may order an appraisal to determine the property's value and charge you for this appraisal. We will give you a copy of any appraisal, even if your loan does not close. You can pay for an additional appraisal for your own use at your own cost" (12 C.F.R. §1026.35(c)(5)(i)).*

If a consumer does not apply for an HPML, but the transaction becomes one for a higher-priced loan after application, the creditor must provide the above disclosure or mail it no later than the third business day after the creditor determines that the loan will be an HPML. The creditor may provide the appraisal copy in electronic form, if the consumer has consented to electronic communications (12 C.F.R. §1026.35(c)(5)(ii)).

Additionally, creditors must provide consumers with a copy of each written appraisal, no later than three business days prior to consummation. In the case of a loan that is not consummated, the appraisal must be provided no more than 30 days after the creditor determines that consummation will not occur. If there is more than one applicant for a loan, the creditor is only required to provide a copy of the appraisal to one of the applicants (12 C.F.R. §1026.35(c)(6)(ii)).

The Rule does not affect, modify, limit, or supersede the operation of any legal, regulatory, or other requirements or standards relating to independence in the conduct of appraisers or restrictions on the use of borrower-ordered appraisals by creditors (12 C.F.R. §1026.35(c)(5)(i)).

Creditors may not charge fees for photocopying appraisals, or postage for providing copies of appraisals. In addition, creditors may not raise the consumer's interest rate or mark up any other fees as a means of covering these costs (12 C.F.R. §1026.35(c)(6)(iv)).

Safe Harbor Appraisal Requirements
In order to qualify for the safe harbor provided under 12 C.F.R. §1026.35(c)(3)(ii), creditors must ensure that the written appraisal:

- Identifies the creditor ordering the appraisal and the property and interest being appraised
- Indicates whether the contract price was analyzed
- Addresses conditions in the property's neighborhood
- Addresses the condition of the property and any improvements to it
- Indicates which valuation approaches were used and includes a reconciliation if more than one approach was utilized
- Provides an opinion of the property's market value and an effective date for the opinion
- Indicates that a physical visit to the interior of the property was performed
- Includes a signed certification from the appraiser that the appraisal was prepared according to USPAP requirements, and
- Includes a signed certification from the appraiser that the appraisal was prepared according to requirements of Title XI of FIRREA and any implementing regulations [38]

Exemptions from Appraisal Requirements (12 C.F.R. §1026.35(c)(2))
The appraisal requirements for HPMLs do not apply to:

- Qualified mortgages
- Transactions secured by a manufactured home
- Transactions secured by a mobile home, boat, or trailer
- Transactions to finance the initial construction of a dwelling
- Bridge loans with terms of 12 months or less, used by a consumer to purchase a new home while selling his/her current principal residence, or
- Reverse mortgages

The general rule created by Regulation Z is that a creditor may not offer an HPML to a consumer without obtaining, before consummation, a written appraisal of the property to be mortgaged.

Special Requirement for Two Appraisals (12 C.F.R. §1026.35(c)(4))

In some cases, a creditor is prohibited from making an HPML to finance the acquisition of a consumer's principal dwelling without obtaining two written appraisals prior to consummation.

These circumstances include those in which:

- The seller acquired the home **90 or fewer days** prior to the consumer's agreement to purchase it, and the price at which the consumer has agreed to purchase the home is **10%** more than the price paid by the seller.

- The seller acquired the home **91 to 180 days** prior to the consumer's agreement to purchase it, and the price at which the consumer has agreed to purchase the home is **20%** more than the price paid by the seller.

The requirement for an additional appraisal is intended to curb the practice of property flipping.

When two appraisals are required, they must meet the following requirements:

- The same certified or licensed appraiser may not perform both appraisals

- Both appraisals must be performed by a certified or licensed appraiser, who must conduct a physical visit of the interior of the dwelling that will secure the loan

- One of the two appraisals must provide an analysis of:

  ○ The difference between the price that the seller paid for the property and the price that the consumer agreed to pay

  ○ Changes in market conditions occurring between the time that the seller purchased the property and the time that the consumer agreed to buy it, and

  ○ Any improvements made to the property after the seller purchased it and before the consumer agreed to buy it

- The creditor may not charge the consumer for the second appraisal

A creditor is not required to order two appraisals if it can demonstrate, through reasonable diligence, that the requirement does not apply (12 C.F.R. §1026.35(c)(4)(vi)). A creditor exercises reasonable diligence in making this determination if it is based on information found in documents such as those that are listed in Appendix O. This Appendix states that a creditor has acted with reasonable diligence under 12 C.F.R. §1026.35(c)(4)(vi)(A) if a determination was made based on information contained in written source documents, such as:

- A copy of the recorded deed from the seller

- A copy of a property tax bill

- A copy of any owner's title insurance policy obtained by the seller

- A copy of the RESPA Settlement Statement from the seller's acquisition

- A property sales history report or title report from a third-party reporting service

- Sales price data recorded in multiple listing services

- Tax assessment records or transfer tax records obtained from local governments

- A written appraisal performed in compliance with 12 C.F.R. §1026.35(c)(3)(i) for the same transaction
- A copy of a title commitment report detailing the seller's ownership of the property, the date of acquisition, or the price at which the seller acquired the property, or
- A property abstract

Reliance on oral statements of interested parties, such as the consumer, seller, or mortgage broker does not constitute reasonable diligence.

Exemptions from the Requirement for Two Appraisals (12 C.F.R. §1026.35(c)(4)(vii))
During rulemaking proceedings for the HPML Appraisal Rule, the CFPB sought comments on situations in which a second appraisal may be unnecessary because the facts surrounding the transaction would not be conducive to property flipping or other types of fraud. As a result of the comments received, the CFPB added a list of eight exemptions to the Rule.

If a transaction for an HPML falls within one of the exemptions listed below, the creditor that is making the loan for a home purchase is not required to obtain a second appraisal.

The exemptions are for transactions involving:
- **Property sold by a local, state, or federal government agency**: this exemption was created because the CFPB determined that properties sold by HUD and other government agencies do not present risks of fraud or flipping that the appraisal rules were intended to address [39]. Noting that sales by government agencies often involve foreclosed properties that are sold quickly to promote homeownership and neighborhood revitalization, the requirement to obtain a second appraisal could interfere with these programs.
- **Purchases from a person that acquired the property through foreclosure**: this exemption applies when the seller acquired the property by exercising the right to foreclose on a defaulted mortgage loan. This exemption includes depository and non-depository lenders and servicers that exercise the right to foreclose.
- **Purchases from nonprofit entities**: this exemption is applicable to nonprofit entities that are allowed to acquire properties for resale from sellers that purchased the properties through a foreclosure [40].
- **Purchases from sellers that acquired property through inheritance**: this exemption also applies to properties that the seller acquired as a result of a court order of dissolution of marriage, civil union, domestic partnership, or partition of joint assets.
- **Purchases from employers or relocation agencies**: this exemption applies when an employer or relocation company acquires a property as a result of relocating an employee.
- **Purchases from a servicemember**: this exemption applies if the servicemember received a deployment or permanent change of station order purchasing the property (12 C.F.R. §1026.35(c)(4)(vii)(F)).
- **Purchases of property in federal disaster areas**: if the property purchased is located in an area that the President designates as a federal disaster area, a second appraisal is not needed.

- **Purchases of property in rural areas**: there are multiple reasons for this exemption, including the difficulty of finding more than one licensed and certified appraiser in some rural areas, which would necessitate the additional cost of hiring appraisers from outside the area where the property is located. Other reasons include the fact that rural areas have not historically been sources of fraudulent real estate flipping activity [41].

Homeowners Protection Act (HPA – 12 U.S.C. §4901 *et seq.*)

HPA Overview

Congress passed the Homeowners Protection Act (HPA) in 1998 to facilitate the cancellation of private mortgage insurance (PMI). Lenders may require borrowers to purchase PMI when they make down payments of less than 20%, and the loan-to-value ratio is high. Borrowers who have little money to invest in the purchase of a home are more likely to default on their loans, and PMI allows lenders to protect their interests while making these riskier loans. PMI helps consumers by enabling them to secure a loan when they have little cash for a down payment. The cost of PMI varies depending on loan product and/or insurer, and is calculated as a percentage of the total amount of the loan.

Generally, borrowers can request that lenders cancel PMI when their loan balance is less than 80%. Based on a borrower's payment history, the lender may honor the request or continue to collect PMI until 78% loan-to-value (22% equity position) is reached. The Homeowner's Protection Act provides for the automatic termination of PMI as borrowers build equity, and the risk of loss from default decreases.

Regulatory Agency
Prior to the transfer of power to the CFPB in July 2011, the federal agencies responsible for enforcing compliance with the HPA were the Federal Deposit Insurance Corporation, the Office of Thrift Supervision, the National Credit Union Administration, and the Farm Credit Administration. The CFPB is now responsible for enforcing the HPA.

Loans and Entities Covered by the HPA
The Homeowners Protection Act applies to residential mortgages on single-family homes used as the borrower's principal dwelling. The law is applicable to lenders, loan servicers, and insurers.

Loans Exempt from the HPA
The provisions of the Homeowners Protection Act do not apply to:

- Government-insured FHA or VA loans
- Loans protected by PMI paid for by the lender

Congress passed the Homeowners Protection Act (HPA) to facilitate the cancellation of private mortgage insurance (PMI).

In addition to these exemptions, there are special exceptions for loans defined under the Act as high-risk loans. For these loans, PMI is in place for a longer period of time but will terminate automatically following the date that is the midpoint of the amortization period if the borrower is current on his/her payments.

Definition of Terms in the Homeowners Protection Act (12 U.S.C. §4903)

Good payment history: A borrower has a "good payment history" if he/she did not make a mortgage payment that was 60 days or more past due during the 12-month period beginning 24 months before the date on which the mortgage reaches the cancellation date and did not make a mortgage payment that was 30 days or longer past due during the 12-month period preceding the date on which the mortgage reaches the cancellation date.

Final Termination: The termination of PMI occurs when the loan does not qualify for earlier cancellation or termination. Final termination takes place on the first day of the month after the mid-point of the loan's amortization period.

High-Risk Loans: Loans that do not meet the conforming loan limits established by Fannie Mae and Freddie Mac.

Disclosures and Notifications Required by HPA

The disclosures required by the law depend on the date that the loan is consummated. For mortgages that closed **before July 29, 1999,** there is only one disclosure requirement. This is the requirement to provide the borrower with an **annual notice** advising him/her that, in certain circumstances, it is possible to request cancellation of PMI. The notice must include an address and a telephone number that the borrower can use to obtain more information on canceling PMI.

For loans that closed **on or after July 29, 1999,** there are numerous disclosure and notification requirements. The primary purpose of the disclosure requirements is to advise borrowers that they have the option of requesting cancellation of their PMI when the loan-to-value ratio on the property securing the loan reaches 80%.

A borrower may request cancellation of PMI if he/she:
- Submits a written request for cancellation
- Has a "good payment history"
- Is current on his/her mortgage payments, and
- Is able to satisfy the lender's requirements to show that the value of the property securing the mortgage has not declined below its original value and the property securing the mortgage is not encumbered by a subordinate lien

(12 U.S.C. §4902)

If borrowers do not pursue the option of canceling their PMI, termination automatically occurs when the loan-to-value ratio reaches 78% of the original value of the property and when the date at which that is projected to occur arrives (based on the initial amortization schedule). A subsequent notification will advise borrowers that the automatic termination has occurred. Note that the requirements differ slightly for fixed-rate loans and ARMs.

Disclosures for Fixed-Rate Mortgages: If PMI applies to a fixed-rate mortgage, the lender must provide the borrower with each of the following at the time of the closing:

- An initial amortization schedule
- Written notice that the borrower can request cancellation of PMI on the *cancellation date* (the date that the loan-to-value ratio will reach 80%)
- Written notice that the borrower can accelerate payment on the loan, thereby reaching an 80% loan-to-value ratio and the ability to cancel PMI ahead of schedule
- Written notice that cancellation of PMI is automatic on the *termination date* (the date when the loan-to-value ratio reaches 78% of the original value of the property)

Disclosures for ARMs: When PMI applies to an ARM, the adjustable rate prevents the lender from knowing the exact date that the loan-to-value ratio will reach 80%. At the time of closing, the lender must provide the borrower with:

- A written notice that the borrower can request cancellation of PMI on the *cancellation date* (the date that the loan-to-value ratio will reach 80%), and that the loan servicer will notify the borrower when the cancellation date is reached
- Written notice that cancellation of PMI is automatic on the *termination date* (the date when the loan-to-value ratio reaches 78% of the original value of the property), and that the loan servicer will notify the borrower when the cancellation date is reached

Disclosures for High-Risk Loans: If PMI applies to a loan defined under the Homeowners Protection Act as a high-risk loan, the lender must provide the borrower with a notification stating:

- PMI is not required when the borrower reaches the midpoint of the amortization of the loan
- Termination of PMI is automatic at the midpoint of the amortization period if the borrower is current on payments

Annual Disclosures: Loan servicers are required to provide borrowers with an annual notice that reminds them of their right to the cancellation or termination of their PMI. The notice must also provide an address or telephone number that borrowers can use to contact their loan servicers with questions about the ability to cancel PMI. The law allows loan servicers to include this annual disclosure with the RESPA disclosure regarding escrow accounts.

Notification of Cancellation or Termination: Within *30 days* of the cancellation or termination of PMI, PMI will automatically terminate when the LTV ratio reaches 78% of the original value of the property and when the date on which that is projected to occur arrives (based on the initial amortization schedule).

Practices Prohibited by the Homeowners Protection Act

The receipt of any payments or premiums for PMI after the date of termination or cancellation is prohibited. Within **45 days** after the cancellation or termination of PMI, the law requires the return of any unearned premiums to the borrower.

Penalties for Violations of the Homeowners Protection Act (12 U.S.C. §4907)

The law provides for higher penalties for entities that are subject to the enforcement authority of the FDIC, the OCC, the NCUA, or the Farm Credit Administration. For these entities, penalties in individual actions are not to exceed $2,000. In a class action lawsuit, penalties may not exceed the lesser of $500,000 or 1% of the net worth of the liable party.

For entities not subject to federal regulators, the penalties in individual actions cannot exceed $1,000, and in class action lawsuits, penalties cannot exceed the lesser of $500,000 or 1% of the gross revenues of the liable entity violating the law.

Borrowers must bring actions for violations of the law within two years of the discovery of the violation.

Secure and Fair Enforcement for Mortgage Licensing Act (S.A.F.E. Act/ Regulation G – 12 U.S.C. §5101 *et seq.* and 12 C.F.R. §1007.101 *et seq.*)

S.A.F.E. Act Overview

In the spring of 2008, the meltdown of the subprime mortgage market led to the introduction of many bills in Congress to address the market conditions that led to the crisis. The combined result of many of these legislative proposals appeared in the Housing and Economic Recovery Act of 2008 (HERA), which was signed July 30, 2008. The goals of HERA include:

- Strengthening regulation of the government sponsored entities
- Providing additional Federal Housing Administration programs to assist homeowners
- Addressing problems caused by the foreclosure crisis
- Establishing a nationwide licensing database and education standards for the mortgage industry

The S.A.F.E. Act is Title V of HERA and has had the most immediate impact on mortgage professionals such as loan originators and brokers. Provisions of the S.A.F.E. Act establish application and reporting requirements for state-regulated loan originators and mortgage brokers. The Act requires each state to participate in the Nationwide Mortgage Licensing System (NMLS) created by the Conference of State Bank Supervisors (CSBS) and the American Association of Residential Mortgage Regulators (AARMR).

Each state has its own version of the S.A.F.E. Act which must meet the minimums required by the federal S.A.F.E. Act, but states may exceed the requirements of the federal Act.

Regulatory Agency and Regulations

The CFPB is responsible for implementation and enforcement of the S.A.F.E. Act. The regulations, referred to as **Regulation G**, are located in 12 C.F.R. §1007.101 through §1007.105.

Requirements of the S.A.F.E. Act

Licensing/Registration

The Act requires federally-regulated loan originators to register with the NMLS and state-regulated loan originators to become licensed through the NMLS. Licensing and registration creates a unique identifying number for each loan originator, enabling regulators to track the activities of registrants/licensees.

License applicants submit their applications through the NMLS for review by the applicable state regulatory agency. The license application forms are standardized Mortgage Uniform (MU) forms, which are available on the NMLS website.

Applicants seeking company licenses must submit:

- An **MU1** form, which requires identifying information about the entity's executive officers and owners, and information regarding any criminal, civil, or regulatory actions against the entity or its control affiliates
- An **MU2** form, which requires a "biographical statement" of each individual designated as a control person and a description of any involvement with a criminal, civil, or regulatory action
- An **MU3** form for branch offices

Applicants for mortgage loan originator licenses must submit an **MU4** form, which requires identifying information and disclosures of any criminal, civil, or regulatory action ever brought against them. By completing and signing this form, applicants give authorization for all current and former employers and law enforcement agencies to provide the information pertinent to the applicant's fitness to serve as a loan originator.

In order for a state to approve a license application, the following minimum standards must be met. The applicant must show that he/she has:

- Never had a loan originator license revoked in any governmental jurisdiction (a revocation that has been vacated will not be deemed a revocation)
- Not been convicted of, or pled guilty or nolo contendere to, a felony in any court:
  - During the seven-year period preceding the date of the application, or
  - At any time if the felony involved an act of fraud, dishonesty, a breach of trust, or money laundering
- Completed the pre-licensing education requirements and passed the applicable licensing test(s)
- Met either a net worth or surety bond requirement or paid into a state fund as applicable

- Demonstrated the financial responsibility, character, and general fitness to command the confidence of the community and warrant a determination that he/she will operate honestly, fairly, and efficiently under reasonable standards established by the individual state

Background Checks

Loan originators must submit to a comprehensive background check including submission of fingerprints, civil and criminal history, and a credit report as part of their application for licensure. Individuals who have been convicted of a felony in the seven years prior to application are not eligible for licensing. Felony convictions involving charges such as fraud, dishonesty, and money laundering may render an individual permanently ineligible for licensure.

Education

Prior to licensing, loan originators are required to obtain at least **20 hours** of NMLS-approved education which covers specific topics relevant to the mortgage profession.

This education must include at least the following:

- Three hours of federal mortgage laws and regulations
- Three hours of ethics, fraud, consumer protection, and fair lending, and
- Two hours of training relating to the nontraditional mortgage marketplace

States may require additional state-specific education.

Following licensure, loan originators are required to obtain at least **eight hours** of NMLS-approved education annually. This education must include at least the following:

- Three hours of federal mortgage laws and regulations
- Two hours of ethics, fraud, consumer protection, and fair lending, and
- Two hours of training related to the nontraditional mortgage marketplace

As with pre-licensing education, states may require additional state-specific education.

Testing

License candidates must also pass an exam administered through the NMLS with a passing score of 75%. Depending on the state in which the candidate wishes to become licensed, he/she will either complete the National test component plus a state-specific test component, or the National and Uniform State Test (UST) components. The NMLS launched the Uniform State Test on April 1, 2013. This new exam replaces the state-specific test components for states that adopt it. Thus, by passing the National and Uniform State Test components, a candidate can satisfy the testing requirements for licensure in those adopting states and any states that choose to adopt in the future.

Applicants are permitted to take the test three consecutive times, provided that at least 30 days pass between examinations. Those who fail the test three times must wait at least six months before taking the examination again.

Demonstration of Financial Responsibility

Individual states will set the guidelines for how loan originators will demonstrate financial responsibility and general fitness. However, examples include net worth requirements, surety bond requirements, payment into a state fund, and minimum credit score requirements.

An applicant will have shown that he/she is not financially responsible when he/she has shown disregard in the management of his/her own financial condition. This may be evidenced by:

- Current outstanding judgments, except judgments solely as a result of medical expenses
- Current outstanding tax liens or other government liens and filings, and/or
- Foreclosures or a pattern of seriously delinquent accounts within the past three years

> *The S.A.F.E. Act requires each state to participate in the Nationwide Mortgage Licensing System (NMLS) created by the Conference of State Bank Supervisors (CSBS) and the American Association of Residential Mortgage Regulators (AARMR).*

Consumer Protection under the S.A.F.E. Act

The S.A.F.E. Act created a number of consumer protection provisions. In addition to encouraging responsible behavior within the industry by mandating licensing/registration and education requirements, the Act also:

- Provides consumers with access to information about registrants/licensees, such as enforcement actions, etc.
- Facilitates collection and distribution of consumer complaints between state regulators

Discussion Scenario: S.A.F.E. Compliant Licensing

On September 23, 2009, Linus Loans applied for his mortgage loan originator license to conduct origination activities in a particular state in the north east. As part of the application, he filed an MU4 form. Linus listed Fantastic Funding Corporation and Laughing Loans, Inc. as his sponsors. Both companies are licensed as correspondent mortgage lenders under the licensing law of Linus's state.

In a previous career, Linus was a securities dealer, making big bucks on Wall Street. However, something was awry with Linus Loans' security transactions. From November 2002 to February 2003, Linus falsely notarized the signatures of two persons without having actually witnessed these signatures. This was a violation of the National Association of Securities Dealers (NASD) Rules of Conduct, and the NASD brought an action against Linus. On October 1, 2007, as a result of the action, he entered into a consent agreement with NASD, barring him from association with any NASD member and subjecting him to a statutory disqualification as defined in the Securities Exchange Act of 1934. Linus Loans did not admit or deny the findings in the consent agreement, and there was not a hearing on the matter.

Discussion Questions

- *What disclosures must Linus Loans make on his Form MU4?*
- *What is the likely outcome of Linus' application and why?*

Discussion Feedback

Linus Loans is required to disclose on his Form MU4 that a state or regulatory agency found that he had made a false statement or omission or had been dishonest, unfair or unethical. Additionally, he must disclose that he was barred from association with entities in the securities industry or from engaging in a financial services-related business.

While the S.A.F.E. Act requires licensing application through the NMLS, state regulators continue to approve or deny applications. Licensing applications that are found to include false information or omissions of material fact are subject to denial or revocation under state licensing laws. Additionally, many states prohibit employment with more than one licensed lender or broker at one time. If Linus was seeking licensure in a state with such a provision, his license could be denied for this reason as well.

Loan originators can ensure they are compliant with licensing requirements by:

- Submitting complete and truthful information on licensing applications
- Obtaining education that is compliant with their state's statutory requirements
- Meeting all other jurisdictional requirements which establish the ethical, financial, and professional fitness to operate in the mortgage industry

Home Mortgage Disclosure Act (HMDA/Regulation C – 12 U.S.C. §2801 *et seq.* and 12 C.F.R. §1003 *et seq.*)

HMDA Overview

The primary goal of the Home Mortgage Disclosure Act (HMDA) is to identify urban areas where the availability of home financing at reasonable terms is limited.

In order to achieve this overall goal, HMDA has three specific purposes, which are to:

- Determine if depository institutions are meeting the housing needs of their communities (particularly in urban neighborhoods)
- Identify discriminatory lending practices and patterns, which can result in enforcement actions to ensure compliance with fair lending laws
- Determine how to distribute public-sector investments where they are needed

The method that HMDA establishes for achieving its goals and purposes is to require both depository and non-depository institutions to collect data at the time that they receive loan applications and submit the data to the federal agency that supervises their lending activities. The Dodd-Frank Act made changes to HMDA by expanding the data collection requirements to include additional information about individual loan applicants, loan applications, and loan originations. These changes have yet to be implemented.

Regulatory Agencies and Regulations

Before the creation of the CFPB, the Federal Reserve was responsible for issuing regulations for implementation of HMDA. Now, the CFPB is primarily responsible for writing implementing regulations. These regulations are known as **Regulation C** (12 C.F.R. §1003 *et seq.*). The supervision of institutions subject to HMDA and enforcement of the law is now shared by the CFPB and the Office of the Comptroller of the Currency, the Board of Governors of the Federal Reserve, the Federal Deposit Insurance Corporation, the National Credit Union Administration, and the Department of Housing and Urban Development.

The Dodd-Frank Act includes language directing the CFPB to write rules to implement the additional requirements that the law created for HMDA data collection. As of the end of 2013, the CFPB has issued no proposed regulations, but mortgage professionals should be on the lookout for developments in this area. The CFPB has issued a Bulletin that emphasizes the importance of having an effective HMDA compliance program in place.

Institutions and Loans Covered by HMDA (12 C.F.R. §1003.1(c))

The law applies to depository institutions such as banks, credit unions, and savings associations that meet the following criteria:

- Assets that exceed an annually published threshold on the preceding December 31st
- A home or branch office in a metropolitan statistical area (MSA) on the preceding December 31st
- Origination of at least one home-purchase loan or refinancing of a home-purchase loan, secured by a first lien on a one-to four-family dwelling within the preceding calendar year
- The institution is federally insured or regulated, or the mortgage loan(s) made by the institution was (were) insured, guaranteed or supplemented by a federal agency, or the loan(s) was (were) intended for sale to Fannie Mae or Freddie Mac

The law also applies to non-depository mortgage lending institutions that meet the following criteria:

- Origination of home-purchase loans and refinances that either equal at least 10% of its loan-origination volume (measured in dollars) or that equal $25 million or more within the preceding year
- A home or branch office in a metropolitan statistical area on the preceding December 31st
- Total assets as of the preceding December 31st of more than $10 million, including the assets of any parent corporation or the origination of at least 100 home purchase loans, including refinances of home purchase loans, within the previous year

The loans that are subject to HMDA include applications for and originations and purchases of the following types of loans:

- Purchase loans
- Home improvement loans
- Refinances

Data collection is also required when a loan origination or the denial of a loan application results from a response to a pre-approval lending program.

Exempt Institutions (12 C.F.R. §1003.3)

The reporting requirements do not apply to:

- Institutions that do not meet the criteria outlined above
- State-chartered or state-licensed institutions that are subject to state disclosure laws with reporting requirements that are substantially similar to those of HMDA

HMDA has three specific purposes, which are to determine if depository institutions are meeting community housing needs, identify discriminatory lending patterns, and determine how to distribute public sector investments.

Definitions of Terms Related to HMDA

Loan Application Register (LAR): A LAR is the form used for the reporting of HMDA data.

Metropolitan Statistical Area (MSA): Urbanized area with a population of at least 50,000 and identified by the Office of Management and Budget based on census data.

Data Collection and Reporting Requirements under HMDA (12 C.F.R. §1003.4)

HMDA requires the institutions that are covered by the law to collect extensive data about each mortgage loan application and origination. The information reported includes:

- The date an application was received, with an identifying loan number
- The type of loan or loan application
- The purpose and amount of the loan, or the amount for which the loan applicant applied
- Whether the application was a request for pre-approval and whether it resulted in a denial or an origination
- The action taken on the loan
- The location of the property related to the loan
- The owner/occupant status of the property
- Ethnicity, race, sex, and income of the applicant

- The type of entity purchasing a loan that the institution originates or purchases and then sells within the same calendar year
- The difference between the loan's APR and the yield on Treasury securities with comparable periods of maturity if the difference is greater than three percentage points for first liens on a principal dwelling or greater than five percentage points for loans secured by subordinate liens
- Identification of a loan that is subject to HOEPA
- Indication of whether the loan is secured by a first or a subordinate lien

As a result of amendments to HMDA that Congress made under the Dodd-Frank Act, there are many additional data collection requirements under the law. However, financial institutions are not required to report additional data until the first January 1 that occurs nine months after the CFPB issues final regulations to implement these provisions of the law.

The collection of HMDA data helps federal regulators to determine if different or more onerous lending terms are offered to different loan applicants on the basis of personal characteristics such as race, ethnicity, or sex. The supervisory agencies, such as federal banking regulatory agencies, compile the information submitted to them by lending institutions and the Federal Financial Institutions Examination Council aggregates, and reports it within each MSA.

As mentioned in the section on ECOA, exceptions are made to fair lending provisions prohibiting inquiries about personal characteristics. In order to meet the reporting requirements of HMDA, a mortgage professional may request information on a loan applicant's race, ethnicity, and sex when completing the loan application. The applicant may decline to answer, in which case the mortgage professional must make a best guess based on visual observation.

The data collected pursuant to HMDA requirements must be presented on the LAR and submitted to the appropriate federal agency by March 1 of the year after the loan data was compiled (12 C.F.R. §1003.5(a)). A public disclosure statement of the information will be prepared by the Federal Financial Institutions Examination Council, and lending institutions must make this information available to the public within three business days after receiving the disclosure statement from the FFIEC.

Penalties for Violations of HMDA

Civil monetary penalties can result from the failure to report data, failure to report data in a timely manner, and failure to report data accurately. The regulatory agencies that monitor compliance use a penalty matrix and consider factors such as good faith compliance efforts, previous violations, the seriousness of current violations, and financial resources of the entity in calculating penalties.

With enforcement actions that it brought in 2013 against both depository and non-depository mortgage lenders, the CFPB has demonstrated its commitment to enforcing HMDA. Richard Cordray, the CFPB Director, emphasized the importance of submitting accurate data and the seriousness with which the agency views violations of the law when he stated that inaccurate information *"...obstructs the purpose of the Home Mortgage Disclosure Act and makes it more difficult for the CFPB to discover and stop discriminatory lending"* [42].

> *The collection of HMDA data helps federal regulators determine if different lending terms are offered to different loan applicants on the basis of personal characteristics.*

Fair Credit Reporting Act (FCRA/Regulation V – 15 U.S.C. §1681 *et seq.* and 12 C.F.R. §1022 *et seq.*)

FCRA Overview

Congress enacted the Fair Credit Reporting Act (FCRA) in 1970 to ensure the accuracy, fairness, and privacy of consumers' personal information that is assembled and used by consumer reporting agencies. In order to protect the rights of consumers, the law creates special obligations and restrictions for Consumer Reporting Agencies (CRAs), and for furnishers and users of consumers' personal information.

Regulatory Agency and Regulations

Prior to the creation of the CFPB, the implementation and enforcement of FCRA was shared by federal banking regulatory agencies and the Federal Trade Commission. The transfer of authority to the CFPB in July 2011 placed general rulemaking authority with the CFPB as well as general authority to enforce compliance with FCRA and its implementing regulations. However, the FTC retains some rulemaking and enforcement authority. In a memorandum of understanding entered between the CFPB and the FTC, the agencies have agreed to give one another a 30-day notice prior to the publication of an advance notice of proposed rulemaking and to "consult promptly" on guidance documents that address unfair, deceptive, or abusive acts or practices under FCRA.

The regulations promulgated pursuant to FCRA are known as **Regulation V** and are found in 12 C.F.R. §1022 *et seq.* One section of the regulations that is of particular importance is Appendix M, which provides model forms for the notices and disclosures required by FCRA.

Covered Transactions (12 C.F.R. §1022.1)

FCRA applies to any transaction that involves the use of credit reports, consumer investigatory reports, and employment background checks.

The privacy requirements do not apply to disclosures of limited information to government agencies, to the FBI, and to counter-terrorism investigations.

Definition of Terms Related to FCRA (15 U.S.C. §1681a)

Consumer Report: The communication of any information from a consumer reporting agency that relates to a consumer's credit worthiness, credit standing, credit capacity, character, personal characteristics, or mode of living which is used or expected to be used in order to determine the consumer's eligibility for credit or insurance to be used for personal, family, or household purposes or to evaluate a consumer for employment.

Consumer Reporting Agency (CRA): Any person who regularly engages for fees or on a cooperative nonprofit basis in the practice of assembling or evaluating of consumer credit information in order to provide consumer reports to third parties. The Dodd-Frank Act authorizes the CFPB to supervise "larger participants" in the market for consumer products and services (12 US.C. §5514(a)(1)(B)). The CFPB adopted a rule in July 2012 in which it defines "larger participants" to include CRAs with annual receipts exceeding $7 million (12 C.F.R. §1009.104(b)). Therefore, the CFPB has the authority to examine large CRAs, such as Equifax, Experian, and TransUnion, for FCRA compliance.

Investigative Consumer Report: A consumer report containing information about a consumer's character, general reputation, personal characteristics, and mode of living that is obtained through personal interviews.

File: All the information about a consumer that is recorded and retained by a CRA.

Adverse Action: This term is given the same meaning under FCRA as under ECOA, meaning a denial of credit or an extension of credit in a substantially smaller amount, or for terms substantially different, than that requested by the loan applicant. It also means any denial or unfavorable change in insurance coverage, or a denial of employment based on an investigative consumer report.

Disclosures and Notifications Required by FCRA

FCRA creates a number of obligations for users and furnishers of credit information as well as the credit reporting agencies (CRAs) which receive and report credit information.

Obligations of CRAs: (Examples of CRAs are Equifax, Experian, and TransUnion, which are often referred to as "The Big Three.")

- **CRA Disclosures to Consumers**: If requested by a consumer, CRAs must clearly and accurately disclose all information in the consumer's file, the sources of the information, and the identification of each person that procured a consumer report. The disclosure must also include a summary of the consumer's rights under FCRA. Unless otherwise authorized by the consumer, the disclosure must be in writing (15 U.S.C. §1681(g)).

- **CRA Notification to Users**: CRAs must provide notices to any person who regularly and in the ordinary course of business furnishes information to a CRA and to any person who receives and uses a consumer report. The notice to furnishers and users must advise them of their responsibilities under the FCRA (15 U.S.C. §1681(d)).

CRAs have the burden of protecting consumer privacy when reporting credit information.

Obligations of Furnishers: (Loan servicers, lenders, and creditors that receive loan and credit line payments are examples of furnishers of information that CRAs place in consumers' files.)

- **Notification to CRAs of Corrections**: If the furnisher of information regularly and in the ordinary course of business provides information to CRAs and determines that the information provided is not complete or accurate, the furnisher has a duty to correct the information and to provide the corrections to all CRAs that received inaccurate information.

- **Notice of Dispute**: If a consumer disputes the accuracy and completeness of information provided by a furnisher, the furnisher cannot report the disputed information to a CRA without providing notice of the dispute.

- **Notice Regarding Delinquencies**: A furnisher that reports information on a delinquent account must provide the CRA with the month and year of the commencement of the delinquency that immediately precedes an action for collection.

- **Duties after Receipt of Notice of Dispute**: Upon receipt of a notice of dispute from a CRA, a furnisher must conduct an investigation, report the results to the CRA that provided notice of the dispute, report any inaccuracies to all CRAs that received the inaccurate information, and delete the inaccurate information. Furnishers have 30 days from the CRA's receipt of a dispute to investigate the dispute and rectify any inaccuracies.

(15 U.S.C. §1681s-2)

> *In order to protect the rights of consumers, the law creates special obligations and restrictions for consumer reporting agencies and furnishers and users of consumers' personal information.*

Obligations of Users: (A lender or mortgage broker that uses a consumer report in the process of making a mortgage loan is an example of a user of information collected by a CRA.)

- **Certification of Permissible Purpose**: Users must provide a Consumer Reporting Agency with a certification that states the permissible purpose for which the user is requesting the consumer report. Permissible purposes include consumer requests for reports, such as a consumer's request for a credit report required by a mortgage lender. Another permissible purpose is to determine a consumer's eligibility for a license, such as the loan officer license under certain state laws.

- **Notification of Adverse Action**: When a user takes any type of adverse action based on information in a consumer report, the user must provide the consumer with written, oral, or electronic notification which includes contact information for the CRA that provided the report. The notification must include a statement that the CRA did not make the adverse decision and must advise the consumer of the right to obtain a free copy of the report used by the creditor in making the decision and of the right to contact the CRA to dispute the accuracy and completeness of the report.

- **Notification of Adverse Action Based on Information from Affiliates**: If adverse action is based on information from an entity that is affiliated with the user by common ownership or control, the user must notify the consumer of the adverse action and of the right to obtain a disclosure of the nature of the information relied on in taking the adverse action.

(15 U.S.C. §1681m)

Lenders, brokers and other "users" of credit information have the burden of protecting consumer privacy when using credit information.

Practices Prohibited by FCRA

- FCRA prohibits a CRA from furnishing a consumer report for any reason other than a permissible purpose. Permissible purposes include providing a report pursuant to the written instructions of the consumer to whom the report relates and providing a report in connection with a credit transaction involving the extension of credit to the consumer (15 U.S.C. §1681b).
- FCRA prohibits those who furnish information to a CRA from knowingly providing inaccurate information (15 U.S.C. §1681s-2).
- No CRA can write a consumer report containing outdated negative financial information such as bankruptcies over ten years old and other negative information such as paid tax liens and civil judgments that are more than seven years old unless the consumer report relates to a credit transaction involving a principal amount of $150,000 or more (15 U.S.C. §1681c(a)).
- CRAs cannot release disputed information in a consumer report without indicating that the consumer disputes the accuracy and completeness of the information (15 U.S.C. §1681c(f)).

Penalties for Violations of FCRA

- **Civil Liability for Willful Noncompliance**: Any person who willfully fails to comply with consumer protection provisions of FCRA is liable to the injured consumer for actual damages or for damages of not less than $100 and not more than $1,000, plus punitive damages, costs of bringing the action, and attorney's fees (15 U.S.C. §1681n(a)(1)(A)).
- **Civil Liability for Obtaining a Consumer Report under False Pretenses**: If a natural person obtains a consumer report under false pretenses or knowingly obtains one without a permissible purpose, he/she will be liable for actual damages or $1,000, whichever is greater (15 U.S.C. §1681n(a)(1)(B)).
- **Civil Liability for Knowing Noncompliance**: Any person who obtains a consumer report from a consumer reporting agency under false pretenses or knowingly obtains one without a permissible purpose is liable to the CRA for actual damages that the CRA incurs or $1,000, whichever is greater (15 U.S.C. §1681n(b)).
- **Civil Liability for Negligent Noncompliance**: Negligent failure to comply with the law may result in the payment of actual damages, costs, and attorney's fees to the injured consumer (15 U.S.C. §1681o).

- **Criminal Penalties for Obtaining Information under False Pretenses**: Any person who obtains information about a consumer under false pretenses will be fined and/or imprisoned for not more than two years (15 U.S.C. §1681q).

- **Criminal Penalties for Unauthorized Disclosures by Officers and Employees**: Officers or employees of a CRA who knowingly and willfully provide information about a consumer to a person not authorized to receive the information will be fined and/or imprisoned for no more than two years (15 U.S.C. §1681r).

Fair and Accurate Credit Transactions Act of 2003 (FACTA – 15 U.S.C. §1681 *et seq.*)

FACTA Overview

In 2003, Congress added additional provisions to FCRA with the enactment of the Fair and Accurate Credit Transactions Act (FACTA). Congress adopted these additional provisions in order to address the problem of identity theft, to facilitate consumers' access to the information retained by CRAs, and to improve the accuracy of consumer reports.

Regulatory oversight and covered and exempt transactions for FACTA are the same as those for FCRA.

Disclosures, Notifications, and Actions Required by FACTA (15 U.S.C. §§1681c-1, 1681c-2)

Obligations for CRAs: Most of the disclosures, notifications, and actions required by FACTA are the duties of consumer reporting agencies.

These statutory duties include:

- **Providing Notice of Consumer Rights**: FACTA creates requirements for the issuance of a Victim's Notice of Rights when a consumer reports identity theft to a consumer reporting agency.

- **Issuing Free Credit Reports**: In order to encourage consumers to self-monitor their credit reports as a means of detecting identity theft, Congress requires each of the three national credit bureaus (Experian, Equifax, and TransUnion) to provide a free credit report annually, when requested by the consumer.

- **Creating a Fraud Alert**: At the request of a consumer who believes that he/she is or may be the victim of fraud, CRAs must create a fraud alert for the consumer's file and include it with any credit scores generated for the consumer. CRAs must keep the fraud alert in the file for 90 days.

- **Creating an Extended Fraud Alert**: After receipt of an identity theft report, CRAs must create an extended fraud alert, maintain it in the file, and include it with any credit report generated for the consumer for a period of seven years.

- **Creating an Active Duty Alert**: At the request of an active duty consumer, CRAs must create a statement that the consumer is on active duty for the military and include the statement with any credit reports generated for the active duty consumer. CRAs must keep the active duty alert in the file for not less than 12 months.

- **Forwarding Fraud Alerts and Active Duty Alerts to Other CRAs**: When one of the three national credit bureaus receives a consumer's request for fraud alert or an active duty alert, it must forward the information to the other CRAs.

- **Disclosing Credit Scores**: Consumers have a right to purchase a copy of their credit scores. With disclosure of a credit score, CRAs must explain that the CRA credit score may be different from a lender's credit score, and provide a list of factors used to compute the score and a list of factors that negatively impacted the score.

- **Blocking Information**: CRAs must block the reporting of any information in a consumer's file that the consumer identifies as information that resulted from identity theft and must notify the furnisher of the information that the blocked information may be the result of identity theft. The block must be effective within four business days of receipt of copies of the consumer's identity, his/her identity theft report, and a description of the information in the consumer's file that relates to transactions that he/she did not make.

- **Notification of Decision to Decline or Rescind a Block**: In certain circumstances in which the CRA reasonably determines there is not a basis for blocking the information, it can decline the request for a block or rescind a block and must provide prompt notification to the consumer.

> *The Fair and Accurate Credit Transactions Act (FACTA) was adopted to address identity theft, facilitate consumers' access to information retained by CRAs, and improve the accuracy of consumer reports.*

Obligations for Mortgage Professionals: FACTA creates some special disclosures, notifications, and actions for mortgage professionals:

- **Disclosure of Credit Score**: In mortgage lending transactions, the "person who makes or arranges loans" must provide mortgage loan applicants with information about the credit score used to evaluate their creditworthiness and must provide this information with a notice that advises them of the importance of reviewing their credit scores and of their right to contact the CRA or the lender that generated the credit score (15 U.S.C. §1681g(g)).

- **Response to Consumer's Request for Information on Fraudulent Transactions**: When identity theft occurs in lending transactions, mortgage professionals must comply with the alleged victim's written request for copies of any records of transactions conducted by a person who made unauthorized use of the victim's identity. The request must include verification of the victim's identity and proof of a claim of identity theft. Response to these requests is due 30 days after receipt of the request (15 U.S.C. §1681g(e)(1)).

- **Rule for the Proper Disposal of Consumer Information**: When it was enacted, FACTA directed the FTC and the federal banking agencies to *"...issue final regulations requiring any person that maintains or otherwise possesses consumer information, or any compilation of consumer information, derived from consumer reports for a business purpose to properly dispose of any such information or compilation"* (15 U.S.C. §1681w). The rule that the

FTC adopted was effective in June 2005, and it applies to all people and businesses that use consumer reports. The preamble to the rule cited mortgage brokers as an example of entities that are subject to the rule, and the stated purpose is to prevent the careless disposal of documents that can lead to identity theft and to other forms of theft and fraud. The "Disposal of Consumer Report Information and Records Rule," also known as the Disposal Rule, applies to all information in a CRA file that a lender or mortgage broker uses to establish the creditworthiness of a consumer, and requires "reasonable measures" to ensure that unauthorized access to, or use of, consumer information cannot occur as a result of its disposal.

The Disposal Rule provides the following examples of reasonable measures to protect consumer information from unauthorized access or use:

- Burning, pulverizing, or shredding papers containing consumer information
- Destroying or erasing electronically-stored information
- Conducting due diligence to verify compliance with the Disposal Rule by any third party that is employed to dispose of consumer information

(16 C.F.R. §682.3(b))

Lenders, mortgage brokers, and other mortgage professionals are subject to the Gramm-Leach-Bliley Act and must also incorporate methods for the disposal of information in their security program as required by the Safeguards Rule.

Definition of Terms Related to FACTA

Active Duty Alert: A statement in a consumer reporting agency's file for a particular individual, stating that the consumer is on active duty for the military (15 U.S.C. §1681g(e)(4)).

Creditor: FACTA and FCRA use the same definition as ECOA for creditor. It is any person who regularly extends, renews, or continues credit.

Identity Theft: Fraud or attempted fraud using the identifying information of another person (15 U.S.C. §1681a(q)(3)).

Identity Theft Report: The FTC defines an identity theft report as *"...a report that alleges theft with as much specificity as the consumer can provide."* FTC regulations list information a theft report *"may"* include, stating that its list is *"for illustrative purposes only,"* and advising consumers that different companies may have different requirements when receiving identity theft reports. Generally, reports must include an affidavit stating general information about the theft and the victim and a list of the fraudulent accounts opened in the victim's name (15 U.S.C. §1681a(q)(4)).

Practices Prohibited by FACTA

If a consumer requests information about transactions, which were allegedly made with the unauthorized use of his/her identity, businesses (including mortgage brokers and mortgage lenders) cannot charge a fee for providing the information. Since the FACTA provisions are codified as part of FCRA, the penalty provisions of FCRA apply to violations of FACTA.

FTC Red Flags Rule

Red Flags Rule Overview

The Red Flags Rule is a measure included in FACTA to address identity theft. **"Red flag"** is defined under federal regulations as *"...a pattern, practice, or specific activity that indicates the possible existence of identity theft"* (16 C.F.R. §681.1 (b)(9)). While the Red Flags Rule was effective January 1, 2008, with compliance required by November 1, 2008, enforcement was delayed several times. A bill signed by President Obama in December 2010, called the Red Flag Program Clarification Act of 2010, narrowed the scope of creditors who must comply with the requirements, and enforcement of the regulations was effective December 31, 2010. In November 2012, the FTC issued an interim final rule to implement the provisions of the Red Flag Program Clarification Act. Neither the 2010 amendments to the law nor the new regulations impact mortgage lenders since the regulations still define the term "creditor" to include "lenders such as banks" and "mortgage brokers" (16 C.F.R. §681.1(b)(5)).

It is worth noting the distinctions offered regarding personal information under the Gramm-Leach-Bliley Act and its Safeguards Rule, and the protections offered under the Red Flags Rule. Both the Safeguards Rule and the Red Flags Rule are intended to prevent the release of personal financial information. The primary difference is that the Safeguards Rule focuses on the methods of securing personal information, and the Red Flags Rule focuses on the methods of detecting a security breach. The Red Flags Rule is still interpreted and enforced by the FTC.

Businesses and Accounts Subject to Rule

The Red Flags Rule applies to financial institutions and to creditors that offer or maintain "covered accounts." Financial institution, creditor, and covered accounts are all terms defined under the regulations, and the meanings of these terms determine the types of business entities and accounts that are subject to the Red Flags Rule.

These terms are defined as follows:

Financial Institutions: A state or national bank, a state or federal savings and loan association, a mutual savings bank, a state or federal credit union, or any other person that, directly or indirectly, holds a transaction account belonging to a consumer.

Creditor: As established under FACTA, a creditor is defined as someone who regularly extends credit or arranges for the extension of credit, including finance companies and mortgage brokers.

Covered Accounts: The types of accounts generated by these entities that are subject to special protection under the Red Flags Rule include accounts:

- Offered or maintained by a financial institution or creditor
- Intended for personal, family, or household purposes
- Designed to permit multiple payments or transactions

Mortgage loans are cited in the regulations as an example of the types of accounts covered by the regulations.

The Red Flags Rule protects **customers**, who are defined as a person who has a "covered account" with a financial institution or a creditor. In the field of mortgage lending, a customer would be a loan applicant or a borrower who applies for or obtains a mortgage from a mortgage broker or a financial institution.

> *The Red Flags Rule was included in FACTA to address identity theft. The Red Flag Program Clarification Act narrowed the scope of creditors who must comply with the requirements.*

Requirements of the Red Flags Rule (16 C.F.R. §681.1(d))

The Red Flags Rule requires creditors and financial institutions to establish an **Identity Theft Prevention Program**. The program must have provisions for:

- Identifying patterns, practices, or specific activities that may indicate the possible existence of identity theft
- Detecting irregularities when obtaining information from a person opening an account or accepting a change of address on existing accounts
- Preventing and mitigating identity theft by responding appropriately to the types of risks posed by particular types of accounts
- Updating the identity theft program periodically to identify new risks to the security of personal information

The Interagency Guidelines on Identity Theft Detection, Prevention, and Mitigation provides comprehensive information for developing an Identity Theft Prevention Program. These Guidelines are located in Appendix A of 16 C.F.R. §681.

The Guidelines:

- Give examples of the specific types of risk factors
- Suggest appropriate responses when evidence of identity theft emerges
- Describe appropriate ways to update the program when new methods of detecting identity theft are available and when mergers and acquisitions or other business changes occur that might impact the security of customer information

Illustrations of Red Flags

The Appendix A Guidelines include an extremely helpful list of "red flags" that financial institutions and creditors can use to identify threats to the security of covered accounts. Individuals responsible for the implementation of an Identity Theft Prevention Program should be acquainted with each red flag on the list.

The Guidelines break these warning signs of security threats into a number of categories:

- **Notifications or warnings from a CRA,** such as a notice that there is activity on an account that is inconsistent with the account's prior history
- **Suspicious Documents,** such as documents that show evidence of tampering or documents containing information that is inconsistent with prior information provided
- **Suspicious Personal Identifying Information,** such as information that does not match the information found in the consumer report
- **Suspicious Activity Related to the Covered Account,** such as irregular payment activity
- **Notices from Customers, Identity Theft Victims, Law Enforcement** that fraudulent activity is associated with the account

The Guidelines are available online through the Government Printing Office [43].

Application to Small Businesses

When publishing the final version of the Red Flags Rule, the FTC noted that small businesses are also vulnerable to identity theft and need to establish programs to prevent it. However, the Small Business Administration (SBA) commented that certain requirements, particularly the production of a written program, could be overly burdensome for small businesses. [2]

The FTC disagreed with the assertion that the requirements are too burdensome. However, in order to facilitate compliance with the rule, the FTC delayed enforcement of the rule to give all creditors and financial institutions time to develop an Identity Theft Prevention Program.

The Dodd-Frank Act

In July 2010, Congress enacted the Dodd-Frank Wall Street Reform and Consumer Protection Act (the Dodd-Frank Act) in response to the collapse of the economy that began with the 2007 meltdown of the mortgage lending market. The law addresses a broad range of issues that relate to financial and investment activities, including mortgage lending and investing.

The Dodd-Frank Act is divided into 16 titles. These titles address a range of financial issues including the improved regulation of banks, savings and loans, non-bank financial companies, hedge fund advisers, and swap dealers and participants. The titles in the law that directly impact mortgage lending and investing include:

- Title IX, or Investor Protections and Improvements to the Regulations of Securities, with provisions authorizing stricter regulation of investors and credit rating agencies
- Title X, or the Consumer Financial Protection Act of 2010, which authorizes the creation of the CFPB, provides for the transition of regulatory authority from other federal regulatory agencies to the CFPB, and outlines the Bureau's regulatory and enforcement responsibilities

---

2   The SBA defines a small business as one that has assets of $165 million or less.

- Title XIV, or the Mortgage Reform and Anti-Predatory Lending Act, with provisions that apply directly to mortgage originators, servicers, and appraisers

These titles in the Dodd-Frank Act set the regulatory boundaries for the origination and securitization of mortgage loans.

> *The Dodd-Frank Wall Street Reform and Consumer Protection Act (the Dodd-Frank Act) is divided into 16 titles. These titles address a range of financial issues including the regulation of banks, savings and loans, and non-bank financial companies.*

As a result of the authority extended to the CFPB under the Dodd-Frank Act, the CFPB is now the principal federal regulator for all depository and non-depository entities that offer home loans to consumers. Title XIV, the Mortgage Reform and Anti-Predatory Lending Act, is the section of the Dodd-Frank Act that poses the principal compliance concerns for loan originators who are not affiliated with depository institutions.

Title XIV is divided into eight subtitles:
- Subtitle A addresses **Residential Mortgage Loan Origination Standards** and creates:
    - A prohibition against incentives for loan originators to earn additional compensation by steering consumers towards particular loans or loans with particular lending terms, and
    - Limitations on loan originator compensation
- Subtitle B addresses **Minimum Standards for Mortgages**, and directs the CFPB to adopt rules addressing:
    - The establishment of standards for determining a borrower's ability to repay a home loan
    - The creation of a rebuttable presumption of the ability of a consumer to repay a home loan if the loan meets the standards that are established for a "qualified mortgage"
- Subtitle C addresses **High-Cost Mortgages** and directs the CFPB to broaden the application of disclosure requirements and prohibited practices to a wider range of loans by:
    - Extending the HOEPA provisions to purchase money mortgages and open-end home equity lines of credit
    - Lowering the interest rate and points and fees thresholds for HOEPA loans
    - Adding a prepayment penalty trigger, which provides that a loan is a high-cost home loan if it includes a prepayment penalty provision that is in force for more than 36 months after closing or if the loan allows prepayment penalties to exceed more than 2% of the amount prepaid
    - Imposing homeownership counseling requirements
    - Strengthening prohibited lending terms and practices
- Subtitle D authorizes the creation of an **Office of Housing Counseling** within HUD

- Subtitle E addresses **Mortgage Servicing**, and requires the CFPB to create new rules for loan servicers. Proposed rules address the following matters that relate to loan servicing:
  - Monthly mortgage statements
  - Reminders to borrowers before interest rates reset
  - Options for forced-place insurance
  - Options for avoiding foreclosure
  - Prompt crediting of payments
  - Accurate recordkeeping
  - Prompt correction of errors
  - Delinquent borrower access to servicer personnel
  - Evaluation of delinquent borrowers for foreclosure options
- Subtitle F addresses **Appraisal Activitie**s, and requires:
  - Stricter appraisal standards for "higher risk mortgages"
  - Stricter standards to ensure the independence of appraisers
- Subtitle G addresses **Mortgage Resolution and Modification**. With so many homeowners in trouble on their mortgages, the Home Affordable Modification Program (HAMP) was authorized under the 2008 Emergency Economic Stabilization Act. Since implementation of the HAMP program seemed unsuccessful, the Treasury Department and the Department of Housing and Urban Development tried to make it easier for consumers to obtain loan modifications by:
  - Requiring mortgage servicers participating in the program to provide data to borrowers that is used in performing a net present value (NPV) analysis if their requests for loan modifications are denied
  - Making a net present value calculator available on the Internet that homeowners can use to determine whether their mortgages would be accepted or rejected for modification
  - Making reasonable efforts to provide a website that homeowners can use to apply for mortgage modifications

  The HAMP program was scheduled to end on December 31, 2013, but has been extended through 2015.

- Subtitle H addresses **Miscellaneous Provisions**, which include:
  - Acknowledgment of the need to reform Fannie Mae and Freddie Mac
  - A directive for an inter-agency study on foreclosure rescue and loan modification scams
  - Reauthorization of the Emergency Mortgage Relief Program
  - Authorization for more funds for the Neighborhood Stabilization Program

As a result of regulatory changes dictated by the Dodd-Frank Act, the CFPB has been engaged in ongoing rulemaking proceedings. Many of the new rules have been finalized and are effective in 2014.

Mortgage Assistance Relief Services (MARS Rule/Regulation O – 12 C.F.R. §1015 *et seq.*)

In 2010, the FTC issued rules that apply to all for-profit companies that offer **mortgage assistance relief services (MARS)** through telemarketing and other marketing media.

The FTC issued these rules in response to:

- Deceptive and abusive practices in the marketing of MARS
- Misrepresentations made by for-profit mortgage relief companies that they are affiliated with the government, a nonprofit organization, a lender, or loan servicers
- The failure of struggling homeowners to realize that they can take advantage of free homeownership counseling services through state or HUD programs

The need for these rules resulted from the growing number of scams that target homeowners who are in default on mortgage payments and facing the possibility of foreclosure. Promising "foreclosure rescues" and loan modifications to reduce monthly mortgage payments, these scams rob homeowners of dwindling financial resources with fraudulent offers for a solution.

In 2011, the CFPB republished the MARS Rule, making technical changes to reflect the transfer of implementation and enforcement authority from the FTC to the CFPB. At the time that it republished the rules, the CFPB did not make any substantive changes to them.

Definition of Terms Related to the MARS Rule

Consumer: Consumers are defined as *"...any natural person who is obligated under any loan secured by a dwelling"* (12 C.F.R. §1015.2).

Mortgage assistance relief service provider: The required disclosures, notices, and prohibited practices under the MARS Rule apply to "mortgage assistance relief service providers," who are defined as any person who *"...provides, offers to provide, or arranges to provide any mortgage assistance relief service..."* (12 C.F.R. §1015.2).

Mortgage assistance relief service: These services include any plan, program, or service offered in exchange for compensation to assist in:

- Stopping, preventing, or postponing foreclosure or repossession of a consumer's dwelling
- Negotiating or arranging for modification of terms in a home loan to reduce the interest rate, principal balance, monthly payments, or fees
- Obtaining a forbearance or modification in the timing of loan payments

- Negotiating for or arranging an extension of time for a consumer to cure a default, reinstate a home loan, or redeem a dwelling
- Obtaining a waiver of an acceleration clause or balloon payment provision in a home loan
- Negotiating, obtaining, or arranging a deed in lieu of foreclosure, short sale, or other alternative disposition of a consumer's home

(12 C.F.R. §1015.2)

Prohibited Representations for MARS Providers (12 C.F.R. §1015.3)

When advertising or marketing MARS services, providers of these services are prohibited from representing that a consumer cannot or should not contact his/her mortgage lender or loan servicer. MARS providers are also prohibited from representing *"...the benefits, performance, or efficacy of any mortgage assistance relief service unless, at the time such representation is made, the provider possesses and relies upon competent and reliable evidence that substantiates the representation is true"* (12 C.F.R. §1015.3(c)). This evidence must be based on tests and research conducted by experts.

MARS providers are also prohibited from making **misrepresentations** related to:
- The likelihood of obtaining or arranging particular results, such as a loan modification
- The amount of time that it will take to achieve results
- The amount of money or debt relief that a consumer may save or realize by using mortgage assistance relief services
- The terms or conditions under which any refund, either full or partial, will be made by the MARS provider

MARS providers are prohibited from misleading consumers by:
- Implying that the provider is affiliated, endorsed or approved by the U.S. government, a governmental homeowner assistance plan, a federal or state agency, a nonprofit housing counselor, or by the lender or loan servicer that made or services the consumer's home loan
- Suggesting that they will receive legal representation
- Stating that the consumer is not obligated to make scheduled payments
- Asserting that the provider has completed services that he/she/it agreed to perform and should receive payment

The MARS Rule absolutely prohibits the collection of any fee or payment until a written agreement between the consumer and the consumer's lender or loan servicer has been executed. This agreement must incorporate the offer of mortgage assistance relief that the provider has negotiated with the lender or servicer (12 C.F.R. §1015.5(a)). At the time that a MARS provider offers this written agreement to a consumer, it must also give the consumer the notice and the disclosure that is described in the subsequent section.

Disclosure Requirements for MARS Providers (12 C.F.R. §1015.4)

The MARS Rule establishes one set of disclosures for "general commercial communications" and another for "consumer-specific communications." Commercial communications are defined as any type of written or oral statement made using any mode of communication or broadcasting and includes examples that range from newspaper advertisement to infomercials (12 C.F.R. §1015.2).

"General commercial communication" is defined as commercial communication that is not directed towards a specific consumer and that occurs before a consumer agrees to allow a MARS provider to seek mortgage assistance relief on his/her behalf.

MARS providers must make the following disclosures in all general commercial communications:

- "(Name of company) is not associated with the government, and our service is not approved by the government or your lender."
- "Even if you accept this offer and use our service, your lender may not agree to change your loan."

"Consumer-specific commercial communication" is defined as commercial communication that is directed at a specific consumer and that occurs before a consumer agrees to allow a MARS provider to seek mortgage assistance relief on his/her behalf. MARS providers must make the following disclosures in all consumer-specific commercial communications:

- "You may stop doing business with us at any time. You may accept or reject the offer of mortgage assistance we obtain from your lender [or servicer]. If you reject the offer, you do not have to pay us. If you accept the offer, you will have to pay us (insert amount or method of calculating the amount) for our services."
- "(Name of company) is not associated with the government, and our service is not approved by the government or your lender."
- "Even if you accept this offer and use our service, your lender may not agree to change your loan."

Both the general and the consumer-specific commercial communications are required to be "clear and prominent." In order to ensure that these disclosures are clear and prominent, the rule requires that printed advertisements have a heading next to the disclosure that states: **"IMPORTANT NOTICE."** These words must be in bold print that is two sizes larger than the font size of the disclosures. Verbal communications, including telephone calls, must include the same disclosures, which must be prefaced with the statement, "Before using this service, consider the following information..." (12 C.F.R. §1015.4 (a)(3)).

All communications, whether general or consumer-specific, that expressly or implicitly represent that consumers should temporarily or permanently discontinue mortgage payments must include a disclosure stating, "If you stop paying your mortgage, you could lose your home and damage your credit rating" (12 C.F.R. §1015.4 (c)). Since the regulations also prohibit MARS providers from stating the consumer is not obligated to make scheduled payments, it would be difficult for MARS providers to make such a representation without violating the rule.

Notice and Disclosure Requirements Due when Offering Mortgage Relief (12 C.F.R. §1015.5)

When securing an agreement between a consumer and the lender or servicer that holds the consumer's home loan, MARS providers must give the consumer a notice from the loan holder or the loan servicer that describes any differences in lending terms between the consumer's existing loan and the modified loan.

Terms that should be addressed in the notice should include:

- The principal balance
- Interest rate
- Number of payments
- Monthly amounts owed for principal, interest, taxes, and insurance
- Loan term
- Any outstanding payments

This notice will allow a consumer to make a quick comparison between the terms of his/her existing mortgage and the loan that he/she will have after the proposed modifications are made. This notice must be "clear and prominent," and must have a heading that states **"IMPORTANT INFORMATION FROM YOUR [name of lender or servicer] ABOUT THIS OFFER."** This heading must be in bold print that is two sizes larger than the font size of the disclosures (12 C.F.R. §1015.5 (c)(2)).

If a MARS provider secures an agreement between a consumer and the lender holding the consumer's home loan or between the consumer and the loan servicer that accepts the consumer's payments, this agreement must include a disclosure stating "This is an offer of mortgage assistance relief we obtained from your lender [or servicer]. You may accept or reject the offer. If you reject the offer, you do not have to pay us. If you accept the offer, you will have to pay us (insert amount or method of calculating the amount) for our services" (12 C.F.R. §1015.5 (b)).

> *When securing an agreement between a consumer and the lender or servicer holding the consumer's home loan, MARS providers must give the consumer a notice describing any differences in lending terms between the consumer's existing loan and the modified loan.*

APPLYING MORTGAGE KNOWLEDGE TO EXAM PREPARATION

Additional Protections under the MARS Rule

The MARS Rule offers additional protections to consumers by:

- **Prohibiting Waivers**: Consumer protections offered through the Rule's notice and disclosure requirements and prohibited practices may not be waived, and attempts to obtain a waiver are a violation of the Rule (12 C.F.R. §1015.8)

- **Extension of Liability**: The Rule extends liability to any person who provides *"substantial assistance or support to any mortgage assistance relief provider when that person knows or consciously avoids knowing that the provider is engaged in any act or practice that violates this rule"* (12 C.F.R. §1015.6)

Recordkeeping Requirements (12 C.F.R. §1015.9 (a))

MARS providers must retain the following records for a period of 24 months. The 24-month period is measured from the date the record is created. The requirements apply to:

- Contracts between consumers and MARS providers

- Copies of all written communication between a consumer and a MARS provider that occurred before the consumer entered into an agreement with the provider

- Consumer files with names, contact information, payments made, and MARS provided *"...to the extent the mortgage assistance relief provider keeps such information in the ordinary course of business"* (12 C.F.R. §1015.9 (a)(4))

- Copies of sales scripts, training materials, commercial communication, websites, weblogs, and other MARS marketing materials

- Copies of required notices and disclosures

- Copies of records to demonstrate compliance with training and monitoring requirements and resolution of consumer complaints

Compliance Monitoring Requirements (12 C.F.R. §1015.9 (b))

MARS providers must "take reasonable steps sufficient to monitor" both employees and independent contractors for compliance with the MARS Rule.

This requirement involves monitoring of all communications with consumers, including:

- Monitoring telemarketing of mortgage assistance relief services with blind recording and testing of verbal communications by sales staff and customer service

- Establishing a procedure for receiving and responding to consumer complaints, including investigating complaints and taking corrective action against an employee or independent contractor who has failed to comply with the Rule

The Rule states that corrective action *"...may include training, disciplining, or terminating..."* an individual who is not complying with the MARS Rule (12 C.F.R. §1015.9 (b)(3)).

Exemptions (12 C.F.R. §1015.7)

Attorneys are exempt from some of the requirements of the MARS Rule if they:

- Provide mortgage assistance relief services as part of their legal practice
- Are licensed to practice law in the state where the consumer who is seeking relief resides or in the state where the consumer's dwelling is located
- Comply with other state laws that require conduct similar to that required by the MARS Rule

There is no doubt that this is an exemption that is subject to interpretation. The definition of "practice of law" varies in each state. In Pennsylvania, the definition frequently alluded to is one provided by the State Supreme Court, which defines the practice of law as the use of knowledge in three areas including advising clients, preparing legal documents, and appearing in public tribunals, such as courts [44]. Attorneys affiliated with MARS providers are likely to be engaged in these types of activities. However, in determining whether an exemption applies, state and federal enforcement agencies are likely to make this determination based on the primary focus of the attorney's professional activities. If the attorney is primarily engaged in the practice of law, the exemption will apply; if he/she is primarily involved in mortgage-related services while employed by a mortgage company, the exemption may not apply.

Some of the provisions of the MARS Rule that exempt attorneys must still comply with are those related to advance fees and disclosures. Attorneys must not accept advance payments, although the restriction on fees does not apply if the attorney deposits consumer funds into a client trust account. Attorneys are also required to comply with the MARS Rule by providing the notices required when offering a contract between the consumer and the lender or servicer, although the restriction on fees does not apply if the attorney deposits consumer funds into a client trust account.

It is important for loan originators to know that most states have adopted laws and rules that regulate the activities of entities and individuals that offer mortgage assistance relief services. The requirements vary greatly from state to state, with some imposing licensing requirements on those who offer to modify loans or to provide other forms of relief and others that create prohibited practices and disclosure requirements that are stricter than those created under the MARS Rule. Therefore, mortgage professionals that offer mortgage assistance relief services should not assume that compliance with the MARS Rule constitutes full compliance with all applicable laws.

While some attorneys may be exempt from provisions of the MARS Rule, they must still comply with those related to advance fees and disclosures.

The USA PATRIOT Act

Overview of the PATRIOT Act

Drafted and enacted in record time, the USA PATRIOT Act (PATRIOT Act) became law only a few weeks after the terrorist attacks of September 11, 2001. The portions of the PATRIOT Act that impact mortgage lending transactions are contained in Title III, which is called the "International Money Laundering Abatement and Anti-Terrorist Financing Act of 2001." Money laundering is the filtering of ill-gotten money through a series of transactions in order to prevent the tracing of the funds to their original illegal source. In the findings that it included in Title III, Congress explained how money laundering and terrorism are related, stating *"...money laundering... provides the financial fuel that permits transnational criminal enterprises to conduct and expand their operations to the detriment of the safety and security of American citizens..."* (H.R. 3162 §302(a)(1)).

The stated purposes of Title III include Congress' goal *"...to strengthen the provisions put into place by the Money Laundering Control Act of 1986..."* (H.R. 3162 §302(b)(2)). Through the PATRIOT Act, Congress made amendments to the Money Laundering Control Act and the Bank Secrecy Act to strengthen these laws and the ability of the U.S. government to take action to address money laundering.

Regulatory Agency

Congress authorized The Department of Treasury to implement Title III of the PATRIOT Act. An agency within the Treasury Department known as the Financial Crimes Enforcement Network (FinCEN) has primary responsibility for investigating, identifying, and reporting information on money laundering and other financial crimes.

Lending Institutions Covered by Title III of the PATRIOT Act

The requirements of Title III of the PATRIOT Act apply to "financial institutions," which are defined to include 24 specific types of entities including:

- Federally-regulated banks
- Branches and agencies of foreign banks located within the U.S.
- Credit unions
- Non-federally regulated private banks
- Persons involved in real estate closings and settlements
- Loan or finance companies

The types of business and financial institutions covered by the law are extensive. The definition of **"financial institution"** is so broad that it includes not only traditional financial institutions, but also businesses such as casinos, pawnbrokers, and automobile salesmen. Despite this broad definition, the first set of regulations that the Department of Treasury and FinCEN wrote in 2002 applied primarily to regulated depository institutions, and the regulations created a "temporary exemption" for ten entities defined as financial institutions. Loan or finance companies were included in the list of temporarily exempt entities (31 C.F.R. §1010.205(b)(ii)).

As of February 6, 2012, the temporary exemption for loan or finance companies came to an end. With a new rule issued on that date, FinCEN defined "loan or finance company" to include **"Residential Mortgage Lender or Originator."** Under the regulations, a "residential mortgage lender" includes persons to whom debt for a residential mortgage loan is initially payable or the person to whom the debt obligation is initially assigned after closing. The regulations define a "residential mortgage originator" as a person who accepts, offers, or negotiates the terms of a residential mortgage loan application (31 C.F.R. §1010.100(lll)(1)). In the preamble to the 2012 rule, FinCen collectively refers to residential mortgage lenders and residential mortgage originators as RMLOs.

These new regulations that are applicable to residential mortgage lenders and originators were effective on April 3, 2012. FinCEN established a delayed compliance date of August 13, 2012 to give those entities and individuals that are subject to its provisions time to implement a plan for complying with the new rules.

> *The portions of the Patriot Act that impact mortgage lending transactions are contained in Title III, the "International Money Laundering Abatement and Anti-Terrorist Financing Act of 2001."*

Actions Required by Title III of the PATRIOT Act and the New Regulations

In order to achieve compliance with the new regulations, which create specific responsibilities for them under Title III of the PATRIOT Act, RMLOs must:

- **Create an Anti-Money Laundering (AML) Program**: This must be a written program, approved by senior management, *"...that is reasonably designed to prevent the loan or finance company from being used to facilitate money laundering or the financing of terrorist activities"* (31 C.F.R. §1029.210(a)). This program must include procedures for complying with the reporting requirements of Subchapter II of the PATRIOT Act, a compliance officer, ongoing training for employees, and independent testing to ensure maintenance of an adequate program.

- **Make Suspicious Activity Reports**: RMLOs must file suspicious activity reports (SARs) if there is evidence that funds involved in a transaction which was conducted or attempted through them involve funds derived from or intended to disguise an illegal activity, was designed to evade the Bank Secrecy Act, was not the sort of transaction that the customer would normally be involved in, or involved the use of the RMLO to conduct criminal activity. SARs are filed with FinCEN.

- **Report Receipt of Currency in Excess of $5,000**: Receipt of currency in excess of $5,000 is reportable.

There are also deadlines, recordkeeping and information-sharing requirements under the regulations. RMLOs must file a SAR within **30 days** after an "initial detection" of suspicious activity. However, if an RMLO has information that requires immediate attention, he/she/it must immediately notify "appropriate law enforcement" by telephone in addition to filing a SAR. RMLOs must retain SARs and supporting documentation for five years from the date of filing a SAR.

In the preamble to the new regulations, FinCEN has indicated that it is likely to expand its definition of "loan or finance company" to other types of businesses. It began its "incremental approach to implementation of regulations" by creating requirements for RMLOs because it has conducted studies which indicate that RMLOs *"...are in a unique position to assess and identify money laundering risks and fraud while directly assisting consumers with their financial needs and protecting the sector from the abuses of financial crime"* [45].

Gramm-Leach-Bliley Act (GLB Act/Regulation P – 15 U.S.C. §6801 *et seq.* and 12 C.F.R. §1016 *et seq.*)

GLB Act Overview

The purpose of the privacy provisions of the Gramm-Leach-Bliley (GLB) Act is to ensure that financial institutions, including mortgage brokers and lenders, protect nonpublic personal information of consumers by:

- Advising consumers of the financial institution's policies with regard to the use and exchange of personal information
- Offering consumers the opportunity to limit the use and exchange of their personal information
- Creating a security program to protect personal information from unauthorized release and disclosure

Regulatory Agency and Regulations

Before the creation of the CFPB, implementation and enforcement of the GLB Act was carried out by the federal banking regulatory agencies and the FTC. Now, the CFPB is responsible for implementation and enforcement of the law and the GLB Act regulations, which are known as **Regulation P** (12 C.F.R. §1016 *et seq.*).

Information and Persons Protected by the GLB Act

The GLB Act applies to "nonpublic personal information," which the law defines as *"...personally identifiable financial information provided by a consumer to a financial institution; resulting from any transaction with the consumer or any service performed for the consumer; or otherwise obtained by the financial institution."* (15 U.S.C. §6809(4)).

Examples of personally identifiable information include:

- Information from a credit report
- Information that a consumer provides to obtain a loan

The GLB Act protects the privacy of "nonpublic personal information" that is provided by individual "consumers" and "customers." The law establishes different standards of privacy protection for consumers and customers, with the strictest standards applying to relationships with customers.

In the context of mortgage lending, a customer relationship and the requirements for protecting customer information exist when:

- A customer completes an application for a loan
- A customer obtains a loan from a lender or mortgage broker
- A financial institution obtains the servicing rights for a loan

Information Exempt from Protection by the GLB Act

The GLB Act does not extend protection to publicly available information, which includes:

- Information in government real estate records
- Information from a telephone book or information included on a public and unrestricted web site
- Listed telephone numbers provided by customers

The purpose of the privacy provisions of the Gramm-Leach-Bliley (GLB) Act is to ensure that financial institutions, including mortgage brokers and lenders, protect nonpublic personal information of consumers.

Definition of Terms Related to the GLB Act (12 C.F.R. §1016.3)

Affiliate: Any company that is controlled by or is under common control with another company.

Consumer: Defined in Regulation P as *"...an individual who obtains, from a financial institution, financial products or services which are to be used primarily for personal, family, or household purposes"* (12 C.F.R. §1016.3(e)). The rule clarifies that consumers are individuals who conduct isolated transactions with a financial institution, such as arranging for a wire transfer, using an ATM, or cashing a check.

Customer: A consumer who has a "customer relationship" with a financial institution.

Customer Relationship: A customer relationship exists when a consumer has a continuing relationship with a financial institution. Regulation P states that a customer relationship exists during the arrangement for or brokering of a mortgage loan and during the servicing of a loan.

Financial Institution: In Regulation P, the term is broadly defined as *"...any institution the business of which is engaging in financial activities..."* (12 C.F.R. §1016.3(l)(1)). As described below, "financial activities" are defined in the regulations to include brokering loans. Therefore, mortgage brokers as well as lenders are subject to the GLB Act.

Financial Activities: The FTC includes "brokering loans" as an example of financial activity covered by the GLB Act.

Nonpublic Personal Information: Regulation P defines the term, "nonpublic personal information" as *"...personally identifiable financial information"* provided by a consumer to a financial institution for a financial transaction or service or personal financial information otherwise obtained by a financial institution (12 C.F.R. §1016.3(p)(1)).

Disclosures and Notifications Required by the GLB Act

The GLB Act requires financial institutions always to notify customers, and sometimes to notify consumers, of their policies and practices regarding the collection of nonpublic personal information and the sharing of it with third parties. Notices must include information on safeguarding the privacy of nonpublic personal information. If financial institutions plan to share consumer or customer information, they must also provide notice of the right to opt-out of the sharing of information.

Following are the requisite notices under the GLB Act:

Initial Privacy Notice: The requirements for the initial privacy notice differ for consumers and customers. Financial institutions are not required to provide consumers with a privacy notice unless they intend to share the consumer's information with nonaffiliated third parties. Financial institutions must always provide customers with a conspicuous privacy notice in writing or in electronic form that clearly describes the financial institution's practice of sharing nonpublic personal information with affiliates and third parties. The notice must specify the types of information shared and the types of affiliated and nonaffiliated parties that will receive the information. The initial privacy notice to customers is due at the time the customer relationship is established (12 C.F.R. §1016.4(a)(1)).

Opt-Out Notices: Financial institutions that intend to share nonpublic personal information must provide consumers and customers with a notice of their right to opt-out of the sharing of information. The notice must include a description of the type of information that the financial institution may disclose, and "reasonable means" to opt-out, such as opt-out forms which are easy to complete or toll-free telephone numbers to representatives who will accept the opt-out information. No specific timeframe is given under the law other than consumers must be provided with a reasonable opportunity to opt-out. Note: The initial privacy document and opt-out notice can be included in one document (12 C.F.R. §1016.6).

The requirement to provide opt-out notices includes some exceptions. The exceptions include:

- Disclosures to a third party in order to complete a transaction requested by a consumer or customer (this exception would include disclosures made by mortgage brokers to settlement service providers in order to close a mortgage loan), and
- Disclosures to financial institutions that share joint-marketing agreements

(12 C.F.R. §1016.13)

Annual Privacy Notices: Financial institutions are required to send annual privacy notices to customers, and these notices must contain the same information that is included in the initial privacy notice, including notice of the right to opt-out and information on exercising the right to opt-out (12 C.F.R. §1016.5).

Practices Prohibited by the GLB Act

- **Prohibition on the Sharing of Account Numbers**: With a few limited exceptions, the GLB Act prohibits the sharing of account numbers for marketing purposes.

- **Limitations on the Re-disclosure and Reuse of Information**: If a third party obtains nonpublic personal information that is released pursuant to an exception or as a result of a customer's failure to opt-out, the third party can only use the information for limited purposes.

The GLB Act does not include specific penalty provisions for violations of the law's privacy provisions.

Safeguards Rule (16 C.F.R. §314)

The provisions of the GLB Act require compliance with the Safeguards Rule. The intention of the Safeguards Rule is to ensure the protection of privacy of personal information with the creation, implementation and maintenance of an effective security program. This rule was adopted by the Federal Trade Commission in 2002.

Institutions Covered by the Safeguards Rule

The FTC's Safeguards Rule covers all the "financial institutions" (as defined under the GLB Act) that are within its jurisdiction. Financial institutions within the jurisdiction of the FTC include mortgage brokers.

Security Program

A company's security program designed to meet the requirements of the Safeguards Rule must include the following elements:

- A designated company representative to coordinate the program

- Identification of internal and external risks which affect the security of customer information

- Regular testing, monitoring and adjustment of the security program

- Oversight of service providers who have access to customer information

The GLB Act requires financial institutions to notify customers, and sometimes consumers, of their policies and practices regarding the collection of nonpublic personal information and the sharing of it with third parties.

Privacy Protection/Do-Not-Call (16 C.F.R. §310)

Privacy rights are a significant concern for mortgage professionals who are involved in the solicitation, origination, processing, closing and servicing of mortgage loans. Multiple laws protect the privacy of borrowers, and violation of these laws can result in serious liability. In addition to the Gramm-Leach-Bliley Act, which protects the financial privacy of consumers, federal and state laws protect consumers from unwanted solicitations from mortgage bankers and mortgage brokers.

The Do-Not-Call Implementation Act was signed into law in 2003 as part of earlier legislation – the Telemarketing Consumer Fraud and Abuse Prevention Act and the Telemarketing Sales Rule. The Do-Not-Call Implementation Act authorized the Federal Trade Commission (FTC) to implement and enforce the Do-Not-Call Registry. The FTC's authority covers interstate calls, while the Federal Communications Commission (FCC) covers calls made to and from points within the same state.

As a result of the Dodd-Frank Act, the CFPB shares enforcement authority for the Telemarketing Sales Rule. In their memorandum of understanding, the FTC and the CFPB will consult on rulemakings under the Telemarketing Sales Rule regarding the use of telemarketing to offer consumer financial products and services.

The telemarketing legislation is intended as a consumer protection law that allows consumers to restrict unwanted sales calls from coming into their homes. Consumers are required to take the initiative to place their names on the Do-Not-Call Registry.

Under the original provisions of the Telemarketing Act, consumers were required to renew their entry in the registry every five years. Following amendments made by the Do-Not-Call Improvement Act of 2007, phone numbers added to the registry become permanent.

The provisions of the Telemarketing Act and Sales Rule apply to any business or individual engaged in the practice of telemarketing. Telemarketing is generally defined as calls made as part of a plan or program to persuade consumers to purchase goods or services.

Requirements of the Do-Not-Call Provisions

Mortgage professionals involved in sales and telemarketing practices must provide a truthful and prompt verbal disclosure of the following information:

- The identity of the caller
- The fact that the purpose of the call is to sell goods or services
- The nature of the good/services being sold
- Assurance that no purchase or payment is required to participate in any type of promotion

One of the most important procedures required by the Telemarketing Sales Rule is the requirement for businesses that conduct telemarketing to access the Do-Not-Call Registry every 31 days. This requirement is aimed at ensuring telemarketing call lists are updated with the names and phone numbers that are newly registered.

Unless a mortgage professional limits his or her calls to individuals with whom there is an established business relationship, or individuals who have provided written agreements to accept calls, it is illegal to initiate calls without obtaining access to the Do-Not-Call Registry. Access to the Registry is available to telemarketing professionals on a fee basis. Fees are assessed based on the number of area codes accessed, and the FTC establishes an annual maximum fee.

Recordkeeping (16 C.F.R. §310.5)

Mortgage professionals engaged in telemarketing are required to maintain records of all telemarketing activities for a period of 24 months from the date the materials were produced.

Examples include:

- Advertising, brochures, telemarketing scripts, and promotional materials
- Name and last known address of each customer, the goods/services purchased and the amount paid for them
- Name, last known home address and telephone number of current and former employees
- Any authorizations or informed consent agreements from consumers who agree to receive telemarketing calls

Prohibitions of the Telemarketing Sales Rule

The Telemarketing Sales Rule and its provisions create a number of prohibited practices for sales and telemarketing professionals. Several important points which can impact mortgage professionals include prohibitions on the following abusive practices:

- Use of threats, intimidation or profane language
- Placing calls to consumers before 8:00 a.m. or after 9:00 p.m. – it is important to consider the local time of the consumer
- Making false or misleading statements
- Requiring payment of a fee in advance of obtaining a loan or other extension of credit
- Charging a consumer for goods or services without consent
- Failing to transmit a telephone number so that it can be read by a call recipient's Caller ID
- Initiating a call to a consumer listed on the Do-Not-Call Registry

Exceptions to the Do-Not-Call Provisions

The requirements of the Telemarketing Sales Rule and its provisions do not apply if a consumer has an established relationship with a mortgage professional. In the case of an established relationship, a mortgage professional is permitted to place calls to customers, even if their phone numbers are on the Do-Not-Call Registry.

A critical component to this exception is the law's definition of an established business relationship. An established business relationship is a relationship between a seller and a consumer based on a financial transaction that they have shared within the 18-month period that immediately precedes any sales call. Additionally, mortgage professionals are permitted to contact consumers for a period of three months following a relationship that is based on an inquiry by the consumer.

Regardless of the existence of an established business relationship, if a consumer specifically asks a mortgage professional not to contact them, the request must be honored.

> *The requirements of the Telemarketing Sales Rule and its provisions do not apply if a consumer has an established relationship with a mortgage professional.*

Penalties for Violations of the Telemarketing Sales Rule

Violations of the Telemarketing Sales Rule are regarded as unfair and deceptive trade practices under the Federal Trade Commission Act. Penalties are $16,000 for each violation, and when violations continue, each day is considered a separate violation.

Under certain circumstances, a company which violates telemarketing provisions may be exempt from liability. The FTC considers whether the mortgage professional has established procedures for complying with the provisions, trains its personnel on the procedures and regularly monitors compliance.

Discussion Scenario: Privacy Concerns

A homeowner comes into the office of a mortgage broker, who operates as a sole proprietor, and makes some general inquiries about interest rates. The homeowner used the services of the mortgage broker one year earlier to secure a first mortgage, and he is now interested in a home equity loan so that he can cash in on the equity that he has gained in his home.

The broker offers the homeowner a loan application, suggesting that the information in the application will enable her to give the homeowner suggestions on products that might suit his needs. The homeowner declines to complete an application. However, he leaves his name and home phone number, suggesting that the broker call him if rates decrease.

A week later, when interest rates drop a quarter of a percentage point, the mortgage broker decides to call the homeowner. Following standard office procedure, the broker's secretary checks the office's recently updated list of numbers compiled from the Do-Not-Call Registry, and finds that the homeowner's name is on the registry. The broker calls the homeowner, telling him that she can give him low interest rates with better lending terms than other mortgage brokers can offer. The homeowner gives the mortgage broker the information necessary to complete the loan application and asks her to begin processing his application as soon as possible. To facilitate the processing of his application, he agrees to mail a copy of his recent tax return to the mortgage broker's secretary.

Because the homeowner is anxious to complete the transaction, the mortgage broker immediately contacts settlement service providers. She calls only those service providers who have adequate security programs, which they have reviewed with her, and who have signed a contract agreeing to secure and protect the privacy of the personal information of customers. In her office, the broker begins assembling the information that is needed in order to proceed with the closing. She asks her secretary to e-mail her a copy of the homeowner's file that she has retained since his last closing, and uses this information to identify mortgage products that she will recommend.

On the day of the settlement, which occurs three weeks after receipt of the loan application, the mortgage broker includes a privacy statement with the other closing documents. She does not include an opt-out notice with the initial privacy notice. The lender that is funding and servicing the loan also provides the homeowner with a privacy statement that includes notice of the right to opt-out and a form for the use in exercising the right to opt out. The homeowner signs the opt-out form when he signs the other closing documents.

Discussion Questions

- *Based on your understanding of privacy laws, what procedures did the broker follow which kept her in compliance?*

- *What procedures did she fail to follow that cause compliance issues?*

- *What are some policies a mortgage professional can put in place to ensure privacy violations are not a concern?*

Discussion Feedback

The mortgage broker was operating in compliance with the Telemarketing Sales Rule by maintaining procedures in the office to prevent calls to persons listed on the Do-Not-Call Registry and maintaining an updated call list. The broker's call to the homeowner was not in violation of the Telemarketing Sales Rule because she had a business relationship with the homeowner that was established for less than 18 months before placing a call to him. Recent inquiries by the homeowner and his request for a call in the event that interest rates dropped are also indicators that the mortgage broker shared an established business relationship with the homeowner, allowing call in spite of the fact that his name was on the Do-Not-Call Registry.

However, the content of her call was not in compliance with the law. Promising low interest rates and the most competitive lending terms without reviewing the homeowner's updated financial information were misleading statements that she used to induce the homeowner to complete a mortgage application. She should have refrained from making these representations until she knew they were true, based on verification of the homeowner's current financial status. Technically, the unrealistic representations were an unfair and deceptive trade practice, subject to action by the FTC.

The mortgage broker provided the homeowner with a privacy notice at the time of the closing but violated the GLB Act by failing to provide an initial privacy notice within the time frame prescribed by the law. The FTC Privacy Rule specifically provides that an initial privacy notice is due when a customer relationship is established and that the establishment of a customer relationship occurs when a consumer *"Enters into an agreement or understanding with you whereby you undertake to arrange or broker a home mortgage loan..."* (16 C.F.R. §313.3(i)(E)).

In its Financial Privacy Rule, the FTC includes an exception for situations in which providing notice will *"...substantially delay the customer's transaction."* (16 C.F.R §313.4(e)(2)(ii)) Under this exception, subsequent delivery of the notice is allowed when the customer relationship is established over the phone and the customer requests *"...prompt delivery of the financial product or service"* (16 C.F.R. §313.4(e)(2)(ii)(A)).

With the homeowner requesting that the mortgage broker process his application right away, delayed delivery of the privacy notice would have been acceptable. However, delayed delivery of the privacy notice until the time of closing rendered the notice meaningless.

As long as she entered into agreements with the settlement service providers stating that they would not disclose the homeowner's personal information, the mortgage broker did not violate the law by failing to provide an opt-out notice. Opt-out notices are not required for the sharing of information with settlement service providers.

Other privacy concerns represented in the scenario relate to the safeguarding of customer information. In order to operate her business in compliance with the Safeguards Rule, the mortgage broker would need a security system that includes: Training for her secretary; protection of nonpublic personal information, such as the mailed or faxed copies of tax returns; and protection of the information stored and transmitted on the mortgage broker's computer.

Mortgage professionals can ensure they are in compliance with privacy concerns by:

- Maintaining policies and procedures which include checking the Do-Not-Call Registry and updating telemarketing lists every 31 days
- Ensuring nonpublic personal information is safeguarded at all times – including during its use, storage and disposal
- Providing disclosures as required by federal and state laws

Mortgage Fraud Laws

The Federal Bureau of Investigations (FBI) defines mortgage fraud as *"the intentional perversion of the truth for the purpose of inducing another person or other entity in reliance upon it to part with something of value or to surrender a legal right"* [46].

Costing the mortgage industry billions of dollars each year, fraud threatens the overall soundness of the entire mortgage market. It is a crime that impacts mortgage lenders, insurers, and purchasers. Often referred to as the fastest growing white collar crime and as a problem of epidemic proportions, mortgage fraud is receiving increasing attention from the FBI, the Internal Revenue Service (IRS), the Department of Housing and Urban Development (HUD) and from federal and state legislators.

Two Types of Mortgage Fraud

The FBI categorizes mortgage fraud in two ways: Fraud for Profit and Fraud for Housing. The focus of most anti-fraud efforts is on Fraud for Profit, also known as Industry Insider Fraud.

Fraud for Profit (also known as Industry Insider Fraud)

This type of fraud involves the conspiratorial involvement of unscrupulous individuals coming from all areas of the mortgage lending industry. Individuals can include mortgage bankers, mortgage brokers, loan officers, underwriters, processors, real estate agents, appraisers, and lawyers. Using inflated appraisals, falsified loan documents, and straw buyers to secure fraudulent loans, these industry insiders are the cause of an estimated *"...80 percent of all reported fraud losses..."* [47].

Fraud for Housing

The FBI distinguishes Fraud for Profit from Fraud for Housing, which occurs when a borrower misrepresents his/her employment history, credit history, intention to occupy a property as a primary residence, or income in order to improve his/her chances of securing a mortgage. Originators should not be tempted to "help" loan applicants to obtain a loan with the use of inaccurate information. They should also advise loan applicants that it is illegal to include false information in an application or to use fraudulent documents for verification of income and employment.

Industry insider fraud and fraud for housing are both illegal, but industry insider fraud results in much greater losses, and is therefore the primary focus of federal anti-fraud operations. Although industry insiders may continue to pocket ill-gotten profits gained in mortgage fraud schemes, those who are caught are certain to face stiff penalties, including imprisonment.

Mortgage Fraud Investigations

The FBI, HUD, and the IRS conduct investigations for mortgage fraud, and make referrals to the Department of Justice when there is sufficient evidence for prosecution.

Federal Laws Relating to Mortgage Fraud

In 2009, Congress responded to the increasing epidemic of mortgage fraud with the enactment of **The Fraud Enforcement and Recovery Act (FERA)**. FERA was enacted to facilitate the prosecution of those who commit mortgage fraud and to increase the financial resources that are available to investigate and prosecute fraud cases. FERA revised the federal criminal code by specifically providing that the law against defrauding a financial institution includes actions related to the "mortgage lending business." FERA defines "mortgage lending business" as *"... an organization which finances or refinances any debt secured by an interest in real estate,* *including private mortgage companies and any subsidiaries of such organizations, and whose activities affect interstate or foreign commerce"* (18 U.S.C. §27).

Other federal laws that are commonly used to address mortgage fraud include statutes against mail fraud, bank fraud, wire fraud, making false statements to a financial institution, money laundering, and conspiracy. These laws are described below. All of them carry stiff criminal penalties. Mail fraud, bank fraud and making false statements to a financial institution also have a statute of limitations of ten years for prosecution – longer than other federal laws.

> *The FBI categorizes mortgage fraud in two ways: Fraud for Profit and Fraud for Housing. The focus of most anti-fraud efforts is on Fraud for Profit, also known as Industry Insider Fraud.*

Mail Fraud (18 U.S.C. §1341)

Mail fraud is the knowing use of the mail system to carry out a fraudulent scheme. Amendments to the law include not just use of the U.S. Postal Service but also the use of any private or commercial mail carrier, such as Federal Express or United Parcel Service.

Penalties for mail fraud can include fines, imprisonment of not more than 20 years, or both. If the violation affects a financial institution, a person can be fined not more than $1 million, imprisoned not more than 30 years, or both.

It is not necessary for a violator to complete the mailing. Prosecutors need only to show that the defendant understood that, in the common course of business, a mail service would be used to carry out a fraudulent scheme.

Bank Fraud (18 U.S.C. §1344)

Bank fraud is the use of a fraudulent scheme to unlawfully obtain money or property from a federally-insured financial institution. Penalties for bank fraud include fines of not more than $1 million, imprisonment of not more than 30 years, or both.

Conspiracy (18 U.S.C. §371)

Federal law contains a general conspiracy statute that protects the government from fraud and other offenses. The law specifically addresses conspiracies *"...to defraud the United States or any agency thereof...."* Therefore, the law applies to fraudulent actions against government agencies such as HUD and the Federal Housing Administration.

Money Laundering (18 U.S.C. §1956 and 18 U.S.C. §1957)

Money laundering is a term that describes financial transactions that are used to distance illegally obtained funds from their original criminal source. It is a common misperception that money laundering laws apply strictly to funds and proceeds from drug trafficking, terrorist activities, and organized crime.

The laws against money laundering are complex, but there are two federal laws that prosecutors are likely to rely on in establishing that a defendant has attempted to launder funds obtained from a fraudulent lending transaction.

Penalties for violations of federal money laundering provisions are severe and can include a fine of $500,000 or twice the value of the property involved in the transaction, whichever is greater, imprisonment for up to 20 years, or both.

Additionally, simply depositing more than $10,000 of fraudulently obtained money in a bank account can constitute money laundering. Penalties for violations of this money laundering provision can include fines and imprisonment for terms of up to ten years.

False Statements to a Financial Institution (18 U.S.C. §1014)

Many actions for mortgage fraud are based on violations of this law, which states that it is a crime to knowingly make false statements or to overvalue land or property in order to influence the decision of lending institutions. Offering false information to a lender in order to obtain a loan is an action that is clearly covered by this law.

Penalties for violations of this law are severe, providing that those convicted "…shall be fined not more than $1,000,000 or imprisoned not more than 30 years, or both." False statements that can lead to fines and imprisonment include inflated appraisals used to secure a mortgage, and any false statements in a lending transaction, such as falsely stating that a home will be used as a primary residence.

Fraud in Connection with Identification Documents (18 U.S.C. §1028)

Many cases of mortgage fraud involve the use of false identification documents, including the use of stolen personal information. It is a violation of federal law to produce or use false identification documents. The law provides for three levels of penalties, depending on the nature of the act. Prison sentences can be as long as 15 years.

General Mortgage Knowledge

GENERAL MORTGAGE KNOWLEDGE

Learning Objectives

This chapter was created based on the General Mortgage Knowledge section of the NMLS National Test Content Outline. There are several topics covered in this chapter, and each has the potential to appear on the NMLS national test in multiple choice question format. In this chapter, students will:

- Review the Guidance on Nontraditional Mortgage Product Risks and the Statement on Subprime Mortgage Lending
- Learn about the mortgage product standards the Nontraditional Guidance and Statement advise
- Examine the characteristics of loans that will be regulated as higher-priced mortgages and the lending practices and prohibitions required for them
- Explore the history and recent developments in subprime lending
- Consider important changes in federal legislation specific to the Home Ownership and Equity Protection Act (HOEPA), including:
  - The special disclosures and notifications required for HOEPA loans
  - The lending terms and practices prohibited by HOEPA and the reasons for these prohibitions
- Explore the basics of fixed-rate and adjustable-rate loans
- Learn the difference between government loan programs and conventional loan programs
- Review second mortgages and subordinate financing
- Gain an understanding of securitization and the role the secondary market plays
- Investigate special needs properties and borrowers, including nontraditional lending
- Take a look at the current mortgage lending landscape
- Review recent developments in the mortgage lending landscape which led to the industry's present condition
- Examine broad pieces of recent federal legislation that directly impact the business of lending and mortgage origination
- Understand the impact a single mortgage loan can have on the greater financial markets
- Learn about the purpose and process of securitization
- Define key players in the securitization process

Introduction

Some knowledge about the history of mortgage lending from the 1920s through 2007 is critical to understanding:

- Why certain mortgage programs and products have disappeared from today's market

- Why other mortgage products that had lost popularity are once again sought by consumers, and

- Why lending standards have changed, making mortgage originations more difficult to complete today than they were six years ago

Course participants should pay particular attention to highlighted terms in the following history of mortgage lending because these terms are likely to appear on the SAFE mortgage loan originator test. While reading this overview of eight decades of lending history, course participants should also note the enormous impact that the secondary mortgage market has had on the availability of loan funds and on the types of mortgage products that are available to consumers.

The history of mortgage lending that is directly relevant to mortgage origination today goes back to the early twentieth century. At that time, most mortgages had short terms of three to five years with a balloon payment due at the end of the loan term. Borrowers who could not refinance faced foreclosure. During this era of mortgage lending, lending took place almost exclusively through depository institutions such as banks. The amount of money that these institutions had for originating new home loans or refinancing existing mortgages was limited to the funds available from current deposits. Even this limited lending activity came to an abrupt halt as the country entered the Great Depression in 1929. The triggering event of the 1929 lending crisis was the stock market crash that led panicked depositors to withdraw their money from banks, leaving lenders with no money to fund loans. Also, banks were experiencing difficulty collecting outstanding loans and, to the extent secured, difficulty selling the collateral at a sufficient price to pay the debt. As a result of this run on the banks, Americans who had no money to meet their balloon payments and who were depending on refinances to hold onto their homes inevitably lost them. Foreclosures were rampant.

> *Historical insight is necessary to understand why lending standards have changed and why mortgage originations are more difficult to complete today.*

The Creation of the Secondary Mortgage Market

The initial step that President Franklin Delano Roosevelt and Congress took to restore confidence in the banking and lending systems was to pass the Banking Act of 1933. This law authorized the creation of the Federal Deposit Insurance Corporation (FDIC). By insuring deposits, the FDIC was able to promote public confidence in the soundness of banks. The next step directly impacted mortgage lending, and it was the creation in 1934 of the **Federal Housing Administration (FHA)**. The FHA encouraged lenders to fund loans by insuring the full value of mortgages for qualified borrowers. The final step towards recovery was the creation of a government-sponsored enterprise, known as the **Federal National Mortgage Association (Fannie Mae)**. Fannie Mae purchased FHA-insured mortgages as investments, thereby creating a **secondary market** for mortgages. The money gained by selling FHA mortgages to Fannie Mae enabled lenders to make more loans.

The secondary market expanded in 1970 when federal legislation authorized Fannie Mae to purchase and invest in home loans other than FHA-insured mortgages. Another development in 1970 that expanded the secondary market was the enactment of federal legislation to create a competitor for Fannie Mae by establishing the **Federal Home Loan Mortgage Corporation (Freddie Mac)**. Both Fannie Mae and Freddie Mac are **government-sponsored enterprises (GSEs)** that have some protection from the U.S. government, while functioning as private shareholder companies.

Beginning in the 1970s, Fannie Mae and Freddie Mac not only purchased mortgage loans, they also securitized them. **Securitization** is the process of collecting loans with similar credit risks, loan terms, and other comparable features into a "pool" and selling an interest in this pool to investors as a **mortgage-backed security (MBS)**. Part of the appeal of an MBS to investors is that Fannie Mae and Freddie Mac guarantee the performance of their MBS products. Furthermore, even though these securities are not backed by the full faith and credit of the government, *"The market perceives an implicit guarantee by the U.S. government, because like other giant financial institutions…the government is unlikely to let these institutions fail in the event of financial problems"* [48].

Another GSE that was created to encourage the purchase of MBSs is the Government National Mortgage Association (Ginnie Mae). Ginnie Mae does not guarantee mortgages. Instead, it guarantees securities that are created from the purchase of non-conventional mortgages. These include securities created from FHA loans, loans guaranteed by the Veteran's Administration, and loans guaranteed by the United States Department of Agriculture. Ginnie Mae securities are the only MBSs that have the "full faith and credit" of the government of the United States.

> *Fannie Mae and Freddie Mac are government-sponsored enterprises (GSEs) that function as private shareholder companies, but have some protection by the U.S. government.*

Expansion of Securitization to the Private Marketplace

In the 1990s, private-label securitization began, and many argue that it was the rapid growth of these investment products between 2000 and 2005 that ultimately led to the collapse of the mortgage lending market. If private-label MBSs had been based on **prime loans** made to well-qualified borrowers with strong credit scores, these investment products would probably have retained their value. However, the growth of the private-label MBSs paralleled the growth of the **subprime lending market**, which was intended to serve borrowers with blemished credit. Private-label MBSs were created from all types of nonprime and subprime loans, including low-doc loans, negative amortization loans, loans with terms in excess of 30 years, and loans made to homebuyers who were not creditworthy. Private investment firms demonstrated little reluctance to turn any type of mortgage debt into an investment.

Private-label MBSs had neither the actual nor the implicit guarantee of government backing, and the debt underlying these securities belonged to borrowers who were more likely than not to default on their loans. These MBSs were very different from those created from the prime loans that Fannie Mae and Freddie Mac had traditionally purchased. In order to sell these investment products, investment firms had to convince consumers that they were safe, and they turned to rating agencies to do this. As one analyst stated, *"...private-label mortgage-backed securities relied on credit rating agencies to inspire confidence in investors that the debt was safe"* [49].

The rating agencies that endorsed private-label MBSs included Standard & Poor's, Fitch, and Moody's. Although these investment products were created from the debt of borrowers who had compromised credit histories, the rating agencies gave most of these securities the highest AAA rating. In fact, *"In 2006, 79.1% of an average subprime MBS was rated AAA"* [50]. As a growing number of investors purchased and securitized subprime loans, more funding for new subprime lending became available.

Securitization of nonprime and subprime loans was not limited to the private market. Fannie Mae and Freddie Mac also engaged in the purchase and securitization of these types of loans, partially in response to government policies to lower the standards for the loans they purchased in order to free up loan funds for lower-income and marginally-qualified homebuyers [51]. However, private investment firms were the primary players in the securitization of subprime loans and *"By 2006, two-thirds or more of subprime mortgages were being securitized through the private-label market"* [52].

Many argue that it was the rapid growth of private-label securitization which ultimately led to the collapse of the mortgage lending market.

Shifting Risk

In the traditional lending setting that existed before such a large percentage of mortgages were securitized, depository institutions such as banks originated, funded, and serviced home loans and held them in their portfolios until they were paid off. With loans kept in a bank's portfolio, loan performance was easy to track, and the success of a loan officer's career depended on demonstrated success in matching borrowers with loans that they could repay on time. Strict underwriting standards were established and followed because all individuals who were engaged in mortgage transactions were held accountable when borrowers defaulted. One analyst described the gravity of a default in this lending environment, *"Lenders earned profits on loans from interest payments as well as from upfront fees. If the loans went into default, the lenders bore the losses. Default was such a serious financial event that lenders took care when underwriting loans"* [53].

As an increasing number of home loans were routinely sold and securitized, there was no meaningful tracking of individual loan performance. With the evaporation of accountability for defaults, lenders faced fewer risks, making them more willing to fund nonprime and subprime loans, despite the fact that they carry a much higher risk of default. Securitization allowed lenders to *"...make loans intending to sell them to investors, knowing that investors would bear the financial brunt if the loans went belly-up"* [54]. Eventually, loan performance became a virtually irrelevant concern, even in the secondary market, where investment bankers were creating extremely speculative investment products out of mortgage debt. Securitization of mortgages was the first level of investment products built on mortgage debt, with more exotic products known as collateralized debt obligations (CDOs) and CDOs-squared built from repackaged pools of mortgages.

Investors did of course "bear the financial brunt," but they did not bear it alone. Mortgage lenders and brokers that built successful businesses on the lending frenzy were suddenly unable to earn a living. Countless borrowers at the brink of foreclosure found that although they might have a claim against their lenders for predatory lending practices, the law prevented them from bringing these claims against the investors who had purchased their loans. When these borrowers sought recourse from the mortgage companies that originated their loans, they often found that these companies were bankrupt and judgment proof. Risk had been shifted from lenders to brokers to investors so many times that many were to blame, but no one could be held accountable.

> *Securitization allowed lenders to shift the financial burden of loans to investors. Because the risk had been shifted so many times between lenders, brokers, and investors, no one could be held fully accountable when the lending crisis hit.*

Sharing Blame

For decades, heavily regulated depository institutions originated most mortgage loans, and the vast majority of these loans were made to borrowers whose credit ratings, income, and employment histories qualified them as prime borrowers. The secondary market's purchase and securitization of the debt of well-qualified borrowers created safe and reliable investments. Many analysts blame the 2007 mortgage lending crisis on the expansion of the secondary mortgage market to include the purchase and securitization of subprime loans, and there is ample evidence to support this claim.

Other analysts lay the blame for the financial crisis on the ratings agencies such as Standard & Poor's, Fitch, and Moody's, arguing that the securitization of subprime debt and the ensuing financial crisis would not have occurred without the inflated ratings that these credit rating agencies (CRAs) gave to risky MBSs. Investors relied on these deceptive AAA ratings when deciding to invest in securitized subprime loans. The inaccurate ratings issued by the CRAs were due, in part, to the conflict of interest that existed between CRAs and the companies that issued MBSs. Issuers of MBSs paid for the ratings of their securities, and some CRAs would *"...inflate ratings for paying issuers in hopes of gaining repeat business..."* [55]. There is also evidence that issuers of MBSs "shopped" for ratings by going to other CRAs if the first rating agency approached did not provide a favorable rating. Furthermore, ratings agencies also served as consultants to investment bankers who were securitizing loans, and *"...were paid to consult investment banks on how to structure the deal to obtain an investment grade rating"* [56].

Challenging the blame that has been directed towards CRAs, some analysts of the mortgage lending crisis argue that investors should have done their own research on securitized subprime loans and that they relied too heavily on the ratings [57]. There is no doubt that most players in the primary and secondary markets were failing to do their homework and operating with too little information. Those in the primary market who bear some of the blame for the market's collapse include loan originators who abandoned lending standards to make low-doc and no-doc loans to unqualified borrowers.

Opinions regarding the roles that Fannie Mae and Freddie Mac played in the subprime debacle differ at opposite ends of the political spectrum. Conservatives argue that the meltdown of the subprime market was precipitated by tax incentives that the government gave to Fannie Mae and Freddie Mac to purchase huge numbers of loans made to low-income borrowers, including risky subprime loans. Liberals reject this theory and claim that Fannie Mae and Freddie Mac had safeguards in place that the private sector did not follow, such as policies against buying subprime loans with predatory features. What is certain is that Fannie Mae and Freddie Mac *"...purchased billions of dollars of subprime backed securities for their own investment portfolios..."* and that these unsound investments were contributing factors to the financial distress of these government-sponsored enterprises [58].

Certainly, the blame for the current lending crisis does not belong to any one sector of the lending or investing community, and consumers should also accept some degree of responsibility. "Creative financing" was a term that represented the overly optimistic attitudes that prevailed among borrowers and lenders. Countless consumers, including borrowers with sterling credit ratings, over-extended themselves buying homes that were beyond their means and taking out home equity lines of credit to finance pursuits other than homeownership.

Lax lending standards facilitated these transactions. The concept of creative financing often meant that lenders were willing to offer **nontraditional mortgages**, such as interest-only loans and payment-option loans to a broad range of borrowers. Historically, these types of products were only available to very well-qualified borrowers who were seeking financing for short term investments. For many of the consumers who used this type of financing to purchase homes, the ultimate results of creative borrowing have been devastating.

Borrowers share some of the responsibility for the recent lending crisis, as well as those lenders offering "creative financing" and ratings agencies which gave inflated ratings to risky MBSs.

The Return to More Traditional Lending Programs and Products

Since February 2007, when the subprime mortgage market collapsed, there have been many changes related to mortgage programs and products. The most immediate and obvious change was the sudden unavailability of subprime mortgage loans. These products were credited with increasing the rate of homeownership in the United States to an all-time high of 69.2% in 2004. Unfortunately, they included risky features such as adjustable interest rates and balloon payments.

Countless borrowers who did not understand the terms of their loans or who were overly-optimistic about their ability to meet the repayment terms of their lending agreements found themselves in default when their interest rates reset or when balloon payments were due and refinancing was unavailable. In fact, one of the triggering events of the crash of the lending industry was the interest rate reset on a large number of subprime loans.

In the wake of the subprime crisis, and for the first time in decades, FHA loans gained popularity. These loans are generally intended to serve the needs of low- to moderate-income consumers and first time buyers. When Congress passed the Housing and Economic Recovery Act of 2008 (HERA), it included provisions to make FHA loans available to more borrowers, including those at higher income levels. These were the same products that helped to revive the lending market during the Great Depression.

The collapse of the lending market has not only limited the types of mortgage products available, but it has also led to a tightening of lending standards. When the mortgage market collapsed, lenders rapidly retreated from practices that included the origination of low-doc and no-doc loans, and returned to previous lending practices that included documented verification of consumers' eligibility for mortgages. In fact, with new laws in place that require verification of consumers' repayment ability in virtually all lending transactions, the origination of exotic products such as low-doc and no-doc loans is now illegal. These new laws and the commitment of the new Consumer Financial Protection Bureau (CFPB) to enforce them are facts that raise compliance concerns for loan originators to an even higher level.

> *The Housing and Economic Recovery Act (HERA) includes provisions to make FHA loans available to more borrowers.*

MORTGAGE PROGRAMS

Conventional Mortgages

A conventional mortgage is a mortgage NOT insured or guaranteed by the Federal Housing Administration (FHA), the Department of Veterans Affairs (VA), or the Rural Housing Service (RHS) of the U.S. Department of Agriculture (USDA). There are two types of conventional mortgages:

- **Conforming loans**, which are mortgages that meet loan limits and other standards that loans must meet to qualify for purchase by Fannie Mae and Freddie Mac. The advantage of these loans is that they have lower interest rates and cost less since they meet the standards required for purchase and securitization by Fannie Mae and Freddie Mac.

- **Nonconforming loans**, which are mortgages that do ***not*** meet loan limits and other standards that loans must meet to qualify for purchase by Fannie Mae and Freddie Mac. An example of a nonconforming loan is a "jumbo mortgage."

Conforming Mortgages

A conforming mortgage conforms to maximum loan amounts (loan limits), down payment requirements, borrower income requirements, debt-to-income ratios, and other underwriting guidelines established by Fannie Mae and Freddie Mac.

Fannie Mae and Freddie Mac purchase mortgages that meet these limits, thereby creating additional funds lenders can use to make new mortgages.

In October 2013, news about lower conforming loan limits appeared in The Wall Street Journal, which reported that *"Federal officials will delay any reduction in the maximum size of home-mortgage loans eligible for backing by Fannie Mae and Freddie Mac until next spring at the earliest..."* [59]. In the spring and summer of 2014, no lowering of the loan limits occurred, leaving them the same as recent years. Though a change in loan limits is not predicted, mortgage professionals should periodically check news sources for developments.

As of July 2014, the conforming loan limits remain at the following levels:

One-Family Properties:	**$417,000** in most locations, but as high as **$625,500** in high-cost areas
Two-Family Properties:	$533,850, but as high as $800,775 in high-cost areas
Three-Family Properties:	$645,300, but as high as $967,950 in high-cost areas
Four-Family Properties:	$801,950, but as high as $1,202,925 in high-cost areas

The exact loan limits actually differ by county, and the list of counties and applicable loan limits is available on the website for the Federal Housing Finance Agency. The $417,000 loan limit for single-family homes that applies in most locations and the $625,500 loan limit in high-cost areas are the most important numbers to remember for test-taking purposes.

The higher loan limits for areas of the country that are designated as **high-cost areas** apply to 250 counties in the United States. Although these represent only 8% of the counties in the country, they are also highly populated areas, such as Washington, D.C. and the metropolitan areas of large cities like New York and San Francisco [60]. There are even higher conforming loan limits for areas that are not a part of the contiguous United States. These areas include Alaska, Hawaii, Guam, and the Virgin Islands, where the conforming loan limits can range from $625,500 to $938,250.

In an effort to stimulate the economy, Congress included provisions in the 2008 Housing Economic and Recovery Act (HERA) to temporarily raise conforming loan limits for properties in high-cost areas from $625,500 to $729,750. These loans were referred to as **super-conforming loans**. By raising the conforming loan limits, Congress enabled Fannie Mae and Freddie Mac to buy mortgages originated in high-cost areas, thereby reducing the interest rates on these loans and the cost of these mortgages. Due to this temporary increase in loan limits, loans such as jumbo loans in high-cost areas became conforming loans. In the fall of 2011, and despite urging from those who believed that it would benefit the economy to keep the higher limits in place, this temporary increase in loan limits was no longer effective, and the loan limit in high-cost areas fell back to $625,500.

The Federal Housing Finance Agency (FHFA), which was created in 2008 under HERA, oversees Fannie Mae and Freddie Mac. Following HERA provisions for establishing loan limits, this agency also calculates the maximum conforming loan limits.

> *A conventional mortgage is a mortgage not insured or guaranteed by the FHA, the VA, or the Rural Housing Service of the USDA.*

General Requirements for Conventional/Conforming Loans

Down Payment Requirements and the Role of Private Mortgage Insurance
Conforming mortgages have down payment requirements of at least 5%. However, lenders often require up to 20%. If a borrower does not have cash for a significant down payment, the purchase of **private mortgage insurance (PMI)** may enable him/her to succeed in securing a conventional/conforming loan. Data shows that borrowers are more likely to default on a home loan when they have invested little to no money in a down payment. Mortgage insurance reduces the risks involved in these types of lending transactions, thereby facilitating the origination and funding of the loan. PMI also reduces risk for loan purchasers, and Fannie Mae and Freddie Mac are more likely to purchase a loan that has PMI to mitigate the losses associated with default.

As a borrower's equity in his/her home increases, the likelihood of default decreases, and PMI becomes an unnecessary expense. Two decades ago, borrowers found it difficult to cancel unnecessary PMI, and Congress addressed this issue with the enactment of **The Homeowners Protection Act of 1998**. This law requires termination of PMI when:

- The LTV reaches 80% based on the value of the home at the time of the loan origination *and the borrower requests termination*

- The LTV reaches 78%, and cancellation is automatic, without any request from the borrower

These provisions apply to mortgages closed on or after July 29, 1999. PMI for loans closed before that date can be cancelled at the borrower's request after he/she has paid 20% of the principal on the loan. The provisions of the Homeowners Protection Act do not apply to FHA-insured or VA guaranteed loans.

Loan-to-Value Requirements
Just as a minimal down payment represents a greater risk, so do high loan-to-value ratios (LTVs). High LTVs are a risk factor that lenders regard more seriously in today's lending market. Fannie Mae and Freddie Mac may not purchase a loan with an LTV above 80% unless the loan is insured or guaranteed to reduce the LTV risk exposure to less than 80%. If the LTV is higher, the use of PMI may be used to reduce the risk associated with the transaction.

Income Qualification

Conforming loan programs require comprehensive income qualification. Each borrower's income must meet standards and guidelines relevant to the loan program. Some general qualification guidelines include:

- Standard income documentation for salaried and hourly individuals typically includes paystubs for the most recent 30-day period and W-2s for the most recent two-year period
- Individuals earning more than 25% of their income in commission must provide up to two years' tax returns
- Individuals who own more than 25% of a business are required to provide up to two years' tax returns
- Individuals who earn non-taxed income such as Social Security, public assistance or disability must provide comprehensive documentation relevant to the type of income. However, they are permitted to "gross up" those earnings by 25% (i.e. multiply the income by 125%).

Credit Qualification

Conforming lenders require a comprehensive review of a potential borrower's credit history in order to determine credit capacity and credit character. Fannie Mae and Freddie Mac publish credit eligibility matrices regularly to provide guidance for manual underwriting. These standards are subject to change and are based on the transaction type, number of units and loan-to-value/combined loan-to-value. However, as an example, the minimum credit scores in today's market may range from 620 – 700.

Seller Financing and Seller Concessions

Fannie Mae and Freddie Mac permit borrowers to obtain seller financing – also known as a seller carry-back – in conforming loan transactions. Seller financing is a loan from the seller which is recorded in the second position, and monthly payments must be made until it is paid back.

Seller concessions are a gift from the seller used to pay for closing costs, and they do not have to be paid back. Seller concessions are limited to 6% for borrowers who make a down payment of 10% - 24.9%. Seller concessions are limited to 3% for borrowers who make a down payment of less than 10%. For down payments of 25% or more, seller concessions are limited to 9%.

Underwriting for Conforming Loans

Fannie Mae uses automated underwriting systems known as **Desktop Underwriter (DU)**, which is used by lenders, and **Desktop Originator (DO)**, which is used by brokers. These systems assess the credit risk represented by individual loan applicants and determine if they meet minimum eligibility requirements. Freddie Mac has a comparable underwriting system known as **Loan Prospector**, used by both lenders and brokers. All of these systems operate by electronically uploading information contained on a potential borrower's loan application, including credit score, income, existing debt and assets. The underwriting system assesses this data to determine whether to approve a loan or to refer it for manual underwriting. Fannie Mae and Freddie Mac periodically update their automated underwriting systems to reflect market conditions.

The ultimate purpose of DU, DO, and Loan Prospector is to determine if a proposed home loan meets the minimum standards for purchase in the secondary market by Fannie Mae or Freddie Mac. However, even if an automated underwriting system approves a loan, and the lender knows that the loan is saleable, this approval is not a guarantee of lender approval. This is particularly true in the current lending environment in which lenders are extremely averse to risk. Lenders are no longer satisfied to rely on guidelines established by GSEs and typically have **credit overlays**, which extend or augment the credit standards established by Fannie Mae and Freddie Mac.

A lender's credit overlays may require a loan applicant to meet higher standards for:

- Credit scores
- Minimum down payments
- Debt ratios
- Assets (with specific requirements for the amount and type of assets)

While credit overlays may limit the exposure of lenders to the risk of defaults, the use of overlays may increase their risk of facing fair lending claims. Consumer interest groups such as the National Community Reinvestment Coalition claim that credit overlays *"...unfairly limit access to credit in low- to moderate-income consumers, African-American and Latino consumers and to communities of color"* [61].

The following sections include an overview of some of the recent highlights and changes to conforming/conventional loan requirements. Fannie Mae's Single Family Selling and Servicing Guides, Announcements and Lender Letters provide extensive details on conforming/conventional loan requirements. These resources may be found at www.eFannieMae.com.

> *Even if an automated underwriting system approves a loan for purchase by Fannie Mae or Freddie Mac, and the lender knows that the loan is saleable, this is not a guarantee of lender approval.*

Non-Conforming Mortgages

A non-conforming loan is a conventional mortgage loan that exceeds current maximum loan limits and underwriting requirements established by Fannie Mae and Freddie Mac. Examples of non-conforming loan include:

- *Jumbo loans*, which exceed the loan limits established by Fannie Mae and Freddie Mac. For example, a jumbo loan in Akron, Ohio would be one with a loan amount that exceeds $417,000 or one in Washington, D.C. with a loan amount that exceeds $625,500. The cost of getting a jumbo loan is typically higher than the cost of getting a conforming loan.

- *Alt-A*, which is a designation for loans made to borrowers who do not represent the high credit risk of subprime borrowers, but who do not quite meet the underwriting requirements for conforming prime rate loans.

- ***Subprime loans***, which are higher-interest loans made to borrowers with blemished credit or other qualification issues that do not conform with Fannie Mae and Freddie Mac underwriting requirements. These mortgage products disappeared with the collapse of the secondary market that purchased subprime loans.

- ***Nontraditional Mortgages***, which are any mortgage product other than a 30-year fixed-rate mortgage. This definition is specifically provided in the federal S.A.F.E. Mortgage Licensing Act of 2008. During the lending boom, the term "nontraditional mortgage" referred to a vast array of creative mortgage products that are no longer available.

- ***Niche loans***, which are loans for borrowers with unique circumstances or needs.

- ***Super Conforming Loans*** - The Housing and Economic Recovery Act of 2008 authorized Freddie Mac to publish higher conforming loan limits for high-cost areas. These higher limits expired in the fall of 2011, and these loans, which allowed borrowers to obtain jumbo loans at the price of conforming loans, are no longer available.

- ***Option ARMs or Nontraditional ARMs***, which offer flexible payment options. Common payment options might include: minimum payments, interest-only payments, fully amortizing 30-year payments, and fully amortizing 15-year payments. After the introductory interest rate for an Option ARM expires, the minimum payment option can result in negative amortization since the payment may not be large enough to cover the amount of interest due. With unpaid interest added to a loan's principal, the total amount of the loan increases over time. The interest-only payment avoids negative amortization but fails to reduce the principal balance of the loan.

Beginning in 2003, and until the subprime mortgage market meltdown in the spring of 2007, Option ARMs gained popularity, and the Federal Reserve Board made revisions to the CHARM booklet in response to growing concerns that borrowers did not understand the risks associated with these products. In particular, many borrowers did not seem to understand that minimum payments do not reduce the principal balance and can result in negative amortization. The origination of these nontraditional ARMs has almost come to a halt as a result of high delinquency and foreclosure rates on these types of mortgage products and renewed commitment to strict lending standards.

> *A non-conforming loan is a conventional mortgage loan that exceeds current maximum loan limits and underwriting requirements established by Fannie Mae and Freddie Mac.*

Non-Conventional/ Government Loans (FHA, VA, USDA/RHS)

Non-conventional mortgages are mortgages guaranteed or insured by government agencies such as the Federal Housing Administration (FHA), the Department of Veterans Affairs (VA) and the Rural Housing Service (RHS) of the U.S. Department of Agriculture.

FHA Loans (24 C.F.R. §203 *et seq.*)

The Federal Housing Administration does not make, buy, or sell loans. It **insures** loans. In the event of foreclosure, the lender is protected by mortgage insurance issued by the government through the FHA. The insurance covers the full value of the loan. Distinctive characteristics of FHA lending include:

- **The Countercyclical Role of FHA Lending**: FHA lending flourishes when private lending recedes and prevents housing markets from crashing. For example, an analysis of the FHA market that was conducted in 2010 showed that in 2005, *"...the share of mortgages insured by FHA was only about 4.5 percent... FHA's market share is now 25 to 30 percent of mortgage loans"* [62]. Four years later, as the market has improved, FHA loan production has dropped.

- **FHA Loans Must Meet Lending Limits**: There are loan limits for FHA loans, which are tied to the GSE conforming loan limits. The link between GSE loan limits and FHA loan limits makes sense because Fannie Mae and Freddie Mac purchase FHA loans but cannot do so unless the loans meet the GSEs' guidelines for purchase.

- **FHA Borrowers Must Carry Mortgage Insurance**: When a borrower secures an FHA loan, he/she must make an upfront mortgage insurance payment, which is payable in a lump sum or financed by the loan. An FHA borrower must also pay a monthly mortgage insurance premium to protect against losses that occur if there is a default on an FHA home loan. The funds from both types of insurance payments are placed in an escrow account with the U.S. Treasury.

- **HUD Oversees FHA Lending**: The Department of Housing and Urban Development (HUD) is the federal agency with authority to implement rules related to FHA lending and to enforce FHA requirements. In March 2012, the agency stated that it has *"significantly increased oversight of lenders and enforcement of FHA requirements..."* and that it *"...will continue aggressive enforcement of our lender requirements"* [63].

- **HUD Uses Mortgagee Letters to Announce Changes**: The term "mortgagee" means lender, and in the context of FHA lending, a mortgagee is an FHA-approved lender. Each year, HUD issues numerous "mortgagee letters" to advise FHA lenders of changes in lending policies, procedures, and operations. The mortgagee letters that are available online date back to 1976, though such letters have been issued by HUD since 1934. Letters from 1976 to the present are available online [64]. On this website, letters are listed in chronological order, beginning with the most recent. Each letter has a numerical designation based on the year in which it was issued and its place in the succession of letters that HUD releases over the course of a given year.

There have been many changes in FHA lending, beginning in 2008. These changes relate to loan limits and to the insurance payments made by FHA borrowers. Rulemaking related to mortgage insurance premiums and to upfront mortgage insurance is currently underway. Mortgage professionals should, therefore, visit the HUD/FHA website periodically to follow these developments.

The History of FHA Loans

As discussed in the introductory section of this course, the FHA was originally created during the Great Depression when the high rate of foreclosures discouraged lenders from making new mortgage loans. President Franklin Delano Roosevelt and Congress established the FHA in 1934 with the enactment of the National Housing Act. The passage of the **National Housing Act** and the establishment of the FHA were components of FDR's New Deal programs to rescue the U.S. economy from the ravages of the Depression. The FHA gave the business of mortgage lending a jumpstart by insuring the full value of mortgages for qualified borrowers. By insuring loans, the FHA eliminated the risk of loss from foreclosure, thereby encouraging lenders to make new mortgages. In 1965, the FHA became a part of the Department of Housing and Urban Development (HUD). HUD continues to be the federal agency that is responsible for issuing the rules that regulate FHA-insured lending. On its website, HUD reports that since 1934, *"The FHA and HUD have insured over 34 million home mortgages..."* [65].

Until the mortgage lending market crumbled, the primary function of the FHA mortgage insurance program was to ensure that low-income families, first-time buyers, and other borrowers who could not qualify for conventional loans could obtain a mortgage. **FHA loan limits** established the maximum amount that a borrower could borrow for an FHA home loan, and by keeping these limits low, the government was able to reserve FHA-insured loans for homebuyers who did not have access to other mortgage products. With the credit crunch that followed the mortgage crisis, the parameters of the FHA lending program changed significantly.

In 2008, Congress sought *"to mitigate the effects from the economic downturn and the sharp reduction of mortgage credit availability from private sources..."* by increasing FHA loan limits [66]. As a result of these changes in FHA loan limits, *"a broader range of applicants are using the FHA program. Middle- and upper-income borrowers as well as the traditional first-time homebuyers are using the program in heavy volumes"* [67]. The changes that opened FHA lending to borrowers from a broader range of income brackets were initially made by Congress through the Economic Stimulus Act of February 2008 and the Housing Economic Recovery Act. Additional adjustments to the conforming loan limits were made through the July 2008 Housing Economic Recovery Act and the American Recovery and Reinvestment Act of 2009.

FHA loans may cost more than conventional mortgages because borrowers must pay for mortgage insurance. However, FHA loans also have many favorable characteristics that have made them popular products in the past and that continue to make them popular mortgage products for today's borrowers. These include:

- Low down payment requirements
- Fee limits on closing costs (e.g. the administrative cost of processing the mortgage cannot exceed 1% of the loan amount)
- More lenient underwriting requirements

The FHA does not make, buy or sell loans; it insures loans. In the event of foreclosure, the lender is protected by mortgage insurance issued by the government through the FHA.

FHA Maximum Mortgage Amounts

Like conforming loan limits for conventional loans, FHA loan limits vary by county and have higher lending rates for high-cost areas.

FHA loan limits were first established under the National Housing Act of 1949 and have since been subject to numerous revisions by Congress.

Today, the law, as amended by current regulations, states that in order to be eligible for FHA insurance, a mortgage must be made by an FHA-approved lender and the amount of the mortgage must be **the lesser of**:

- 115% of the median house price in an area, or
- 150% of the national conforming loan limit of $417,000

(12 U.S.C. §1709(b))

As an example of how these loan limitations impact FHA financing, imagine that a borrower requests an FHA loan amount of $730,000 in Westchester County, New York. Her loan originator knows that the median house price in Westchester County for a single family home is $598,000 and that 115% of this price equals $687,700. However, he also knows that 150% of the $417,000 national conforming loan limit is $625,500, and with the FHA mortgage amount limited to the lesser of these two numbers, the borrower cannot get FHA financing for $730,000 in Westchester County.

FHA loan limits are divided into lower-cost areas, referred to as **"the floor,"** and high-cost areas, referred to as **"the ceiling."** Current FHA loan limits (floors and ceilings) are:

- One-Family Properties: $271,050 floor and $625,500 ceiling
- Two-Family Properties: $347,000 floor and $800,775 ceiling
- Three-Family Properties: $419,425 floor and $967,950 ceiling
- Four-Family Properties: $521,250 floor and $1,202,925 ceiling
- Alaska, Hawaii, Guam, and the Virgin Islands: 150% of the loan limit ceiling

These numbers are tied to the conforming loan rate established for Fannie Mae and Freddie Mac by the Federal Housing Finance Agency. For example, under the Economic Stimulus Act:

- The loan limits for single family homes cannot exceed 150% of the GSE conforming loan limit of $417,000, and 150% of $417,000 = $625,500.
- The loan limits for single family homes and for two-, three-, and four-unit properties cannot be less than the greater of:
  - The dollar amount limitation established under provisions of the National Housing Act in 1998, or
  - 65% of the GSE conforming loan limit of $417,000 (65% of $417,000 = $271,050)

With 65% of the GSE conforming loan limit being the greater of these two amounts, this language establishes that in any part of the country, qualifying borrowers should be able to borrow up to $271,050 for the purchase of a single family home or for the purchase of two-, three-, or four-unit properties.

For the many areas that have housing prices between the floor and the ceiling, the loan limit is calculated by multiplying the area's median house price by 115%. HUD provides a list of "Areas Between the Floor and Ceiling," and this list provides information on median house price by county.

As an example of how this list of areas between the floor and ceiling is used, imagine that a borrower is moving into Bartow County, Georgia, which is well outside of the Atlanta metropolitan area. The borrower hopes to secure FHA financing for a home in the range of $350,000 to $375,000. Her loan originator knows that this price point is above the $271,050 "floor" and well below the $625,500 "ceiling." However, he is not sure that a loan of $350,000 or more will qualify for FHA financing. Looking at the list of "Areas Between the Floor and the Ceiling," he sees that the median home price in Bartow County is $279,000. Knowing that the conforming FHA loan limit for the area will be 115% of the median house price, he does the math: $279,000 x 115% = $320,850. He then advises his client that if she really wants to take advantage of FHA financing, she needs to look at homes with prices that do not exceed $320,850.

Generally, loan limits are established on a county-by-county basis. However, for large metropolitan statistical areas (MSAs) where a city is spread across several counties, the maximum loan size is based on the county in the MSA with the highest maximum. Originators that live in an area potentially defined as an MSA must determine whether an MSA loan limit or a county limit is applicable in FHA lending transactions. FHA mortgage limits are accessible online on the HUD website.

Again, one of the primary reasons for complying with lending limits is to ensure that mortgage loans meet the requirements for purchase by Fannie Mae or Freddie Mac. Since the crash of the housing market, FHA loan limits have been an ongoing subject of concern for loan originators since the limits continue to change based on politicians' perceptions about what is best for the economy. Although the Economic Stimulus Act established increased loan limits for FHA loans, Congress pushed the loan limits even higher in 2009 under the American Recovery and Reinvestment Act. These higher limits were intended to be temporary, and on October 1, 2011, the size of a mortgage that the FHA could guarantee was reduced from $729,750 to $625,500. However, in November 2011, President Obama signed the Consolidated and Further Continuing Appropriations Act, which included provisions that restored the higher limits of $729,750 through December 31, 2013. On December 6, 2013, HUD released Mortgagee Letter 43, which announced the reduction in the FHA loan limits in high-cost areas from $729,750 to $625,500.

Like conforming loan limits for conventional loans, FHA loan limits vary by county and have higher lending rates for high-cost areas.

Originating FHA Loans

The origination of an FHA loan begins with completing a loan application and obtaining an **FHA Case Number.** FHA case numbers are assigned through HUD's FHA Connection website. Only approved FHA lenders have access to this website, and they must use it to request an FHA case number and to submit borrower information and information on the property that a borrower hopes to purchase. This site is also used for updating an existing "case." The completion of a loan application prior to submitting a request for a case number is a critical first step because lenders have been required since April 2011 to certify that they have an "active loan application" for the property and borrowers listed in the case number request.

After the completion of a loan application and the obtaining of an FHA case number, FHA loan originators will need to get information on the borrower's credit score and employment history. Although late payments and collections are evaluated more leniently under an FHA lending program, there is no leniency with regard to delinquent federal debt, such as tax liens and unpaid student loans, or for child support or unpaid judgments. The best source for information on underwriting FHA loans is the FHA Lender Manual, which is available online.

While lenders do the underwriting and manage the closings for FHA loans, it is the role of the FHA to **endorse** them. Direct endorsement programs allow approved lenders to underwrite and close loans without prior approval from the FHA. Within 60 days after the closing of a loan under a direct endorsement program, the lender must submit the closing package to HUD, where the agency will either endorse the case and issue a **mortgage insurance certificate (MIC)** or issue a notice of return (NOR). Lenders may attempt to resolve a notice of return by submitting additional information and requesting reconsideration for endorsement.

Insuring FHA Loans

The lasting success of FHA lending is due in part to the fact that it is a program that does not depend on appropriations from Congress and on taxpayer dollars. The program is funded entirely by insurance payments made by FHA borrowers. These funds are held in the **Mutual Mortgage Insurance Fund (MMIF)**. When a homeowner defaults on an FHA loan, funds are drawn from the MMIF to repay the lender. In order to ensure that funds are always available to pay claims resulting from defaults on FHA loans, the law requires that the MMIF *"keep capital reserves equivalent to its estimated losses over the next 30 years, plus an additional 2 percent"* [68]. The additional 2% of outstanding FHA loans is known as the FHA's emergency reserve fund.

Unfortunately, as a result of the sharp increase in defaults that has occurred since the crash of the housing market, the FHA has paid many claims from the MMIF. The FHA has reported that *"About 24 percent of FHA loans were in default in 2007 and 20 percent in 2008..."* [69]. Paying these claims has required the MMIF to take funds from its reserves, resulting in losses that have prevented the FHA from keeping the Congressionally-mandated minimum in its reserve fund.

Congress and the FHA have taken measures to address these losses and to store up the MMIF. Most of these measures are related to reducing the default rate on FHA loans, thereby reducing the number of claims paid from the MMIF.

These measures include:

- **Increasing FHA Insurance Premiums**: HUD has increased the insurance premiums that it collects from borrowers. The most recent changes apply to both annual mortgage insurance premiums and to upfront mortgage insurance premiums. The most recent increases were announced by HUD on January 31, 2013. The additional funds from insurance payments will help to rebuild the MMIF emergency reserve fund.

- **Prohibiting Seller-Financed Down Payment Assistance**: When Congress adopted the Housing and Economic Recovery Act, it included a provision in the law that bans the FHA from insuring loans in which the borrower receives down payment assistance from the seller. The reason for this prohibition is that defaults related to these transactions were very high, "… suffering three times the claims rate of cases without down payment assistance" [70].

- **Increasing Oversight of Lenders**: The FHA reports that it has increased its oversight of lenders, citing the fact that it has *"…terminated and suspended several lenders whose default and claim rates were higher than the national default and claim rate"* [71]. In 2010, the FHA also increased the minimum net worth requirements for FHA lenders, increasing them to $1 million and $500,000 for small businesses (24 C.F.R. §202.5(n)).

- **Increasing the Minimum FICO Scores for FHA Borrowers**: The FHA has attempted to reduce the risk for default on FHA loans by lending to borrowers who represent a safer credit risk. In 2010, the FHA changed the combination of FICO scores and down payment requirements for borrowers, stating that a borrower must have a minimum credit score of 580 to qualify for a 3.5% down payment program. A borrower with a credit score below 580 must make a down payment of at least 10%.

In addition to these changes that the FHA has already made to ensure that its capital reserves remain intact, HUD has been considering adopting a rule that will limit seller concessions.

The Housing and Economic Recovery Act prohibits seller-funded down payment assistance for FHA loans. However, other seller concessions, such as interest rate buy-downs, discount points, and contributions to closing costs are legal if they do not exceed 6% of the sales price. HUD issued a proposed rule in 2012 to lower the percentage of allowable seller concessions to the greater of 3% or $6,000. However, this rule has not been finalized. The primary reason cited for limiting seller concessions is that the current 6% level creates incentives for inflated appraisal values.

In an article on this proposed rule, a reporter for the *Los Angeles Times* explained why the FHA views seller concessions as a concern:

> *"When FHA officials announced the policy change this year, they said the long-standing 6% maximum 'exposes the FHA to excess risk by creating incentives to inflate appraised value.' That would occur when sellers agree to pay buyers' closing and other expenses but merely tack those costs onto the final sale price of the house. Rather than agreeing to a $200,000 price… with $12,000 worth of concessions, the final contract price of the house would instead be $212,000.*

If an appraiser did not detect and report the price boost, the FHA would effectively be insuring a mortgage on a house worth less than the sales price. In fact, since the rules allowed a 6% seller concession and the down payment was just 3.5%, the FHA would be insuring an underwater loan from the start" [72].

Many critics of the proposed rule argue that a lower cap on seller concessions is not necessary because of the other measures that HUD has taken to reduce the risk of defaults on FHA loans and the withdrawals from the MMIF to cover the losses that these defaults represent to lenders. HUD's rule addressing seller concessions was published in the Federal Register on February 23, 2012. Mortgage professionals who engage in FHA lending should watch for developments related to this proposed regulation.

> *FHA lending is funded by insurance payments made by FHA borrowers. These funds are held in the Mutual Mortgage Insurance Fund (MMIF). When a homeowner defaults on an FHA loan, funds are drawn from the MMIF to repay the lender.*

Borrower Contributions to the MMIF
Borrowers cannot secure an FHA loan without paying:

- **Upfront Mortgage Insurance Premiums (UFMIPs)**, and
- **Annual Mortgage Insurance Premiums (annual MIPs)**

These insurance payments are held in the MMIF and are withdrawn to pay claims filed by lenders when borrowers default on FHA-insured loans. HUD has used its authority to increase these premiums in order to protect the MMIF. The higher costs for UFMIPs and for annual MIPs are effective for FHA case numbers assigned on or after **April 9, 2012**. These increases apply to single family mortgage insurance.

The **UFMIP** is a premium that borrowers pay in full at the time of closing, although many borrowers take advantage of the option of financing this premium by adding it to the loan amount. HUD has increased upfront premiums by **75 basis points** (.75%), raising the premium from 1% of the loan amount to **1.75%**.

FHA borrowers also pay an annual premium, which is calculated as a percentage of the average outstanding loan balance. For FHA mortgages that have a term of more than 15 years (as is the case for most FHA loans), annual MIP can range from 1.30% to 1.55%, dependent upon the LTV in the transaction [73].

The following table shows the previous and new annual MIP rates by amortization term, base loan amount, and LTV ratio. The MIPs in this table are effective for case numbers assigned on or after April 1, 2013 [74].

Term > 15 Years			
Base Loan Amt.	LTV	Previous MIP	New MIP
≤ $625,500	≤ 95.00%	120 bps	130 bps
≤ $625,500	> 95.00%	125 bps	135 bps
> $625,500	≤ 95.00%	145 bps	150 bps
> $625,500	> 95.00%	150 bps	155 bps
Term ≤ 15 Years			
Base Loan Amt.	LTV	Previous MIP	New MIP
≤ $625,500	78.01% - 90.00%	35 bps	45 bps
≤ $625,500	> 90.00%	60 bps	70 bps
> $625,500	78.01% - 90.00%	60 bps	70 bps
> $625,500	> 90.00%	85 bps	95 bps

The following table shows the previous and new effective annual MIP rates for loans with an LTV of less than or equal to 78% and with terms up to 15 years. The annual MIP for these loans is effective for case numbers assigned on or after June 3, 2013.

Term ≤ 15 Years			
Base Loan Amt.	LTV	Previous MIP	New MIP
Any Amount	≤ 78.00 %	0 bps	45 bps

Loan amount is not the only factor that is relevant to the calculation of the annual MIP. A determination of the exact amount also requires consideration of the loan-to-value ratio and the loan term. MIP calculators are available online to help loan originators to calculate the premiums accurately.

HUD's Mortgagee Letter includes tables with the current mortgage insurance rates. Note that in the HUD tables showing annual MIPs, the rates are expressed as basis points and represent a percentage of the loan amount. For example, 75 basis points represent .75% of the loan amount.

Cancellation of Mortgage Insurance

HUD regulations permit the voluntary termination of MIP if the lender and the borrower agree to terminate the FHA insurance. Requests for insurance cancellation must be forwarded to the FHA Commissioner. If the borrower and lender jointly request the cancellation of insurance and the Commissioner grants the request, the lender must cancel the insurance *"upon receipt of notice from the Commissioner that the contract of insurance is terminated"* (24 C.F.R. §203.295). However, there are new limitations to the cancellation of MIP for FHA loans made on or after **June 3, 2013**.

According to Mortgagee Letter 2013-04, dated January 31, 2013, HUD announced the following changes related to the cancellation of MIP for mortgages with FHA case numbers assigned on or after June 3, 2013:

- For all mortgages regardless of their amortization terms, any mortgage involving an original principal obligation (excluding financed UFMIP) less than or equal to 90% LTV, the annual MIP will be assessed until the end of the mortgage term or for the first 11 years of the mortgage term, whichever occurs first.

- For any mortgage involving an original principal obligation (excluding financed UFMIP) with an LTV greater than 90%, FHA will assess the annual MIP until the end of the mortgage term or for the first 30 years of the term, whichever occurs first [75]. This policy replaces past practices of cancelling MIP when the outstanding principal balance reached 78% of the original principal balance. Now, annual MIP based on the outstanding loan balance is due for the life of the loan.

> *HUD regulations permit the voluntary termination of MIP if the lender and the borrower agree to terminate the FHA insurance.*

Down Payment and Credit Score Requirements for FHA Loans

One of the principal advantages of an FHA loan is the fact that down payment requirements are lower than those for conventional mortgages. This is a particular advantage in today's lending market in which a down payment of 10% to 20% is required for conventional mortgages. HUD/FHA requires the borrower to invest in the loan transaction by making a 3.5% down payment based on sales price or appraisal (whichever is less). The down payment can come from the borrower's own funds, gift funds or housing authority grants. However, as previously noted, down payment assistance from sellers is prohibited.

In its January 20, 2010 announcement "FHA Announces Policy Changes to Address Risk and Strengthen Finances," HUD tightened down payment requirements. Under these requirements (which were part of HUD's program for strengthening the MMIF by reducing the payment made from the fund for defaults on home loans), borrowers are required to have a minimum FICO score of 580 to qualify for the FHA's 3.5% down payment program. Borrowers with less than a 580 FICO score will be required to put down at least 10%. Borrowers with a credit score of less than 500 are not eligible for FHA loans.

Unfortunately for homebuyers with credit scores that fail to meet or exceed the minimum FHA requirements, an FHA loan may be unattainable. Credit scores in the 580 range are proving not to be good enough to secure a mortgage in today's market. In fact, it is reported that credit scores below 620 are unlikely to secure an FHA loan. Despite FHA guidelines and the fact that FHA loans are insured, lenders are using higher lending standards than those that are outlined for FHA home loan programs. These higher standards, which are referred to as "credit overlays," are greatly reducing the number of FHA loans made to borrowers with credit scores below 620. Fair lending challenges regarding the use of overlays are on the horizon for FHA loans just as they are for the use of credit overlays under conventional lending programs.

Additional changes came in 2013, including stricter requirements related to credit scores and debt-to-income ratios. In Mortgagee Letter 2013-05, HUD announced that if a borrower's credit score is below 620 and his/her debt-to-income ratio exceeds 43%, the loan must be underwritten manually [76].

FHA Programs

FHA offers a number of programs to meet the needs of eligible borrowers. Several popular programs include:

203 (b) Home Mortgages: FHA's primary program, 203 (b) is a fixed-rate program used to purchase or refinance one- to four-unit family dwellings. The 203 (b) program may also be used to purchase a unit in a condominium. FHA has a number of specific requirements regarding the condo project. For example, the condo must be part of a project with at least two units, and 50% of the units must be owner-occupied. More information on FHA mortgages for condos may be found in Mortgagee Letter 2009-46 B.

251 Adjustable-Rate Mortgages: The 251 program is based on 203 (b), with the added feature of an adjustable rate. FHA offers a number of different types of ARMs, including one-, three-, five-, seven- and ten-year versions.

Energy Efficient Mortgages: These loans are allowed for improvements to existing and new construction properties to increase their energy efficiency. Financing is the greater of 5% of the loan or $4,000, with the maximum capped at $8,000.

245 (a) Growing Equity Mortgages and 245 Graduated Payment Mortgages: Similar in structure, these programs are intended to assist borrowers by lowering the initial costs of their mortgage. Payments increase each year, so the programs are best for borrowers expecting a steady increase in their income over time.

2-1 Buy Downs: FHA permits borrowers to buy down the rate on their fixed-rate loan. Lenders are required to qualify the borrower at the note rate and not the buy down rate. In this type of buy down, the borrower deposits funds in an escrow account in order to offset lower interest payments the first two years of the loan. For example, the borrower might qualify at 6.5%. He/she would make payments based on a 4.5% interest rate the first year and make payments based on a 5.5% interest rate the second year. The note continues to carry the 6.5% interest rate throughout the term. The fact that the borrower (or some other party, such as the seller) has "prepaid" enough interest to supplement the reduced payment so that the lender receives the full payment each month is what allows the smaller payment. The 2-1 buy down is not a permanent buy down, and FHA lenders are likely to discuss the benefits of a permanent buy down instead of a 2-1 buy down and its temporarily-reduced rate.

203 (g) Officer and Teacher Next Door: The 203 (g) program is intended to revitalize communities by offering homes for sale at a 50% discount off the HUD appraised value to teachers, law enforcement officers and firefighters/EMTs. HUD requires a mortgage agreement to be signed for the discounted amount although no payments or interest is charged as long as the borrower fulfills a three-year owner occupancy requirement. It is important to note that this program is only for the sale of properties which HUD and FHA own.

Cash-Out Refinance: An FHA cash-out refinance is a loan that is appropriate for a borrower whose home has increased in value and who wants to use the home equity for improvements or to pay bills. This mortgage product allows borrowers to secure a new mortgage for more than is owed on an existing mortgage. FHA has specific limits on the maximum LTV for cash-out refinance transactions:

- If a borrower has owned a property as his/her principal residence for at least 12 months or more, he/she is eligible for a maximum of 85% of the appraised property value for a cash-out refinance transaction
- If the borrower has owned a property for less than 12 months, he/she is limited to 85% of the lesser of the appraised value or the initial sales price for a cash-out refinance transaction

A borrower who secures a cash-out refinance uses the funds from the new loan to pay off the old loan and has access to the remaining cash for other expenditures.

Home Equity Conversion Mortgage: A Home Equity Conversion Mortgage (HECM) is the FHA's version of a reverse mortgage. It is only available to homeowners who are 62 or older and who have a low mortgage balance or no mortgage on their homes. It allows homeowners to receive monthly payments or a lump sum, which is drawn against the equity in their home through a line of credit. The home that is used to secure the mortgage must be the borrower's principal residence. Borrowers cannot secure a HECM without completing reverse mortgage counseling from a HUD-approved counselor and receiving a signed and dated certificate that verifies the completion of counseling. Borrowers who secure a HECM must pay UFMIPs and annual MIPs.

A number of changes to the FHA reverse mortgage program occurred in 2013 as a result of the **Reverse Mortgage Stabilization Act of 2013**. The need for this legislation arose from losses of up to $5 billion that occurred when millions of homeowners took out reverse mortgages, took lump sum payments, and then ran into financial problems [77]. Since borrowers with reverse mortgages are not required to make periodic payments on their loans, defaults on HECMs result from other types of delinquencies, which include failing to pay homeowners' insurance and property taxes. Failure to maintain these payments is a breach of the borrower's lending agreement with his/her FHA lender, and this breach may provide the lender with a basis for accelerating the loan and ultimately foreclosing. When the FHA has to tap into its MMIF to cover the losses sustained by a large number of lenders, it runs the risk of depleting its reserves, which are required by law to meet statutory minimums. Currently, the MMIF reserve funds are significantly below the required amount.

As of 2014, there are limits on the initial disbursements allowed for HECMs, including lower limits on single disbursement lump sum payment options. Also, effective September 30, 2013, there have been changes to the initial mortgage insurance premium for HECMs. Under the new rules, the initial MIP is determined by the amount of funds that the borrower plans to draw during the first 12 months of the loan.

Loan originators that work for FHA-approved lenders should regularly visit the HUD website, where mortgagee letters are issued announcing changes to the HECM program. In 2013 and 2014, a number of mortgagee letters addressed changes in the HECM program, including a letter issued in July 2014 which adds special counseling considerations regarding *"...the potential benefits of the HECM in light of the total cost of obtaining the HECM"* [78]. This letter also informs FHA-approved lenders of lending limits that may result from the fact that a non-borrowing spouse is younger than 62 years of age. The reason for considering the younger age of non-borrowing spouses is that many surviving spouses have found themselves evicted from their homes when an older spouse who was an HECM borrower passes away.

Streamline Refinancing: With a streamline refinancing, an existing FHA loan is refinanced with another FHA insurance loan. The lending process is "streamlined" because it does not involve the complete underwriting process associated with a new FHA loan. For example, income verification is not required with an FHA streamline refinancing and in some cases, a credit report may not be necessary. One of the greatest benefits of a streamline refinance is that it does not require a home appraisal. Instead, the FHA will allow the borrower to use the original purchase price of the home in the refinance, regardless of its actual value. These mortgages are available at fixed and variable rates.

A streamline refinance requires a good payment history for the 12 months preceding the loan application (the loan cannot be delinquent), and payment of UFMIP and annual MIP. The insurance rates for FHA loans endorsed before June 1, 2009 are less than those endorsed after that date. The other requirement for a streamline refinance is proof of a net tangible benefit from the refinance. A net tangible benefit exists if an adjustable-rate mortgage is refinanced into a fixed-rate loan or if the payment for the principal, interest and mortgage insurance on an FHA loan is reduced by at least 5%. For borrowers with new FHA loans, there is a requirement to complete a waiting period of 210 days before refinancing their existing FHA loans with a streamline refinance.

> *A number of changes to the FHA reverse mortgage program occurred as a result of the Reverse Mortgage Stabilization Act of 2013, which affects areas such as initial disbursements and mortgage insurance premium standards for HECMs.*

VA Loans (38 C.F.R. §36.4300)

The U.S. Department of Veterans Affairs (the VA) does not make loans to veterans; it establishes eligibility requirements for VA loans and guarantees them. The guarantee that the government offers with VA loans is a promise to repay lenders a portion of a loan balance if a veteran's loan goes into foreclosure.

Advantages and distinctive characteristics of VA loans include:

- 100% financing
- No prepayment penalties
- More lenient underwriting requirements than those that apply in transactions for conventional loans
- Limited closing costs

- Seller concessions are allowed
- VA assistance available if it becomes difficult to make mortgage payments

History of VA Loans

VA loans are a product of President Franklin Delano Roosevelt's 1944 Servicemen's Readjustment Act, which is also known as the "G.I. Bill." One of the benefits that this law provided to veterans was a federally-guaranteed home, with no down payment. Relief from a down payment requirement is still a characteristic of VA loans today. The credit and loan guarantees that the law offered to World War II veterans was considered a way to compensate them for their inability to build credit while serving in the Armed Forces. The need to give veterans a chance to "catch up" as they reenter civilian life remains an important objective of laws that address veterans' benefits.

In the decades since the G.I. Bill was passed, Congress has adopted a number of other laws to update and expand the provisions in the G.I. Bill. The most recent law that addressed the needs of veterans, including home lending needs, was the Veteran's Benefits Improvement Act of 2008. Title V of this law made many revisions to the VA loan program.

These revisions include:
- Increasing the LTV for refinances of VA loans to 100%
- Extending the availability of certain home loan guaranty programs, including one for adjustable-rate mortgages and one for hybrid adjustable-rate mortgages
- Requiring the VA to assess the ability of the home loan guaranty program to protect veterans from foreclosure

The Veteran's Benefits Improvement Act temporarily increased the maximum loan guaranty amount for home loans. The period for this temporary increase expired by law on December 31, 2011.

Although maximum loan guaranty amounts are not as high as they were in 2011, VA loans still have many benefits, with 100% financing and the absence of an absolute down payment requirement topping the list. Veterans should, however, be aware that securing any type of mortgage in today's market is challenging, and VA loans are no exception. Ultimately, the decision of whether or not to fund a VA loan is the lender's. Veterans may find that they need to enhance their applications with a strong credit score and by making financial commitments that are beyond the requirements of the VA lending program.

For example, if a veteran finds a home that he/she really wants to purchase, making a down payment can determine whether or not a lender is willing to make the loan.

The U.S. Department of Veterans Affairs (VA) establishes eligibility requirements for VA loans and guarantees to repay a portion of a loan balance if a veteran's loan goes into foreclosure.

Maximum Loan Guaranty Amount for VA Loans

The VA does not limit how much a veteran can borrow in a home lending transactions. It does, however, limit the amount that it can guarantee to repay a lender in the event of a default on the loan. The amount that the government will guarantee to a lender is known as a veteran's **"entitlement."** The basic entitlement for eligible veterans is $36,000, and those who are seeking to purchase a home in a high-cost area may qualify for a "bonus entitlement" that is an additional $68,250.

The size of the government's VA loan guarantee depends on the size of the loan. For example, the government offers a guarantee of:

- **50% of the loan**, if the loan is not more than $45,000
- **$22,500,** if the loan is more than $45,000, but no more than $56,250
- **The lesser of $36,000 or 40% of the loan,** if the loan is more than $56,250
- **The lesser of "the maximum guaranty amount" or 25% of the loan amount,** if the loan is more than $144,000

(38 U.S.C. §3703 (a)(1))

The law defines the **"maximum guaranty amount"** as the dollar amount that is equal to 25% of the Freddie Mac conforming loan limit (38 U.S.C. §3703 (a)(1)(C)). Since the current GSE conforming loan limit for most locations is $417,000, the guaranty for most counties is limited to 25% of $417,000, which equals $104,250. Following GSE conforming loan limit guidelines, in some high-cost areas the guaranty is 25% of $625,500, or $156,375.

Note once again, that just as government insurance for FHA loans is tied to GSE conforming loan limits, VA guarantees are also related to these loan limits, and the reason for this connection is to ensure that after lenders fund a government loan, they will have the option of selling it to Fannie Mae or Freddie Mac in the secondary mortgage market.

Originating VA Loans

The first step for a veteran who wants to secure a VA loan is to obtain a **Certificate of Eligibility (COE)**. Determinations of eligibility are based on the length of service and are issued to veterans who were not discharged dishonorably. Eligibility is extended for wartime and peacetime service, with longer service requirements for those who were in the military in times of peace. Lenders who are working with veterans can obtain an automatic certificate of eligibility (ACE) by using an online system that provides the certificate immediately.

The certificate of eligibility contains information on the amount of entitlement that is available to the veteran. A veteran who has used all or part of his/her entitlement may restore the entitlement and use it to purchase another home after showing that:

- He/she has sold the home for which the entitlement was previously used and paid the mortgage in full
- A qualified veteran is buying the home for which the entitlement was previously used and is assuming the outstanding balance on the loan and using his/her own entitlement in the transaction

- He/she has paid in full the prior loan for which the entitlement was used
- He/she has reimbursed the VA for any claims paid as a result of default or foreclosure

After an originator establishes that a veteran is eligible for a loan, completes an appraisal of the property used to secure the loan, and evaluates the creditworthiness of the veteran, the transaction may proceed. The federal regulations that address limitations on interest rates and fees for VA loans are found in 30 C.F.R. §§36.4312-36.4313. These are important regulations for originators to understand when negotiating VA loans. While this course does not provide a full review of these regulations, originators should know the following regarding interest rates and fees for VA loans.

Interest Rates

After a lender and veteran negotiate an interest rate, the veteran may pay reasonable discount points to reduce the loan's rate (38 C.F.R. §36.4312(b)). If the loan has an adjustable interest rate, there are special rules that apply, including those that require:

- The use of one-year constant maturity Treasury bills as the index when calculating changes in the interest rate
- No initial interest rate adjustment until 36 months from the date of the borrower's first mortgage payment
- No single rate adjustment that *"...may result in a change in either direction of more than one percentage point from the interest rate in effect for the period of maturity immediately preceding that adjustment"* (38 C.F.R. §36.4312(d)(4)(i))
- No rate adjustment over the loan term that exceeds *"...more than five percentage points from the initial contract interest rate"* (38 C.F.R. §36.4312(d)(4)(i))
- A special disclosure for the veteran which explains that the interest rate will change and that states the frequency of changes, the method of computing the new rate, and a hypothetical payment schedule showing the maximum potential increase during the first five years of the loan's term

Charges and Fees

As an origination fee, lenders may charge veterans a flat fee of no more than 1% of the loan amount (12 C.F.R. §36.4313(c)(2)). They must use this fee and cannot charge veterans additional amounts for costs such as the lender's appraisal and inspection, document preparation, interest rate lock-in fees, escrow fees, mailing charges, and closing or settlement fees.

In addition to the VA loan funding fee, veterans can be required to pay "customary and reasonable" fees for the following services and items:

- Their own appraisals
- Recording fees and recording taxes
- Credit reports
- Taxes and assessments
- Hazard insurance

- Title examination and insurance
- Flood zone determinations, as long as they are not made for the lender or made by a VA appraiser

(12 C.F.R. §36.4313(c)(1))

Funding fees are veterans' contributions to mortgage lending transactions. Although there are a few exemptions, including exemptions for veterans with disabilities, most VA loans include a non-refundable funding fee. The funding fee ranges from 0.50% to 3.30%, depending on the type of loan the veteran is obtaining and whether the transaction involves his/her first use of loan eligibility or the subsequent use.

For example, the following are the current funding fees for home loan purchases:

- **2.15%** for first-time users of an entitlement who are not making a down payment
- **1.5%** for first-time users who are making a down payment between 5% and less than 10%
- **3.3%** for subsequent users making no down payment
- **1.25%** for subsequent users who are making a down payment of 10% or greater

These fees are effective through September 30, 2016, when new fees for loans closed after that date will come into effect [79].

The VA funding fee can be financed. Disabled veterans, spouses of disabled veterans, and surviving spouses of veterans who died in service do not pay the funding fee. The funding fee is considered non-refundable unless the borrower is overcharged or inadvertently charged.

The veteran is required to occupy as his/her primary residence the property that is used to secure the VA loan. However VA loans are assumable. The buyer must qualify for the assumption but does not need to be a veteran. However, the full entitlement of the original borrower is not available for use again until the assumed loan is repaid.

VA Debt-to-Income Ratios

VA loans are made based on a total debt-to-income ratio, or back-end ratio of up to 41%. A back-end ratio shows the amount of a borrower's gross income that will go towards all of his/her indebtedness, including mortgage expenses. (A front-end ratio focuses on how much income is used to cover mortgage expenses and no other expenses). While VA underwriting does not look at the housing (front) debt ratio, it does consider residual income when qualifying borrowers. Based on the geographic area, the borrower must be guaranteed a certain amount of income every month after expenses.

VA Programs

VA loans can be for purchases or refinances and can be used for a number of different transactions including:

- Traditional purchases
- Construction refinances

- Installment land sales contracts
- Loan assumptions
- Traditional refinances
- Interest rate reduction refinance loans (IRRRLs)

The laws and regulations that apply to these transactions are numerous, and the information in this course is only a starting point for identifying the guidelines for originating VA home loans. Each program has its own requirements and limitations, and these are subject to legislative changes that Congress inevitably makes to address economic and social demands of the time.

> *The VA does not limit how much a veteran can borrow in a home lending transaction; however, it does limit the amount that it can guarantee to repay a lender in the event of a default on the loan.*

USDA (RHS) Loans (7 C.F.R. §§3550; 1980.301 *et seq.*)

The Rural Development Housing & Community Facilities Programs of the United States Department of Agriculture make and guarantee loans to qualified applicants. Loans made under the USDA program are referred to as Section 502 loans because these "Direct Single Family Housing Loans and Grants" are described under Section 502 of the Housing Act of 1949. Section 502 loans are made for the purpose of assisting low-income borrowers purchase homes in rural areas. There are two basic versions of 502 loans, and these include:

- **RHS Direct Loans,** which are funded directly by the U.S. Government, and
- **RHS Guaranteed Loans,** which are funded by private lenders, but are guaranteed by the RHS in the event that the borrower's loan goes into foreclosure

History of RHS Loans

The availability of home loans through the U.S. Department of Agriculture (USDA) was initially authorized under the Housing Act of 1949. At that time, eligibility for a loan through the USDA *"...was limited to persons who lived in dwellings on land capable of producing at least $400 worth of agricultural products annually"* [80]. In 1961, Congress amended the Housing Act of 1949 to make nonfarm rural properties eligible for RHS loans. Land used to secure RHS loans was simply required to be in a "rural area" which was defined in 1965 as having a population below 2,500 or as having a population of up to 5,500 if the area was "rural in character."

Clearly, as the division between suburban and rural areas became less distinct, this definition that was tied to such low population levels could stand the test of time. The current definition is more complex and is based on higher population levels and such factors as an area's location inside or outside of a metropolitan statistical area (MSA), its rural character, and a *"serious lack of mortgage credit for low- and moderate-income households as determined by the Secretary of Agriculture and the Secretary of HUD ..."* (7 C.F.R. §3550.10).

The USDA's rural lending programs were originally administered by the Farmers Home Administration. Congress created the Rural Housing Service in 1994 with the adoption of the Department of Agriculture Reorganization Act. Like other government insured and guaranteed lending programs, the RHS home lending programs grew in popularity when the mortgage lending market began its precipitous decline in 2007.

One of the most important recent changes in the RHS lending program occurred when the USDA launched a program in October 2011 to make its single-family housing guarantee loan program (SFHGLP) self-sustaining. Until October 2011, this program was subsidized by tax dollars. Beginning with loans made on October 1, 2011, the RHS has been using annual fees charged to borrowers with 502 guaranteed loans to create a self-funding SFHGLP program.

> *Loans made under the USDA program are referred to as "Section 502 loans." Section 502 loans are made for the purpose of assisting low-income borrowers purchase homes in rural areas.*

Originating RHS Loans

Eligibility requirements for 502 direct loans and 502 guaranteed loans include income limitations and the location of the property used to secure the loan in a rural area. Although both types of loans are only available to borrowers with low to moderate income, the direct loans are reserved for low- and very low-income borrowers. There are many rules for the origination of both types of loans, and these regulations are located in the Code of Federal Regulations in the following sections:

- Direct Single Family Housing Loans: 7 C.F.R. §3550.1-3550.100
- Single Family Rural Housing Loan Guarantees: 7 C.F.R. §1980.301-367

These rules also include additional provisions that address the servicing of RHS loans. There are numerous provisions related to RHS loan servicing, and the primary goal of these provisions is *"...to provide borrowers with the maximum opportunity to become successful homeowners"* (7 C.F.R. §1980.370) and to *"...reduce the number of borrower failures that result in liquidation...."* (7 C.F.R. §3550.201)

An outline of all of the requirements for the origination of direct and guaranteed RHS loans is beyond the scope of this course. However, an efficient means of providing an overview of the requirements of both types of loans is to outline the differences between the two lending programs. The principal differences between the 502 direct loans program and the 502 guaranteed program are as follows:

- **Loan Funding**: The USDA funds direct loans, and private lenders fund guaranteed loans.
- **Income Limitations**: Borrowers under the direct loan program must not have income levels that exceed the low income limit for their rural area. Borrowers under the guaranteed program must not have income levels that exceed 115% of the median income for their rural area.

- **Interest Rates**: Borrowers who secure a loan under the direct loan program may receive subsidies that can lower the interest to 1%. Subsidies are not available to borrowers with guaranteed loans.

- **Loan Terms**: The loan term for a direct loan is 33 years or 38 years. The loan term for a guaranteed loan is 30 years.

- **Mortgage Insurance Requirement**: Borrowers with direct loans are not required to secure or pay for mortgage insurance. Borrowers with guaranteed loans must pay an up-front "guarantee fee," which serves as insurance to cover lender losses in the event of default. The amount of the upfront guarantee fee is 2% of the loan amount, and the law allows borrowers to finance this fee. On October 1, 2011, borrowers with guaranteed loans were required to pay an annual fee for the first time in the history of RHS SFHGLP. This annual fee is .4% of the outstanding principal balance. These annual fees are charged every year for the life of the loan and cannot be cancelled.

- **Limited Access to Credit**: Direct loans are only available to borrowers *"...who cannot obtain credit from other sources..."* (7 C.F.R. §35550.51). Guaranteed loans are available to borrowers who may have other lending options.

Of course, there are also a number of important similarities between direct and guaranteed loans. Both types of RHS or 502 loans must:

- Be secured by property that the RHS has designated as a **"rural area"**
- Be secured by a dwelling that is **"modest"**
- Have a **fixed interest rate**
- Be offered to a borrower who can demonstrate **repayment ability**

Finally, one of the most significant benefits that both direct and guaranteed RHS home loans offer is 100% financing.

Guidances

The downturn in the subprime market began in the fourth quarter of 2005. Growing numbers of defaults and foreclosures contributed to market decline, and there was pressure from those within and outside of the mortgage lending industry to offer an immediate response to the emerging subprime crisis.

Months and years of political debate and administrative procedures are involved in the enactment of laws and the adoption of new regulations. Knowing that legislative and regulatory solutions were long-term goals, the federal banking regulatory agencies responded to the crisis by writing:

- *The Interagency Guidance on Nontraditional Mortgage Product Risks, and*
- *The Statement on Subprime Lending*

These guidances have never had the force and effect of laws or regulations, but they were important at the time of their adoption, since they encouraged the reestablishment of common-sense lending practices and promoted standards that were ultimately codified in new and revised lending laws and regulations.

Guidance on Nontraditional Mortgage Product Risks

In 2006, the Government Accountability Office (GAO) conducted a study to assess how much consumers understand about nontraditional mortgage products. The GAO concluded that nontraditional mortgages are complex products that borrowers did not understand and that the disclosures offered with these loans failed to provide adequate explanations of the lending terms.

The first response to these concerns was a joint effort by the federal banking regulatory agencies to create the *Interagency Guidance on Nontraditional Mortgage Product Risks*, which they issued in October 2006. This guidance was applicable to the practices of depository institutions, such as banks and credit unions.

There were concerns that a large percentage of mortgage professionals, including state-licensed entities such as mortgage brokers and loan originators, were left without guidance standards. States regulators worked quickly to fill the regulatory gap. On November 16, 2006, the Conference of State Bank Supervisors (CSBS) and the American Association of Residential Mortgage Regulators (AARMR) published their *Guidance on Nontraditional Mortgage Product Risks for State-Licensed Entities*.

The federal and state guidances are almost identical. Both address risky lending practices and recommend safer origination standards and practices. Since the guidance issued by CSBS and AARMR addresses the actions of mortgage brokers, mortgage lenders, and loan originators, the following summary of the standards suggested by the guidances will focus on the State Guidance. Even though new laws and regulations have effectively replaced the guidances, it is worthwhile to look at their provisions since they directly address lending practices that have proven to be detrimental for both borrowers and mortgage professionals, and have served as a starting point for the laws and regulations that the federal government ultimately adopted.

> *The Interagency Guidance on Nontraditional Mortgage Product Risks was created in response to concern that borrowers did not understand nontraditional mortgage products being offered in the lending market.*

Loan Terms and Underwriting Standards

The State Guidance defines "nontraditional mortgages" as those that allow borrowers to exchange lower payments during an initial period for higher payments during a later amortization period, and it addresses the need for stricter underwriting standards for them.

While emphasizing the importance of a more thorough repayment analysis for nontraditional loans, the State Guidance urges the most stringent repayment analysis for:

- Nontraditional mortgages that include reduced documentation and/or the simultaneous origination of a first- and second-lien loan, known as "piggy-back loans"

- Nontraditional loans offered to subprime borrowers
- Nontraditional loans that finance the purchase of non-owner-occupied investment properties

Types of loans the State Guidance specifically cites as risky products include interest-only loans and payment-option adjustable-rate mortgages.

The State Guidance strongly discourages certain lending practices, such as the making of a collateral-dependent loan in which the borrower has no source for repayment other than the collateral, which is a practice that is essentially prohibited. The Guidance also discourages lenders from making loans characterized by a large spread between low introductory rates and the fully indexed rate. As the Guidance notes, with these types of loans, "…borrowers are more likely to experience negative amortization, severe payment shock and an earlier-than-scheduled recasting of monthly payments" [81].

Risk Management Practices

The State Guidance suggests that effective risk management practices should include:

- Establishing appropriate limits on risk layering (An example of risk layering is offering a nontraditional mortgage to a borrower with poor credit scores and using reduced documentation, thereby assuming three distinct types of risk in making the loan)
- Setting growth and volume limits by loan type
- Monitoring compliance with underwriting standards
- Overseeing the practice of third parties such as mortgage brokers
- Considering how to respond if the secondary market decreases its purchase of nontraditional loans
- Anticipating the need to repurchase nontraditional loans if the sold loan losses exceed expectations

Unfortunately, as the events of 2007 and 2008 showed, these types of risk management practices were neither adopted nor implemented by enough lenders to reverse the inevitable and devastating impact of too many years of risky lending.

Consumer Protection Issues

The State Guidance urges originators to provide consumers with information on the risks of nontraditional mortgages even before they receive disclosures required under the Truth-in-Lending Act. Ideally, consumers should have information about the risks associated with products like interest-only loans and payment-option loans while shopping for a mortgage. It also discourages the use of promotional materials that emphasize the benefits of nontraditional mortgages without describing their liabilities. Misleading advertisements are not only a disservice to consumers, but place the advertiser at risk for administrative enforcement actions, lawsuits, and penalties under the Truth-in-Lending Act, the Federal Trade Commission Act, and consumer protection laws enacted at the state level.

Recommended Practices

Recommended practices for addressing the risks associated with nontraditional mortgages include the following.

Communication with Consumers: One of the most important aspects of good client communication is advising loan applicants of the risks associated with nontraditional ARMs. These risks include:

- Payment shock when amortizing payments begin
- Loss of equity in the home used to secure the mortgage if the payment agreement allows negative amortization to occur
- The inclusion of prepayment penalty terms in the agreement (the use of these is now severely limited)

Borrowers need the guidance of a mortgage professional to help them understand that even with traditional ARMs there are risks and that it is important to understand provisions in a lending agreement that may not be clear to them, such as payment increases that will result from interest rate resets.

Control Systems: Control systems for the origination of nontraditional mortgage products should include:

- Employee training to ensure that originators communicate effectively with loan applicants about the risks and benefits of nontraditional mortgages
- Use of compensation programs that do not encourage originators to direct loan applicants to expensive, risky products
- Measures by mortgage companies to ensure that third parties, such as independent brokers, are effectively managed and are operating in compliance with the law

As a result of legislation passed in the wake of the lending crisis, the mortgage industry is now subject to statutory requirements for loan originator training and for the use of compensation systems that remove incentives for making risky or unnecessarily expensive loans.

> *The State Guidance urges originators to provide consumers with information on the risks of nontraditional mortgages even before they receive disclosures required under the Truth-in-Lending Act.*

Statement on Subprime Mortgage Lending

Six months after publishing the *Guidance on Nontraditional Mortgage Product Risks*, the Federal Bank Regulatory Agencies determined that it was important to provide a direct response to the crisis unfolding in the subprime lending market. They drafted a supervisory guidance that focused on the risks of making subprime ARM loans to subprime borrowers. The Federal Reserve published the final version of the *Statement on Subprime Mortgage Lending* on June 28,

2007. Once again, CSBS and AARMR took part in drafting a parallel statement for state-licensed loan originators.

Both the federal and state Statements describe subprime borrowers as those who demonstrate a higher credit risk due to:

- Two or more 30-day delinquencies within the prior 12 months
- One or more 60-day delinquencies within the prior 24 months
- Foreclosure, repossession, or charge-off within the prior 24 months
- Bankruptcy within the previous five years
- Credit scores that represent a high risk of default
- Debt-to-income ratio of 50% or higher

Often, these borrowers are desperate for debt relief and are attracted to ARMs with low introductory rates. These ARMs soon adjust to much higher rates, resulting in payment shock and even default for the borrower. The Statement identifies the riskiest loans as ARMs that include any of the following features:

- A low introductory rate that expires after a short period
- High interest rate caps or no rate caps
- No documentation or limited documentation of the borrower's income
- High prepayment penalties or prepayment penalties that are in force for an extended period of time

Changes to HOEPA rules and the adoption of new regulations for higher-priced mortgages address some of these concerns directly. First, they prohibit lending without using specific types of documents to verify repayment ability. Second, they prohibit prepayment penalties after the first two years of a loan's term. In 2014, as a result of provisions included in the Dodd-Frank Act, there will be further limitations on prepayment penalties.

Like the *Guidance on Nontraditional Mortgage Product Risks*, the *Statement on Subprime Lending* warns against risk layering and suggests the use of control systems and effective communication with consumers as recommended practices for reducing the risks associated with mortgage lending transactions.

The Statement on Subprime Mortgage Lending was created as a supervisory guidance in response to the crisis unfolding in the subprime lending market.

Current and Future Relevance of the Guidances

Students should be familiar with the Guidances for a number of reasons. First, these documents provide insight into past lending practices that led to the origination of loans that were likely to fail. Second, they give loan originators a checklist of general lending considerations, such as risk factors to look for when evaluating a loan applicant and information to share with clients when helping them to identify appropriate mortgage products. Third, the NMLS National Component Content Outline lists the *Statement on Subprime Lending* and the *Guidance on Nontraditional Mortgage Product Risks* as subjects that the test may address.

Laws adopted through the Dodd-Frank Wall Street Reform and Consumer Protection Act reflect policies adopted under the Guidances. For example, it is now illegal to:

- **Originate Negative Amortization Loans Without Disclosures and Counseling**: This prohibition applies not only to closed-end loans but also to open-end loans secured by a dwelling. These loans cannot include provisions that allow negative amortization to occur without providing the borrower with a disclosure that explains that negative amortization will increase the principal balance due on the loan and reduce home equity. If the borrower is a first-time home borrower, he/she must complete HUD-approved homeownership counseling before accepting this type of loan [82].

- **Originate a Loan with Prepayment Penalties**: The law creates very strict limitations on prepayment penalties in all "residential mortgage loans."

- **Finance Single Premium Credit Insurance**: This prohibition applies to closed-end and open-end loans such as HELOCs that are secured by the borrower's principal dwelling. These loans cannot include a provision that finances credit life, credit disability, credit unemployment, or credit property insurance, or debt cancellation coverage.

- **Originate a Home Loan Without Consideration of Repayment Ability**: When offering a residential mortgage loan to a consumer, lending decisions must be based on "a reasonable and good faith determination" of the consumer's ability to repay. This determination must:
    - Be based on verified credit history, income, obligations, debt-to-income ratios, and employment status
    - Include an assessment of the consumer's ability to pay not only principal and interest but also taxes, insurance, and assessment
    - Be based on the consumer's ability to repay at the time the loan is consummated and on a payment schedule that fully amortizes the loan during the loan term

If a borrower is considering a "nontraditional mortgage," which is broadly defined as any loan other than a fixed-rate 30-year loan, the assessment of repayment ability must be based on a fully amortizing repayment schedule and on payment amounts that fully amortize the loan by the end of the loan term.

MORTGAGE LOAN PRODUCTS

Fixed-Rate Loans

With a fixed-rate mortgage, the interest is set at the time of closing and does not change during the life of the loan. Although a borrower's interest rate will not change, monthly payments may change if the loan servicer finds that there is a shortage or surplus in the escrow account.

Lenders will make fixed rate loans for terms of any length although 10-, 15-, 20-, 25- and 30-year terms are common. In many cases, the shorter the loan term, the lower the interest rate. Loans made for non-standard terms such as 12 years or 27 years generally revert to the interest rate for the next longest standard loan term.

FHA Fixed-Rate Loans: The FHA offers 15- and 30-year fixed-rate mortgages to qualifying borrowers. These mortgages are available for one- to four-unit homes.

VA Fixed-Rate Loans: VA fixed-rate loans are made for 15-, 20-, 25- or 30-year periods.

USDA (RHS) Fixed-Rate Loans: RHS or 502 loans always have fixed interest rates. Direct RHS loans may have terms of 33 or 38 years, and guaranteed RHS loans have 30-year loan terms.

> *With a fixed-rate mortgage, while a borrower's interest rate will not change, monthly payments may change if the loan servicer finds that there is a shortage or surplus in the escrow account.*

Prepayment of Fixed-Rate Mortgages

Prepayment penalties allow lenders to recoup some of the interest that they do not earn on a loan if the borrower prepays the balance before the end of the loan term. Most often, early repayment or prepayment of the full loan amount takes place during the refinancing of a mortgage. Prepayment penalties can discourage refinances, since the need to pay them can be triggered by paying off an existing loan with a new loan. Since fixed-rate mortgages have rarely included prepayment penalties, the ability to prepay these loans without incurring a penalty has historically been one of their greatest advantages.

This benefit of fixed-rate mortgages is far less significant now that prepayment penalty provisions are prohibited in most lending transactions. As a result of amendments to federal lending laws that were dictated by the Dodd-Frank Act, prepayment penalties are prohibited in:

- Closed-end loans that are not fixed-rate qualified mortgages
- Adjustable-rate mortgages
- High-cost mortgage loans regulated under HOEPA, and
- Higher-priced mortgage loans

(12 C.F.R. §1026.43(g))

Today, prepayment penalties are only allowed in qualified mortgages that have a fixed rate for the full term of the loan (12 C.F.R. §1026.43(g)(1)(ii)(A)). Even with a fixed-rate qualified mortgage, prepayment penalties are limited to:

- 2% of the outstanding loan balance if the prepayment is made within the first two years after consummation of the loan

- 1% of the outstanding loan balance if the prepayment is made within the third year after the consummation of the loan, and

- No prepayment penalty if the prepayment is made three years or more after consummation

Bi-Weekly Mortgage Payments – Another Prepayment Strategy

If a borrower cannot prepay his or her loan balance, but wants to repay a loan within a shorter period of time, it is possible to reduce the loan term by making an "extra" mortgage payment each year. This reduces the loan with a term of 30 years to about 24.5 years. The process of making an extra payment every year forms the basis of the bi-weekly mortgage payment plan.

Making a payment every two weeks is the same as making an extra mortgage payment every year because there are 26 bi-weekly periods in a year (13 monthly payments). Many loan servicers do not apply the mid-month payment to the loan until after a full monthly payment has been received. Therefore, there are no additional interest savings from a mid-month principal reduction.

The bi-weekly payment plan can be applied to both fixed-rate and adjustable-rate loans with a payment plan that allows borrowers to make a payment every two weeks instead of once a month. Theoretically, this helps people who are paid every two weeks to manage their cash flow.

However, it may be more practical to utilize an independent prepayment strategy as opposed to using a bi-weekly mortgage payment plan because:

- There is a greater potential for late payments due to the fact that there are twice as many payments to make and the fact that servicers may not credit a "full payment" until the monthly required minimum is received, and if the "full monthly payment" is not received before the grace period expires, the payment is considered late

- The rates for a loan utilizing a bi-weekly payment plan are often not as competitive as those for standard monthly plans

- Lenders may charge a fee for administering the bi-weekly program

Adjustable-Rate Mortgages (ARMs)

A variable-rate or adjustable-rate mortgage (ARM) is a mortgage with an interest rate that may change one or more times during the life of the loan. ARMs are often initially made at a lower interest rate than fixed-rate loans although, depending on the structure of the loan, interest rates can potentially increase to exceed standard fixed-rates.

There are two types of protection, one that is mandatory and one that is voluntary, which are intended to ensure that borrowers understand the amount of interest that they will pay during the term of a variable-rate loan:

- **Mandatory Protection for Borrowers**: The Truth-in-Lending Act requires lenders to provide applicants for ARMs with The Consumer Handbook on Adjustable-Rate Mortgages (CHARM). In 2006, the Federal Reserve Board revised the CHARM booklet and use of the new booklet was mandatory on October 1, 2007. Lenders must also offer ARM applicants information on every variable-rate loan program in which the consumer expresses an interest.

- **Voluntary Protection for Borrowers**: Interest rate caps ensure that payments will remain at a manageable level by limiting the extent to which lenders may increase interest rates. Most loan agreements for ARMs include some type of cap, but caps are NOT mandatory, and lending laws do not establish a limit on the allowable increase on variable interest rates.

New Rules for Qualifying Borrowers for ARMs

Although loan qualification is discussed in greater detail in Module 3 of this course, it is important to note that amendments to the Truth-in-Lending Act and the adoption of new regulations have changed the requirements for qualifying for an ARM. Since they became available in the 1980s, ARMs have appealed to consumers because they were usually offered with low introductory rates. These low introductory interest rates improved the ability of borrowers to secure home loans. These days are now over. As a result of changes that Congress made to TILA through the Dodd-Frank Act, the law and its implementing regulations no longer allow borrowers to qualify for mortgages based on introductory rates.

Today, applicants for ARMs must qualify for these loans based on the **"fully indexed rate."** The requirement to qualify for a mortgage based on the fully indexed rate of a loan is one of the many requirements of the **Ability to Repay Rule (ATR Rule)**, and it applies to all transactions involving ARMs except for open-end home equity loans. The purpose of this Rule is to prevent consumers from accepting mortgages that they are unable to pay when the introductory loan rate expires and rate adjustments lead to higher periodic payments.

There is no doubt that the requirement to qualify borrowers based on the fully indexed rate will have an impact on the origination of ARMs. As all lenders are forced by law to adopt this tougher standard, fewer ARMs will be approved.

> *The Ability to Repay Rule (ATR Rule) imposes requirements for borrower qualification in order to prevent consumers from obtaining mortgages that they ultimately cannot afford to repay.*

Calculation of Interest Rate Increases for ARMs – Index and Margin

All lending agreements for ARMs include an **adjustment frequency** (or adjustment period) to establish how often an adjustment to the interest rate can occur. The adjustment usually occurs annually, but may occur monthly or only once every few years.

The starting point for the adjustment is the **index**, which lenders must disclose to borrowers. The index is a common way of measuring the cost of borrowing money. The specific index used to determine the rate adjustments must be disclosed to a potential borrower on the early ARM disclosure provided at application. The index also appears on the promissory note when the loan goes to closing.

Common indices include the **Treasury Bill Index**, the 11th District Cost of Funds Indexes **(COFI)** or the London Interbank Offered Rate **(LIBOR)**. The index is subject to change and is therefore likely to be different each time that there is an adjustment period. An index with a long term offers borrowers more protection from short-term fluctuations in the economy than an index with a short term. For example, a borrower with an ARM that uses a six-month U.S. Treasury bill for the index has less protection from increases in the interest rate than a borrower who uses a three-year Treasury bill as the index.

The other number which lenders must disclose to borrowers in lending agreements is the **margin**. The margin is a fixed number that is not subject to change during the term of a loan. The margin is a number, expressed in percentage points, and selected by the lender. The margin represents the lender's operating costs and profit margin. Margins vary from lender to lender and range from 2.5% to 3%. After the initial fixed period of an ARM expires, the calculation of an increase is made by adding the index to the margin.

Consumer protections which limit the amount the interest rate or payment on an ARM may change. There are four caps in common use:

- **Initial Rate Cap**: A limit on the amount that the interest rate can increase or decrease at the first adjustment date for an ARM.

- **Periodic Rate Cap**: A limit on the amount that the interest rate can change up or down on any adjustment date.

- **Lifetime Rate Cap**: A limit on the amount that an interest rate can change over the life of an ARM, aka Rate Ceiling.

- **Payment Cap**: A limit on the amount that the payment can change on any adjustment date from the current or previous payment amount on an ARM. Payment caps do not limit the amount the interest rate may adjust, but rather place a limitation on the amount the required minimum payment may change per adjustment period. The borrower may not know that while the required payment has not changed or can only change a certain amount, their monthly payment may not be sufficient to pay all of the interest due. When this occurs, it is referred to as negative amortization.

Negative amortization occurs when the accrued but unpaid interest is added to the principal balance of the loan. Most loan programs are positive-amortizing, meaning that a portion of the balance is retired with each payment. Negative amortization is the reverse—instead of paying off the balance of the loan, the balance increases. An additional risk is that, when limiting his/her payments to the minimum in a rising rate environment, at some point, the lender will require that the loan be "recast" meaning the required minimum payment will be adjusted to an amount which will fully retire the loan over its remaining term at the then effective rate. This will generally produce a much larger minimum required payment because the balance has increased above the amount at which it started, the term has shortened, and the interest rate is likely to be higher.

With negative amortization, the borrower ends up paying interest on interest since it is added to the principal when unpaid, and the new required accrued interest each month will increase; thus costs increase over the life of the loan. Current lending laws and regulations prohibit payment programs that can lead to negative amortization for:

- High-cost mortgages regulated by HOEPA (12 C.F.R. §1026.32(d)(2))
- Qualified mortgages, including qualified ARMs (12 C.F.R. §1026.43(2)(i)(A))

Hybrid ARMs

A hybrid ARM is a mortgage loan with a rate that does not adjust during the first three to five years of the loan's term. After the initial rate period expires, the loan adjusts based on the index and margin specified in the lending agreement. Lenders offer a variety of hybrid loans, which are referred to by their initial fixed period and adjustment period. For example, a 3/1 hybrid loan is a loan in which the interest is fixed for a period of three years and then adjusts once each year for the duration of the loan term. Other hybrid loan products include 5/1, 7/1, and 10/1 ARMs. Hybrid ARMs may be especially valuable products for borrowers who know that they will only live in a home for a few years.

Interest-Only ARMs and Payment-Option ARMs

Interest-only and payment-option ARMs were popular during the lending boom, but these types of mortgages are no longer commonly available. By combining the risks of an adjustable-rate mortgage with other risks, such as payments that do not reduce the loan balance, these loans are examples of the "risk layering" that the federal and state guidances condemned and that new lending laws prohibit.

Qualified mortgages prohibit payment schedules that allow borrowers to defer payments of principal, as well as those that lead to an increasing principal balance (negative amortization). Therefore, as more and more lenders seek to make qualified mortgages, loan products such as interest-only and payment-option loans may become increasingly difficult to find.

FHA ARMs

Section 251 of the National Housing Act authorizes the FHA to insure ARMs. Amendments to the National Housing Act in 2003 allowed HUD to also begin insuring hybrid ARMs. Under current HUD regulations, the FHA can insure hybrid ARMs that offer fixed rates for one, three, five, or ten years before annual adjustment to the rate of interest begins.

One-, three-, and five-year ARMs allow for caps of 1% and 5%. Seven- and ten-year ARMs allow for caps of 2% and 6%.

VA ARMs

The Veterans Benefits Improvement Act of 2004 reinstated a program from the early 1990s that allowed the VA to guarantee traditional adjustable-rate mortgages. The Act also allows the VA to guarantee hybrid ARMs. Traditional ARMs guaranteed by the VA typically limit annual adjustment to 1% and include a cap of five percentage points on the maximum interest rate increase over the life of the loan. The VA also guarantees a hybrid mortgage product that sets a fixed interest rate for the first three to five years and then adjusts annually.

Balloon Mortgages

A balloon mortgage requires a borrower to make one large payment at the end of the loan term. This payment may be referred to as a "call" or a "bullet." Borrowers usually pay the balance by refinancing. In some loans, the risk of the balloon payment may be minimized by the existence of an option for converting the loan to a fixed-rate loan at its maturity date. This is referred to as a conditional refinance provision. Conditional refinance provisions are similar to provisions contained in ARMs that offer a "conversion option," which is the ability to convert to a fixed-rate mortgage for the remainder of the loan. A loan with a conditional refinance provision allows the borrower to request modification of the terms of the loan at the time of maturity, which is often five to seven years after the closing on the loan. A conditional offer to refinance a balloon mortgage at maturity does not guarantee refinancing. The borrower must qualify for the conditional refinance by meeting conditions which show that the risk of extending the loan does not adversely affect the lender.

Balloon program terminology is sometimes a source of confusion. Mortgage products that have a balloon payment due within five or seven years may be referred to as 5/25 and 7/23 loans, respectively. This indicates that the loan is fixed for five or seven years and has a conditional refinance option for the remaining 25 or 23 years. Notations of 5/30, 7/30, 10/30, or 15/30 indicate there is a balloon feature without a conditional refinance provision.

High-cost mortgages that are regulated under HOEPA may not include a balloon payment (12 C.F.R. §1026.32(d)(1)(i)). Qualified mortgages, which are discussed in the next section of the course, are not allowed to include a balloon payment unless the loan is a **"balloon payment qualified mortgage,"** which is a fixed-rate loan with a term of no less than five years that is made by a small creditor.

> *A balloon mortgage is a mortgage which requires one large payment at the end of the loan term. Qualified mortgages may not include a balloon payment unless they have a fixed rate, a term of no more than five years, and are made by a small creditor.*

Qualified Mortgages

After the failure of so many loans that were originated during the lending boom, Congress adopted laws that are intended to give lenders and other loan originators the incentive to make certain that borrower repayment ability is thoroughly evaluated and that other steps are taken to ensure that borrowers are able to repay their loans. These new laws offer an incentive for following sound lending practices by creating a **"safe harbor"** from liability for lenders that make loans that meet the characteristics of a qualified mortgage. This safe harbor is provided by presuming that a creditor that makes a qualified mortgage has complied with ability-to-repay standards. There are two presumptions of compliance:

- A **"conclusive presumption of compliance"** applies to prime mortgages, and not to subprime or higher-priced mortgage loans.

- A **"rebuttable presumption of compliance"** is extended to higher-priced mortgage loans. In order to successfully rebut or challenge the presumption of a creditor's compliance with ability-to-repay standards, a borrower must prove that the creditor failed to make a reasonable and good faith determination of repayment ability by showing that the consumer's income, debt obligations, alimony, child support, and monthly payment on the covered transaction would leave the consumer with insufficient residual assets.

(12 C.F.R. §1026.43(e)(1)(ii))

The Qualified Mortgage Rule (QM Rule) was released by the CFPB in January 2013, and became effective on January 10, 2014.

What Are Qualified Mortgages?

A qualified mortgage is one that meets the following product feature prerequisites:
- The periodic payments are sufficient to pay the principal and interest due and will not result in negative amortization
- The loan does not allow the borrower to defer repayment of the principal (e.g. interest-only loans)
- The loan does not include a balloon payment feature (with some exceptions)
- The loan's term does not exceed 30 years
- The points and fees for the loan do not exceed **3%** of the total loan amount, and
- The borrower's debt-to-income ratio does not exceed **43%**

The underwriting standards for qualified mortgages are strict, and are intended to ensure that the creditor has thoroughly assessed the borrower's repayment ability. Underwriting must include:
- Calculation of monthly payments using:
  - The maximum interest rate that may apply during a loan's first five years, measured from the date that the first periodic payment is due, and
  - Periodic payments that will repay the principal balance that is outstanding after the interest rate adjusts to the maximum rate applicable during the loan's first five years, and the loan amount over the term of the loan
- Verification of the consumer's current or reasonably-expected income or assets
- Calculation of the consumer's current debt obligations, alimony, and child support, and
- Calculation of the consumer's monthly debt-to-income ratio, which cannot exceed 43%

(12 C.F.R. §1026.43(e)(2))

Scope of the Qualified Mortgage Rule

The QM Rule applies to **"covered transactions,"** which are defined as consumer credit transactions secured by a dwelling other than an open-end home equity line of credit, a mortgage related to a timeshare plan, a reverse mortgage, or a bridge loan of 12 months or less (12 C.F.R. §1026.43(b)). This definition is the same definition that TILA gives to a "residential mortgage."

Qualified mortgages may be fixed-rate mortgages or adjustable-rate mortgages, and, in limited circumstances, they may include balloon mortgages. What distinguishes these mortgages from others is sound underwriting and the absence of risky lending terms.

Balloon Payment Qualified Mortgages

Balloon payment qualified mortgages are those that meet the following requirements for a qualified mortgage:

- No negative amortization
- A loan term that does not exceed 30 years
- Compliance with the 3% points and fees cap that is established for qualified mortgages
- Verification of the consumer's reasonably expected income or assets, and
- Determination of the consumer's debt-to-income ratio, although the 43% limit does not apply

Underwriting for balloon payment qualified mortgages must establish repayment ability based on the borrower's ability to make substantially equal monthly payments using an amortization period of no more than 30 years, including all mortgage-related obligations. Furthermore, the creditor must be a **small creditor serving a rural or underserved area**, and:

- The loan must have a **fixed interest rate**
- The loan must have a term that is **five years or longer,** and
- The small creditor must hold the loan for **three years,** unless it sells the loan to another small creditor (selling earlier or selling to a creditor that is not a small creditor will result in the loss of qualified mortgage status)

(12 C.F.R. §1026.43(f))

There are a number of criteria for determining if a creditor is a small creditor, but for purposes of understanding the rules for balloon payment qualified mortgages, it is most important to know that in order to be "small," more than 50% of the creditor's mortgages must be secured by properties in areas that are designated as rural or underserved. Creditors are required to use the CFPB's *List of Rural and Underserved Counties* in order to determine if they are serving a rural or underserved area. This list is updated annually.

For a two-year period of time, small creditors that do not predominantly serve rural or underserved areas will also be allowed to make balloon payment qualified mortgages. In addition to meeting the characteristics of balloon payment qualified mortgages, this temporary category of qualified mortgages must also meet an APR limitation. Temporary balloon payment qualified mortgages may not have an APR that is more than **3.5 percentage points** over the average prime offer rate.

This two-year period during which small creditors in non-rural areas can make temporary balloon payment qualified mortgages will expire in January 2016. These rules were issued by the CFPB in a concurrent rulemaking that took place at the same time that it issued its Qualified Mortgage Rule.

> *Qualified mortgages may be fixed- or adjustable-rate mortgages and, in limited circumstances, they may include balloon mortgages. These mortgages are distinct from other types because they feature sound underwriting standards and exclude risky lending terms.*

Other Types of Mortgages

Second Mortgages and HELOCs

Second Mortgages
A second mortgage – also known as a junior mortgage or subordinate lien – is a lien that ranks in priority below the first mortgage. It is also important to note that not all subordinate liens are second mortgages – the term subordinate lien can also refer to debt that sits in priority below a second mortgage. The priority of liens is significant if foreclosure occurs because liens are paid in the order in which they are recorded. In the event of foreclosure by the holder of the first mortgage, no funds are released for payment of the second mortgage until all foreclosure expenses are paid and the first mortgage is paid in full. Home equity loans and home equity lines of credit (HELOCs) are examples of home financing that are generally second liens.

Home Equity Loans
The loan is *closed-end*, meaning that the borrower receives a lump sum and does not continue to make withdrawals. The lender gives the borrower a check, based on the equity in the borrower's home, and the borrower begins repayment. These types of loans are usually second mortgages.

Home Equity Lines of Credit (HELOCs)
HELOCs are considered *open-end credit* – similar to credit cards – and as a borrower pays off the principal, he/she can continue to make withdrawals. Although a HELOC is often a second mortgage, it can also be a first mortgage. For example, a borrower can refinance a first mortgage with a HELOC in order to secure a line of credit.

Piggyback Loans
Borrowers with loans of greater than 80% loan-to-value (LTV) are required by conforming lenders to obtain private mortgage insurance (PMI). In a piggyback loan scenario, a borrower often takes a simultaneous second mortgage in order to avoid paying PMI. An 80-10-10 loan is an example of this type of transaction.

In an 80-10-10 transaction, the borrower obtains a first mortgage at 80% LTV and a simultaneous second mortgage at 10% LTV. The remaining amount is a 10% down payment or 10% equity in the property.

Construction Loans

A construction loan is an interim loan used to pay for the construction of buildings or homes. Interim financing is short-term financing (i.e. three – nine months) made to cover costs while waiting for the requirements of a permanent loan to be met. Construction loans are usually designed to provide periodic disbursements to the builder/developer as construction progresses and are often handled as interest-only transactions.

The temporary construction loan takes the equity in the raw land into consideration as a down payment for the construction lender. At the conclusion of construction, the loan is converted into permanent financing, although construction-permanent loan options also exist. In the case of a construction-permanent loan, all the financing is wrapped up in one closing although the loan terms are not always the most favorable for the borrower.

Bridge Financing

Bridge financing may include loans such as the construction loans that are discussed in the previous subsection. A bridge loan can include a range of short-term loans that are taken out by homeowners who are waiting for long-term financing. In addition to using a bridge loan while constructing a home, some borrowers need a bridge loan to help themselves through the transition from an existing home into a new home when the existing home has not yet sold. These borrowers can use a bridge loan to secure the funds needed for a down payment while waiting for their home to sell. The loan is secured by the existing home that the borrowers are trying to sell. The underwriting for bridge loans is generally less strict than the underwriting for permanent loans since these loans have short terms.

Reverse Mortgages

Reverse mortgages are popular products for older homeowners who have equity in their homes and little or no income. They allow an older homeowner to use equity in their homes to meet the expenses of living, or to pay for home improvements. Borrowers are not required to repay the loan as long as they continue to live in the home. Additionally, in 2008, FHA announced a purchase program for HECMs which permits qualifying borrowers to purchase a principal residence using reverse mortgage proceeds.

There are three types of reverse mortgages. The common features of all three are:
- Loans are only available to borrowers that are 62 or older
- The borrower must live in his/her home
- The mortgage is payable in full when the home is sold or the last surviving homeowner dies
- Interest is charged on the outstanding balance and added to the debt
- Debt increases with each payment advanced and with accrued interest

The three types of reverse mortgages are:

Single Purpose Reverse Mortgages: These are low-cost loans offered to low income borrowers by state and local agencies or non-profit organizations. Borrowers can only use them for the purpose specified by the lender such as payment for home improvements or payment of property taxes.

Home Equity Conversion Mortgages (HECM): These are reverse mortgages that are regulated and insured by HUD. They allow borrowers to receive fixed monthly payments, a line of credit, or a combination of payments and a credit line. These loans are available to homeowners who owe little or no money on their home payments. Borrowers must complete counseling with a HUD-approved HECM counselor in order to obtain the loan.

Proprietary Mortgages: These are private loans. They are more expensive but often allow homeowners to borrow more than they can borrow with a HECM. Homeowners with expensive homes who want to borrow more than they can borrow with a HECM may consider this type of reverse mortgage.

There are a number of reasons why a reverse mortgage might become due and payable, some of which are:

- The homeowner dies
- The homeowner moves out of the home (for a period of one continuous year)
- The homeowner sells the home
- The homeowner fails to pay property taxes or keep the home insured
- The homeowner fails to maintain or repair the home
- The homeowner declares bankruptcy
- The homeowner abandons the property
- Perpetration of fraud or misrepresentation
- Eminent domain or condemnation proceedings

Additionally, default clauses may be added, which make the reverse mortgage due and payable:

- Renting all or a portion of the home out
- Adding a new owner to the home's title
- Taking out any new debt against the home
- Zoning classification changes

Reverse mortgages allow older homeowners to use equity in their homes to meet the expenses of living or to pay for home improvements. Borrowers are not required to repay the loan as long as they continue to live in the home.

Nontraditional Products

The SAFE Act defines a nontraditional mortgage product as any mortgage product other than a 30-year fixed-rate mortgage (12 U.S.C. §5102(7)). Therefore, a wide range of loans, including "traditional" straightforward ARMs and fixed-rate mortgages with a loan term of more or less than 30 years, are nontraditional products. Outlined below are examples of the exotic nontraditional products that were popular during the mortgage lending boom. Today, none of these is readily available to consumers, and with strict rules now in place that prohibit lending in any transactions without assessment of the ability of borrowers to repay their loans at the fully indexed rate, borrowers no longer have the incentive to pursue these types of transactions. The primary incentive for these loans was the ability to qualify for a loan using a low introductory rate. Now, this practice is not permitted.

Interest-Only Loans

Interest-only (I-O) loans developed during the mortgage industry and housing boom. They were typically used by individuals who wished to keep monthly payments low by only paying the interest due on the loan. Other borrowers obtained interest-only loans in order to qualify for a larger loan amount. Interest-only loans enabled them to do this since the interest-only payment is much lower than a fully-amortized principal and interest payment. Before the lending boom, typical candidates for interest-only loans were investors who purchased and sold properties within a short period of time. During the lending boom, many borrowers used these products to secure homes that were not realistically within their reach.

Because the structure of the loan requires payments of interest only, the borrower never builds equity in the property unless the value of the property increases. At the end of the loan term, the borrower essentially owes a balloon payment of the entire principal of the loan.

These loans are unlikely to ever find their way back into the consumer mortgage market, because new laws and regulations prevent borrowers from qualifying for interest-only loans based on initial amortizing payments. As discussed in greater detail in Module 3 of this course, the new Ability to Repay Rule (ATR Rule) requires an assessment of repayment ability in all closed-end mortgage transactions, and this assessment must be based on the ability of borrowers to repay their loans at the **"fully indexed rate"** (12 C.F.R. §1026.43(c)). The fully indexed rate is the rate that will apply after the introductory rate expires. With the ATR Rule eliminating any possibility of qualifying for an I-O loan based on its low introductory rate, consumers will no longer turn to these products as a way to secure a larger loan.

Reduced Documentation/No Documentation Loans

Reduced documentation loans – also known as "low doc" or "no doc" loans – are another type of mortgage that has become virtually unavailable in the marketplace. Low doc and no doc loans were initially used for self-employed individuals and other borrowers with income, debt and assets which were difficult to verify through standard underwriting documentation. However, as the housing market and mortgage industry growth increased, these programs were used by all types of borrowers.

The ATR Rule severely restricts the availability of these products by requiring verification of the information that a creditor relies on to determine a consumer's ability to repay a loan using reasonably reliable third-party records. Reduced documentation for most lending transactions is illegal, and these nontraditional mortgages are highly unlikely to return to the consumer mortgage market.

The other variations on nontraditional mortgages that are listed below are also unlikely to be a part of any negotiations for home loans, since provisions in the ATR Rule render them illegal. When these types of products were available, borrowers often paid additional fees that were intended to cover the risk of lending without full verification of income or assets. However, so many of these loans failed that the additional fees paid for their origination could not begin to cover the losses incurred.

No Ratio: Conforming loans require an underwriting analysis of a borrower's debt ratios, including the ratio of housing debt-to-income and ratio of total debt-to-income. In this type of nontraditional loan, the borrower's debt ratios were not considered.

No Income, No Assets (NINA): In a NINA loan program, no income or assets information was provided by the borrower, nor verified by the lender. Although income was not verified, the lender verified that the borrower was employed. Other requirements were also verified by the lender.

Stated Income, Stated Assets (SISA): In a SISA loan program, the borrower provided information about his/her income and assets. However, no documentation was provided, and the lender performed no verification of the information. Although income was not verified, the lender verified that the borrower was employed. Other requirements were also verified by the lender.

No Income, Verified Assets (NIVA): No income information was considered, however, assets were verified. Although income was not verified, the lender verified that the borrower was employed. Other requirements were also verified by the lender.

Stated Income, Verified Assets (SIVA): The borrower provided information on his/her income, however, no documentation was required, or verification on the actual income figures was performed. Assets, employment and other requirements were verified by the lender.

No Doc: In a no doc loan, the only documentation used was the credit report and appraisal. These loan programs relied on the value of the home and the borrower's credit history.

Nontraditional products are no longer readily available to consumers. With strict rules in place that prohibit lending without assessment of borrower repayment ability, consumers no longer have the incentive to pursue these types of transactions.

The New Mortgage Product Landscape

As noted earlier in this course, dramatic changes in the mortgage industry have eliminated or reduced many of the loan products that were available during the mortgage lending boom. Many lenders have drastically changed the way they make loans including much tighter underwriting guidelines and less availability of loan products. In many cases, the focus of FHA and the GSEs has been on keeping people in their homes versus supporting expansion of the housing market. The spotlight is primarily on **loss mitigation**, which involves avoiding lender losses due to default and foreclosure, as well as attempting to prevent a borrower's loss of his/her home.

In early 2008, Congress passed the Housing and Economic Recovery Act of 2008. The legislation was an amendment to the National Housing Act and was aimed at shoring up the failing economy by providing assistance and relief to the American public. A number of programs have emerged as part of the legislation as well as in response to troubles in the mortgage industry. Generally targeted at consumers with existing loans, they are intended to refinance or modify mortgage debt in order to prevent default or foreclosure. Programs such as President Obama's Home Affordable Refinance Program (a program that is intended to help homeowners who owe more on their homes than they are worth) are still available to consumers as a result of legislation that has extended them.

Loan Modifications

While loan modification is not a loan program, it is a hot topic in today's mortgage landscape. Many large lenders have a loan modification department or policy, although it is not always a procedure the average borrower is able to negotiate. Controversy has also surrounded the practice of loan modifications.

The basic definition of a loan modification is a permanent change in the terms of a loan (either term, interest rate or both) in response to a borrower's long-term inability to make payments. Additionally, loan modification may involve a change to the outstanding principal if the lender is willing/able to write a portion of the loan off. The controversy that has emerged is that lenders often will not consider a borrower eligible for a loan modification until he or she is already defaulting on the loan. Homeowners who are merely projecting a future inability to make payments have been turned away.

Freddie Mac's Single-Family News reports the following steps for lenders to take in a loan modification:

- Create a loan modification agreement and deliver two copies to the borrower – both copies require signatures and notarization
- Execute the loan modification within 25 days of Freddie Mac approval
- Submit the new loan terms for recordation, obtain title policy endorsement as needed and file the loan modification agreement
- Determine if the loan is active or inactive (for accounting and investor purposes)
- Report the loan modification to the investor

Fannie Mae suggests a number of options, in addition to loan modification, when a borrower is unable to make his or her mortgage payments:

Short Sale (or Pre-foreclosure Sale): A short sale occurs when the lender agrees to a reduced payoff on a loan when the subject property is sold. In other words, the borrower is allowed to sell the property for an amount that is less than the principal amount due on the mortgage and the lender releases its lien.

Forbearance: In a forbearance, the lender agrees to a reduction or suspension of loan payments for an agreed upon period of time. At the end of the period, the borrower is responsible for resuming payments and for making up past due amounts.

Assumption: Some mortgages are eligible for assumption. This is a method transferring the property to a new owner who takes over the outstanding mortgage debt.

Deed-in-lieu of Foreclosure: Obviously a last resort to other foreclosure avoidance methods, this method results in the homeowner voluntarily giving the deed to their property to the lender.

The most important regulatory development related to loan modification is the promulgation of rules by the Federal Trade Commission (FTC). These rules regulate the actions of individuals and companies that offer mortgage assistance relief services (MARS). The primary purpose of the MARS Rule is to protect consumers from falling prey to solicitations from businesses offering loan modification and foreclosure rescue programs. Countless consumers have found that they have given the last of their financial resources to fraudulent businesses or to individuals or companies that are unlikely to be able to offer the services promised. For example, many foreclosure rescue scams involve a request for upfront fees and a promise of foreclosure relief as soon as the fee is paid. Until they have parted with an advance payment and the promised relief fails to follow, consumers do not realize that they have been scammed.

The MARS Rule absolutely prohibits the solicitation or payment of advance fees for mortgage assistance relief services. Payment to a MARS provider is not allowed until the homeowner and his/her lender have executed an agreement that provides some form of mortgage assistance relief. The Rule also includes strict disclosure requirements, recordkeeping requirements, and prohibitions against making any misrepresentations.

Prohibited misrepresentations include:

- Misrepresentations about the likelihood of achieving results
- Misrepresentations about the time that it will take to achieve results, and
- Misrepresentations that lead the consumer to believe that the MARS provider is affiliated with or approved or endorsed by the federal government or by any state or federal agency

Understanding all of the provisions of the MARS Rule and establishing a compliance program that addresses the Rule is an important concern for all companies and for all individuals, including loan servicers and licensed loan originators who are attempting to meet some of the current needs of consumers in the mortgage market by providing loan modifications and other types of mortgage assistance relief services.

> *The basic definition of a loan modification is a permanent change in the terms of a loan (either term, interest rate or both) in response to a borrower's long-term inability to make payments.*

Terms Used in the Operation of the Mortgage Market

Loan Terms

Amortization: Periodic payments on a loan requiring payment of enough principal and interest to ensure complete repayment of the loan by the end of the loan term.

Negative Amortization: An amortization method in which the monthly payments are not large enough to pay all the interest due on the loan. This unpaid interest is added to the balance of the loan.

Closing Costs: At the time of closing, payment is due for a number of fees that relate to the cost of obtaining a loan, the transfer of ownership to the borrower, and the taxes and fees owed to the state and local government. Closing costs normally include an origination fee, property taxes, charges for title insurance and escrow costs, appraisal fees, etc. Closing costs will vary according to the area of the country and the lenders used. The borrower does not always cover all of the costs of closing. The parties to a lending transaction can negotiate the payment of certain closing costs.

Debt-to-Income Ratio: The relationship, expressed as a percentage, between a borrower's monthly obligations on long-term debts and his or her gross monthly income.

Discount Point: A fee paid in exchange for a reduction in the rate to something below the lender's quoted market rate. The payment "offsets" the lender's loss of return of interest over time from the reduced rate.

Earnest Money: Money paid by a buyer to a seller at the time of entering a contract to indicate intent and ability of the buyer to carry out the contract.

Equity: The difference between the fair market value of a property and the current balances of any liens against the property.

Escrow Account: An account held by the lender, on behalf of a borrower, into which the borrower deposits money for taxes and/or insurance payments. Escrow accounts may also hold other funds related to a real estate purchase such as earnest money.

Fees: Any kind of money paid in conjunction with a mortgage loan, other than the actual loan amount and interest. "Fees" might include third-party fees such as those for credit reports or appraisals, or origination/broker fees. Fees affect the total cost of credit when obtaining a loan.

Finance charge: Any kind of fees or charges associated with obtaining credit and paid to the lender, broker or for their benefit. Finance charges can include many items, including loan fees, broker fees, miscellaneous fees, per diem interest, and mortgage insurance, including the escrows for mortgage insurance, etc.

PFC: Prepaid finance charge.

POC: Paid outside of closing.

Prepayment Penalty: Fees charged for an early repayment of debt. Prepayment penalties are subject to laws that restrict the amount of the penalty and that limit the imposition of prepayment penalties to the early years of a loan.

Sales Contract: A legally binding agreement between a buyer and seller detailing the terms and conditions of the sale of real estate.

Seller Carry-Back: A purchase transaction, often involving an assumable mortgage, in which the party selling the property provides all or part of the financing.

Service Release Premiums (SRPs): Service release premiums (SRPs) are fees which lenders may receive for selling or transferring their right to service a mortgage loan.

Servicer: An individual or entity that services a loan by performing responsibilities such as sending statements to borrowers, accepting payments, issuing late payment notices, and managing escrow accounts.

> *"Negative amortization" occurs when the monthly payments are not large enough to pay all the interest due on the loan. This unpaid interest is added to the balance of the loan.*

Disclosure Terms

Adverse Action: The term used to describe a decision by a lender not to extend credit to a consumer on the terms that the consumer requested. Adverse action may be taken if it is determined that the potential borrower is not creditworthy or does not meet the requirements of a particular loan program – factors such as income, credit history, etc. may be considered when taking adverse action. It is illegal for a lender or creditor to take adverse action based on a consumer's personal characteristics such as race, gender, marital status, etc. ECOA requires that consumers are properly notified of their loan status within 30 days.

Affiliated Business Arrangement: An arrangement in which (A) a person who is in a position to refer business incident to or a part of a real estate settlement service involving a federally related mortgage loan, or an associate of such person, has either an affiliate relationship with or a direct or beneficial ownership interest of more than 1% in a provider of settlement services; and (B) either of such persons directly or indirectly refers such business to that provider or affirmatively influences the selection of that provider.

Annual Percentage Rate (APR): APR is a uniform measurement of the cost of a loan, including interest and financed costs of closing, expressed as a yearly percentage rate.

Finance Charge: A finance charge is a uniform measurement of the cost of a loan expressed as a dollar amount. It is the total of all fees and charges paid to lender or broker or for their benefit required to bring a loan to settlement.

Good Faith Estimate (GFE): The GFE is a disclosure due to a potential borrower within three business days of loan application (or immediately if the loan application is made via a face-to-face interview). It outlines a reasonable estimate of the costs and fees associated with the loan.

HUD-1 Settlement Statement: The HUD-1 is the standard settlement statement used to itemize all the payees and costs, fees, interest, etc. associated with a loan. It meets the requirements established by RESPA for a "uniform settlement disclosure."

HUD-1A: Is the version of the HUD-1 Settlement Statement used when there is no seller involved in the real estate transaction, such as with a refinance.

Loan Estimate: Effective August 1, 2015, this disclosure replaces the GFE and the Early Truth-in-Lending Disclosure.

Closing Disclosure: Effective August 1, 2015, this disclosure replaces the HUD-1 Settlement Statement and the final Truth-in-Lending Disclosure.

Note Rate: The note rate is the stated interest rate on a mortgage or loan agreement.

> *"APR" stands for "annual percentage rate," a uniform measurement of the cost of a loan, including interest and costs of closing, expressed as a yearly percentage rate.*

Financial Terms

Deed: A written instrument properly signed and delivered that conveys Title to real property.

Deed of Trust: In many states, a form of security agreement used to pledge a borrower's real property as security for the payment of a note. It is a three-party instrument in which the borrower assigns his/her ownership interest to a trustee who may sell the property and apply the net proceeds of the sale to the outstanding debt if the borrower fails to pay the note as agreed. This is in contrast to a mortgage (a two-party instrument) which assigns the borrower's ownership interest to the lender who may sell the property for non-payment of the debt.

Mortgage: A two- party instrument which assigns the borrower's ownership interest to the lender who may sell the property for non-payment of the debt.

Foreclosure: Foreclosure is the sale of property after a borrower's default on payments to satisfy the unpaid debt or breach of the loan contract. The exact procedure that the lender follows in order to foreclose on a piece of property depends on the presence or absence of a ***power of sale clause*** in the mortgage or deed of trust and the jurisdiction in which the property is located. If the mortgage or deed of trust does not include a power of sale clause, the lender must file a lawsuit, requesting the court to enter an order of foreclosure. This type of foreclosure is known as a ***judicial foreclosure***. When the mortgage or deed of trust includes a power of sale clause, the lender is not required to file a lawsuit in order to begin foreclosure proceedings. The power of sale clause authorizes the lender or trustee to sell the property to pay off the balance on the loan. This type of foreclosure proceeding is known as a ***non-judicial foreclosure***. Many non-judicial foreclosures proceed, with variations among states, along the following steps:

- At least 120 days before the foreclosure sale date, the lender must serve the borrower with a notice of default and record a notice of default in the county where the property is located.

- The lender must publish a notice of default once a week for four consecutive weeks, with the last notice appearing at least 20 days prior to the sale of the property.

- Sale of the property takes place by public auction, and the property must be sold to the highest bidder for cash.

- Prior to the sale, the borrower can cure the default by paying all past due amounts.

Interest: Interest is the money that a lender earns from a loan. The rate of interest that a lender charges for a mortgage depends on the current market rates for the type of loan that the borrower is seeking and the qualifications of the borrower.

The portion of each mortgage payment that represents a payment of interest on the loan depends on the type of mortgage that the borrower has chosen. The most common payment program includes monthly payments of the interest due and payment of enough of the principal to ensure that the principal is paid in full at the end of the loan term. This type of payment program is known as **mortgage amortization**. Amortization tables allow lenders to look up pre-calculated monthly payments for loans with fixed interest rates.

Other payment programs include:

- **Negative Amortization**: Negative amortization occurs when the mortgage payment is less than the interest currently due. The payment does not include any amount to reduce the principal balance, and because it does not include enough to pay the interest due, the loan balance increases over time. The primary reason that a borrower would agree to a payment plan that includes negative amortization is to reduce the size of payments at the beginning of the term of a loan. Many predatory lending laws try to protect consumers by prohibiting the use of negative amortization in high-cost loans.

- **Partial Amortization**: Partial amortization occurs when the mortgage payment includes the interest due and a small payment towards the principal that is not adequate to reduce the principal balance to zero by the end of the loan term.

- **Interest-Only Loan**: With an interest-only loan, the borrower pays the amount of interest due each payment period but makes no payment toward the principal. Therefore, at the end of the loan term, the borrower owes as much principal as he/she owed at the beginning of the term.

Discount Points: Discount points are a tool that borrowers can use to adjust the price of a loan. Points or discount points are fees that borrowers can pay to a lender to lower the interest rate on a mortgage. Each discount point costs 1% of the amount of the loan. The use of discount points to lower the rate of interest for the full term of a loan is known as a **Permanent Buy Down**. Whether it makes sense financially to pay points to obtain a permanent buy down will depend on how long the borrower intends to hold onto the property he/she is purchasing. Lenders or mortgage brokers can help borrowers to determine how long it will take them to recoup the cost of the points paid to reduce the interest rate.

Promissory Note: Neither a mortgage nor a deed of trust contains a borrower's contractual promise to repay a loan. The *note*, or *promissory note*, is the borrower's promise to repay the loan. The note includes:

- Identification of the borrower and the lender
- The borrower's promise to repay the loan
- Amount of the loan
- Interest rate charged on the unpaid principal
- Period of the term for repayment of the loan
- Reference to the real estate used to secure the loan
- Provisions for the imposition of late charges for overdue payments
- Signature(s) of borrower(s)

As the document that contains the borrower's promise to repay the loan, the note is the most important document in a lending transaction. Furthermore, the note is one of the documents that determines the rights of the parties if a dispute arises regarding the terms of the loan; the other is the security agreement or mortgage/deed of trust.

Fully Indexed Rate: In an ARM, the interest rate indicated by adding the current index value and the margin.

Index: A published interest rate used, when combined with a margin, as the basis upon which the note rate of ARM will adjust.

Securitization: The process of pooling similar types of loans to create mortgage backed securities for sale in the financial markets.

General Terms

Conforming Loan: A loan that meets the lending limits and other criteria established by Fannie Mae or Freddie Mac.

Conventional Loan: A mortgage that is not made under any federal program (i.e. not insured by the FHA or guaranteed by the VA or the USDA).

PITI: Principal, Interest, Taxes and Insurance are the monthly housing expenses that a lender calculates in order to determine a borrower's housing expense ratio.

Purchase Money Mortgage: A mortgage loan obtained by a borrower for the purchase of a residential property in which the property is the collateral for the loan.

Qualifying Ratios: Investor specific calculations used to determine if a borrower can qualify for a mortgage. They consist of two separate calculations: a housing expense ratio and total debt ratio.

Reconveyance: A clause in a mortgage that conveys title to a borrower once the loan is paid in full. This concept also applies to reconveyance contracts where homeowners have the option to repurchase their home pursuant to foreclosure assistance.

Refinance: Obtaining a new mortgage loan on a property already owned.

Revolving Debt: A type of credit arrangement in which a consumer is pre-approved for a line of credit and he/she may make purchases against that credit. Credit cards are a common form of revolving credit.

Subordinate Lien: A lien on property that is junior, or subsequent, to another lien, or liens based on the order of recordation or by agreement among the lenders. In the event of foreclosure, subordinate financing does not receive funds until prior liens are paid. Aka subordinate financing, junior lien, junior financing.

Subprime: Below the qualifications set for prime borrowers. Loans for borrowers who have either poor credit, an unstable income history, or high debt ratios.

Table Funding: The process whereby the broker closes a loan "using its own funds," so that the note and security agreement show it as the lender, but immediately (generally within one business day) assigns the loan to the ultimate lender, who actually brings the funds, as payment to the broker for the assignment, to the table and these are actually the monies which fund the loan.

Underwriting: The process of evaluating a loan applicant's financial information and facts about the real estate used to secure a loan to determine whether a potential loan is an acceptable risk (and on what terms) for a lender.

> *A "conventional loan" is a mortgage that is not made under any federal program (i.e. not insured by the FHA or guaranteed by the VA or the USDA).*

Discussion Scenario: Loan Products and Programs 1

Read each scenario and answer the question(s) based on the information you are provided.

Scenario 1: Jack Jackson and David Davidson are best friends who have decided to purchase homes in a popular development in their town. They are thrilled to find ranch-style homes for sale which are next door to each other on a shady tree-lined street. They are excited about their families growing up together and feel great about the long-term investment. They are able to purchase each property for $325,000 and they both have $25,000 available for down payment and closing costs.

Jack is a hardcore traditionalist. He has no problem with higher interest rates – he just doesn't like risk and doesn't want his payment to change. Because he has small children, he and his family are on a budget, and he hopes to keep his payments as low as possible.

David is also a traditionalist. He is adamant that he does not want an adjustable rate. However, his wife has a part-time job and they are not as concerned about their monthly payment. The Davidsons are willing to accept a higher monthly payment if they can pay their mortgage off faster.

Discussion Questions
- *What is the best loan product for the Jacksons?*
- *What about for the Davidsons?*

Scenario 2: Newlyweds Jeff and Jen Jefferson just moved to a new city and are excited to purchase their first home. Jeff struggled with some credit card debt coming out of college and has been working on improving his credit. Jen just got a new job with great earning potential, but based on their expenses, they are concerned about keeping their payments low for awhile. Over the past few years they have both worked on and off as freelancers, so at times their tax returns were filed as self-employed. Jen also had a period of unemployment following a massive layoff at her former employer. As a wedding gift, Jeff's parents have offered to provide them with a sizeable down payment.

They spoke with one loan originator who made some suggestions that seemed too good to be true – loans with deceptively low interest rates where they could potentially owe more over time, loans with payments that do not address the loan principal, loans where they would have larger payments in the future and loans where they do not need to provide employment documentation. They have been reading about loan programs that have led to loss of equity and foreclosure and have decided to get a "second opinion."

Discussion Questions

- *What are some of the risk factors an underwriter is going to want to consider with the Jeffersons?*
- *What kind of loan products might the other loan originator have been discussing with them?*
- *What kind of loan program might you suggest based on the information provided?*

Discussion Feedback

Scenario 1: Based on the information provided in the scenario, a 30-year fixed-rate is likely the best loan product for the Jacksons. It provides the least amount of risk and is generally a solid product for someone who will be living in a property for a long period of time. For the Davidsons, a fixed-rate loan is also appropriate. However, since they are more concerned about paying their loan off faster, a 15-year fixed-rate might be a good product for them to consider.

Scenario 2: Some of the Jefferson's risk factors that could be a concern include damaged credit, self-employment income and gaps in income. With their desire to keep their payments low, they might also have a high debt-to-income ratio.

Based on the limited information in the scenario, the first loan originator could have been recommending option ARMs, interest-only loans, loans with a balloon payment (or an adjustable-rate loan) and low doc loans, most of which are virtually unavailable in the current mortgage marketplace. These nontraditional loan products, combined with their risk factors, may create layers of risk which are unacceptable from an underwriting standpoint.

While more information may be needed, the Jeffersons might be good candidates for an FHA loan. Or, depending on the size of their down payment and how much "repair" Jeff has been able to do to his credit score, they could qualify for a conventional/conforming loan. While an option ARM is not a wise decision for these borrowers, an FHA or conventional adjustable-rate product such as a 3/1 ARM might be a good choice.

Securitization

Asset securitization began in the 1970s when banking institutions struggled with the traditional lending model and began to seek additional means for funding an increased demand for mortgage loans. To attract investors, investment bankers eventually developed vehicles that isolated defined mortgage pools, segmented the credit risk, and structured the cash flows from the underlying loans [83].

The Comptroller of the Currency lists a number of benefits of securitization:

For Loan Originators: Turns a lending business into an income stream that is less capital intensive, lowers borrowing costs.

For Investors: Offers attractive yields and increases secondary market liquidity.

For Borrowers: Makes credit available on terms that lenders may not be able to provide without securitization.

Securitization results in the lender being able to transfer active loans to another entity in exchange for new funds. When the active loans are sold, the lender has a renewed source of funds with which to make more loans. Instead of waiting for years over the course of a loan term for payments to come in, the lender has access to the funds all at once.

> *Asset securitization began when banking institutions struggled with the traditional lending model and began to seek additional means for funding an increased demand for mortgage loans.*

Discussion Scenario: Loan Products and Programs 2

Read the following descriptions and discuss/determine what type of loan product or program each borrower may have.

1. Sergeant Simpson just purchased a home. He was required to pay a funding fee and qualify based on a total debt ratio of 41%. His loan is: _____.

2. Retired veteran Sam Samuels and his wife Sarah have reached their golden years. They are both 70 and were disappointed when their investments fell short and did not adequately supplement Sam's Navy pension. They obtained a loan to help with their living expenses. The Samuels have: _____.

3. The Montgomerys just purchased 15 acres with a loan from a farm credit institution with no down payment. They will build a farmhouse on the land. They likely have: _____.

4. The Smiths had some credit problems for a few years but qualified for a loan program with a higher interest rate their lender offered in order to offset the increased credit risks. The Smiths have: _____.

5. The Morrisons have a loan with a fixed interest rate for seven years. At the end of seven years, they will be required to pay the remainder of their loan in full, although they have a conditional

refinance provision. The Morrisons have: _____.

6. Henry Henson and his wife Henrietta have decided to make a few upgrades around their home. Their kids are gone, they are ready to retire and they feel like it is time to add the things they have never had the money to do. They want to remodel their kitchen and add a whirlpool tub to their master bath. To pay the contractors, they take out a loan based on their equity. The loan is similar to a credit card – they only make payments based on funds they withdraw from the loan. The Hensons have: _____.

7. ABC Mortgage Company wants to take advantage of the safe harbor that it will enjoy from liability when it originates mortgages that amortize fully by the end of the loan's 30-year term, have points and fees that do not exceed 3% of the total loan amount, and that include no negative amortization features or balloon payments. It will also limit these transactions to borrowers whose debt-to-income ratios do not exceed 43%. The type of loan that it plans to focus on making is known as: _____.

Discussion Feedback

1. Sergeant Simpson has a **VA loan**. VA loans require payment of a funding fee and only consider the total debt ratio which must be 41% or less.

2. The Samuels have a **reverse mortgage**. The key indicators are the fact that they are both over 62 and need the loan to pay for living expenses. They will not have to repay the loan as long as they live in the home.

3. The Montgomerys likely have an **RHS loan**. These loans do not require a down payment and can be used to purchase a lot/home site in rural areas.

4. The Smiths have a **subprime loan**. Subprime loans were obtained by borrowers who had impaired credit or other qualification problems. A higher interest rate was intended to protect the lender in the event the borrower defaulted.

5. The Morrisons have a loan with a **balloon payment**. 7/23 is a typical loan with a balloon payment after seven years and a conditional refinance provision.

6. The Hensons have a **home equity line of credit** (HELOC). A HELOC acts like a credit card – the borrower is approved for a line of credit and only makes payments based on withdrawals they make from the credit line.

7. ABC Mortgage plans to focus on making **qualified mortgages**. Qualified mortgages must meet certain product feature prerequisites, including a loan term that does not exceed 30 years, points and fees that do not exceed 3% of the total loan amount, no balloon payments, no payment schedules that lead to negative amortization, and origination limited only to borrowers whose debt-to-income ratios do not exceed 43%.

Page left intentionally blank.

Mortgage Loan Origination Activities

Page left intentionally blank.

MORTGAGE LOAN ORIGINATION ACTIVITIES

Learning Objectives

This chapter was created based on the Mortgage Loan Origination Activities section of the NMLS National Test Content Outline. The topics found in this chapter, as in all other chapters, could likely appear on the NMLS national test in multiple choice question format. In this chapter, students will:

- Review the key players and steps in the loan origination process
- Achieve insight into the origination process and obtain tips on effective loan application communication
- Gain perspective on what underwriters look for in loan files in order to anticipate and avoid problems
- Practice some of the important financial calculations associated with the origination process
- Review the importance of borrower communication and how it can make or break successful loan origination
- Investigate each step of the loan cycle, from origination through funding and servicing, and learn about the roles of various individuals involved in the loan process
- Explore the Uniform Residential Loan Application in detail to ensure compliance
- Discover how to meet underwriter requirements and avoid underwriting pitfalls
- Learn about the responsibilities of the title company and information on the post-closing process
- Review the fundamentals of property ownership
- Explore the property appraisal process
- Review calculations as they pertain to debt ratios, borrower income, and loan amount
- Examine the components of a credit report

Introduction

The operational procedures for mortgage professionals align with federal and state laws, customer service best practices, mathematical concepts and documentation. In this course, students will review the importance of the loan application, qualification, processing, underwriting, qualifying ratios, specific program guidelines, closing and more.

APPLICATION INFORMATION AND REQUIREMENTS

Application Accuracy and Required Information (e.g. 1003)

Loan applicants must complete a mortgage loan application and provide documentation to show the veracity of the information provided in the application. In order to complete an application, it is also necessary to obtain documentation on the value of the property used to secure the loan.

The Uniform Residential Loan Application, also known as Form 1003, is the standard form that applicants must complete when applying for a mortgage.

Customer

The customers that mortgage professionals serve are most often referred to in federal lending laws and regulations as **"consumers."** While the purpose of lending laws has always been to protect consumers, defaults on home loans that led to millions of foreclosures in the United States resulted in efforts to offer more aggressive protection to consumers. The ultimate protection offered to consumers was the creation of the Consumer Financial Protection Bureau (CFPB), which officially began its operations on July 21, 2011.

By adopting legislation to create an agency that is singularly focused on protecting consumers in the financial marketplace, Congress replaced a system in which seven federal banking regulatory agencies regulated the offering of consumer financial products and services. Under this system, *"no single agency had effective tools to set the rules to oversee the whole market, and that is part of what led to an economic crash of epic proportions"* [84]. The "whole market" that the CFPB regulates includes non-depository lenders and mortgage brokers, as well as the loan originators employed by these entities. The federal banking regulatory agencies lacked jurisdiction over these "nonbanks." The CFPB has the authority to protect consumers in lending transactions that take place with these entities, as well as the authority to protect them during their transactions with banks, credit unions, and other traditional lenders.

Though the current lending market is characterized by a renewed focus on consumer protection, consumers must understand the responsibilities that they have to provide truthful information on a loan application and to make responsible borrowing decisions. Form 1003 contains an Acknowledgement and Agreement section which includes the borrower's (and co-borrower's) signature(s). This section requires the borrower to attest to the truthfulness of the information contained in the application. While honest mistakes may be corrected, it is important that all parties involved in a loan transaction understand the importance of truthfulness and accuracy in completing the loan application, as well as the legal implications of failing to be truthful and accurate. The gravity of failing to provide truthful information on a loan application is emphasized on the last page of the application with the following statement that borrowers must sign and acknowledge: *"We fully understand that it is a Federal crime punishable by fine or imprisonment, or both to knowingly make any false statements concerning any of the above facts as applicable under the provisions of Title 18, United States Code, section 1001, et seq."*

While not confirming all of the statements in the application, the mortgage loan originator is required to sign and essentially verify that all the questions were asked, answered, and recorded properly. By signing, the loan originator is indicating responsibility for his/her actions in completing the application.

When asking loan applicants to sign this final acknowledgment on their mortgage applications, loan originators should explain that under Title 18, Section 1001, it is a crime to knowingly and willfully make any verbal or written statement to the government that is materially false, fictitious or fraudulent. A loan application constitutes a statement to the government because it is used to secure a "federally-related mortgage." [1] A false statement on a loan application is "material" if it *"...has the 'natural tendency to influence or [is] capable of influencing the decision of the decision-making body to which it is addressed'...in other words, it is not necessary to show that your particular lie ever really influenced anyone"* [85].

Loan originators should also tell loan applicants that a violation of Title 18, Section 1001 may lead to a **five-year** jail term.

In conjunction with the loan application, some lenders may provide borrowers with the FBI Mortgage Fraud Warning Notice, which includes the following language:

> *Mortgage fraud is investigated by the Federal Bureau of Investigation and is punishable by up to 30 years in federal prison or $1,000,000, or both. It is illegal for a person to make any false statement regarding income, assets, debt, or matters of identification, or to willfully overvalue any land or property, in a loan and credit application for the purpose of influencing in any way the action of a financial institution.*

The Warning Notice was issued in March 2007 as a joint effort of the Mortgage Bankers Association and the FBI in combating mortgage fraud. Use of the FBI Warning Notice is not mandatory and is *"...completely voluntary. It is the lender's decision as to if and how the form should be worked into the loan origination process"* [86].

Fannie Mae and Freddie Mac are also involved in the fight against mortgage fraud [87]. Both of these GSEs have email addresses and phone numbers available for reporting mortgage fraud.

Freddie Mac has also created two forms for reporting mortgage fraud, and these are forms for:

- Reporting fraud affecting the servicing of Freddie Mac loans, which could include loan modification or foreclosure rescue scams
- Reporting fraud affecting the origination of Freddie Mac loans, which could include the submission of inaccurate information regarding the value of property used to secure a loan or the qualifications of a borrower

After completing these forms, they must be submitted to: mortgage_fraud_reporting@freddiemac.com.

> *Form 1003, the Uniform Residential Loan Application, is the standard application that applicants complete when applying for a mortgage.*

---

1   Recall that under RESPA, a "federally-related mortgage" is one that is made with funds insured by the government (such as FHA and VA loans), made with funds from a federally-regulated lender, intended for sale to Fannie Mae or Freddie Mac, or made by a creditor regulated under TILA.

Loan Originator

As mortgage brokers and other nonbank providers of mortgage loans and services became a growing presence, state legislators began paying attention to this unregulated group of professionals. The first licensing laws that appeared in state codes in the 1990s required licensing for mortgage companies. During the mid-2000s, state licensing requirements became stricter and began to include education and licensing programs for individual loan originators. In 2008, the federal government weighed in on the licensing of nonbanks and their employees by adopting the S.A.F.E. Mortgage Licensing Act, which requires loan originators in every state to meet education and licensing requirements.

Loan originators play a critical role in the mortgage lending process, since they are the individuals who interact directly with consumers to help them complete a loan application and to identify the supporting documentation required. Since most consumers only engage in the lending process a very limited number of times, they will look to loan originators for advice and guidance while completing the Uniform Residential Loan Application and considering loan product options.

Completing the Loan Application

The purpose of the application interview with the potential borrower is to obtain information to complete the loan application. This may take place in a face-to-face meeting, over the phone or even over the Internet.

The 1003 is a fairly extensive document and is used to compile a broad range of personal information about a potential borrower and the loan for which he or she is applying. Sections of the 1003 are discussed in the following sections.

As lenders, mortgage brokers, and their loan originators help borrowers to complete loan applications, compliance with the new Ability to Repay Rule (ATR Rule) and the Qualified Mortgage Rule (QM Rule) should be an ongoing consideration. These rules were mandated by the Dodd-Frank Act and are directly responsive to the pre-recession lending environment in which there was an epidemic of inaccurate disclosure of income and assets, failure to verify income and assets, and reliance on inaccurate appraisals. Now, the law prohibits creditors from entering a consumer credit transaction that is secured by a dwelling *"...unless the creditor makes a reasonable and good faith determination at or before consummation that the consumer will have a reasonable ability to repay the loan according to its terms"* 12 C.F.R. §1026.43(c)(1)). New regulations also provide that a creditor's "reasonable and good faith determination" must be based on verified and documented information (12 C.F.R. §1026.43(c)(2)). The section of this course on "Qualification: Processing and Underwriting" will review some of the specific requirements of these rules.

Section I: Type of Mortgage and Terms of Loan

Section I of the 1003 is the **"Type of Mortgage and Terms of Loan"** section. This section allows borrowers to choose the type of loan for which they are applying. There are specific boxes on the loan application for each loan type that must be checked. Borrowers will also fill out the loan amount that they are requesting.

The agency case number box is designated for the Federal Housing Administration (FHA), the Veterans Administration (VA) or the Rural Housing Service (RHS) case numbers. There is also a section for the lender's case numbers. Borrowers will not have these numbers, and loan originators need to apply for them.

After discussing the applicant's goals and while completing the application, the loan originator will fill out the interest rate and the length of time – also known as the term – that the borrower is requesting. The amortization type (fixed-rate, graduated payment, adjustable-rate) is also set forth in this section.

I. TYPE OF MORTGAGE AND TERMS OF LOAN						
Mortgage Applied for:	☐ VA ☐ FHA	☐ Conventional ☐ USDA/Rural Housing Service	☐ Other (explain):		Agency Case Number	Lender Case Number
Amount $	Interest Rate %	No. of Months	Amortization Type:	☐ Fixed Rate ☐ GPM	☐ Other (explain): ☐ ARM (type):	

Section II: Property information and Purpose of Loan

Section II of the 1003 – **"Property Information and Purpose of Loan"** - is used to provide information concerning the property address and how the loan proceeds will be used. The property address for the loan collateral is the address of the property that will be used to secure the loan. The address may be different from the applicant's primary address. The property address must include the city, state and zip code. Designation of the property type – a single-family home or a multi-unit – is disclosed here.

After the potential borrower provides the street address for the property securing the loan, a **"legal description"** is required. However, the legal description may not be immediately available since it is necessary to obtain it from the county recorder's office or through a title insurance company. A legal description of rural property is provided through the "metes and bounds system" or the "rectangular survey system," and property located in subdivisions is described using the **"subdivision lot and block system."** Under this system, land is surveyed and platted into blocks and/or numbered lots on a survey plat that is filed in the county recorder's office. An example of a legal description under the subdivision lot and block system is "Lot 6 of Block 2 of the Sunny Vale Subdivision Plat as recorded in May, Book 30, Page 22 at the Recorder of Deeds."

Section II requires the borrower to indicate whether the purpose of the loan is to purchase, construct, or refinance a home and to state whether the home will be a primary or secondary residence or an investment property. The information in this section varies, based on the purpose of the loan:

- **Construction or Construction-Permanent Loan**: The loan applicant must state the year the lot was acquired, the original cost, any existing liens against the lot, and the present value of the lot plus the cost of improvements. Borrowers may have questions regarding these types of loans. They need to understand that a construction loan is a loan of limited duration that allows the borrower to make several draws as funds are needed to complete construction of a new home. Some construction loans may have a balloon payment that is due at the period for construction, and borrowers must refinance the loan to make the balloon payment and secure a long-term mortgage. The mortgage that replaces the short-term loan is sometimes referred to as a "take-out loan." Another product that requires only one application and closing is a construction-to-permanent loan. This loan automatically converts from a construction loan to a long-term mortgage when the construction is complete. Borrowers may be required to pay a "conversion fee."

- **Refinance**: The loan applicant must state the year of acquiring the property, the original cost, the amounts of existing liens (such as a first mortgage), the purpose of the refinance (such as securing a better interest rate, making home improvements, or paying off debt), and the cost of improvements made or to be made.

The request in Section II for "Title" is a request for the borrower's legal name(s). Information provided under "Manner in Which Title Will be Held" is particularly important when the applicants are married. If the name of both the husband and wife will be on the title, the application should state that the title will be held by "Husband and Wife." If the borrower is single and unmarried, "Single" is the appropriate entry in this section of the application.

Section II also asks if estate will be held in "Fee Simple" or "Leasehold." While originating residential mortgage loans, it is not likely that loan originators will encounter a transaction involving a leasehold. Black's Law Dictionary defines **"leasehold"** as *"An estate in realty held under a lease; an estate for a fixed term or years"* [88]. A leasehold agreement may secure a purchaser's interest in real estate for many decades and can be sold. However, ownership is not permanent, and there may be limitations related to the use and disposition of the property. A **"fee simple"** is *"…one in which the owner is entitled to the entire property, with unconditional power of disposition during his life, and descending to his heirs…upon his death…"* [89]. Fee simple is the desired form of holding ownership to property because it has the fewest restrictions. Virtually every residential transaction involves an estate that is held in fee simple.

The final information requested in Section II is information on the "Source of Down Payment, Settlement Charges, and/or Subordinate Financing."

The source of funds for a down payment and for closing costs may be indicated as "Checking/Savings" if the borrower is using his/her own funds or as "Gift Funds" if the borrower is receiving a gift from a family member or friend to cover these costs.

Subordinate financing is debt that has a lower rank than a borrower's first mortgage. The ranking of debt is important because it determines the order in which a consumer's debt will be paid off. In its data entry instructions for Desktop Underwriter, Fannie Mae explains that the information that it is seeking from loan applicants on subordinate financing includes *The outstanding balances of subordinate liens, including drawn Home Equity Lines of Credit (HELOC) amounts and closed-end second mortgages that are secured by the subject property"* [90].

An example of a situation in which a lender needs to know about subordinate financing is a transaction in which a borrower wants to refinance a first mortgage and to hold on to a second mortgage that provides him/her with a line of credit. When the first mortgage is paid off during the refinancing, the second mortgage becomes the loan that has first priority. The lender may not agree to complete the refinance of the existing first mortgage unless the holder of the second mortgage agrees to allow its mortgage to remain in second place.

II. PROPERTY INFORMATION AND PURPOSE OF LOAN

Subject Property Address (street, city, state & ZIP)					No. of Units

Legal Description of Subject Property (attach description if necessary)					Year Built

Purpose of Loan	☐ Purchase ☐ Construction ☐ Other (explain): ☐ Refinance ☐ Construction-Permanent		Property will be: ☐ Primary Residence ☐ Secondary Residence ☐ Investment

Complete this line if construction or construction-permanent loan.

Year Lot Acquired	Original Cost	Amount Existing Liens	(a) Present Value of Lot	(b) Cost of Improvements	Total (a + b)
	$	$	$	$	$

Complete this line if this is a refinance loan.

Year Acquired	Original Cost	Amount Existing Liens	Purpose of Refinance	Describe Improvements ☐ made ☐ to be made	
	$	$		Cost: $	

Title will be held in what Name(s)	Manner in which Title will be held	Estate will be held in: ☐ Fee Simple ☐ Leasehold (show expiration date)

Source of Down Payment, Settlement Charges, and/or Subordinate Financing (explain)

Section III: Borrower Information

Section III of the loan application – **"Borrower Information"** – asks for the borrower's personal information. If the applicant has lived in his/her home for less than two years, residency information must be provided for the past two years. This information includes the other addresses where the borrower resided and an indication of whether the home was owned or rented. Contact information for the applicant is also necessary.

The applicant must provide personal information including social security number, age and number of dependents. Even though the age and number of dependents of the applicant is requested, the information cannot be used to discriminate in the mortgage transaction. Age is requested because the applicant must be of age to execute a contract. Information on the borrower's age may also be used as allowed under the Home Mortgage Disclosure Act (HMDA).

Borrower				III. BORROWER INFORMATION	Co-Borrower			
Borrower's Name (include Jr. or Sr. if applicable)					Co-Borrower's Name (include Jr. or Sr. if applicable)			
Social Security Number	Home Phone (incl. area code)	DOB (mm/dd/yyyy)	Yrs. School		Social Security Number	Home Phone (incl. area code)	DOB (mm/dd/yyyy)	Yrs. School
☐ Married ☐ Unmarried (include ☐ Separated single, divorced, widowed)		Dependents (not listed by Co-Borrower) no. ages			☐ Married ☐ Unmarried (include ☐ Separated single, divorced, widowed)		Dependents (not listed by Borrower) no. ages	
Present Address (street, city, state, ZIP)		☐ Own ☐ Rent ___ No. Yrs.			Present Address (street, city, state, ZIP)		☐ Own ☐ Rent ___ No. Yrs.	
Mailing Address, if different from Present Address					Mailing Address, if different from Present Address			
If residing at present address for less than two years, complete the following:								
Former Address (street, city, state, ZIP)		☐ Own ☐ Rent ___ No. Yrs.			Former Address (street, city, state, ZIP)		☐ Own ☐ Rent ___ No. Yrs.	

Section IV: Employment Information

Section IV of the loan application – **"Employment Information"** – is for the applicant's current and/or two-year employment history. Current employer's information must be provided; if the applicant has more than one employer, all must be listed. If the applicant has not been at his/her current job for two years or more, he/she must provide information on employment for the past two years. If the applicant is self-employed, this must also be specified. When two borrowers are signing the loan application, and using both of their incomes to qualify for a mortgage, it is necessary to include the two-year employment history of both. The application also asks for information on "Years employed in this line of work/profession." Continuous employment in the same line of work or profession is an attribute that lenders like to see on a loan application because it shows that the potential borrower has marketable skills and job stability.

Borrower			IV. EMPLOYMENT INFORMATION	Co-Borrower		
Name & Address of Employer	☐ Self Employed	Yrs. on this job	Name & Address of Employer	☐ Self Employed	Yrs. on this job	
		Yrs. employed in this line of work/profession			Yrs. employed in this line of work/profession	
Position/Title/Type of Business	Business Phone (incl. area code)		Position/Title/Type of Business	Business Phone (incl. area code)		

If employed in current position for less than two years or if currently employed in more than one position, complete the following:

Borrower			IV. EMPLOYMENT INFORMATION (cont'd)	Co-Borrower		
Name & Address of Employer	☐ Self Employed	Dates (from – to)	Name & Address of Employer	☐ Self Employed	Dates (from – to)	
		Monthly Income $			Monthly Income $	
Position/Title/Type of Business	Business Phone (incl. area code)		Position/Title/Type of Business	Business Phone (incl. area code)		
Name & Address of Employer	☐ Self Employed	Dates (from – to)	Name & Address of Employer	☐ Self Employed	Dates (from – to)	
		Monthly Income $			Monthly Income $	
Position/Title/Type of Business	Business Phone (incl. area code)		Position/Title/Type of Business	Business Phone (incl. area code)		

Section V: Monthly Income and Combined Housing Expense Information

Section V – **"Monthly Income and Combined Housing Expense Information"** – covers the information required to calculate an applicant's front and back debt-to-income ratios. When the applicant is asked for his/her income information, all income that the applicant wishes to reveal (applicants are not required to list child support or alimony payments received) should be listed. Income may come from sources other than regular or full-time employment that is identified in IV. Other sources of income, which must be documented if they are used for qualification, may include:

- Regular full-time and part-time employment, including second jobs
- Social security
- Child support
- Alimony
- Investment/rental property income

Housing expenses are also addressed in this section. The calculation for housing expenses should include mortgage payments, property taxes, association or condominium fees, mortgage insurance and homeowners/hazard insurance payments.

> *Section V, "Monthly Income and Combined Housing Expense Information," covers the information required to calculate an applicant's front and back debt-to-income ratios. Applicants are not required to list child support or alimony payments received.*

V. MONTHLY INCOME AND COMBINED HOUSING EXPENSE INFORMATION

Gross Monthly Income	Borrower	Co-Borrower	Total	Combined Monthly Housing Expense	Present	Proposed
Base Empl. Income*	$	$	$	Rent	$	
Overtime				First Mortgage (P&I)		$
Bonuses				Other Financing (P&I)		
Commissions				Hazard Insurance		
Dividends/Interest				Real Estate Taxes		
Net Rental Income				Mortgage Insurance		
Other (before completing, see the notice in "describe other income," below)				Homeowner Assn. Dues		
				Other:		
Total	$	$	$	Total	$	$

* Self Employed Borrower(s) may be required to provide additional documentation such as tax returns and financial statements.

Describe Other Income

Notice: Alimony, child support, or separate maintenance income need not be revealed if the Borrower (B) or Co-Borrower (C) does not choose to have it considered for repaying this loan.

B/C		Monthly Amount
		$

Section VI: Assets and Liabilities

Section VI – **"Assets and Liabilities"** – addresses the applicant's assets and liabilities, and the purpose of itemizing both is to calculate the borrower's net worth.

When completing this section of the loan application, loan originators need to ask the potential borrower if he/she is combining assets with a spouse, partner, or other co-borrower in order to qualify for a loan. If the loan applicant does not intend to include the assets of a co-borrower, he/she must check the "Not jointly" box in Section VI. The application states that the assets of another person cannot be used on the application unless *"...their assets and liabilities are sufficiently joined so that the Statement can be meaningfully and fairly presented on a combined basis...."* Obviously, if the application includes the assets of a spouse, partner or co-borrower, the application must indicate that the Statement of Assets and Liabilities is prepared "Jointly."

Liquid assets include:

- Deposit or "Earnest Money" held in escrow towards the purchase of the home
- Cash
- Checking accounts, with account numbers provided
- Savings accounts, with account numbers provided
- Stocks and bonds, and the loan applicant can state how much he/she believes they are worth. If the value of these assets becomes an important factor in securing the loan, the lender may ask for an investment statement.
- Cash value and face amount of life insurance policies

Below the area where cash, checking and savings accounts, stocks and bonds and life insurance are listed, there is a space for providing "Subtotal Liquid Assets." These assets are referred to as "liquid" because they are readily accessible. Even stocks, bonds, and investment grade life insurance policies may be cashed in without great difficulty.

After the itemization of "liquid assets," the application provides a space for the non-liquid assets represented by:

- Real estate
- Retirement accounts (such as IRAs, 401Ks, etc.)
- Net worth of businesses
- Automobiles

These assets are regarded as "non-liquid" because they are not readily converted into cash. Borrowers may provide their opinion of what these assets are worth. The space for "Other Assets" may include personal property. "Total Assets" include the grand total of liquid, non-liquid, and other assets.

Liabilities include:

- Debts for medical bills
- Credit cards
- Mortgages
- Judgments
- Consumer loans
- Student loans
- Alimony payments
- Child support payments

Asking loan applicants to produce monthly statements for mortgages and consumer debt such as credit cards and car payments can help the loan applicant and originator to accurately represent the applicant's liabilities.

Section VI, "Assets and Liabilities," addresses the applicant's assets and liabilities, in order to calculate the borrower's net worth. If the loan applicant does not intend to include the assets of a co-borrower, he/she must check the "Not jointly" box in Section VI.

VI. ASSETS AND LIABILITIES

This Statement and any applicable supporting schedules may be completed jointly by both married and unmarried Co-Borrowers if their assets and liabilities are sufficiently joined so that the Statement can be meaningfully and fairly presented on a combined basis; otherwise, separate Statements and Schedules are required. If the Co-Borrower section was completed about a non-applicant spouse or other person, this Statement and supporting schedules must be completed about that spouse or other person also.

Completed ☐ Jointly ☐ Not Jointly

ASSETS	Cash or Market Value	Liabilities and Pledged Assets. List the creditor's name, address, and account number for all outstanding debts, including automobile loans, revolving charge accounts, real estate loans, alimony, child support, stock pledges, etc. Use continuation sheet, if necessary. Indicate by (*) those liabilities, which will be satisfied upon sale of real estate owned or upon refinancing of the subject property.		
Description				
Cash deposit toward purchase held by:	$			
List checking and savings accounts below		LIABILITIES	Monthly Payment & Months Left to Pay	Unpaid Balance
Name and address of Bank, S&L, or Credit Union		Name and address of Company	$ Payment/Months	$
Acct. no.	$	Acct. no.		
Name and address of Bank, S&L, or Credit Union		Name and address of Company	$ Payment/Months	$
Acct. no.	$	Acct. no.		
Name and address of Bank, S&L, or Credit Union		Name and address of Company	$ Payment/Months	$
Acct. no.	$	Acct. no.		

VI. ASSETS AND LIABILITIES (cont'd)			
Name and address of Bank, S&L, or Credit Union		Name and address of Company	$ Payment/Months	$
Acct. no.	$	Acct. no.		
Stocks & Bonds (Company name/ number & description)	$	Name and address of Company	$ Payment/Months	$
		Acct. no.		
Life insurance net cash value	$	Name and address of Company	$ Payment/Months	$
Face amount: $				
Subtotal Liquid Assets	$			
Real estate owned (enter market value from schedule of real estate owned)	$			
Vested interest in retirement fund	$			
Net worth of business(es) owned (attach financial statement)	$	Acct. no.		
Automobiles owned (make and year)	$	Alimony/Child Support/Separate Maintenance Payments Owed to:	$	
Other Assets (itemize)	$	Job-Related Expense (child care, union dues, etc.)	$	
		Total Monthly Payments	$	
Total Assets a.	$	Net Worth (a minus b) ▶	$	Total Liabilities b.	$

Schedule of Real Estate Owned (If additional properties are owned, use continuation sheet.)

Property Address (enter S if sold, PS if pending sale or R if rental being held for income) ▼	Type of Property	Present Market Value	Amount of Mortgages & Liens	Gross Rental Income	Mortgage Payments	Insurance, Maintenance, Taxes & Misc.	Net Rental Income
		$	$	$	$	$	$
Totals		$	$	$	$	$	$

List any additional names under which credit has previously been received and indicate appropriate creditor name(s) and account number(s):

Alternate Name	Creditor Name	Account Number

Section VII: Details of Transaction

Section VII – **"Details of Transaction"** – is for specific information about the proposed transaction. The transaction information section is used to display how much money the borrower will need in order to get the loan to closing. The following information is detailed in this section:

- **Purchase Price** – The purchase price is the sale price of the property outlined in the sales contract.
- **Alterations, Improvements, Repairs** – Estimated cost for alterations, improvements and repairs are identified.
- **Land** – The cost of land, if purchased separately, from the cost noted in the purchase price.
- **Refinance** – Debts to be paid off in a refinance transaction.
- **Estimated Prepaid Items** – These are items paid in advance. Examples of prepaid items

are homeowner's insurance, escrows, interest and tax payments.

- **Estimated Closing Costs** – Costs charged in a loan transaction such as origination fees, processing fees, appraisal fees, title fees and recording fees.

- **Private Mortgage Insurance (PMI), Mortgage Insurance Premiums (MIP), Funding Fee** – This is the upfront private mortgage insurance fee, upfront mortgage insurance premium or VA funding fee that is charged to the borrower as a part of the loan transaction.

- **Discount** – The discount fee is a charge paid by the borrower to reduce the interest rate on the mortgage. It is generally expressed in percentages or points. A point is 1% of the loan amount.

- **Total Costs** – The above items are added together to get the estimated total cost of the loan.

- **Subordinate Financing** – Financing that a borrower will receive in addition to the loan amount identified in Section I of the 1003. Subordinate financing may include a second mortgage or a Home Equity Line of Credit (HELOC).

- **Borrower's Closing Costs Paid by Seller** – This will identify contributions that will be made by the seller to the borrower at the time of closing. It generally appears on the HUD-1 Settlement Statement as a seller's contribution or a seller's credit.

- **Other Credits** – May appear as a grant, a gift, a broker's credit or a lender's credit.

- **PMI, MIP, Funding Fee Financed** – For the purpose of calculating cost, the PMI, MIP or funding fee can either be paid by the borrower out of pocket, or it can be financed as a part of the loan. This line identifies whether the PMI, MIP or funding fee will be financed.

- **Loan Amount** – The amount identified in Section I of the 1003.

- **Cash From/To Borrower** – The cash from or to the borrower is identified by subtracting the cost of the loan from the credits. The result is what needs to be communicated to the borrower prior to closing, after preparing the final 1003. The amount may vary slightly, but it will serve as a good estimate.

VII. DETAILS OF TRANSACTION		
a.	Purchase price	$
b.	Alterations, improvements, repairs	
c.	Land (if acquired separately)	
d.	Refinance (incl. debts to be paid off)	
e.	Estimated prepaid items	
f.	Estimated closing costs	
g.	PMI, MIP, Funding Fee	
h.	Discount (if Borrower will pay)	
i.	Total costs (add items a through h)	

VII. DETAILS OF TRANSACTION		
j.	Subordinate financing	
k.	Borrower's closing costs paid by Seller	
l.	Other Credits (explain)	
m.	Loan amount (exclude PMI, MIP, Funding Fee financed)	
n.	PMI, MIP, Funding Fee financed	
o.	Loan amount (add m & n)	
p.	Cash from/to Borrower (subtract j, k, l & o from i)	

Section VIII: Declarations

Section VIII – **"Declarations"** – contains questions that enable a lender to determine if the potential borrower is subject to other matters that may impact his/her ability to repay the loan. Such matters include:

- Outstanding judgments
- Involvement as a party to a lawsuit
- Financial obligations as a cosigner or endorser on a loan for which another borrower is principally responsible
- Obligations to repay money borrowed for use as a down payment in the current transaction
- Obligations to pay alimony or child support

The loan applicant must make other declarations that serve as evidence of his/her financial responsibility. These declarations include:

- Any bankruptcies within the past seven years
- Any foreclosure within the past seven years
- Surrender of deed in lieu of foreclosure within the past seven years
- Delinquencies of federal debt, which would include student loan debt
- Ownership interest in another property within the past three years (answering this question is only required if the loan applicant intends to occupy the dwelling that will secure the present loan as his/her primary residence)

The declarations also require the loan applicant to disclose his/her status as a U.S. citizen or as a permanent resident alien.

It is important to remind the borrower that the questions must be answered truthfully and completely, and that untruthful responses may be considered fraud, subjecting the loan applicant to prosecution.

The lender may ultimately verify the responses through a third party verification process. If the verification reveals something contrary to the applicant's response, the applicant should be notified and the 1003 should be adjusted accordingly. The underwriter may request additional information or mitigating information pursuant to underwriting guidelines.

> *Section VIII, "Declarations," contains questions that enable a lender to determine if the potential borrower is subject to other liabilities that may impact his/her ability to repay the loan.*

VIII. DECLARATIONS				
If you answer "Yes" to any questions a through i, please use continuation sheet for explanation.	Borrower		Co-Borrower	
	Yes	No	Yes	No
a. Are there any outstanding judgments against you?	☐	☐	☐	☐
b. Have you been declared bankrupt within the past 7 years?	☐	☐	☐	☐
c. Have you had property foreclosed upon or given title or deed in lieu thereof in the last 7 years?	☐	☐	☐	☐
d. Are you a party to a lawsuit?	☐	☐	☐	☐
e. Have you directly or indirectly been obligated on any loan which resulted in foreclosure, transfer of title in lieu of foreclosure, or judgment?	☐	☐	☐	☐

(This would include such loans as home mortgage loans, SBA loans, home improvement loans, educational loans, manufactured (mobile) home loans, any mortgage, financial obligation, bond, or loan guarantee. If "Yes," provide details, including date, name, and address of Lender, FHA or VA case number, if any, and reasons for the action.)

VIII. DECLARATIONS				
If you answer "Yes" to any questions a through i, please use continuation sheet for explanation.	Borrower		Co-Borrower	
	Yes	No	Yes	No
f. Are you presently delinquent or in default on any Federal debt or any other loan, mortgage, financial obligation, bond, or loan guarantee?	☐	☐	☐	☐
g. Are you obligated to pay alimony, child support, or separate maintenance?	☐	☐	☐	☐
h. Is any part of the down payment borrowed?	☐	☐	☐	☐
i. Are you a co-maker or endorser on a note?	☐	☐	☐	☐
--				
j. Are you a U.S. citizen?	☐	☐	☐	☐
k. Are you a permanent resident alien?	☐	☐	☐	☐
l. Do you intend to occupy the property as your primary residence?	☐	☐	☐	☐
If "Yes," complete question m below.				
m. Have you had an ownership interest in a property in the last three years?	☐	☐	☐	☐
(1) What type of property did you own—principal residence (PR), second home (SH), or investment property (IP)?	_____		_____	
(2) How did you hold title to the home— by yourself (S), jointly with your spouse (SP), or jointly with another person (O)?	_____		_____	

Section IX: Acknowledgment and Agreement

Section IX – **"Acknowledgment and Agreement"** – allows applicants to affirm that they understand the purpose of the loan application and any loan that is offered as a result of the application will be secured by a deed of trust on the property described in the application. Applicants are required to sign this section and acknowledge that all information contained in the 1003 is true and correct to the best of their knowledge. As previously noted, loan originators should advise loan applicants that failure to truthfully complete the application could result in civil liability or criminal prosecution for mortgage fraud.

IX. ACKNOWLEDGEMENT AND AGREEMENT

Each of the undersigned specifically represents to Lender and to Lender's actual or potential agents, brokers, processors, attorneys, insurers, servicers, successors and assigns and agrees and acknowledges that: (1) the information provided in this application is true and correct as of the date set forth opposite my signature and that any intentional or negligent misrepresentation of this information contained in this application may result in civil liability, including monetary damages, to any person who may suffer any loss due to reliance upon any misrepresentation that I have made on this application, and/or in criminal penalties including, but not limited to, fine or imprisonment or both under the provisions of Title 18, United States Code, Sec. 1001, et seq ; (2) the loan requested pursuant to this application (the "Loan") will be secured by a mortgage or deed of trust on the property described in this application; (3) the property will not be used for any illegal or prohibited purpose or use; (4) all statements made in this application are made for the purpose of obtaining a residential mortgage loan; (5) the property will be occupied as indicated in this application; (6) the Lender, its servicers, successors or assigns may retain the original and/or an electronic record of this application, whether or not the Loan is approved; (7) the Lender and its agents, brokers, insurers, servicers, successors, and assigns may continuously rely on the information contained in the application, and I am obligated to amend and/or supplement the information provided in this application if any of the material facts that I have represented herein should change prior to closing of the Loan; (8) in the event that my payments on the Loan become delinquent, the Lender, its servicers, successors or assigns may, in addition to any other rights and remedies that it may have relating to such delinquency, report my name and account information to one or more consumer reporting agencies; (9) ownership of the Loan and/or administration of the Loan account may be transferred with such notice as may be required by law; (10) neither Lender nor its agents, brokers, insurers, servicers, successors or assigns has made any representation or warranty, express or implied, to me regarding the property or the condition or value of the property; and (11) my transmission of this application as an "electronic record" containing my "electronic signature," as those terms are defined in applicable federal and/or state laws (excluding audio and video recordings), or my facsimile transmission of this application containing a facsimile of my signature, shall be as effective, enforceable and valid as if a paper version of this application were delivered containing my original written signature.

Acknowledgement. Each of the undersigned hereby acknowledges that any owner of the Loan, its servicers, successors and assigns, may verify or reverify any information contained in this application or obtain any information or data relating to the Loan, for any legitimate business purpose through any source, including a source named in this application or a consumer reporting agency.

Borrower's Signature	Date	Co-Borrower's Signature	Date
X		X	

> *Applicants are required to sign Section IX, acknowledging that all information contained in the 1003 is true and correct to the best of their knowledge.*

Section X: Information for Government Monitoring Purposes

The final section on the 1003 – **"Information for Government Monitoring Purposes"** – is related to government statistics. The section is referred to as the Home Mortgage Disclosure Act (HMDA) Section. It requests information regarding race, sex and ethnicity. The application includes a paragraph explaining that none of this information can be used to discriminate against the loan applicant, stating that the applicant can opt not to complete this section. If the applicant decides not to furnish this information, it will be up to the loan originator to make an "educated guess" concerning the demographic information to report to the government (only in regards to face-to-face applications; not internet, mail, or telephone).

| X. INFORMATION FOR GOVERNMENT MONITORING PURPOSES | | | | | |

The following information is requested by the Federal Government for certain types of loans related to a dwelling in order to monitor the lender's compliance with equal credit opportunity, fair housing and home mortgage disclosure laws. You are no t required to furnish this information, but are en couraged to do so. The law p rovides that a le nder m ay not discriminate ei ther on t he basis of this information, or on whether you choose to furnish it. If y ou furnish the information, please provide both ethnicity and race. Fo r race, you m ay check m ore than one designation. If you do not furnish ethnicity, race, or sex, under Federal regulations, this lender is required to note the information on the basis of visual observation and surname if you have made this application in person. If you do not wish to furnish the information, please check the box below. (Lender must review the above material to assure that the disclosures satisfy all requirements to which the lender is subject under applicable state law for the particular type of loan applied for.)

BORROWER ☐ I do not wish to furnish this information			CO-BORROWER ☐ I do not wish to furnish this information		
Ethnicity: ☐ Hispanic or Latino ☐ Not Hispanic or Latino			**Ethnicity:** ☐ Hispanic or Latino ☐ Not Hispanic or Latino		
Race:	☐ American Indian or Alaska Native ☐ Native Hawaiian or Other Pacific Islander	☐ Asian ☐ White ☐ Black or African American	**Race:**	☐ American Indian or Alaska Native ☐ Native Hawaiian or Other Pacific Islander	☐ Asian ☐ White ☐ Black or African American
Sex: ☐ Female ☐ Male			**Sex:** ☐ Female ☐ Male		

To be Completed by Loan Originator:
This information was provided:
- ☐ In a face-to-face interview
- ☐ In a telephone interview
- ☐ By the applicant and submitted by fax or mail
- ☐ By the applicant and submitted via e-mail or the Internet

Loan Originator's Signature X		Date
Loan Originator's Name (print or type)	Loan Originator Identifier	Loan Originator's Phone Number (including area code)
Loan Origination Company's Name	Loan Origination Company Identifier	Loan Origination Company's Address

If information is missing from the application, the loan originator should make an effort to notify the applicant immediately and allow him/her a reasonable amount of time in which to furnish it. Applicants must be made aware of the status of their loan application in writing within **30 days** of the date of application. Evidence of this notification must be kept in the loan file.

Verification and Documentation

After completing a loan application, an applicant must provide documentation to support the information disclosed in the application. These documents include:

- **Requests for Verification of Employment (VOE)**: If the applicant is salaried and is not self-employed, he/she will sign a VOE, which the lender will forward to the applicant's employer for verification of employment and income. If the applicant has not held his/her current employment for two years, the lender will also send a VOE to the previous employer. Lenders may also request W-2 forms, pay stubs, and tax forms.

  Lenders are not likely to consider overtime and bonus pay as part of a loan applicant's income unless the applicant can show that he/she has received the additional income consistently for at least two years, and the employer indicates that the overtime or bonus pay is likely to continue.

- **Requests of Verification of Deposit (VOD)**: A Verification of Deposit is a document signed by the loan applicant's bank or other depository institution verifying the applicant's balance in the account and the account history.

- **Special Considerations for Applicants with Commission Income or Self-Employment**: Lenders ask for additional documentation when calculating the income of loan applicants who earn commission income and when calculating the income of self-employed loan applicants.

- **Commission Income**: Lenders will require copies of income tax returns for the past two years and information on current income if commissions represent 25% or more of an applicant's annual income. In order to account for the variability of an applicant's commissions, lenders will average the past two years of income.

- **Income of Self-Employed Applicants**: A self-employed applicant must show that he/she has maintained an income for two years in order to qualify for a mortgage loan. Lenders will not rely on a verification of employment from a self-employed applicant. Lenders will request additional documentation to verify income. These documents may include:
  - Tax returns for the past two years
  - A year-to-date profit and loss statement
  - Balance sheets for the past two years
  - A self-employed income analysis

Suitability of Products and Programs

"Loan suitability" is a term that refers to the diligent matching of loan programs with the financial circumstances of consumers. The debate over loan suitability began when a booming mortgage market offered loan applicants a wide range of exotic mortgages, including interest-only and payment-option loans. The question of loan suitability seemed to be particularly relevant in transactions involving first-time and subprime borrowers who were unable to qualify for safer and more traditional mortgages. The debate heated up in 2007, when record numbers of borrowers began to default on these loans. Some lenders, legislators, and consumer groups advocated the adoption of new laws requiring a more rigorous analysis of borrower repayment ability and consideration of borrowers' long-term and short-term goals. Others argued that borrowers must ultimately bear the responsibility for deciding what type of loan product is best suited to meet their individual needs.

When the housing and mortgage markets began collapsing in 2007, market and legislative responses had the effect of creating loan suitability standards. With a record number of defaults occurring on home loans, products such as subprime loans and exotic nontraditional mortgages rapidly disappeared from the market. When this happened, originators were no longer able to offer consumers risky mortgages, and lending decisions were once again limited to the suitability of fixed- versus adjustable-rate loans. The Congressional response to the debate over loan suitability is found in the Dodd-Frank Act. This law includes provisions that create higher lending standards for all mortgages, and it imposes requirements for a thorough analysis of repayment ability in most transactions for home loans. These provisions of the law are implemented through the Ability to Repay Rule (ATR Rule), which became effective in January 2014. Other provisions of the Dodd-Frank Act encourage consumers to make safer borrowing choices by requiring homeownership counseling for riskier loan products.

The Ability to Repay Rule and Loan Suitability

From the late 1990s through 2006, housing prices were escalating, and many consumers were afraid that by hesitating to buy a home, they would soon be priced out of the market. It was this fear that led many to accept loans with artificially low introductory rates and payment schedules that allowed principal loan balances to increase. Undoubtedly, many loan originators believed that by providing "creative financing options," they were making the dream of homeownership a reality for many consumers.

While these transactions enabled many borrowers to finance the purchase of a home, the products failed in terms of long-term suitability. As the introductory interest rates on creatively-financed loans expired, countless borrowers were unable to make payments based on their new rates. These events demonstrated the importance of looking at the long-term suitability of a loan.

The most critical component of long-term loan suitability is matching a borrower with a loan that he or she can repay. New laws and regulations, including the Ability to Repay Rule, have made it illegal to approve a consumer for a loan based solely on his or her ability to make the initial payments calculated at the introductory rate. The ATR Rule prohibits a creditor from entering a consumer credit transaction that is secured by a dwelling *"...unless the creditor makes a reasonable and good faith determination at or before consummation that the consumer will have a reasonable ability to repay the loan according to its terms"* (12 C.F.R. §1026.43(c)(1)). The Rule also provides that a creditor's "reasonable and good faith determination" must be based on verified and documented information (12 C.F.R. §1026.43(c)(2)).

The ATR Rule applies to all mortgages other than open-end home equity loans, reverse mortgages, and timeshare plans (12 C.F.R. §1026.43(a)). It is the ATR Rule that no longer allows borrowers to qualify for a mortgage based on its introductory rate. Instead, they must qualify based on their ability to make payments when the interest rate on their loan resets.

> *"Loan suitability" is a term that refers to the diligent matching of loan programs with the current financial circumstances of each customer. Revisions to some laws have made loan suitability a legal standard that originators are required to meet.*

Financial and Homeownership Counseling

Homeownership counseling is a prerequisite for obtaining a home loan in certain types of lending transactions. The purpose of these provisions is to provide borrowers with information that they need in order to understand whether a loan product is suitable for them.

Loan counseling requirements include:

- **Counseling Requirement for Accepting High-Cost Home Loans**: Amendments to the Home Ownership and Equity Protection Act (HOEPA) and its implementing regulations impose a requirement on borrowers to complete counseling with a HUD-approved counselor before accepting a loan that is a high-cost mortgage under HOEPA (12 C.F.R. §1026.32(a)(5)).

- **Counseling Requirement for Accepting Negative Amortization Loans**: First-time borrowers must complete counseling with a HUD-approved counselor before accepting a negative amortization loan (12 C.F.R. §1026.36(k)).

- **Counseling Requirement for FHA HECMs**: A borrower who is seeking a reverse mortgage from the FHA must complete counseling with a HUD-approved counselor.

HUD has always encouraged counseling for borrowers who consider an adjustable-rate mortgage (ARM) instead of a fixed-rate loan. As discussed below, resources are readily available that can help loan originators to counsel customers on the advisability of accepting these riskier mortgage products.

Counseling for ARMs

When adjustable-rate mortgages became increasingly popular mortgage products in the 1980s, the Federal Reserve Board created the *Consumer Handbook on Adjustable-Rate Mortgages* (the CHARM booklet) to ensure that consumers would not enter lending agreements for ARMs without considering their risks as well as their advantages. The Federal Reserve updated the CHARM booklet in 2006 to address the risks of new types of ARMs such as interest-only ARMs and payment-option ARMs. A copy of the CHARM booklet is available online at the CFPB website [91].

Use of the CHARM booklet is mandatory under TILA. When loan originators give the booklet to customers, they should strongly encourage them to read the contents and to ask any questions that arise after completing a review of the brochure.

> *Homeownership counseling is a prerequisite for obtaining several different types of home loans. These include high-cost home loans, negative amortization loans, and HECMs.*

Disclosures

As a consumer protection measure, and as a legal compliance measure, the timing and accuracy of disclosures is an important component of loan origination. Lending laws and regulations create long lists of obligatory disclosures. The disclosures are intended to:

- Educate consumers
- Provide consumers with information on loan costs
- Notify consumers of risky lending terms
- Notify consumers of their rights under federal lending laws
- Ensure that consumers know the status of their loan applications
- Give notice to consumers about changes in the servicing of their loans

Following is a list of the requisite disclosures, grouped according to their purposes.

Informational Disclosures to Educate the Consumer

The reason for requiring informational disclosures, such as the CHARM booklet, is that the information contained in the disclosures can educate consumers, and educated consumers may make better decisions when choosing between different mortgage products.

- **Settlement Cost Information Booklet**: Required by RESPA and due three business days after the completion of a loan application for a purchase transaction, this booklet reviews the settlement process and outlines the rights and protections that the law creates for borrowers (12 C.F.R. §1024.6(a)).

- **CHARM Booklet**: Required by TILA within three business days of application for all ARMs, this booklet alerts consumers to the risks of accepting an ARM (12 C.F.R. §1026.19(b)(1)).

- **Early ARM Disclosure (Adjustable-Rate Disclosure)**: Required by TILA and due within three business days of application, this disclosure must include a clear notice that payment or loan terms can change, and details on calculation of rate changes and the impact of rate changes on payments and loan amortization. A model disclosure form is provided in Regulation Z (12 C.F.R. §1026.19(b)(2)).

- **Loan Estimate**: Effective August 1, 2015, this disclosure, which integrates TILA and RESPA disclosures, replaces the Early ARM Disclosure and the Good Faith Estimate.

- **When Your Home is On the Line**: What You Should Know About Home Equity Lines of Credit: This booklet is required by TILA for loan applicants who are considering home equity loans (12 C.F.R. §1026.40(e)).

Disclosures to Inform the Consumer about the Costs of a Loan

Disclosures regarding the cost of a loan and the fees associated with its closing are intended to provide the consumer with information that he/she can use to shop competitively for a mortgage loan and for settlement service providers. Other disclosures are intended to help consumers anticipate costs associated with a loan that will occur after closing and throughout the loan term.

- **Good Faith Estimate**: Required by RESPA and due within three business days after the submission of a loan application, the GFE provides an estimate of settlement costs that will be due at the time of closing (12 C.F.R. §1024.7).

- **Loan Estimate**: Effective August 1, 2015, this disclosure, which integrates the RESPA and TILA disclosures, replaces the Good Faith Estimate and the early TIL Disclosure.

- **HUD-1 Settlement Statement**: Required by RESPA and due at the time of closing, borrowers may request a copy of the HUD-1 one business day prior to settlement. Copies of the HUD-1 are prepared for both the buyer and seller at closing. The HUD-1A is used in refinance transactions where there is no seller (12 C.F.R. §1024.8).

- **Closing Disclosure**: Effective August 1, 2015, this disclosure, which integrates TILA and RESPA disclosures about the costs of a loan and settlement fees, replaces the HUD-1 and the final TIL Disclosure.

- **Initial Escrow Statement**: Required by RESPA and due 45 days after closing, this disclosure is often provided at the time of closing. The initial escrow statement provides an estimate of escrow payments (taxes, insurance, etc.) that will be required in the first 12 months of the loan (12 C.F.R. §1024.17(g)).

- **Annual Escrow Statement**: Required by RESPA, this disclosure on the amounts needed to cover escrow disbursements is due annually (12 C.F.R. §1024.17(i)).

- **Escrow Closing Notice**: This notice is required prior to the closing of an escrow account. When a borrower requests cancellation of an escrow account, the notice is due three business days before the closing of the consumer's escrow account. When a creditor or servicer cancels an escrow account, the Escrow Closing Notice is due no later than 30 business days before the account closes (12 C.F.R. §1026.20(e)(5)(i), (ii)).

- **Affiliated Business Arrangement Disclosure**: Required by RESPA and due at the time of referring a loan applicant to a settlement service provider, this disclosure advises the consumer that the referring party and the settlement service provider share an ownership interest and the potential to realize some profit as a result of that ownership interest (12 C.F.R. §1024.15(b)).

- **Initial Truth-in-Lending Disclosure Statement (TIL)**: Required by TILA and due within three business days after the receipt of a completed loan application, this is the critical disclosure that provides consumers with the cost of credit expressed as a dollar amount (the finance charge) and as an annual percentage rate (12 C.F.R. §1026.18(c)).

- **Final Truth-in-Lending Disclosure Statement**: Required by TILA, this disclosure must be delivered or placed in the mail no later than the seventh business day before settlement. If there are any changes within the seven-business-day period, a new disclosure must be provided at least three business days before closing (12 C.F.R. §1026.19(a)(2)).

- **Re-disclosure of APR**: For a regular transaction, re-disclosure is required at least three business days prior to closing anytime the APR varies by more than one-eighth of 1% (12 C.F.R. §1026.22(a)(2)). For an irregular transaction, re-disclosure is required if the APR varies by more than one-fourth of 1% (12 C.F.R. §1026.22(a)(3)).

- **Initial Rate Change Disclosure**: This is a disclosure that TILA requires for ARMs, and it is intended to provide borrowers with information to prepare them for interest rate adjustments that will result in changes in payment amounts. The disclosure must also provide an explanation of how the rate is calculated, disclose the index and margin used to make this calculation, and identify any caps that will limit the increase in the rate. It must be provided at least 210 days, but no more than 240 days, before the first payment based on the new rate is due. This disclosure may be made at consummation if the first rate and payment changes are due within 210 days after consummation (12 C.F.R. §1026.20(c)(2)).

Although it will be servicers or lenders, and not loan originators, that will provide these disclosures, loan originators should advise borrowers with ARMs to look out for these important notices. They should also advise them that subsequent rate change disclosures are generally due no less than 60 days, and no more than 120 days, prior to an interest rate and payment change (12 C.F.R. §1026.20(d)).

Disclosures regarding loan costs and closing fees are intended to provide the consumer with information to shop competitively for a mortgage loan and settlement service providers.

Disclosures to Advise Consumer of Risky Lending Terms or Agreements

Some disclosures are offered to consumers to make certain that they understand the risks associated with specific types of lending terms and agreements:

- **Balloon Payment Notice**: Required by HOEPA, and due at least three business days prior to closing, this notice is required in those transactions in which balloon payments are allowed. Notice regarding the presence of a balloon payment provision is also required in the GFE for all residential mortgage transactions (12 C.F.R. §1026.18(5)).

- **Notice Regarding Insurance Premiums**: Required by HOEPA for a mortgage refinancing if the "amount borrowed" includes financing to cover optional insurance products, this notice is intended to prevent "packing" the cost of unnecessary insurance in high-cost home loans (12 C.F.R. §1026.32(c)(5)).

- **Notice that Completion of Loan Application and Receipt of Disclosure Does Not Obligate Borrower to Complete Transaction:** Previously required only with HOEPA loans, this disclosure is required by TILA and due within three business days of application. It advises consumers of the risks of losing their home when signing a lending agreement for all loans (12 C.F.R. §1026.32(c)(5)).

Disclosures to Alert Consumers of Their Rights

The purpose of some disclosures is to alert consumers that they have legal rights that they are entitled to exercise within a particular time frame.

- **Notice of Right to Receive Appraisal Report**: Creditors must provide loan applicants with notice of their right to receive a copy of the appraisal, and this disclosure is due no later than **three business days** after a creditor receives an application for credit that will be secured by a first lien on a dwelling (12 C.F.R. §1002.14(a)(2)).

- **Notice Regarding Monitoring Programs**: Required by ECOA and due when obtaining information on race, ethnicity, sex, marriage, and age (12 C.F.R. §1002.9(b))

- **Notice of Right to Rescind**: Required by TILA and due at the time of closing in transactions that are *not* related to a home purchase or to a refinance with the lender who made the loan being refinanced (12 C.F.R. §1026.23(b))

- **Notice of Right to Cancel PMI**: Required by the Homeowner's Protection Act at the time of closing and required in annual disclosures (12 U.S.C. §4903(a))

- **Notice of Right to Receive Credit Score and to Dispute Its Accuracy**: Required by FACTA and due during the loan transaction (15 U.S.C. §1681(g))

- **Notice of Right to Financial Privacy and Right to Opt-out of the Sharing of Personal Information**: Required by the GLB Act at the time of establishing a customer relationship (at the time of application) (15 U.S.C. §6802(b))

Disclosures to Alert Consumers about the Status of a Loan Application

- **Notice of Action Taken**: Required by ECOA and due 30 days after the receipt of a loan application (12 C.F.R. §1002.9(a)(1)(i))

- **Notice of Adverse Action**: Required by ECOA and due 30 days after the receipt of a loan application (12 C.F.R. §1002.9(a)(1)(iii))
- **Notice of Incomplete Application**: Required by ECOA and due 30 days after the receipt of an application (12 C.F.R. §1002.9(a)(1)(ii))

Disclosures Relating to Loan Servicing

RESPA creates a set of disclosures to ensure that borrowers receive notification if there are any changes related to the servicing of their loans.

- **Mortgage Servicing Disclosure Statement**: Required by RESPA and due three business days after completion of a loan application (12 C.F.R. §1024.21(b))
- **Servicing Transfer Statement**: Required by RESPA and due 15 days prior to the effective date of the transfer (12 C.F.R. §1024.21(d))

It is important to note that if certain circumstances change during the processing period of a loan application, the loan applicant must be provided with new disclosures. For instance, TILA requires re-disclosure of the APR on a regular loan if it varies by more than one-eighth of 1% at least three business days prior to closing. Another important example would be if the potential borrower decides to switch from a fixed-rate to an adjustable-rate loan. In this scenario, the potential borrower would need to receive an updated GFE and TIL Disclosure, as well as the CHARM booklet and the program disclosures related to adjustable-rate loans.

> *It should be noted that if certain circumstances change during the processing period of a loan application, the applicant must receive new disclosures.*

Discussion Scenario: Loan Application and Qualification

Larry is a loan originator for EZ Mortgages, and he is meeting with Bob Lightfeather to help him complete a loan application for a home purchase. Bob tells Larry that he has already met with a loan originator at another mortgage company and that he is beginning the process with a new mortgage broker because his former originator did not succeed in securing him a mortgage *"...even though everything was in order."* Larry learns that in Bob's earlier attempt to secure a loan, he applied for a conventional mortgage to purchase a $150,000 home. Bob has approximately $2,500 to use as a down payment, and he believes that his father will lend him another $2,000. The seller of the home is a friend of Bob's, and he has also offered to lend him money for the down payment if that is the only way to make the deal happen.

As the interview proceeds, Larry learns that three years ago, Bob earned a degree in landscape architecture. He has spent the three years since graduation working for three different home project stores in their gardening departments. He is now in his fifth month as an employee for a small private firm that prepares landscape designs and completes installations of these designs at office parks and new residential developments. Bob says that he likes this job because it allows him to use his degree. Hoping to improve his chances of securing a loan, Bob says that he would like to use his wife's income to help him qualify. Her earnings are irregular because they come primarily from providing day care services when a friend has to travel out of town for work. She also works at a bakery during the holidays and has just earned her certification to work as a substitute teacher at the local elementary school.

Bob has a credit score of 580. When Larry asks him about his assets, he states that he has never owned his primary residence but that he owns one third of an interest in a small mountain cabin that he purchased two years ago with his brothers. He also owns a truck that he uses for his business. He does not have investments or life insurance.

Bob is impatient to submit the loan application, so Larry offers to help him complete it. Larry suggests that with his limited cash and marginal credit score, Bob should apply for an FHA loan. He provides Bob with information on fixed-rate and variable-rate FHA loans. He lists Bob's wife as co-borrower. Larry lists Bob's "line of work/profession" as a landscaper when providing the history of his employment for the past three years. Larry lists the employment of Bob's wife as a teacher. For income, Larry lists Bob's income from his regular full-time employment and his wife's irregular income.

Larry completes the assets and liabilities table listing Bob's checking account balance and Bob's estimated value of his truck and his cabin. He strongly suggests that Bob invest in life insurance, and hands him the card of a *"...a buddy of mine who knows the business. He'll take good care of you."* Larry does not mention that he has an investment in his friend's insurance company and realizes some earnings as the business grows.

As Larry begins going through the declarations, Bob is impatient and asks, *"Can't I just sign this now? I'm due on a new job in 20 minutes."*

Larry tries to hurry the process by saying, *"I assume you haven't had any recent bankruptcies or foreclosures and that you're not named in any lawsuits? And, let's see, will you definitely need to repay your dad if you borrow money from him for a down payment? Would he agree to write a letter saying that the money's a gift?"*

"Sure, he'll say whatever I need him to say to help me get the house."

"Well, you're short on the amount needed, even for an FHA loan," Larry says as he hurries to finalize the form.

Based on Bob's last name, and without asking for confirmation, Larry checks Bob's race as American Indian.

Bob asks, *"Where do I sign?"* Larry offers him a pen saying, *"I guess you know about the acknowledgments since you've already been through this process."*

As he leaves, Bob hands Larry copies of his pay stubs for the past five months and of his tax returns for the past two years. Three business days after his hurried meeting with Bob, Larry sends him a Good Faith Estimate, an initial TIL disclosure for the variable-rate loan that Larry thinks Bob is most likely to get, and a mortgage servicing disclosure statement. Bob also includes another business card from his "insurance buddy" in the package, stapling it to a piece of paper on which he has scribbled, *"I work closely with this guy and he's the best in the business. He can also help you out with mortgage insurance, which you may need to get this loan."* Larry also encloses a cover letter that states *"I am notifying you that I have ordered an appraisal and a title report. Please note that all of the disclosures that I am required to provide to you are enclosed."*

Shortly after submitting the loan application to two of the lenders with whom he regularly does business, Larry learns that both have declined to extend credit to Bob. Despite the impatience that Bob showed to complete the application, Larry does not hear from him for two months, when he finally calls to ask about the loan status. Bob decides to try applying for a loan with a third mortgage company.

Discussion Questions

- *Was Larry's recommendation that Bob apply for an FHA loan good advice?*
- *Were Larry's descriptions of Bob and his wife's employment accurate?*
- *Did Larry handle the disclosures and acknowledgements in the loan application properly?*
- *Did Larry act or fail to act in any way that may represent his failure to comply with the law?*
- *Are there any recommendations that Larry should make to Bob to help him to improve his chances of securing a loan?*

Discussion Feedback

Bob is the type of first-time borrower that has typically benefitted from FHA financing. However, with Congress maintaining high lending limits for FHA loans and with a growing number of well-qualified borrowers applying for them, Bob is not likely to secure one of these loans with his credit score of 580. Cautious lenders are now demanding credit scores of at least 620 for FHA loans.

Another reason that FHA loans have been popular with first-time homebuyers is that the down payment requirements are only 3.5% of the loan amount. Unfortunately, even if Bob secures an additional $2,000 in cash from his father to add to his savings of $2,500, he will be $750 short of the $5,250 that he needs for the down payment. Larry should have advised Bob of the importance of securing the full amount needed for a down payment.

Larry apparently left out another important piece of information related to the down payment. When advising Bob to apply for an FHA loan, Larry should have told him that since 2008, seller-assisted down payment assistance has been prohibited for FHA loans. This is information that may have helped Bob decide between applying for a government loan or trying once again to secure a conventional loan.

Larry's suggestion for Bob to pursue FHA financing was sound, but he failed to provide important information regarding market conditions and information on down payment requirements and restrictions that could have helped Bob decide how to proceed with his loan application.

Larry mischaracterized the employment of both Bob and his wife. Describing Bob as a landscaper creates the impression that he performs manual labor exclusively and fails to highlight the fact that Bob completed a degree to attain additional knowledge and skills in his line of work. Although Bob has not held one job for a two-year period, he has consistently performed work in an area for which he is trained, and a careful description of his employment history will show that he has progressed from working as sales staff to earning a position in a firm that allows him to use all of his training. Although Larry may be attempting to enhance the qualification of Bob's wife by stating that she is a teacher, this notation is misleading and deceptive since she had not worked as a teacher at the time that the application was prepared and does not have guaranteed employment in this field.

When Larry's client became impatient, Larry should have suggested meeting at another time and may have encouraged Bob to do so by explaining that a hurriedly prepared application is less likely to be successful than one that is carefully prepared and accurate. Larry made a number of errors regarding the disclosures and notices contained in the application. First, Larry should have given Bob a chance to provide his own response to the question on the application regarding his race and ethnicity. The law only allows loan originators to use a loan applicant's surname or visual appearance to provide HMDA information when the loan applicant refuses to provide it him/herself.

Next, Larry rushed through the most important notices contained in the application. These are the acknowledgment that alerts applicants to their legal obligations under a mortgage and the notice that reminds them that giving false information may lead to serious legal action, including fines and imprisonment. Knowing that Bob had recently been through the loan application process does not excuse Larry of the responsibility for encouraging Bob to read these notices. He could have encouraged him to do so by saying, *"I know that you have seen this information recently, but it is important that you understand that both lenders and regulators are taking a closer look at loan applications, and you need to protect yourself by understanding the importance of providing accurate information."* Larry also missed the opportunity to use these notices to protect himself from liability. When failing to make sure that a loan applicant understands the legal obligation to provide truthful information, a loan originator risks his/her license and credibility and exposes him/herself to potential liability for providing inaccurate information on a loan application.

Larry violated the disclosure requirements of multiple federal laws. First, he violated RESPA by referring Bob to his "insurance buddy" without providing an affiliated business disclosure. Another immediate violation was the failure to provide an initial privacy notice. Furthermore, if Larry's mortgage company shares information with nonaffiliated third parties, Larry should also have provided Bob with the opportunity to opt out of the sharing of nonpublic personal information.

Larry violated TILA by failing to give Bob the CHARM booklet, even though he recommended a variable-rate loan. Finally, Larry violated ECOA by failing to provide Bob with timely notice of action taken on his loan application. This notice was due 30 days after completing the loan application. Larry also violated ECOA by failing to provide Bob with a notice of the right to receive a copy of the appraisal.

Finally, Larry violated a host of federal and state laws against misrepresentation and fraud by suggesting to Bob that he ask his father to misrepresent the amount of money loaned for a down payment and to hide the fact that he wanted Bob to repay the $2,000 loan. Instead of making this suggestion to misrepresent the money as a gift, Larry should have explained to Bob that he was required to list cash borrowed for a down payment as a liability on the schedule of assets and liabilities.

As soon as Bob complained that another mortgage broker failed to find him a loan, Larry should have realized that Bob may not be creditworthy in today's market. After learning that Bob's cash resources were limited and that his credit score was below 620, Larry probably needed to engage in a serious discussion with Bob about a long term, instead of a short term, strategy for securing a home loan. Obvious suggestions for a long term strategy include saving the rest of the money needed for a 3.5% down payment and even striving to set aside enough for a higher down payment. Larry's advice to Bob on securing life insurance was good, but he should have made the recommendation with the proper disclosures. As Bob spends more time in his present job, and if his wife assumes regular employment, they will be far more likely to secure a mortgage. If Larry took the time to persuade Bob to make homeownership an ultimate, instead of an immediate, goal, both parties would benefit.

QUALIFICATION: PROCESSING AND UNDERWRITING

Borrower Analysis

Assets and Liabilities

Financial statements list an applicant's assets and liabilities side by side to facilitate the lender's assessment of the applicant's financial situation. As discussed in the section-by-section review of the Uniform Residential Loan Application, the form includes a table for the itemization of liquid and non-liquid assets and liabilities. Course participants should look again at the outline of requirements for completing Section VI of the loan application to see what they must include in the schedule of assets and liabilities.

Income

Borrower income is an important consideration for almost all loan types. In the recent past, there were loan programs which allowed borrowers to state their income with no or minimal documentation to verify it. These no-doc and low-doc stated income loans have all but disappeared due to rampant misuse and the occurrence of fraud.

Today, lenders take a close look at a borrower's ability to repay a loan and are under the obligation of state and federal laws to do so. The amount of income the borrower makes in a month is analyzed against the total amount of debt he/she currently has as well as the prospective mortgage payment. This is called the debt ratio. Conventional/ conforming loans and nonconventional government loans have different standards as to what constitutes an acceptable ratio. Fannie Mae, Freddie Mac, and lenders establish guidelines for acceptable debt-to- income ratios in order to control the degree of risk associated with lending transactions.

One of the most important developments under the Qualified Mortgage Rule is the establishment of a 43% debt-to-income ratio requirement for qualified mortgages. Lenders that want the protection from liability that comes with the origination of qualified mortgages need to comply with this requirement. Note, however, that for the next seven years, there will be some leniency in enforcing the qualified mortgage standards, and **"temporary qualified mortgages"** will not be subject to the 43% debt-to-income ratio.

The new QM and ATR Rules also include requirements for the verification of income. The ATR Rule requires creditors to verify income and assets using copies of tax returns, IRS W-2 forms, payroll statements, bank statements, records from government agencies regarding entitlements, and receipts from the use of check cashing services (12 C.F.R. §1026.43(c)(3)).

Examples of other types of income documentation that is commonly used include:

- Paystubs for the most recent 30-day period and W-2s for the most recent two-year period
- Up to two years' tax returns for individuals earning more than 25% of their income in commissions. Their tax returns must document receipt of commission payments for a period of up to 12 months.
- Up to two years' tax returns for individuals who own more than 25% of a business
- Comprehensive documentation relevant to the type of income received for individuals who earn non-taxed income such as Social Security, public assistance, or disability income

Due to the prevalence of overstated income and the potential for tampering with income documents, many lenders require authorization from a loan applicant to conduct an independent verification of tax records. This independent verification is often performed for self-employed borrowers but is becoming more common with other types of borrowers. The IRS form 4506-T is used to obtain a transcript of tax returns. IRS form 8821 is used to authorize the release of other tax information.

In addition to documentation and verification of current and past employment, income analysis can also take a number of other factors into consideration. Analysis of factors such as economic stability of a profession, potential increases in income due to education and training, relocation, and guaranteed bonuses can all be used to help a borrower work with his/her loan originator to determine the appropriate loan product for his/her circumstances.

Income Calculations

The first calculations an originator typically makes during the loan interview regard income. Most applicants are paid on either an hourly basis or a salary. The salary might be given on an annual, monthly, or bi-weekly basis. Applicants who are self-employed or commissioned sales people require special considerations. This discussion will follow standard conforming guidelines in the consideration of income. A pay stub will provide most of the needed information. However, the originator will need to ask questions about the frequency of any overtime pay, how the employer handles vacation time, and when the potential buyer last received a raise. Once these questions are answered, the rest is just basic math!

Hourly
To compute the income of an hourly worker, you need to know the base hourly rate of pay, the number of hours worked in a typical week, the number of overtime hours received on average, and the number of weeks worked each year.

The formula is as follows:

$$\{base\ rate\} \times \{hours\} = \{weekly\ base\ income\}$$
$$\{OT\ rate\} \times \{OT\ hours\} = \{OT\ weekly\ income\}$$
$$\{weekly\ base\} + \{OT\ income\} = \{weekly\ income\}$$
$$\{weekly\ income\} \times \{weeks\ worked\} = \{annual\ income\}$$
$$\{annual\ income\} \div 12 = \{monthly\ income\}$$

Overtime income can only be used to qualify for a loan if the applicant can show a history of receiving overtime and the employer verifies that overtime is likely to continue. Two continuous years typically constitutes a history of overtime. Annual vacation days are included at the base rate.

Bi-weekly Salary
To compute a bi-weekly salary, all you need to know is the applicant's salary and how the applicant's vacation time is treated. If the applicant receives a paid vacation (as most do), the calculation is simple. Remember that there are 26 bi-weekly pay periods in a year.

The formula is as follows:

$$\{bi\text{-}weekly\ salary\} \times 26 = \{annual\ income\}$$
$$\{annual\ income\} \div 12 = \{monthly\ income\}$$

If the applicant does not receive a paid vacation, determine the typical amount of days that he or she takes off each year and subtract that income from the annual income before calculating the monthly income.

There is a difference between bi-weekly payments of salary and **semi-monthly payments**. While a bi-weekly payroll has 26 pay periods, one that is semi-monthly has **24** pay periods. Therefore, computations of income will differ for loan applicants who are paid on a bi-weekly payroll and those that are paid semi-monthly.

Annual Salaries
An applicant's income will occasionally be reported as an annual salary. This is common for educators and business executives.

If this is the case, the formula is as follows:
$$\{annual\ income\} \div 12 = \{monthly\ income\}$$

Self-Employed, Commissioned, and Trade Workers
Self-employed, commissioned, and trade workers are treated in much the same way. Their income is usually averaged over a two-year period. For the self-employed, the originator uses the income shown on the individual's tax return. For commissioned and trade workers, the originator uses the income shown on their W-2 form. In both cases, the calculation begins with adding the income from the previous two years and dividing it by 24.

The formula is as follows:
$$\{year\ one\ income\} + \{year\ two\ income\} = \{income\ base\}$$
$$\{income\ base\} \div 24 = \{monthly\ income\}$$

This more restrictive standard is used because the income of these workers is less stable than the income of hourly or salaried workers. Therefore, a lender must be more cautious when evaluating the capacity of these prospective borrowers' ability to repay a loan. When evaluating a person's tax returns, remember to add back into the annual income those expenses that will not recur and any depreciation taken on capital expenditures.

For example, a person might have relocated his or her office, which would be expensed and lower the net income. However, this expense is unlikely to recur, so the originator can add those costs back into the net income when determining the applicant's annual income.

Other Income
Annual bonuses, summer income, or other recurring additional income may be averaged over a two-year period and included in an applicant's annual income prior to calculating the monthly income. Child support and alimony may be used if it is court-ordered and if the applicant can show a stable history of receiving the payments.

Credit Report

Will the prospective borrower repay the debt? In order to weigh the risk of default, creditors also look at potential borrowers' credit history: how much they owe, how often they borrow, whether they pay bills on time, and whether they live within their means. Creditors also look for signs of borrowers' stability, and these include how long they have lived at their present address, whether they rent or own their home, and the length of their present employment.

In the past, it was possible for creditors to reach different conclusions based on the same set of facts. Based on individual experience or even instinct, one creditor may have found an applicant to be an acceptable risk, whereas another may have denied the same applicant a loan. However, new technologies have emerged that have altered this individualized lending process.

For better or worse, the development by Fair Isaac and Company (FICO) of credit-scoring software in the early 1990s produced what is purportedly an objective credit score. The use of analytical programs to generate credit scores like the FICO score resulted in the identification of an increasing number of consumers with some type of blemish on their credit histories, thereby reducing the number of prime borrowers. Credit scoring systems have also reduced the ability of creditors and loan originators to use experience and instinct to make lending decisions.

The automated credit score facilitated the development of automated underwriting programs. Fannie Mae's *Direct Underwriter* and Freddie Mac's *Loan Prospector* quickly set the standard for the industry. Each relies heavily on an applicant's credit score to make the credit decision. In addition, each eliminates the subjective decision-making process that manual underwriting allows.

> *In order to weigh the risk of default, creditors examine the credit histories of potential borrowers for signs of stability or possible risk.*

How is Credit Identified?
Consumer Reporting Agencies (CRAs) gather and sell information regarding an applicant's credit in the form of credit reports. The information is available to individuals, who are entitled to a free credit report annually, when they request one. It is also available to creditors, employers, insurers, banks, lenders, and similar entities. A credit report evaluates the financial responsibility of prospective borrowers. The applicant's credit report contains information with different levels of detail and specificity depending on the type of report requested. The highest level and most detailed report, called a **tri-merged report**, uses data from the three major repositories: Experian, Equifax, and TransUnion, otherwise known as the Big Three.

Scores are developed through a statistically validated system designed to evaluate any available information about an individual's payment history. The score assigns a number to this objective analysis. The report also contains relevant information beyond the score that is supportive of the loan origination and underwriting process. The ability to cross verify information that the repositories report with the information the customer provides is key to loan integrity and fraud prevention.

The credit report will provide the following:

- Applicant information
- Content summary of the report
- Credit scores
- All known public records
- Filed collections actions data
- Derogatory trade lines information
- Credit inquiries
- Fraud verification alert information

It is important for applicants to realize that having negative information on their credit report does not mean they are doomed forever. Despite late payments—or even bankruptcy—they can still make credit their friend. In general, account information, including late payments and other adverse information reported by creditors, is kept on a credit report for no longer than seven years. However, there are certain exceptions to this rule:

- Bankruptcy information may remain on credit reports for up to 10 years
- Unpaid tax liens might, depending on where the applicant lives, remain on credit reports indefinitely
- Certain states require that adverse credit information remain on credit reports no longer than five years

Although the importance of a prospective borrower's credit score should not be underestimated, borrowers may need the assurance that successful originators never end their analysis of a loan application based on score alone.

Scores only help them identify appropriate loan products for individual borrowers. That said, the available options are far more limited now than they were in 2006.

A credit report evaluates the financial responsibility of prospective borrowers. The applicant's credit report contains information with different levels of detail and specificity depending on the type of report requested.

Getting Permission to Access Credit Information

By obtaining a consumer report, the originator has instant access to a powerful tool that can determine the direction of the loan application process and has, in hand, critical information to determine what loan might suit the applicant's needs. To make a credit inquiry, along with consumer consent, a loan originator must have a "permissible purpose" identified under the federal Fair Credit Reporting Act (FCRA). A permissible purpose for obtaining a consumer report includes a mortgage lender's need for a consumer's credit history.

How is the Information Formatted and Provided?

Each repository presents personal identification and credit information in a different format. In addition, most mortgage lenders, mortgage brokers, and banks use repository information consolidators that provide the information in the formats required by the originators. Different CRAs provide a varied menu of services, including those that compile information from the "The Big Three" and combine it in an easy-to-read format.

How Do You Evaluate a Credit Report?

The first step of an evaluation is to carefully check all the identifying information. Multiple name spellings, addresses, or Social Security Numbers suggest errors in the report or possible identity theft. Loan originators should alert loan applicants of these types of discrepancies. After reviewing the report itself, loan originators should compare it to information provided by the loan applicant in the loan application and discuss any discrepancies with the applicant. If the report includes liens, debts, or judgments that the loan applicant believes to be paid off, the loan originator may need to solicit the help of a title agent and/or a court clerk to resolve inaccuracies.

If a lender decides not to make a loan based on information found in a consumer report, the Fair Credit Reporting Act requires the lender to advise the loan applicant that:

- The CRA did not make the decision to deny the loan application

- The consumer has a right to a free copy of his/her credit report

- The consumer may contact the CRA to dispute the accuracy and completeness of the report

Tax Liens and the Credit Score

Many consumers do not think about the impact their taxes have on their credit and are actually not aware that an impact even exists. When taxes go unpaid, the IRS can place a lien on a consumer's assets. If tax liens go unpaid, they will remain on a credit report for 15 years or more. Paid tax liens remain on a credit report for seven years.

Credit Accounts

There are variations in how each of the CRAs release information and how third party credit services may collate and document the information. However, credit accounts greatly impact a consumer's credit score and provide insight into credit character for loan qualification.

The following areas are typically found in the credit accounts section of a credit report:

- **Company Name**: The name of the creditor

- **Account Owner**: Will indicate whether the consumer is a joint account owner, authorized user, co-signor, etc.

- **Date Opened**: The month and year the credit account was established

- **Date Reported**: The date the last report was made to the CRA on the account – this can be an area of importance if there has not been a recent report establishing up to date payments

- **Months Reviewed and Date of Last Activity**: The number of months that have been reported and the last time any activity (including payment) occurred on the account

- **High Credit**: Usually means the credit limit on the account
- **Balance and Past Due Amounts**: The amount the consumer owes on the credit account and any amount that has been reported past due
- **Type of Account**: Such as open (for utilities), revolving (credit cards), installment (car loans), etc.
- **Timeliness of Payment**: The consumer's payment history regarding the account. As a rule, the following codes correspond to timelines:

  0 = Credit is open but has not been used (or reported)

  1 = Paid on time

  2 = 30+ days past due

  3 = 60+ days past due

  4 = 90+ days past due

  5 = 120+ days past due and/or referred to collections

  7 = Making payments via wage garnishment

  8 = Repossession

  9 = Charged off bad debt

There are variations in how each CRA releases information and how third-party credit services may collate and document the information. However, credit accounts greatly impact a consumer's credit score and provide insight into credit character for loan qualification.

Identifying Problems in the Credit Report and Fraud Alert

Examining the credit report is the originator's first line of defense to identify potential discrepancies and fraud. The Federal Trade Commission's Red Flags Rule requires financial industry professionals to identify and mitigate instances of identity theft as they pertain to credit reports. Some standard underwriting red flags, as well as red flags established by the FTC, include:

- Recently opened accounts
- All balances in round numbers
- Changes of addresses, especially recent
- P.O. Box addresses
- Recent payoff of a large number of accounts
- Misspellings and errors
- Large numbers of recent credit inquiries
- Uncharacteristic use of credit or sudden increase in use of credit
- A credit history that does not match the consumer's age

The originator and the processor, through verification of assets, employment, and the veracity of information provided on the application, are the first to sense that either the application is accurate or that fraud may be present. Under current federal law, all participants in the application and submission of a fraudulent loan are liable regardless of when the fraud was subsequently discovered. It is better to be cautious.

The Credit Score and Credit Risk

The Big Three

Industry consolidation has whittled what used to be scores of local and regional credit bureaus down to the three that we know of today: Equifax, Experian, and TransUnion. Over the past two decades, the "big three" gobbled up all of the smaller credit bureaus in an effort to become truly national in their coverage. A national credit bureau is beneficial because consumers will not lose any of their solid credit history simply because they have moved to another part of the country. Likewise, moving will not rid them of a negative credit history. Even if they were to move from the U.S. to Canada (or vice versa), their credit history would still follow them.

Equifax, Experian, and TransUnion are three separate and competitive companies. As such, they do not share information. It is very unlikely that a potential borrower's credit report is the same at all three credit bureaus because:

- **Not all lenders report to all three of the CRAs**: Lenders are not required to report to all three CRAs. Therefore, there will usually be omissions in an applicant's credit history at one or more of the credit bureaus.

- **Even if every lender DID report to all three CRAs, the information would probably be different**: Lenders that do report to all three credit bureaus do so by sending data tapes to them each month. Credit bureaus do not receive or "run" the tapes at the same time. As such, account information may be different at each CRA depending on the time of the month.

- **Not all lenders pull a credit report from all three credit bureaus when they are processing a credit application**: A lender will likely pull only one credit report when an applicant applies for a credit card or auto loan. This means that the "inquiry" is only going to show up on one of the three credit reports. The exception to this rule is a mortgage application. Most mortgage lenders will pull all three credit reports during their loan processing practices.

> *Equifax, Experian, and TransUnion are three separate and competitive companies. It is very unlikely that a potential borrower's credit report is the same at all three credit bureaus.*

Discussion Scenario: Income Calculations

Determine the qualifying income for the borrower in each of the following scenarios.

Borrower 1: Steve Stephens is a draftsman for a local architectural firm. He works 40 hours each week and is paid an hourly wage of $16.85 with no history of overtime. He receives a two-week paid vacation each year and has been with the company for six years. ***What is his monthly qualifying income?***

Borrower 2: Jamie James is a mid-level executive with a local utility company. She is paid bi-weekly. Her pay stub shows a base rate of $2,307.89 per pay period. It also shows a discretionary bonus income with a year-to-date total of $4,500. ***What is her monthly qualifying income?***

Borrower 3: Tommy Thomas is a maintenance worker for a local sign company. He is paid a weekly salary of $765 and works an average of 46 weeks each year. ***What is his qualifying income?***

Borrower 4: Cassie Cassidy is a self-employed graphic artist. Her tax returns show net taxable earnings of $67,890 for 2009 and $59,540 for 2008. The returns also show she is depreciating her studio, which she owns at a level annual rate of $6,700. ***What is her qualifying income?***

<u>Discussion Feedback</u>

Borrower 1: The calculation for Mr. Stephens' income is fairly straight forward. In the example, it is fine to use 52 weeks per year since we know his vacation is paid.

The basic calculation is as follows:

(Hourly Rate × Hours Worked Per Week) × Weeks Worked Per Year = Annual Income
Annual Income ÷ 12 = Monthly Qualifying Income

Mr. Stephens' calculation:

($16.85 × 40) × 52 = $35,048
$35,048 ÷ 12 = $2,920.67

Steve Stephens' monthly qualifying income is: **$2,920.67**

Borrower 2: In the calculation for Ms. James, it is important to note that she is paid bi-weekly. This means she receives 26 paychecks per year. (Alternately, someone who is paid semi-monthly receives 24 paychecks per year.) With regard to her bonus, it would not be used for qualifying income since it is noted that it is "discretionary" (meaning the amount can change or she may not receive it at all), and we do not have evidence that there is a two-year history of receiving the bonus.

The calculation is as follows:

$$Bi\text{-}weekly\ Pay\ Amount \times 26 = Annual\ Salary$$
$$Annual\ Salary \div 12 = Monthly\ Qualifying\ Income$$

Mrs. James' calculation:

$$\$2,307.89 \times 26 = \$60,005.14$$
$$\$60,005.14 \div 12 = \$5,000.43$$

Jamic James' monthly qualifying income is: **$5,000.43**

Borrower 3: Mr. Thomas' calculation is fairly straightforward. However, it is important to remember that we have been told he works 46 weeks per year. It is easy to forget and perform the calculation based on 52 weeks.

The basic calculation is as follows:

$$Weekly\ Salary \times Weeks\ Worked\ Per\ Year = Annual\ Salary$$
$$Annual\ Salary \div 12 = Monthly\ Qualifying\ Income$$

Mr. Thomas' calculation:

$$\$765 \times 46 = \$35,190$$
$$\$35,190 \div 12 = Monthly\ Qualifying\ Income$$

Tommy Thomas' monthly qualifying income is: **$2,932.50**

Borrower 4: Ms. Cassidy's calculation has a twist – you are dealing with annual salaries based on tax documents along with self-employment expenses, versus straightforward payroll documents.

The basic calculation is as follows:

$$(Year\ One\ Net\ Income + Year\ Two\ Net\ Income) \div 24\ Months = Monthly\ Income$$

If we assume that the studio depreciation can be applied to both years, it would be added to the Net Income:

$$((Year\ One\ Net\ Income + Depreciation) + (Year\ Two\ Net\ Income + Depreciation)) \div 24\ Months$$
$$= Monthly\ Income$$

Ms. Cassidy's calculation:

$$((\$59,540 + \$6,700) + (\$67,890 + \$6,700)) \div 24\ Months = \$5,867.92$$

Cassie Cassidy's monthly qualifying income is: **$5,867.92**

Qualifying Ratios

The evaluation of an applicant's ability to qualify for a loan involves the consideration of his/her income, credit history, credit scores, assets, and liabilities. Lenders require documentation and verification in order to verify that a loan applicant has accurately represented his/her qualifications. After this information is assembled, the lender applies mortgage industry formulas, such as debt-to-income ratios, to determine the size of the loan for which a loan applicant may qualify. Other numerical assessments, such as credit scores, help lenders to determine whether the loan applicant is likely to repay the loan in accordance with the terms in the lending agreement, and this determination directly impacts the interest rate charged on the loan.

Evaluating Applicants Using the Front End Ratio

The front end ratio, which is also known as the ***housing ratio***, is a calculation that allows lenders to compare the monthly housing expense that a loan applicant will assume with a new mortgage to his/her income. This may include flood insurance, homeowners' dues, condo assessments, or PUD assessments. The lender calculates the ratio by dividing the monthly housing expense by gross monthly income. In order to accurately calculate the monthly housing expense, the lender adds the following expenses, which are collectively referred to as ***PITI***: **P**rincipal, **I**nterest, **T**axes and **I**nsurance.

For conventional mortgage loans that conform to Fannie Mae and Freddie Mac guidelines, the maximum front end ratio has traditionally been 28%. Front end ratios for FHA loans and VA loans are less difficult to meet. Applicants for FHA loans must meet a front end ratio of 31%. Lenders who make VA loans look primarily at the back end ratio.

Evaluating Applicants Using the Back End Ratio

The back end ratio, which is also known as the ***total debt ratio***, compares the total monthly obligations to gross monthly income. Lenders calculate total monthly obligations by adding monthly housing expenses and all recurring debt such as car payments, credit card payments, child support, and student loans. Lenders who make conventional loans that conform to Fannie Mae and Freddie Mac guidelines have traditionally used a maximum back end ratio of 36%.

The back end ratios for FHA loans and VA loans are less difficult to meet. Applicants for FHA loans must meet a back end ratio of 43%. The back end ratio for VA loans is 41%. Some lenders of nonconforming loans have allowed the back end ratio to be as high as 55%.

Under the new QM Rule, a mortgage cannot be a qualified mortgage if the consumer's debt-to-income ratio exceeds 43% (12 C.F.R. §1026.43(e)(2)(vi)). The specific information required for the calculation of debt-to-income ratios for qualified mortgages is found in **"Appendix Q to Part 1026 – Standards for Determining Monthly Debt and Income."** Use of this Appendix is mandated by a provision in the QM Rule which states that in making a qualified mortgage, creditors must verify "The consumer's current debt obligations, alimony, and child support in accordance with appendix Q…." (12 C.F.R. §1026.43(e)(2)(v)(B)).

The standards set forth in Appendix Q are based on FHA standards, which are outlined in the HUD Handbook that is used to verify monthly debt and income when underwriting FHA loans.

Using the Appraisal to Calculate the LTV Ratio

After obtaining an accurate appraisal from a licensed appraiser, the loan originator uses formulas, such as the *loan-to-value ratio (LTV)*, to determine the type of loan for which the loan applicant will qualify.

The LTV ratio is calculated by dividing the amount of the mortgage by the appraised value or the purchase price of the home, whichever is less. For example:

A loan applicant applies for a mortgage to purchase a home which the seller has agreed to sell for $350,000. The purchase price is $5,000 less than the home's appraised value of $355,000. The loan applicant has savings of $70,000 to use for a down payment. The lender performs the following calculations:

{Purchase Price} – {Down Payment} = **{Mortgage Amount}**
{$350,000} – {$70,000} = **{$280,000}**
{Amount of Mortgage} ÷ {Purchase Price} = **{LTV}**
{$280,000} ÷ {$350,000} = **{80%}**

It is important to note, however, if the appraisal is less than the purchase price, the borrower will have to increase his/her down payment or obtain mortgage insurance.

Most lenders that offer conventional conforming mortgages will not allow the LTV to exceed 80% because Fannie Mae and Freddie Mac will not purchase a mortgage with an LTV over 80%. However, Fannie Mae and Freddie Mac will purchase a mortgage with an LTV that exceeds 80% if the borrower purchases *mortgage insurance* in the amount prescribed by these agencies' guidelines. For example:

If the loan applicant in the preceding example had a down payment of only $35,000, the lender would make the following calculations:

{Purchase Price} – {Down Payment} = **{Mortgage Amount}**
{$350,000} – {$35,000} = **{$315,000}**
{Amount of Mortgage} ÷ {Purchase Price} = **{LTV}**
{$315,000} ÷ {$350,000} = **{90%}**

With an LTV of 90%, the lender would not be likely to make the loan unless the borrower purchased private mortgage insurance. With mortgage insurance, the lender knows that it is possible to sell the mortgage in the secondary market, and insurance will mitigate additional risks that the lender incurs when making a loan with a high LTV. The amount of mortgage insurance that the borrower must purchase depends on the LTV; a higher LTV will require more insurance.

The LTV for FHA loans and VA loans is higher than the LTV for conventional mortgages. The LTV for FHA loans can be as high as 96.5%, although the FHA published a notice in February

2013 soliciting comments on its proposal to limit the LTV for loans in excess of $625,500 to 95%. The LTV for some VA loans is 100%. Two additional ratios that compare the loan amount to the value of the property are the combined loan-to-value ratio and the high loan-to-value ratio.

Combined Loan-to-Value Ratio (CLTV)

The CLTV is a ratio which lenders use when an applicant requests a second mortgage. Lenders calculate the CLTV by combining the cost of all mortgages on a home and comparing the combined cost to the value of the home securing the loans.

A loan applicant applies for a second mortgage for $40,000. He has a $200,000 mortgage on a home with an appraised value of $300,000. The lender will perform the following calculation:

$$\{(\text{First mortgage} + \text{Second mortgage})\} \div \{\text{Appraised value of home}\} = \{\textbf{CLTV}\}$$
$$\{(\$200,000 + \$40,000)\} \div \{\$300,000\} = \{\textbf{80\%}\}$$

With a CLTV of more than 80%, the interest rate on the second mortgage is likely to be higher.

High Loan-to-Value Ratio (HLTV)

An HLTV is the ratio determined when the borrower has a first mortgage and a home equity line of credit with the balance not fully drawn, which produces a lower CLTV (using the outstanding balance) than that computed when the available balance is used, which produces the HLTV ratio.

Studies show that the default rate is higher on high LTV, CLTV, and HLTV loans. Furthermore, a lender may not be able to fully recoup the losses associated with a default on a loan with a high loan-to-value ratio. For example, if the LTV is over 90%, the net sales proceeds may not be sufficient to cover the costs associated with the foreclosure, repair, and resale of the property. Due to the additional risks associated with a high LTV ratio and knowing that a borrower with little equity to protect is more likely to default, lenders will scrutinize the loan application with a high loan-to-value ratio to determine if the additional risk is acceptable and at what increased rate.

> *The HLTV ratio is produced when the borrower has a first mortgage and home equity line of credit with the balance not fully drawn, producing a lower CLTV.*

Ability-to-Repay/Qualified Mortgage Rule

Leading up to the 2008 mortgage crisis, mortgages were extremely easy to obtain, with dwellings often secured by "no-doc" and "low-doc" loans, which did not require thorough documentation before selling loans to investors. As a result of the crisis, since 2009, creditors were required to follow rules that prohibited making higher-priced mortgage loans without assessing the consumer's ability to repay the loans. In the 2010 Dodd-Frank Wall Street Reform and Consumer Protection Act (the Dodd-Frank Act), Congress adopted similar but not identical ability-to-repay (ATR) requirements for virtually all closed-end residential mortgage loans.

Congress also established a presumption of compliance with the ATR requirements for a certain category of mortgages, called qualified mortgages (QMs). The final Ability-to-Repay and Qualified Mortgage Rule, issued in January of 2013, was amended in May and July of 2013 and went into effect on January 10, 2014. The Rule requires residential mortgage lenders to consider the borrower's ability to repay before extending credit, and defines "qualified mortgages" that are subject to a presumption of compliance with the ability-to-repay rules. The Rule generally applies to closed-end consumer credit transactions that are secured by a dwelling, for which an application is received on or after January 10, 2014.

Transactions Covered by the Rule

The ATR Rule applies to almost all closed-end consumer credit transactions secured by a dwelling, including any real property attached to the dwelling. The ATR Rule is not limited to first liens or to loans on primary residences.

The following loans are **excluded** from the ATR Rule:
- Open-end credit plans (home equity lines of credit, or HELOCs)
- Timeshare plans
- Reverse mortgages
- Temporary or bridge loans with terms of 12 months or less (with possible renewal)
- A construction phase of 12 months or less (with possible renewal) of a construction-to-permanent loan

(12 C.F.R. §1026.43(a))

In addition to the types of loans outlined above, certain extensions of credit made by certain creditors are also exempt from the ATR requirements. The following types of extensions are generally exempt:
- Extensions of credit made by creditors designated by the U.S. Department of the Treasury as Community Development Financial Institutions and creditors designated by HUD as either a Community Housing Development Organization or a Down Payment Assistance Provider of Secondary Financing
- Extensions of credit made by creditors designated as nonprofit organizations under section 501(c)(3) of the Internal Revenue Code of 1986 that extend credit no more than 200 times annually, provide credit only to low- to moderate-income consumers, and follow their own written procedures to determine that consumers have a reasonable ability to repay their loans
- Extensions of credit made by housing finance agencies directly to consumers, as well as extensions of credit made by other creditors pursuant to a program administered by a housing finance agency
- Extensions of credit made pursuant to an Emergency Economic Stabilization Act program, such as extensions of credit made pursuant to a state Hardest Hit Fund

Since the ATR requirements do not apply to these loans, they are not eligible for QM status (12 C.F.R. §1026.43(a)(3)(iv), (vi)).

Ability-to-Repay and the ATR Requirements

According to the CFPB, in order to meet the ATR standards, a creditor must make a reasonable, good faith determination before or at consummation of a covered mortgage loan that the consumer has a reasonable ability to repay (12 C.F.R. §1026.43(c)(1)). A reasonable, good faith effort must use eight underwriting factors, including:

- Current or reasonably-expected income or assets, other than the value of the property that secures the loan, that the consumer will rely on to repay the loan
- Current employment status (if employment income is relied on when assessing the consumer's ability to repay)
- Monthly mortgage payments for the loan. This is calculated using the introductory or fully-indexed rate, whichever is higher, and monthly, fully-amortizing payments that are substantially equal
- Monthly payments due on any simultaneous loans secured by the same property
- Monthly payments for property taxes and insurance the consumer is required to buy, plus certain other costs related to the property, such as homeowners association fees or ground rent
- Debts, alimony, and child support obligations
- Monthly debt-to-income ratio or residual income, calculated using the total of all of the mortgage and non-mortgage obligations listed above, as a ratio of gross monthly income, and
- Credit history [92]

> *In order to meet the ability to repay standards, a creditor must make a reasonable, good faith determination that the consumer has a reasonable ability to repay the loan.*

The documents used when determining ATR must be reasonably reliable third-party records [93]. Creditors must verify a consumer's income by using W-2s or payroll statements. The Rule provides flexibility concerning these documents, provided that the creditor reviews each of the eight factors described above. When verifying income, a creditor can also use bank statements, employer records, or receipts from check-cashing services. Oral confirmation of employment is acceptable if received directly from the consumer's employer and the creditor makes a note of the phone call. Rental payment history may also be used to confirm credit history if a consumer does not have a credit score or history from a major credit bureau. The following are considered reasonably reliable third-party records:

- Records from government organizations
- Statements provided by a cooperative, condominium, or homeowners association
- A ground rent or lease agreement

- Credit reports
- Statements for student loans, auto loans, credit cards, or existing mortgages
- Court orders for alimony or child support
- Copies of the consumer's federal or state tax returns
- W-2 or other IRS forms for reporting wages or tax withholding
- Payroll statements
- Military leave and earnings statements
- Financial institution records
- Records from the consumer's employer or a third party that obtained consumer-specific income information from the employer
- Check-cashing receipts, and
- Remittance-transfer receipts

(12 C.F.R. §1026.43(c)(3))

Determining ATR (12 C.F.R. §1026.43(c)(1))

The CFPB does not require a creditor to develop specific underwriting standards, but it does provide examples demonstrating how internal policies can influence ATR determinations. The examples below are illustrative of factors that may show that an ATR determination was based on good faith.

Underwriting standards: the creditor used underwriting standards that have historically resulted in comparatively low rates of delinquency and default during adverse economic conditions.

Payment history: the consumer paid on time for a significant time after origination or reset of an adjustable-rate mortgage.

When determining ATR, it is important to consider the specific facts and circumstances relevant to each loan.

Income and Debt Considerations in Determining ATR
The general ATR standard requires creditors to consider debt-to-income (DTI) ratio or residual income, but does not contain specific DTI or residual income thresholds (12 C.F.R. §1026.43(c)(2)(vii)). Information on the consumer's income and debts will be used in determining ATR. Any income a creditor relies upon must be verified. Wages, unearned income, and regular payments such as child support may be considered as income. Various types of employment (full-time, part-time, seasonal, and self-employment), but only the income used to determine ATR, should be verified.

According to the CFPB, when assessing a consumer's ATR, four underwriting factors help in evaluating the consumer's debts.

A creditor should determine the following monthly payments:

- The loan subject to underwriting
- Any simultaneous loans secured by the same property
- Mortgage-related obligations, and
- Current debt obligations [94]

The consumer's debt and income are then used to calculate the DTI ratio.

> *Any income a creditor relies upon to determine a borrower's ability to repay must be verified.*

COMMITMENTS AND UNDERWRITING CONDITIONS

Lock-in and Float Agreements

Lock-in agreements, which are also known as **rate-lock agreements** or rate commitments, are agreements made by a lender to hold an interest rate and a specified number of points while processing an applicant's loan. Lock-in agreements should be made in writing. True lock-in agreements lock in the interest rate and the points. Other types of agreements, known as float agreements, allow the interest rate or points to rise and fall with the market.

Lenders may charge a fee for a lock-in. The fee may be a flat fee or a percentage of the mortgage amount, payable upfront or at the time of closing. Some lenders may finance the fee by adding a fraction of a percentage of a point to the interest rate. The fees for long lock-in periods are higher than the fees for a lock-in that is effective for only a short period of time. Lock-in fees may not be refundable. Therefore, approved applicants who choose not to accept a loan risk the loss of the fees that they paid for a lock-in.

Expiration Date for Lock-in Agreements
Lock-in agreements may be effective for as little as seven days from the date of loan approval up to 120 days. Most agreements are effective for 30 to 60 days. If an applicant's loan is not settled and funded within the period of time that the agreement is effective, he/she will obtain a loan at the current rate. However, it is usually to the advantage of the borrower for the originator to request an extension to the agreement. Lock-in extensions must be approved by the lender, and a fee is charged for the extension, but it is usually worth the effort and cost so that the applicant is guaranteed the interest rate to which he/she agreed.

Float Agreements
Lenders may allow loan applicants to lock in an interest rate without locking in the points. This type of float agreement, which is known as **floating points**, benefits the loan applicant if points fall. However, if interest rates also fall, the lender may charge extra points to make more money from the mortgage transaction.

Lenders may agree to float both the interest rate and the points, allowing the loan applicant to lock in the rate and points between the time of the loan application and the date of closing. The applicant can choose to lock in the rate and points at the time that appears most advantageous.

It is important to note that the decision to lock or float the interest rate is up to the borrower. It is an ethical issue if an originator does not act upon a borrower's request to lock a rate. Additionally, some states have strict rules governing rate lock agreements – an originator may face legal or regulatory ramifications for failing to honor such an agreement.

> *Lock-in agreements, also known as "rate-lock agreements" or "rate commitments," are agreements made by a lender to hold an interest rate and a specified number of points while processing an applicant's loan.*

Underwriting

An underwriter's principal responsibility is to ensure that the proposed loan meets the requirements set forth by the investor who will purchase the mortgage. This includes assessing a borrower's ability and willingness to repay the mortgage debt and examining the property being offered as security for the mortgage. It must be determined that the prospective borrower not only has the ability to pay but has also proven a willingness to repay their debts, thus limiting the probability of default and collection difficulties.

The underwriter's job is to confirm that potential borrowers have sufficient cash assets available to close the mortgage. The property must also be examined to see that it is sufficient collateral for the mortgage and that it meets the investor's minimum acceptable guidelines. Much of the underwriter's decision-making has now been taken over by an Automated Underwriting System (AUS). These underwriting systems are known by many names, but they all play the same role. They make an automated underwriting decision based on information entered into the AUS.

If loans are submitted via the AUS, it is then the underwriter's responsibility to make sure that the information entered into the AUS is indeed the information provided on the URLA and that all information is documented and accurate. It is the originator's responsibility to ensure that the loan file includes all information and documentation necessary to aid the underwriter in accomplishing this task.

An underwriter looks for complete and accurate information on the loan application and loan package and addresses any questions raised by lack of documentation or information in order to make an underwriting decision. The major areas that an underwriter examines are credit, income, assets, and collateral.

Prospective Borrower's Credit History and Explanations of Derogatory Credit

Past credit performance serves as the most useful guide in determining a potential borrower's attitude toward credit obligations and in predicting his or her future actions. A borrower who has made payments on previous and current obligations in a timely manner represents reduced risk. Conversely, if the credit history shows continuous slow payments, judgments, and delinquent accounts, despite an adequate income to pay off those obligations, then strong compensating factors will be necessary to approve the loan.

An underwriter examines the overall pattern of credit behavior and isolated occurrences of derogatory credit. If the prospective borrower's history reflects a bankruptcy, the underwriter will be looking to see what items on the credit report might be included in the bankruptcy, when the bankruptcy occurred, the reason for bankruptcy, and the type of credit history the borrower has had since the bankruptcy.

When derogatory credit is revealed, the underwriter will be looking for explanations for the derogatory credit, which the originator must document. The applicant's explanation must make sense and be consistent with the other credit information in the file. The underwriter will also check for items not listed on the credit report but disclosed on other documents, such as automatic deductions for loan payments on paycheck stubs or on bank statements. The originator and applicant must address these items.

If there are recent inquiries that could result in new credit, the applicant must address this. Many originators fail to ask the applicant about a credit inquiry that may turn into a debt. For example, an applicant purchased a new car shortly before closing escrow. The sales agent told him that the inquiry would not show on his credit report for at least 30 days.

As part of a quality control check, the lender ran another credit report. The new credit report showed a credit inquiry by the car dealership and the car manufacturer's lending subsidiary. Upon the lender's request to the credit reporting agency, the lender confirmed that a loan had been authorized for the applicant. Further investigation resulted in the applicant being denied the loan as his new car payment put his ratios over guideline limits.

> *A credit report which shows timely payments on past and current obligations represents reduced risk. A report which shows repeated slow payments, judgments, or delinquent accounts will require strong compensating factors to receive loan approval.*

Income Analysis

All income must be supported with the proper documentation. During the lending boom, low-doc or no-doc loans were made with little to no documentation, but these are products that lenders can no longer make now that the Truth-in-Lending Act and Regulation Z prohibit the origination of a residential mortgage loan unless the creditor can make a reasonable and good faith determination of the borrower's repayment ability, and bases this determination on documented and verified information (12 C.F.R. §1026.43(c)(1), (2)).

When completing income analysis, the underwriter must develop an average of income and bonuses or overtime for the past two years, and then evaluate the probability of its future continuance to be used in calculating income. The underwriter will verify the calculations used to confirm the applicant's income. This area seems to be of particular concern as many times the income is calculated incorrectly. It is the underwriter's responsibility to verify that the income used when calculating the debt-to-income ratio is accurate.

The underwriter looks not only at the length of time that the prospective borrower has been working but also how long he/she has been with the same employer. The originator must address any job-hopping, job gaps, and any change in the line of work. The originator should document the reason for any job gaps or lack in length of time on the job. This could be due to the borrower being in school, the military, or a seasonal worker. The originator should document this in the file so that it leaves no questions for the underwriter.

The underwriter will review W-2s and 1040s to evaluate income consistency. This is particularly important when calculating commission and self-employed applicants. If the applicant is self-employed or commissioned, the underwriter will be looking at the 1040s for the non-reimbursed employee expenses or Schedule C and the adjusted gross income.

Any substantial increase or decrease in income must be addressed. The underwriter may even ask for current profit and loss statements. This is all required to provide evidence that the income is consistent with the previous year's earnings. If the income shows considerably greater or lower than what is supported by the previous year's tax returns, the underwriter will ask for an explanation as to the increase or decrease. This may be due to a large one-time investment for the business, or it may be due to additional product lines or clients that the business recently acquired. Whatever the reason, explanations are in order. Also, if the applicant must pay quarterly taxes, then the originator must be sure to include proof that estimated taxes were paid as required.

The underwriter will calculate other non-taxable income and confirm that the correct adjustments have been used. One area that originators must pay attention to is the term "grossing up." The originator should be careful that the correct grossing up percentages are used. The underwriter will look for documentation to support income. This includes, but is not limited to, W-2s, paycheck stubs, 1040s, retirement statements, social security awards benefit letters, divorce decrees, and settlements.

The underwriter will also review the 1040s for other income or expenses not documented in the loan file. This may include rental income (Schedule E), self-employment tax and income (Schedule C), farming expenses and income (Schedule F), and corporate or partnership returns. If an originator reviews the tax returns before submission, he or she should address any items that may become concerns of the underwriter in the loan file.

For rent received for properties owned by the prospective borrower, the originator must include documentation to support the rental amount. Documentation may include a current lease or rental agreement. As a standard rule, the underwriter will use 75% of rental income stated on the rental or lease agreement unless otherwise documented by 1040s. If 1040s are provided and the underwriter verifies less than 75% adjusted rental income, then the lower amount must be used for qualification purposes. If there is a negative rental income, the negative income will be considered a liability and treated as a debt.

> It is the underwriter's responsibility to verify that the income used when calculating the debt-to-income ratio is accurate.

Assets – Cash to Close the Transaction

The cash investment in the property must equal the difference between the amount of the mortgage and the total cost to acquire the property. All funds for the applicant's investment must be verified and documented. If the applicant has placed an earnest money deposit, the underwriter may ask to see a receipt from the escrow company holding the funds. This is to verify that the monies are in escrow and that these funds have or have not already been removed from any bank statements that are being submitted as evidence of funds available to close the transaction.

An underwriter is going to examine the asset documents to verify that there are enough funds available to close the transaction. During the underwriter's examination, an applicant's saving history and use of funds will also be reviewed. The underwriter will be looking for non-sufficient funds, use of credit lines, undisclosed loans, large deposits, and debits that may suggest undisclosed debts. Any of these areas need to be addressed by the applicant and originator in the loan file.

If funds are proceeds from the sale of a home, the underwriter may ask to see evidence in the form of a HUD-1 Settlement Statement. If the property has not sold at the time of underwriting, loan approval may be conditioned upon verifying that the applicant has actually received the proceeds.

Stocks, bonds, 401Ks, and retirement accounts are only to be counted at 60% of their face value. If any of these accounts are to be used for the purchase of the home, the underwriter may ask for the current statements along with proof of liquidating the account, stock, or bond. If the applicant intends to sell personal property items (cars, RVs, etc.) to obtain funds to close the transaction, the applicant must provide satisfactory evidence of the actual cash value of the property being sold. This estimated cash value must be realistic and at the current market value. If the estimated value of an item being sold seems unrealistic, the underwriter may ask to see an appraisal of the item or further documentation to provide evidence of the higher value.

If the prospective borrower is using rent credit (a portion of monthly paid rent credited towards his/her down payment by the seller), it must be documented. The underwriter may ask for verification of rent paid and applied towards the credit. If credit has been for a specific term, the underwriter may ask the prospective borrower to provide proof of residency in the form of utility bills or other documents such as bank statements for the term of the credit given.

The Subject Property Collateral

The underwriter must ensure that the property is eligible and meets lender guidelines for collateral. To do this, the underwriter relies on the appraisal report, preliminary title report, and any inspections requested by the prospective borrower or required by the lender. The underwriter must determine that the appraiser is properly licensed and has Error and Omission (E&O) insurance and that his or her resume substantiates competence to appraise this type of property.

The Sales Contract

While reviewing the sales contract, the underwriter will look for credits or personal property included in the sales contract that will affect the value of the collateral. All personal property should be excluded from the sales contract or notated that it is to be sold with no value. However, if the item being sold with property is such that value must be considered, it will affect the value and the loan amount.

The Underwriting Review of the Appraisal

The appraisal report is used to determine the value of the property being mortgaged and to advise of deficiencies that affect the continued marketability of the property should the lender need to foreclose on it. The underwriter looks to confirm that the names, address, and property description are accurate. The loan agent should check these areas before submitting to underwriting. Errors caught upfront will eliminate problems during underwriting.

The underwriter will be looking at the location of the subject property and any possible hazards or deficiencies that may affect the marketability of the property if the lender should have to foreclose. They will also compare the location of the subject property with the location of the comparable properties (comps) used. If the underwriter feels that they are too far from the subject property or that there should be more comps near the subject property, the underwriter may ask for additional comps to validate the value given by the appraiser. A review appraisal may also be required.

If there are any contract issues that affect the sales price or value of the home, the appraisal will note that. An underwriter will look at the floor plan (footprint) to check for functional obsolescence of the property. Photos will also be carefully examined. The underwriter is looking for any visible signs of health and safety hazards or damage to or near property that may affect the lender's collateral. It is important to check for addresses in photos and to be sure that the subject property in the photo is the same as described in the appraisal.

The effective age will be reviewed. The last thing that a lender wants is collateral with a remaining economic life less than the term of the loan. This would mean that the property would not be there when the loan matures. The underwriter will also verify that an approved appraiser has completed the appraisal and that it is correctly signed and dated by the appraiser.

> *The appraisal report is used to determine the value of the property being mortgaged and advise of deficiencies that affect the continued marketability of the property.*

The Title Report

The underwriter will check to see if the subject property is a condominium or planned unit development, which would affect the loan documents and what title policy endorsements will be required. The underwriter may ask for the Home Owners Association (HOA) documentation, Consumer Confidence Report (CCR) on the drinking water, and Deed Restrictions.

The underwriter will be looking at other items that may cloud the title or affect the marketability of the property. Those items might be easements, land locks, vesting, and leaseholds. An originator must be cautious on leaseholds, as the term of the loan cannot be more than the remaining term of the leasehold.

Safety Issues

If the property is a manufactured home, the underwriter will check to make sure that the manufactured home tags required by HUD are noted on the appraisal. Additionally, evidence is required to prove that the manufactured home is titled as real property and not personal property. A structural engineer's certificate may also be required. The originator needs to make sure that he/she knows the lender's guidelines regarding manufactured homes prior to submitting the loan file to underwriting to avoid any suspensions or delays in approval.

If the property being financed is a new home under construction, the underwriter will require a completion notice from the appraiser. The underwriter may also require proof or evidence by the local building authority. The originator should be aware of this, plan ahead and order these items before the scheduled closing date. This will avoid last minute delays.

Flood Zone Verification

The underwriter will also verify the flood zone. This is necessary to assure that if the property is in a flood prone area, that the proper flood insurance is required to protect the lender's collateral and the prospective borrower's purchase. The appraiser is responsible for determining if a property is located in a flood zone.

Other Required Inspections

After reviewing the contract and appraisal, the underwriter may ask for verification that repairs were done or require further inspections to be performed. This is all to ensure the collateral of the lender or to meet program guidelines, such as those in an FHA or VA loan. This may include termite, well, septic, roof, or other inspections noted on the appraisal.

Documentation and Verification

The underwriter has a difficult job of ensuring that the loan application is properly documented and substantiated. An underwriter does not try to find ways to deny loans, but rather looks to see what loans meet the guidelines and have sufficient documentation to support the information provided by the applicant. Many times an underwriter is left to guess what the originator is trying to submit.

Questions will arise out of incomplete information either on the URLA or documentation provided in the loan file. The better information and documentation the originator can provide in the loan package, the better chance there is of having their loan sail through underwriting smoothly and efficiently.

The URLA captures most of the information needed to obtain a risk assessment from an AUS or manual underwriting decision. It is crucial that all information provided on the URLA for an underwriting decision is accurate. It is the underwriter's role to verify the accuracy of the information that is entered. The loan originator plays a big part in underwriting by ensuring information gathered and submitted to the lender has been reviewed for accuracy and comprehensiveness. Looking for discrepancies against the URLA and documentation is a key way of finding inaccurate or false information.

Faxed and Internet documents must be verified. The originator should look at the heading on the top of a faxed document. Does it have the sender's name and phone number? Is it from the company that should be sending it? Does the Internet document have the URL? If it is not a secured website, this might be a sign of a fraudulent document, especially if it is being provided as evidence of employment, income, or assets.

> *The underwriter must ensure that the loan application is properly documented and substantiated. The better the information and documentation provided in the loan package, the better the chance of a smooth and efficient underwriting process.*

Common Underwriting Pitfalls

Some Underwriting Quicksand and Common Pitfalls to Avoid

- Incomplete files with no documents to back up what is stated on the URLA
- Inaccurate data. Many times these are just calculation errors in income or not using proper percentages for rental income, non-taxable income, or stocks, bonds, and retirement statements.
- Cash-out refinance loans submitted as no-cash-out
- Property is not the applicant's principal residence
- Qualifying ratios exceeded without compensating factors given
- Obligations of all applicants; non-purchasing spouse not included, inaccurate or unreported borrower debt
- Insufficient assets to close transaction
- Assets not documented
- Applicant's income not calculated correctly
- Applicant's income not substantially documented, such as self-employment
- Loan program not provided

- New construction documentation not provided. This can result in delays in closing.
- Sales contract not fully executed by all buyers and sellers
- Major repairs needed and not addressed in loan file
- Repair or compliance clearances not provided according to sales contract or lender guidelines
- Alimony or child support not included in debts
- Secondary financing not disclosed
- Real estate obligations not disclosed
- Delinquent federal debts that showed up on title report but not credit report
- Incorrectly calculated loan amounts

The importance of having a complete and accurate URLA and sufficient documentation in loan files cannot be overstated.

APPRAISALS

In addition to evaluating a loan applicant, it is necessary to evaluate the property used to secure a loan. Lenders rely on appraisals to ensure that the value of the property is adequate to serve as security, or collateral, for the loan. A licensed appraiser must prepare the appraisal.

Accurate appraisals are of great importance. The overvaluation of real property used to secure home loans is an issue of great concern. Critics point to overvaluation as a factor contributing to the meltdown of the real estate market. Overvaluation is also at the root of many predatory lending transactions and mortgage fraud schemes, allowing many unscrupulous mortgage professionals to profit at the expense of borrowers and lending institutions.

Overvaluation can also result from pressure exerted by sellers who hope to sell high, or from borrowers in refinance transactions who hope to secure a generous line of credit based on the equity in their homes. These demands from consumers are often directed towards loan originators who may feel pressured to pass their clients' demands for a favorable appraisal on to appraisers.

> *Many critics point to overvaluation as a factor contributing to the meltdown of the real estate market.*

URAR/1004

There are a number of forms used by appraisers, and it is important to be able to identify them. The lender's underwriting guidelines for the specific property type is the driving force behind what forms must be included in the appraisal order. Credit and valuation models will also affect what is required of the appraiser.

The **Uniform Residential Appraisal Report (URAR)**, or 1004, is the most common and comprehensive appraisal form. It is generally used on all single family homes and may also be used for row homes and townhouses if the property is situated on a fee simple lot.

Other appraisal forms include:
- **1070**: A condensed version of the 1004; often used with rate/term refinances
- **1073**: Used for condominiums, PUDs and row homes/townhouses situated on common ground
- **1007**: Used for single family properties which are intended as investment properties
- **1025**: Used for two- to four-unit properties which are intended as investment properties

A **property inspection waiver** is occasionally permitted instead of a full appraisal for certain refinances. The waiver would be granted for a borrower who is refinancing his or her property within a specified time after a previous loan transaction. Under these circumstances, a conventional lender may permit an abbreviated or "drive by" appraisal if it is comfortable with existing data on the subject property.

Appraisal Approaches

There are a number of approaches an appraiser may use to determine the value of a property. The most common method of conforming loans is the **sales comparison approach**, or market approach. This is based on a comparison with similar, recent property sales in the same vicinity as the subject property. The **cost approach** is another method. It is commonly used to appraise new home construction. Finally, the **income approach** is used for investment properties.

In order to comply with the Uniform Appraisal Guidelines, the appraiser must consider all three approaches. When the appraisal is completed, the appraiser must justify the use of one approach over the others in his/her final conclusion of value.

Sales Comparison Approach

This approach is an analysis of recent sales that are the most comparable to the subject property. An appraiser must analyze a minimum of three comparable sales that were settled or closed within the last 12 months. An appraiser must comment on sales that are more than six months old.

Adjustments to Comparable Sales
The appraiser's analysis must take into consideration all factors that have an impact on value, recognizing that a well-informed buyer will not pay more for this property than the price he/she would pay for a similar property of equal desirability and utility. To accomplish this, the appraiser must analyze all closed and settled sales, contract sales, and current listings of properties that are the most comparable to the subject property.

Because the appraiser's estimate of market value is no better than the reliability of the comparable data that is utilized, the appraiser must exercise diligence to ensure that the comparable sales data is reliable. The appraiser must report each comparable sale on the appropriate appraisal report form and must report a minimum of three comparable sales as part of the sales comparison approach.

Each comparable sale that is utilized must be analyzed for differences and similarities between it and the property being appraised. The appraiser must make appropriate adjustments for location, terms, and conditions of the sale, date of sale, and physical characteristics.

Specific guidelines have been set for adjustments regarding proximity to subject, date of sale, and net or gross adjustments:

- **Proximity to the Subject Property**: Sales should be located within one mile of the subject.

- **Date of Sale**: Comparable sales should have closed within 12 months of an appraisal's effective date.

- **Net & Gross Adjustments**: Adjustments are changes in the value of a comparable property made when comparing the features of the comparable property to the subject property. A net adjustment is the positive or negative value assigned to each feature. The gross adjustment is the sum of those values for each property. The dollar amount of the net adjustments for each comparable sale should not exceed 15% of the sales price of the comparable. The dollar amount of the gross adjustment for each comparable sale should not exceed 25% of the sales price of the comparable.

- **Sales or Financing Concessions**: The dollar amount of sales or financing concessions paid by the seller. Examples of sales or financing concessions include interest rate buy downs, loan discount points, loan origination fees, and closing costs customarily paid by the buyer. The appraiser must obtain this information from the individual who is a party to the concessions. The dollar amount of the concessions is adjusted negatively in the sales grid. Sales concessions are limited on conforming loans based on loan-to-value (LTV). Transactions with LTV over 90% are limited to 3% seller concessions. Concessions on loans with LTV under 90% are limited to 6%.

Rural Properties

Because rural properties are often situated on large lots, and rural neighborhoods can be relatively underdeveloped, there may be a shortage or absence of recent comparable sales in the immediate vicinity of the subject property. This means that the appraiser will often need to select comparable sales that are located a considerable distance from the subject property.

In such cases, the appraiser must use his or her knowledge of the area and apply good judgment in selecting comparable sales that are the best indicators of value for the subject property. The appraiser should include an explanation in his or her report of why the particular comparables were selected in his or her analysis.

What is Considered a Good Comparable Sale?

Your subject property is a 1,200 square foot rancher built in 1990. It is situated on a 10,000 square foot lot in an established residential subdivision. You run a comparable sales search through the local data bank and multiple-listing service you subscribe to. You find ten comparable sales situated in the subject subdivision ranging in gross living area from 1,000 square feet to 1,400 square feet, ranging in age from 10–20 years old, and situated on lot sizes ranging from 5,000 square feet to 15,000 square feet. All sales closed within the past six months.

From the database of ten comparable sales, the appraiser will analyze the properties and choose three that best represent the subject in lot size, room count, gross living area, and amenities. Remember, the adjustments made in the sales grid must fall within the net and gross percentage adjustment guidelines. Lower net and gross adjustments are the best indicators of the most reliable comparable sales.

> *The sales comparison approach, or market approach, is the most common appraisal method for conforming loans.*

Cost Approach

This approach assumes that a potential purchaser would consider building a substitute residence that has the same utility and use as the subject property being appraised. The appraiser arrives at the indicated value of the property by estimating the reproduction cost of improvements, subtracting the amount of depreciation by all causes, and adding the estimated value of the site as if it were vacant. The appraiser estimates land value by analyzing comparable sized land sales.

Income Approach

Normally this approach is not applicable to single-family properties. However, if a single-family home is being utilized as an investment property, the appraiser must prepare a single-family comparable rental schedule in addition to the appropriate appraisal report.

TITLE AND INSURANCE

Title Report

Reasons for Title Insurance

When a lender decides to lend money to a borrower, the lender must be satisfied that there are no liens, judgments or other mortgages on the property which could take a priority interest over that of the lender's security interest. It is likewise important for the borrower to be satisfied that the property is unencumbered at the time of the transfer of title. If the borrower is purchasing a home, he/she will want to be assured that there are not any pre-existing liens, encumbrances or defects affecting the property. It must also be ascertained that the borrower is obtaining the title from the correct individuals.

Lenders require title insurance in order to protect themselves from risks that arise when securing a loan with a property. There are two main differences between title insurance and other types of insurance. First, title insurance protects against events that may have happened in the past, while other insurances protect from future events. Second, with title insurance, there is only a one-time insurance premium paid at the loan closing, while other insurance types typically require on-going premiums. Title insurance is regulated by state agencies and the Department of Housing and Urban Development.

> *Lenders require title insurance in order to protect themselves from risks that arise when securing a loan with a property.*

Types of Title Insurance

Lender's insurance and homeowner's title insurance policies are the two types of title insurance available. Homeowners or "owners" insurance provides protection for the borrowers against many potential liabilities, including mechanics liens, unreleased mortgages, improper subdivisions and other third party rights affected on the property over the course of its prior ownership.

Lender's policies provide protection against lender loss from title defects or liens that should have been cleared up prior to the policy being issued. To perfect a lien, the borrower executes a deed of trust or mortgage which is subsequently recorded among the land records in the jurisdiction where the property is located. Deed of trust laws and theories vary among the states and U.S. territories.

Key Elements of Title

In order to understand title, it is important to know the key components. The title history of a property is composed of recorded instruments on the land records on each property and other statutory interests, i.e. tax liens or mechanics liens. Each record tells a story on the property, such as, when the property was acquired, the amount it was sold for etc. It is the job of the title company to review this information on the history of the property and to identify any defects that are in the title history of the property. These defects must be cured prior to closing, or the title company may elect to insure over them. A defect on title can be anything from a lien or judgment to a break in the chain of title.

Real Property vs. Personal Property

There is a major difference between real property and personal property. Real property is comprised of land and anything that is affixed to the land. Personal property is anything that is transitory and can be moved. Title to real property is maintained at local county courthouses and recorders' offices. These courthouses have collected information on every property in the United States since the early 1800s.

There may be a question as to whether a mobile home is considered real property or personal property. If the mobile home is affixed to the land in a permanent fashion, it may be considered an improvement and would be considered real property. It is important to note that the mobile home must also be properly converted from personal property to real property for title, tax, and insurance purposes. If the mobile home is not affixed to the land, it is considered personal property.

> *Real property is comprised of land and anything affixed to the land. Personal property is anything that is transitory and can be moved.*

Steps in the Title Process

Just as the loan process has different steps to get to closing, so does the title process. The steps are as follows:

- **Order Title Search**: The originator should provide to the title company the subject property address and borrower's name (in the case of a refinance) or the seller's name (in the case of a purchase transaction). Based on this information, the abstractor or attorney will conduct a search of the county records to determine the status of the property, including ownership, liens and judgments.

- **Legal Review**: The chain of title is prepared by the abstractor (or attorney) and examined by a title attorney. The attorney certifies any areas of concern to the title company to determine ownership, open liens, open judgments, exceptions and requirements that must be satisfied in order to issue a title commitment.

- **Issue Binder/Commitment**: Once all open liens, judgments and ownership are determined, the title company will issue a title binder to the lender. The title binder will identify ownership, open liens, open judgments, exceptions and items that must be satisfied in order for the title company to issue a title policy. When the title commitment is submitted to the lender, it usually comes in a package that includes the insured closing letter.

- **Closing**: This occurs when the parties meet to execute documents related to the loan transaction. In the case of a purchase, the parties may include the borrower, seller, real estate agents and the settlement agent. In the case of a refinance, the parties may only be the borrower and the title company representative. In some instances, the loan originator may attend settlement to assist the borrower with any questions.

- **Funding**: This occurs once all documents are executed and loan conditions are met. The settlement agent receives funds for disbursement.

- **Issue Short Form Policy**: A short form policy is an abbreviated version of a long form title policy that does not require the recording of the deed or deed of trust prior to issuance. Many lenders request that a short form policy is issued at the time that the loan disburses. The title company will later provide an addendum to the lender showing the recording information.

- **Recording**: Recording is when the deed, deed of trust or other recordable documents are submitted to the courthouse for filing. It is customary for the settlement agent to record documents immediately after closing to ensure priority of lien.

- **Issue Long Form Policy**: If a short form policy is not issued at the time that the loan is disbursed, a long form policy will be issued once the documents that are required to be recorded are stamped with a book and page number and returned from the recorder's office.

Liens

Liens are monetary claims that may provide the creditor with the right to foreclosure. Liens can come in the form of voluntary liens or involuntary liens. Voluntary liens are liens in which an owner has given consent to having the lien attached to his/her property. A mortgage is a perfect example of a voluntary lien. An owner consents to the terms of a mortgage and understands that there is a lien on the property until the mortgage is paid off. An involuntary lien is a lien that is imposed on the property for the owner's unpaid debt.

A good example of an involuntary lien is a tax lien. A tax lien is imposed by statutory right and is imposed on the property when the owner has not paid the real estate taxes on the property. Mechanic's liens are another form of involuntary lien. Mechanic's liens secure payment for a contractor's labor and materials for home improvements that have been completed but not paid for by the property owner. When there is a mechanic's lien placed on a property, the contractor must send the owner a notice of lien within the statutory time period of the completion of the improvements. Contractors are required to record the notice of their lien within a prescribed number of days of the completion of work.

A judgment, which is a decree issued by a court, is considered a lien. Judgments often have limited lives; generally 10 years, unless they are renewed (renewals usually may only occur once). In order to perfect the lien, the judgment must be recorded in the circuit court for the county where the property is located. A judgment lien is typically enforceable for many years from the date of filing.

An attachment is defined as a "seizing of a person's property to secure a judgment or to be sold in satisfaction of a judgment." An attachment is also considered a lien.

Lien priority is the chronological order in which liens are filed against a property. When a property is foreclosed to satisfy a lien, lien priority becomes an important issue for lenders and lien holders. Since there is only a limited amount of value in a property, a higher priority lien is more likely to be satisfied than a lower priority or later-filed lien. This is why lenders always require that prior liens be paid off as a condition of closing. In a purchase transaction, the primary lender always requires that its mortgage is in first lien position.

> *Liens are monetary claims that may provide the creditor with the right to foreclosure. Liens can come in the form of voluntary liens or involuntary liens.*

Priority of Liens:

- Generally, real estate taxes and special assessments take priority over all other liens
- Other liens follow in the order of recordation
- There are some exceptions, particularly for mechanic's liens which can relate back in time even though filed or recorded later in time
- Subordination agreements between lien holders can change priority (for example, a first mortgage vs. second mortgage)

Title Theory States

In title theory states, mortgages are executed and the borrower gives legal title to the lender while retaining equitable title. Theoretically, the lender owns the property via a deed of trust until the debt is paid. Upon default, the lender has a right to possession. When the debt is paid and satisfied, legal title is returned to the borrower.

Lien Theory States

In lien theory states, the borrower retains both legal and equitable title. The mortgage serves as a lien against the property. In the case of default, the lender will be required to institute a foreclosure proceeding in order to obtain legal title to the property.

Subordination Agreement

If a customer has a second mortgage or a HELOC that is not being paid off in the case of a refinance, a subordination agreement may be needed to ensure the lender's priority of lien. A subordination agreement is a document that changes the order of priority. If a lender wishes to maintain a first lien position, it must receive permission from the second mortgage holder to do so by requesting a subordination agreement.

If a subordination agreement is needed, the originator or the title company should contact the subordinating lien holder to determine what is required to obtain a subordination agreement. In some instances, the subordinating lender may require a processing fee. The subordination agreement may be prepared by the title company or the subordinating lender. Ultimately, the agreement must be recorded with the new deed of trust to ensure priority.

Insurance: Hazard, Flood, Mortgage

There are a number of different types of insurance which are required in conjunction with the origination of a mortgage loan. Hazard, flood, mortgage and title insurance are four common types. The beneficiary of the insurance depends on the purpose of the insurance.

Mortgage Insurance

There are two types of mortgage insurance: private mortgage insurance and FHA's mortgage insurance premium policy.

Private Mortgage Insurance (PMI): Generally required by lenders on conventional loans when the loan-to-value (LTV) is higher than 80%. The intention of PMI is to provide some security to the lender in the event of default, the theory being that higher LTV poses a greater risk of default. Borrowers also qualify for a loan with a lower down payment when they are willing to pay PMI. Per federal legislation known as the Homeowners Protection Act (HPA), borrowers may request discontinuation of PMI when they reach 20% equity position. HPA requires automatic discontinuation once the loan has reached 78% LTV.

When the borrower requests discontinuation at 80% LTV, it is at the lender's discretion to grant the request. The law allows lenders to consider the payment history of the borrower in determining whether to discontinue PMI at the higher LTV. A good payment history includes no payments more than 60 days late in the period beginning 24 months prior to the request. A good payment history also includes no payments more than 30 days late in the 12-month period immediately preceding the request.

Mortgage Insurance Premium (MIP): MIP is required on all FHA loans and is intended to serve the same purpose that PMI serves for conventional loans. Upfront MIP is collected on all FHA loans, in addition to annual MIP, which is collected on a monthly basis. In January 2013, HUD issued Mortgagee Letter 2013-04, creating stricter requirements for MIP. Under the new standards, for FHA case numbers assigned on or after June 3, 2013, the following rules for MIP apply:

- Mortgages involving an original principal obligation less than or equal to 90% LTV will be subject to an annual MIP that *"...will be assessed until the end of the mortgage term or for the first 11 years of the mortgage term, whichever occurs first."*

- Mortgages involving an original principal obligation with an LTV greater than 90% will be subject to an annual MIP *"...until the end of the mortgage term or for the first 30 years of the term, whichever occurs first."*

There are a few exceptions to this rule, including one for home equity conversion mortgages [95].

> *Private Mortgage Insurance (PMI) is generally required by lenders on conventional loans when the LTV is higher than 80%. Mortgage Insurance Premium (MIP) is required on all FHA loans in addition to annual MIP.*

Hazard Insurance

Hazard insurance is required to protect the security of the collateral property from damage caused by fire and other risks. It is also commonly known as homeowner's insurance. A **loss payee clause**, or lien holder clause, is included in hazard insurance policies in order to protect the lender. The clause requires insurance claims to be made jointly payable to the lender and the homeowner so the lender can ensure its collateral is repaired or its debt is retired in the event of damage to the property.

Flood Insurance

Flood insurance is also used to protect the security of the collateral property, although its use is determined by the geographic location of the real estate. Flood insurance was first made available by the National Flood Insurance Act of 1968. Homeowners who are required to carry flood insurance can obtain it through the Federal Emergency Management Agency's National Flood Insurance Program.

As part of the process of determining whether or not a property is suitable as collateral for the specified loan, the appraiser has a responsibility to determine the flood zone designation for the property's location. The originator, processor, and underwriter must ensure that if the property is located in a zone designated with an "A" or "V" prefix, proper flood insurance is in place.

The Federal Emergency Management Agency (FEMA) has undertaken a massive effort of flood hazard identification and mapping to produce Flood Boundary and Floodway Maps (FBFMs). One of these areas is a Special Flood Hazard Area (SFHA), which is defined as an area of land that would be inundated by a flood having a 1% chance of occurring in any given year. This is also referred to as the base or 100-year flood. All flood zones with an "A" or "V" prefix fall into this area.

Development may take place within an SFHA if the development complies with local floodplain management ordinances that meet minimum federal requirements. Flood insurance is required for insurable structures within an SFHA to protect federal financial investments and assistance used for acquisition and/or construction purposes within communities participating in FEMA's National Flood Insurance Program (NFIP).

Mandatory Flood Insurance
Flood zones with an "A" or "V" prefix are considered SFHAs and require mandatory flood insurance under federally regulated loan programs. Other flood zones may or may not require insurance due to special circumstances.

Zone V and Zone VE are the zones that correspond to areas within the 1% annual chance coastal floodplains that have additional hazards associated with storm waves. Mandatory flood insurance purchase requirements apply.

Zone D designation is used for areas where there are possible but undetermined flood hazards. In these areas, no analysis of flood hazards has been conducted, but while mandatory flood insurance requirements do not apply, coverage is available.

Zones B, C, and X are the zones that correspond to areas outside the 1% annual chance floodplain; areas of 1% annual chance sheet flow flooding where average depths are less than one foot; areas of 1% annual chance stream flooding where the contributing drainage area is less than one square mile; or areas protected from the 1% annual chance flood by levees. Insurance purchase is not required in these zones.

SPECIFIC PROGRAM GUIDELINES

FHA, VA, USDA, HECM

The requirements for nonconventional government loans including FHA, VA, and USDA mortgage loans are discussed in detail in the section of the course on "General Mortgage Knowledge," and thorough preparation for the examination should include a review of this section. Following is a brief review of these program guidelines.

FHA Guidelines

The purpose of the Federal Housing Administration (FHA) has always been to assist lower-income borrowers and first time homebuyers in obtaining affordable loans. Although the goals of FHA lending have not changed, higher FHA lending limits and limited loan availability in the conventional market have caused a greater number of affluent consumers to apply for FHA loans. It is important to recall that FHA does not make loans. Instead, the agency insures loans made by approved lenders against loss from a foreclosure which does not produce sufficient proceeds to retire debt in full.

FHA supports a number of different loan programs, and recent federal legislation has expanded the agency's product offerings in an attempt to assist more borrowers. FHA's two primary programs are 203B – the fixed-rate program – and 251 – the adjustable-rate program.

The following is a broad overview of some of the FHA program guidelines:

- **Lending Limits**: The FHA has lending limits that vary by county and that are higher for multi-family properties. Since 2008, Congress passed a series of laws to raise and maintain higher lending limits to ease the credit crunch. Currently, the lending limit for single family properties in most areas of the country cannot exceed 150% of the GSE conforming loan limit of $417,000, making $729,750 the FHA loan limit ceiling [96]. Note that FHA lending limits are tied to the GSE conforming loan limit to ensure that FHA loans are suitable for purchase by Fannie Mae and Freddie Mac.

- **Debt Ratios**: The debt ratios that FHA requires are not set by law or regulation and may vary. However, examples of debt ratios that the FHA has used in the wake of the financial crisis include debt-to-income ratios of 31% for housing and 43% for total debt.

- **Down Payment**: FHA requires borrowers to invest in the loan transaction by making a 3.5% down payment based on sales price or appraisal (whichever is less) – it can be from the borrower's own funds, gift funds or housing authority grants.

  In its January 20, 2010 announcement, "FHA Announces Policy Changes to Address Risk and Strengthen Finances," HUD explained that this guideline would change in the early summer of 2010. The new guideline states that new borrowers will be required to have a minimum FICO score of 580 to qualify for the FHA's 3.5% down payment program. New borrowers with less than a 580 FICO score will be required to put down at least 10%. The current reality of the mortgage lending market is that few lenders will make a loan to a borrower with a FICO score below 620.

- **Seller Concessions**: Loans are permitted to contain up to 6% seller concessions. HUD is considering limiting concessions to 3%, which is the amount allowed in conventional mortgage lending transactions, however this has not been finalized.

- **Mortgage Insurance Premiums (MIP)**: MIP is collected as an upfront mortgage insurance premium (UFMIP) at closing as well as on a monthly basis (annual MIP, divided into 12 equal payments). Both are expressed in basis points and calculated based on loan amount, loan term and loan-to-value ratio. As discussed in the foregoing section on insurance, MIP requirements became stricter in 2013. Now, annual MIP is assessed until the end of the loan term or for the first 11 years of the term (whichever comes first) for FHA loans with an LTV of 90% or less, and MIP is assessed until the end of the loan term or for the first 30 years (whichever comes first) for loans with an LTV of more than 90%.

Home Equity Conversion Mortgage (HECM)
The HECM is the FHA's version of a reverse mortgage. The HECM:

- Is available to borrowers who are 62 or older

- Is secured by the borrower's principal dwelling

- Allows borrowers to receive monthly payments or a lump sum drawn from the equity in the home

Borrowers seeking HECM mortgages must complete borrower counseling and pay upfront and annual MIPs. In 2013, HUD made changes to the HECM program, and these changes include limitations on lump sum disbursements, requirements for stricter financial assessments of loan applicants, and new formulas for calculating MIPs. These changes were issued through two Mortgagee Letters that HUD released on September 3, 2013: Mortgagee Letter 2013-27 and Mortgagee Letter 2013-28.

VA Guidelines

The Department of Veterans Affairs (VA) supports affordable loan programs for our nation's active veterans discharged under conditions other than dishonorable, disabled veterans, and spouses of deceased veterans. It is important to note that the VA does not make loans but provides a guaranty for a specific portion of the loan amount made by approved lenders.

The following is a broad overview of some of the VA program guidelines:

- **Certificate of Eligibility (COE)**: In order to originate a VA loan, the veteran must obtain a COE which establishes the qualification to participate and lists the veteran's entitlement.

- **Entitlement and Guaranty**: VA guarantees up to four times the amount of the veteran's entitlement. The basic entitlement is $36,000.

- **Debt Ratios**: For VA loans, lenders are only required to consider the total debt-to-income ratio. The agency uses a total debt ratio of 41%.

- **Seller Concessions**: Loans are permitted to contain up to 4% seller concessions.

- **Loan Limit**: The VA does not publish a maximum loan limit for loans it guarantees, however, there are limits for certain types of loan transactions. The agency uses the loan limits established by Fannie Mae and Freddie Mac.

- **Funding Fee**: Instead of mortgage insurance, every VA loan includes a nonrefundable funding fee, which ranges from .50% to 3.30% of the loan amount and is smaller for those borrowers who make a down payment. The fee depends on the type of loan transaction and whether the veteran has previously used his/her eligibility for a loan. The fee is not charged to disabled veterans and can be financed into the loan.

USDA Guidelines

The United States Department of Agriculture (USDA) makes and guarantees loans for lower-income borrowers in rural areas. The program is administered by the Rural Housing Service (RHS), and the loans originated under this program are known as RHS loans or 502 loans. RHS or 502 loans include direct and guaranteed loans. The government actually funds direct RHS loans, and it insures RHS guaranteed loans.

The following is a broad overview of some of the USDA program guidelines for RHS guaranteed loans:

- **Debt Ratios**: RHS utilizes debt-to-income ratios of 29% for housing and 41% for total debt.

- **Funding Fee**: All RHS loans include a nonrefundable 2% funding fee, also known as a guaranty (or guarantee) fee. RHS loans also require an annual funding fee of 0.40% of the loan amount, paid monthly.

- **100% Financing**: RHS loans do not require a down payment. Borrowers are also permitted to finance the required funding fee, allowing financing up to 102%.

- **30-Year Fixed**: The USDA loan program offers 30-year fixed-rate loans only.

Additional underwriting requirements for USDA loans are available on the USDA website [97].

Fannie Mae, Freddie Mac

Conforming Loan Guidelines

The Federal National Mortgage Association, also known as Fannie Mae, and the Federal Home Loan Mortgage Corporation, also known as Freddie Mac, are government-sponsored enterprises (GSEs) that help to provide lenders with an ongoing source of funding by purchasing loans that conform to GSE guidelines. Fannie Mae and Freddie Mac pool or bundle mortgages with similar characteristics to create mortgage-backed securities that investors can sell on Wall Street. They also sell loans directly to investors that securitize and sell the mortgages under private labels.

The most important factor in determining if a loan is suitable for purchase by Fannie Mae or Freddie Mac is whether it meets the GSE conforming loan limit. Currently, the conforming loan limit for single family homes in most areas of the country is $417,000, and the limit goes up to $625,500 for a single-family residence in high-cost areas.

Other factors that are relevant in determining whether a loan is suitable for purchase by Fannie Mae and Freddie Mac include:

- **Debt Ratios**: The GSEs utilize debt-to-income ratios of 28% for housing and 36% for total debt, although there is some flexibility for higher ratios depending on additional factors.

- **Down Payment**: Fannie Mae and Freddie Mac guidelines include down payment requirements of at least 5%. In today's market, even higher down payments are often required.

- **Mortgage Insurance**: Conforming loans may require private mortgage insurance when the borrower makes a down payment of less than 20%.

> *Fannie Mae and Freddie Mac are government-sponsored enterprises (GSEs) that help to provide lenders with an ongoing source of funding by purchasing loans that conform to GSE guidelines.*

CLOSING

Title and Title Insurance

The title to a property is a document that provides evidence of conveyance of an individual's transfer of ownership of property to another individual. Information affecting property title must be recorded in public records in order to provide a clear lineage of the ownership and transfer of a property. A deed, which is a written agreement transferring property from one person to another, is an example of information that affects title and must be properly recorded. The title company is a key player in the loan origination and settlement process which provides information and services relevant to a property's title. A title company may also provide the legal description of property that is needed for a loan application.

The title company's responsibilities begin with a title search performed by an attorney or abstractor. The title search is an examination of county or municipal records to determine the legal status of the property. Items that an abstractor will search for include easements (such as utility easements or rights of way to another property), unpaid tax liens, or mortgage liens. The title search results in a title abstract which is a report containing the history (or chain) of title associated with the property. The title company will issue a title binder which acts as temporary title insurance until an actual title insurance policy is issued.

Title Insurance

The purpose of title insurance is to provide coverage for undisclosed liens or other title defects that did not turn up in the title search. Title insurance is available in two forms: lender's insurance and owner's insurance. Lender's insurance protects the lender and is generally mandatory for loan approval.

Owner's insurance is voluntary on the part of the borrower. It protects the borrower from lawsuits and other harmful scenarios resulting from title defects. The borrower bears the cost of both lender's and owner's title insurance. Title insurance has the unique characteristic of covering losses that a homeowner may suffer as a result of past acts or omissions, unlike every other type of insurance, which covers potential losses resulting from future events.

Closing Agent

The closing agent is often employed by the title company, although in some cases, he or she may be an employee of the lender, an attorney, or an attorney that represents the lender. State law determines which types of professionals can serve as settlement agents, with some states having much more restrictive requirements than others. For example, in some states, attorneys must handle closings. The responsibilities of the closing agent include:

- Coordinating the closing process
- Verifying transaction amounts
- Ensuring all parties to the transaction (borrower/buyer, seller, etc.) have copies of forms and disclosures required for settlement
- Verifying identity of parties and notarizing documents
- Discussing closing requirements with parties to the transaction including fees, dates, funding, rescission, etc.

Verifying the identity of parties has become an issue of increasing concern since the number of cases of mortgage fraud has reached epidemic proportions. Parties have the right to give power of attorney to another individual and may not be present at closing, and all documents and disclosures prepared for closing may be signed before a notary and returned to the loan originator. If loan originators never meet the borrower and there are other indicators that the lending transaction is suspicious, it is advisable for the loan originator to alert the office manager or underwriter and to contact an attorney to determine what legal obligations he/she may have to report suspected fraud to banking regulators or to other enforcement authorities. Reports go to the Financial Crimes Enforcement Network (FinCEN), which will involve the FBI if appropriate.

> *The closing agent may be an attorney, an attorney representing the lender, or an employee of the title company or the lender. State law determines which types of professionals can serve as settlement agents.*

Explanation of Fees and Documents

While the closing agent's responsibilities include the duty to provide a comprehensive explanation of closing documents and related fees, the borrower should not be hearing these explanations for the first time at settlement. The services of a mortgage broker or loan originator should include full disclosure and discussion of all fees and obligations with the borrower.

A number of states have amended their licensing laws to expressly provide that mortgage brokers have fiduciary obligations or agency relationships with borrowers. In these states, a mortgage broker is responsible for ensuring that its individual loan originators/employees are carrying out these fiduciary duties, which include acting in the borrower's best interests, following the borrower's lawful instructions, disclosing all material facts to the borrower, and using reasonable care in the performance of duties. Making certain that borrowers understand the fees they are paying and the documents they are signing is one way in which a mortgage broker and its loan originators can make certain that they are disclosing material facts to the borrower and using reasonable care in performing the duties associated with loan origination.

Even if a loan originator is not practicing in a state that has adopted laws imposing fiduciary duties on mortgage brokers, the failure to provide open and honest communication about fees and other obligations may constitute careless or even predatory and unethical mortgage origination. Providing a comprehensive and accurate explanation of all fees ensures that a mortgage professional is meeting obligations under RESPA, TILA and other consumer protection laws. Neglecting to explain any of these items to a borrower can place a mortgage professional at risk for violating disclosure requirements of these federal laws as well as state and federal laws pertaining to deceptive trade practices.

Notice of Right to Cancel (Right to Rescind)

Rescission is a legal remedy that voids a contract between two parties, restoring each to the position held prior to the transaction. TILA gives borrowers the right to rescind some types of lending agreements, and in those transactions in which this right exists, loan originators should make certain that borrowers understand the right of rescission, particularly since they have only three business days to exercise it.

The right to rescind does not apply to all types of lending transactions. No right to rescind exists for:

- Residential mortgages to purchase or construct a home
- Refinancing of credit already secured by the borrower's principal dwelling with the same creditor that made the first loan

HELOCs and home improvement loans are the types of loans that are the most likely to be subject to a right of rescission. Notice to the borrower of the right to rescind is due at the time of closing. The notice must be given in a document that is separate from other TILA disclosures, and two copies must be given to each party who has a right to rescind.

Parties with Rights of Rescission
In order to exercise a right to rescind, the consumer is not required to be a signatory to the note, but he/she must have an ownership interest in the dwelling subject to the lien.

Expiration of Right to Rescind in Closed-End Transactions
If the loan is for closed-end credit, the consumer can exercise his/her right to rescind the transaction until midnight on the third business day after the signing of the lending agreement.

Expiration of Right to Rescind in Open-End Transactions
In open-end transactions, such as home equity credit lines, when the lender has a security interest in the borrower's principal dwelling, a consumer can exercise his/her right to rescind the transaction **until midnight on the third business day** after the following events occur:

- The credit plan is open
- A security interest is added or increased to secure an existing plan
- Increasing the dollar amount of the security interest taken in the residence used to secure the plan
- The credit limit is increased

In calculating the time limitations for the right to rescind, note that **"business days" include Saturdays**. Only Sundays and federal public holidays are excluded from the definition of "business days."

Extended Right to Rescind
For both closed-end and open-end credit, a **three-year right to rescind** exists for the following violations by the creditor:

- Failure to provide a rescission notice that meets the TILA requirements for notification
- Failure to disclose all the terms of the lending transaction as required by TILA

> *Rescission is a legal remedy that voids a contract between two parties, restoring each to the position held prior to the transaction. TILA gives borrowers the right to rescind some types of lending agreements.*

Funding

The first step in the post closing process is funding. Generally, funding occurs after the recordation of documents with purchase transactions and refinances involving investment properties. Funding practices vary from state to state. If a refinance transaction involves a principal residence, the loan will fund after the three-business-day rescission period, provided the borrower does not decide to rescind the loan.

When funding occurs, the lender usually wires funds to the closing agent. The closing agent is responsible for disbursing funds to the appropriate parties according to the HUD-1 Settlement

Statement. Payoff statements related to mortgages and to judgments and liens are generally provided to the title company by the lien holder or judgment creditor.

If the transaction involves a refinance to allow the borrower to pay off debt, the borrower generally verifies credit card bills by providing the title company with a copy of the most recent bill statements. If the borrower needs to pay off any debt, the closing agent must make the check payable to the party to ensure that the lender's interest is protected.

Disbursements and payoffs may include payments to the following:
- First mortgage payoffs
- Second mortgage payoffs
- HELOC payoffs
- Tax payments
- Municipal charges
- Creditors
- Lender fees
- Broker fees
- Judgments and liens

Wet Settlement
A wet settlement is when the parties to a loan transaction meet to execute documents, and afterwards, funds are disbursed. When a wet settlement occurs, lenders involved in purchase transactions are required to ensure that the closing agent has funds with which to close. Regarding refinance transactions, loans are to be funded the day after the rescission period expires.

Dry Settlement
A dry settlement is the opposite of a wet settlement. A dry settlement occurs when the parties meet to execute documents, but funds are not disbursed. With dry settlements, the parties are made aware that the funds are not disbursing and the property will not be conveyed until certain conditions are satisfied. Some state recordation statutes even require that the mortgage or deed of trust be recorded prior to disbursing funds.

Table Funding
Table funding is a process that allows a broker to originate and close a loan under his/her name. However, at the time of closing, the loan is transferred to a lender who provides the funds for disbursement. This scenario and similar situations occur when a broker has correspondent lender status or is accessing a line of credit for the purposes of closing the loan.

> *Funding generally occurs after the recordation of documents with purchase transactions and refinances involving investment properties. Funding practices vary from state to state.*

Servicing

Once the file is returned to the lender by the closing agent, loan servicing begins. A loan servicer is the company who will be responsible for accepting loan payments.

In addition to accepting loan payments, the servicer is responsible for:
- Disbursing funds out of the escrow account to pay taxes and insurance
- Maintaining records related to payments and balances
- Managing delinquent accounts

If the original lender on a loan will not be servicing the loan, the borrower must be informed. RESPA requires lenders to provide borrowers with a Mortgage Servicing Disclosure Statement. The statement discloses to the borrower whether the lender intends to sell or transfer the loan servicing to another servicer. The statement must be provided to the borrower within three business days of receiving the loan application.

If a loan servicer transfers, or assigns the right to service the loan, the servicer must notify the borrower at least 15 days before the effective date of the loan servicing transfer. If the borrower makes a timely payment to the old servicer within 60 days of the loan transfer, the borrower cannot be penalized by the new servicer [98].

RESPA now includes new servicing rules that are intended to improve the servicing of mortgage loans with requirements for crediting mortgage payments promptly, resolving errors quickly, responding to borrower inquiries within specified timeframes, and facilitating loss mitigation efforts.

FINANCIAL CALCULATIONS USED IN MORTGAGE LENDING

Periodic Interest

The periodic interest rate, also referred to as the nominal rate, is the amount of interest calculated each payment period (like monthly) when the payment periods occur more frequently than the quoted rate. Since mortgage payments are calculated monthly but based on an annual rate, this is the method used to calculate the interest collected on mortgage payments. The annual rate must first be converted to a "periodic rate" in order to calculate the interest due for that month.

The formula to calculate the "periodic rate" is as follows:
{Annual Rate} ÷ {Number of Payments in a Year} = **{Periodic Rate}**

Example: A mortgage has an annual interest rate of 6% and is due monthly. What would the periodic rate be?
{.06} ÷ {12} = **{.005}, or .5%}**

Once the periodic rate is established, the interest compounded for that month is determined by multiplying the periodic rate by the balance of the loan.

{Periodic Rate} x {Loan Balance} = **{Periodic Interest}**

Example: What is the periodic interest due on a mortgage loan balance of $106,000 with a 30-year rate of 5.325%?

First, find the periodic rate, as shown below:

{.05325} ÷ {12} = **{.0044375}**

Then, multiply the periodic rate by the current loan balance, as shown below:

{.0044375} x {106,000} = **{470.375}, or $470.38**

Credit card payments also use the "periodic interest" formula; however, the interest is often compounded "daily" and based on the APR, so the formula would look like this:

{APR} ÷ {365} = **{Periodic Rate}**

Example: What is the interest on a credit card compounded daily with an APR of 22% and a balance of $1,100?

First, find the daily periodic interest, as shown below:

{.22} ÷ {365} = **{.0006027}**

Next, multiply the periodic rate by the current balance, as shown below:

{.0006027} x {1,100} = **{.66297}, or 66 cents**

Interest Per Diem

Per diem, or daily interest, is calculated by dividing the annual interest rate by the number of days in a year, then multiplying the result by the outstanding balance of the loan. Many lenders will use 360 days, but some require the use of 365/366 days. The lender will provide information on which calculation is correct. Others allow the use of either number. Originators must be sure to know what his/her lender requires before making the calculation.

The formula is as follows:

{Interest Rate} × {Loan Balance} = **{Annual Interest}**
{Annual Interest} ÷ 365 = **{Daily Interest Amount}**

If the loan is amortized, the per diem interest will change every month as the loan balance declines. For the figures included on a Good Faith Estimate, the calculation is made on the anticipated loan amount.

Generally, loans are amortized using a 30-day month or 360 days in a year, and interest is collected in arrears. Therefore, to get the loan on schedule with the payments, per diem interest is collected at closing to put the loan on schedule. For example, if a loan is closing on the 20th day of a month, the closing agent will collect 11 days of per diem interest to pay the interest cost until the end of the month, and the first payment will be due the first day of the next month. That payment will include interest for the preceding month.

The number of days per year used in this calculation may vary by lender. The lender will provide information on which calculation is correct. Originators must be sure to know what the lender requires before making the calculation.

Payments (PITI, Mortgage Insurance)

Amortized mortgage payments are calculated using a financial calculator designed to compute loan amortization. Calculating payments is generally a very simple process when the originator has the total loan amount, interest rate and loan term. Based on the functions of the calculator, the originator will enter these three factors and ask the calculator to solve for a P&I (principal and interest) payment.

Many financial calculators allow a person to enter any three of the variables to return the fourth. For example a person may enter a loan amount, desired payment, loan term and ask the calculator to solve for the required interest rate. Likewise, entering the desired payment, loan term and interest rate will allow a person to solve for the corresponding loan amount.

A more important calculation to borrowers is the PITI (principal, interest, taxes and insurance) payment. It is based on the same principles as the P&I payment but more accurately portrays a borrower's potential monthly payment because it includes the required escrow amounts for taxes and insurance.

Financial calculator models differ in their functions, but many models include a taxes/insurance function for adding these variables into the payment calculation. Regardless of calculator functions, taxes and mortgage insurance are simple calculations that can be added to a P&I payment to advise a borrower of his/her monthly PITI payment.

Calculating Taxes

Taxes are fairly simple to calculate. They are typically obtained as an annual, semi-annual or monthly amount from the locality where a property is located. They are based on the locality's assessed value of the property.

The annual tax amount is divided by 12 to arrive at a monthly tax payment (semi-annual is divided by 6), which can be added to a P&I payment or entered along with the other variables into a financial calculator.

$$\{\text{Annual Property Taxes}\} \div \{12\} = \{\textbf{Monthly Property Taxes}\}$$

Calculating Mortgage Insurance

Mortgage insurance varies based on the borrower's loan-to-value ratio and the type of loan being originated. Fixed-rate loans will have a different mortgage insurance rate than adjustable-rate loans. This is true for both private mortgage insurance (PMI) and FHA mortgage insurance premiums (MIP). HUD sets the rates for FHA insurance, and these rates were subject to an increase in the spring of 2013. Changes to MIP rates are made through the issuance of Mortgagee Letters, and loan originators should visit HUD.gov to follow these and other changes related to FHA lending.

In transactions in which a lender requires the borrower to obtain PMI, the calculation of monthly fees for this insurance is required until the LTV reaches 78%. The monthly PMI is calculated by finding the rate for the specific loan product and multiplying it by the loan amount to find the annual PMI. The annual premium is divided by 12 to arrive at the monthly PMI.

The formula is as follows:

$$\{\text{Loan Amount}\} \times \{\text{Mortgage Insurance Rate}\} = \{\textbf{Annual PMI}\}$$
$$\{\text{Annual PMI}\} \div \{12\} = \{\textbf{Monthly PMI}\}$$

Monthly PMI can be added, along with monthly taxes (and monthly homeowner's insurance), to a P&I payment to arrive at a PITI payment.

> *Mortgage insurance varies based on the borrower's LTV ratio and the type of loan being originated.*

Example

Assume a borrower is purchasing a home for $200,000 and putting $15,000 down on a 30-year fixed loan at 6% interest. The PMI requirement for 93% LTV on a 30-year fixed is 0.78%. Property taxes are $1,500 annually, and the homeowner's insurance premium is $800 annually. What would this borrower's PITI payment be?

The loan amount {185000}, term {30} and interest rate {0.6} are plugged into the financial calculator to solve for a P&I payment of {**$1109.17**}.

Monthly property taxes are calculated as follows:
$$\{1500\} \div \{12\} = \{\textbf{\$125}\}$$

Monthly homeowner's insurance is calculated as follows:
$$\{800\} \div \{12\} = \{\textbf{\$66.67}\}$$

Monthly PMI is calculated as follows:
$$\{185000\} \times \{.0078\} = \{\textbf{\$1,443}\}$$
$$\{\$1443\} \div \{12\} = \{\textbf{\$120.25}\}$$

The PITI payment is calculated as follows:

$$\{\text{Monthly P\&I}\} + \{\text{Monthly Taxes}\} + \{\text{Monthly Homeowner's Insurance}\} + \{\text{Monthly PMI}\} = \textbf{\{PITI Payment\}}$$
$$\{1109.17\} + \{125\} + \{66.67\} + \{120.25\} = \textbf{\{\$1,421.09\}}$$

Down Payment

Down payment is often a component of determining loan-to-value ratios for the purposes of various loan programs or for figuring a maximum loan amount. For instance, FHA borrowers are required to have a 3.5% investment/down payment in their loan transaction. Conventional lenders usually require borrowers to pay PMI if they make a down payment of less than 20%, or otherwise have less than 20% equity in their property.

Example

Assume a borrower is purchasing a property for $237,000 and the lender will require PMI unless the LTV is 80% or less. What is the minimum down payment for this property so that the borrower can avoid PMI?

The calculation is as follows:

$$\{\text{Purchase Price}\} \times \{\text{Maximum LTV}\} = \textbf{\{Loan Amount\}}$$
$$\{237000\} \times \{.80\} = \textbf{\{\$189,600\}}$$
$$\{237000\} - \{189600\} = \textbf{\{\$47,400\}}$$
Or, more simply:
$$\{\text{Purchase Price}\} \times \{\text{Down Payment \%}\} = \textbf{\{Minimum Down Payment\}}$$
$$\{237000\} \times \{.20\} = \textbf{\{\$47,400\}}$$

Loan-to-Value (LTV, CLTV, Total LTV)

There are two loan-to-value (LTV) calculations. The first describes the relationship between the first, or primary, mortgage and the property's value. This is the LTV ratio. The second describes the relationship between all liens and encumbrances and the property value. This is called the combined loan-to-value ratio, or CLTV ratio.

The LTV formula is as follows:

$$\{\text{Loan Amount}\} \div \{\text{Lesser of the Property Value or Purchase Price}\} = \textbf{\{LTV\}}$$

The CLTV formula is as follows:

$$\{\text{1st Loan Balance}\} + \{\text{2nd Loan Balance}\} + \{\text{All Other Lien Balances}\} = \textbf{\{Total Encumbrance\}}$$

$$\{\text{Total Encumbrance}\} \div \{\text{Lesser of the Property Value or Purchase Price}\} = \textbf{\{CLTV\}}$$

A property with only one mortgage or lien will only have an LTV. The CLTV applies only when subordinate financing is, or will be, in place.

> *The LTV ratio describes the relationship between the first (primary) mortgage and the property's value. The CLTV describes the relationship between all liens and encumbrances and the property value.*

Examples

Loan-to-Value

Assume a borrower is purchasing a home appraised at $280,000. The purchase price is $278,000, and the borrower is going to make a 25% down payment. What is the LTV for this transaction? The calculation is as follows:

Determine the loan amount based on the purchase price and down payment:

$$\{Purchase\ Price\} \times \{Down\ Payment\ \%\} = \{\textbf{Down Payment}\}$$
$$\{278000\} \times \{.25\} = \{\textbf{\$69,500}\}$$
$$\{Purchase\ Price\} - \{Down\ Payment\} = \{\textbf{Loan Amount}\}$$
$$\{278000\} - \{69500\} = \{\textbf{\$208,500}\}$$

Determine the LTV (note that the purchase price is used in this particular example since it is lower than the property value):

$$\{Loan\ Amount\} \div \{Purchase\ Price\} = \{\textbf{LTV}\}$$
$$\{208500\} \div \{278000\} = \{\textbf{75\%}\}$$

Combined Loan-to-Value

Assume a borrower is looking to refinance and consolidate some of his debts. He has a first mortgage balance of $115,000 and a home equity loan with a balance of $21,000. He also has a tax lien of $4,000 against his property. His property has appraised at $192,000. What is his CLTV?

The calculation is as follows:

$$\{1st\ Loan\ Balance\} + \{2nd\ Loan\ Balance\} + \{All\ Other\ Lien\ Balances\} = \{\textbf{Total Encumbrance}\}$$
$$\{115000\} + \{21000\} + \{4000\} = \{\textbf{\$140,000}\}$$
$$\{Total\ Encumbrance\} \div \{Property\ Value\} = \{\textbf{CLTV}\}$$
$$\{140000\} \div \{192000\} = \{\textbf{73\%}\}$$

Debt-to-Income (DTI) Ratios

The front ratio is calculated by adding all housing related monthly expenses and dividing them by the gross monthly income. Expenses that are added include the proposed PITI payment, subordinate financing, housing association dues, and any other fixed housing expense. Utilities and maintenance costs are not included.

This basic calculation is:

$$\{Housing\ Expense\} \div \{Income\} = \{\textbf{Front Ratio}\}$$

For example, if a family earning $6,780 per month was seeking a new mortgage with a PITI payment of $1,756 and there were no association dues or subordinate financing, the ratio would be calculated by dividing $1,756 by $6,780, as shown below:

Housing Expense:	$1,756
Income:	÷ $6,780
Ratio:	0.26

This would be expressed as a 26% housing or front ratio. This ratio would be acceptable to most lenders. However, experience has shown that the front ratio is not the most important ratio. The back-end ratio, or total debt ratio, is far more predictive of future default. It is calculated by adding the payments for all long-term debts. A long-term debt is generally defined as one that will take more than 10 months to repay using the standard or minimum payment.

That calculation is:

$$\{\text{Total Monthly Debts}\} \div \{\text{Income}\} = \{\textbf{Back Ratio}\}$$

To continue our example, we could assume that this family has a $358 monthly car payment with 22 months remaining and $3,500 in credit card debt. Unless there is evidence of a higher minimum payment, Freddie Mac and many other investors require the use of a 5% minimum payment on revolving debt. To calculate the total debt ratio, begin by calculating the total monthly payments:

Credit Cards:	$3,500
Minimum:	× .05
Payment:	$175

Next, add the three payments:

Credit Cards:	$175
Car loan:	+ $358
PITI:	+ $1,756
Total:	$2,289

Finally, divide the result by the income:

Total monthly:	$2,289
Income:	÷ $6,780
Total Debt Ratio:	0.34

In order to originate a qualified mortgage, the borrower's debt-to-income ratio at the time of consummation may not exceed 43% (12 C.F.R. §1026.43(e)(2)(vi)).

Temporary and Fixed Interest Rate Buy-Down (Discount Points)

Temporary and fixed interest rate buy-downs are handled differently. In a fixed interest rate buy-down, the borrower pays fees to permanently reduce the note rate of a loan. For instance, the lender may offer an interest rate of 7.75% with no discount points or a rate of 7% with three points. The "three points" are equal to 3% of the loan amount and are paid as closing costs, which affect the APR of the loan. The calculation for points is as follows:

$$\{Loan\ Amount\} \times \{0.01\} = \textbf{"1 point"}$$

A temporary buy-down is created when funds are placed in escrow to offset the monthly payment required by the terms of the loan. The escrow funds reduce the payment rate for a period of time but not the note rate.

> *In a fixed interest rate buy-down, the borrower pays fees to permanently reduce the note rate of a loan. A temporary buy-down occurs when funds are placed in escrow to offset monthly payments.*

Examples

Discount Points
Assume a borrower qualifies for a $175,000 loan at 6.50%. The lender offers a discount rate of 6% for two points. How much will the borrower pay at closing to obtain a 6% note rate?

The calculation is as follows:

$$\{Loan\ Amount\} \times \{Points\} = \{\textbf{Cost of Discount}\}$$
$$\{175000\} \times \{.02\} = \{\textbf{\$3,500}\}$$

Temporary Buy-Down
Assume a borrower has qualified for a $125,000 loan, 30-year fixed at 8.25% interest. She is expecting an increase in her salary over the next three years and would like to save money on her monthly mortgage payment for that period of time by using a seller concession to pay for a 2-1 buy-down. If the borrower receives the maximum concession (6% of $125,000), this would equate to $7,500 to use for closing costs, so essentially the buy-down fee will be paid by the seller, costing the borrower nothing. The payment analysis and total cost for her transaction is as follows.

The total cost would be the escrow amount required to maintain the temporary buy-down:

	Payment Rate	Borrower's Payment	Note Rate Payment	Difference	Difference × 12 = Cost Per Year
Year 1	6.25%	$769.65	$939.08	$169.43	$2,033.16
Year 2	7.25%	$852.72	$939.08	$86.36	$1,036.32
Year 3	8.25%	$939.08	$939.08	$0.00	$0.00
				Total Cost	$3,069.48

Closing Costs and Prepaid Items

Fees associated with loan closing, fees owed to state and local government for real estate related transactions and prepaid items such as per diem interest are funds that a borrower often needs to have available at settlement.

Determining the amount of money that needs to be brought to closing by the buyer in a purchase transaction or owner in a refinance transaction is calculated as follows:

{Loan Amount} – {Payoff} – {Financing Costs} – {Government Charges} – {Prepaid Costs} =
{Cash Needed, or Overage Available as Cash, to Borrower}

If a borrower is struggling to come up with the funds to cover these costs, he or she may accept a higher interest rate in order to secure the cash needed for closing costs. These funds will appear on the Good Faith Estimate as a lender credit to reduce closing charges. Originators are absolutely prohibited from retaining any portion of the fee that is issued as a credit to the borrower.

ARMs (e.g. Fully-Indexed Rate)

Adjustable-rate mortgages (ARMs) are products that were not available in the modern mortgage market until the 1980s. They were enormously popular during the lending boom, when borrowers were able to qualify for a mortgage based on its low introductory rate. Countless borrowers accepted these loans under the optimistic assumption that they would increase their income and be able to make the more expensive periodic payments when their interest rates reset. As a back-up plan, they assumed that with housing prices rising so rapidly, they could tap into the growing equity on their homes to meet the increasing costs of their loans.

When these assumptions proved to be false for many homeowners, Congress rewrote federal mortgage laws to require lenders to calculate periodic payments using the fully-indexed rate. The CFPB has written regulations to implement these statutory requirements, known as the Ability to Repay Rule. Under the ATR Rule, the **"fully-indexed rate"** is the interest rate that will apply when the introductory rate expires and the rate resets (12 C.F.R. §102.43(b)(3)). This requirement forces borrowers to consider whether they can make payments on an ARM when rate adjustments lead to payment increases. In the past, this was an optional exercise; now, it is required by law.

In order to comply with the ATR Rule, lenders are not only required to determine the ability of a borrower to repay a mortgage at the fully-indexed rate, but also to make monthly, fully-amortizing payments that are substantially equal (12 C.F.R. §1026.43(c)(5)). Lenders must calculate the monthly debt-to-income ratio using verified income and assets and the sum of the loan applicant's mortgage-related obligations, including payments on the loan sought, any simultaneous loans, other current debt obligations, alimony, and child support (12 C.F.R. §1026.43(c)(7)).

Types of ARMs

There are numerous types of ARMs. True ARMs have rates that adjust every year of the loan's term. Hybrid ARMs have an initial period during which the interest rate (and payment) is fixed and not subject to adjustment. Once the initial introductory period is over, the loan rate and payment adjust annually. These popular loan products are usually characterized or described through a fraction or ratio. For example, hybrid ARMs include a 3/1 ARM, 5/1 ARM, and even 7/1 and 10/1 ARMs.

With a hybrid ARM, the first number indicates the period of time during which the rate is not subject to adjustment. The second number refers to the time period, after expiration of the introductory rate, in which the rate is permitted to adjust. For example, a 3/1 ARM would have an initial rate not subject to adjustment for the first three years, after which the rate would adjust on an annual basis for the remainder of the loan term.

During the lending boom, many other types of ARMs were available. These mortgages included interest-only and payment-option loans. These products are now extremely hard to come by.

Common Features of ARMs

There are many types of ARMs, but all have common features. These include:

- Periodic adjustments or changes in the interest rate after the initial rate expires
- An adjustment period that determines how often the interest rate will change
- The use of an index and margin to calculate the new interest rate
- The use of rate adjustment caps

The **adjustment period** for an ARM may be defined as the period between one rate change and the next. Typical adjustment periods range between six months and five years. The adjustment period of an ARM may be used to distinguish different ARM products. For example, a loan with an adjustment period of one year may be referred to as a "one-year ARM," and one with an adjustment period of five years may be referred to as a "five-year ARM."

When it is time for a lender to calculate an interest rate adjustment, it must add the **index**, which is an interest rate determined by the market, and the **margin**, which is a set number of percentage points that the lender selects to cover the cost of its services and to compensate it for the risk associated with the loan. Numerous indices are used to compute interest rate adjustments for ARMs, and they include, but are not limited to:

- The LIBOR (London Interbank Offered Rate)
- The COFI (Cost of Funds Index)
- The COSI (Cost of Savings Index)
- The CMT (Constant Maturity Treasury Rate)

Margins do vary between lenders and, since a higher margin will result in higher payments, borrowers are encouraged to look at the margin that a lender sets for a loan. Some lenders may use the borrower's credit rating to determine the margin for particular transactions. If a borrower has strong credit and the risk of default is low, the lender may use a lower margin. Higher margins allow lenders to cover the risk of transactions with borrowers who are less qualified.

Rate adjustment caps help lenders to sell ARMs. With the use of caps, they can assure borrowers that there is a limit to how much their interest rates can increase. Caps come in several forms, and they include:

- **Periodic rate adjustment caps**: a rate adjustment cap focuses on the amount that the interest rate is allowed to change from one adjustment period to the next, and creates a limit on the size of the change. For example, assume that a borrower has a 3/1 ARM with a fixed rate of 2.5% for the first three years of the loan. The index is the six-month LIBOR, and the margin is 3%. The loan also includes a periodic rate adjustment cap of 2%. When the rate adjusts for the first time, the LIBOR is 2.75%. Adding this rate to the 3% margin results in an adjusted rate of 5.75%. However, with the cap on periodic adjustments, the rate may only increase to 4.50%.

- **Lifetime caps**: a lifetime cap establishes a maximum amount that the interest rate may reach over the life of the loan. For example, assume that a borrower has a 3/1 ARM with a rate of 2.5% for the first three years of the loan term, and a lifetime cap of 9%. If rates rise by 2% each year, the fifth adjustment would result in an interest rate of 10.50%; however, the lifetime cap would limit the rate to 9%.

- **Payment caps**: during the lending boom, payment caps were used in some loans. However these caps come with a significant risk to the borrower. If payments are capped and interest rates continue to rise, monthly payments may not be sufficient to cover the interest due, and the lender will add this unpaid interest to the principal. This results in negative amortization. Payment programs that lead to negative amortization are no longer allowed for:
    - HOEPA high-cost home loans, and
    - Qualified ARMs

Remember that before a first-time borrower accepts a loan that includes a negative amortization feature, the borrower must complete counseling with a HUD-approved counselor (12 C.F.R. §1026.36(k)).

Sample Rate Calculations

John and Mary Smith are borrowing $280,000 toward the purchase of a home. The loan is a 3-1 ARM with a start rate of 5.625%, a periodic rate cap of 2% thereafter, and a lifetime rate cap of 6%. What is the highest interest rate that could be charged in the fifth year of the mortgage?

Step 1: Maximum Rate
> (Start Rate) 5.625% + (Lifetime Rate Cap) 6% = (Maximum Rate) **11.625%**

Step 2: Adjustment Periods

In a 3/1 ARM, the first adjustment occurs at the end of the third year and applies to the fourth year. The rate adjusts each year thereafter. In this example, which asks what the rate will be in year five, the rate would have adjusted twice, once after the third year and once after the fourth year.

The calculation is as follows:

Step 3: Maximum Rate for Adjustment Period

$$2 \times 2\% = \textbf{4\%} \text{ (Maximum Periodic Adjustment)}$$
$$5.625\% + 4\% = \textbf{9.625\%} \text{ (New Rate for 5th Year)}$$

Step 4: Comparison with Maximum Rate

$$\textbf{9.625\%} < 11.625\%$$

Using the Margin and Index

You might be asked a question in which the margin and index are given, as well as a hypothetical change in the index. In our previous example, the margin on the loan might be 2.75% and the index might have risen to 5.50% at the time the second adjustment occurred. In this case, the actual new rate would have been computed by adding the margin and index, then comparing the result to the maximum rate.

The calculations are as follows:

$$2.75\% + 5.50\% = \textbf{8.25\%}$$
$$\textbf{8.25\%} < 9.625\%$$

Because 8.25% is less than or equal to 9.625%, the new rate for year five would be 8.25%.

Discussion Scenario: General Mortgage Calculations

The following scenarios require you to apply several mathematical concepts to solve real world questions.

Scenario 1: A property is valued at $342,000. There is a first and second mortgage with a CLTV of 85%. The second mortgage has an 8% LTV. What is the approximate amount of the first mortgage?

Scenario 2: The Gonzales family is closing on a 30-year 1/1 ARM of $295,000 with rate caps of 1 and 6. The start rate is 6.125%. What is the most the interest rate could be following the third adjustment? What is the most the interest rate could be in the second year of the loan?

Scenario 3: The Jackson family is closing on a conventional mortgage for a property valued at $272,225 with an LTV of 90%. They will pay a private mortgage insurance premium of 1.35%

at closing and an origination fee of 1.5 points. What is the dollar amount of the PMI premium? What is the dollar value of the origination fee?

Discussion Feedback

Scenario 1: The calculation is fairly straightforward – the second mortgage LTV can be subtracted from the combined loan-to-value and the resulting % can be used to determine the amount of the first mortgage.

The calculation is as follows:

$$85\% \text{ [CLTV]} - 8\% \text{ [2nd mortgage LTV]} = 77\% \text{ [1st mortgage LTV]}$$
$$\$342,000 \text{ [property value]} \times .77 \text{ [1st mortgage LTV]} = \$263,340$$

The approximate value of the first mortgage is: **$263,340**.

Scenario 2: The calculations for the Gonzales' scenario are very simple – you just need to be clear on what is being asked. Since the ARM has a cap of 1% on the annual adjustment (referenced by "1" in "rate caps of 1 and 6" – "6" refers to the lifetime cap), each annual adjustment cannot exceed 1%. So, beginning with a start rate of 6.125%, the highest that the third adjustment could be is **9.125%**.

For the second question in the scenario, you need to reference the fact that it is a 1/1 ARM – the interest rate is 6.125% for the first year of the loan. In the second year, it will begin adjusting. Again, referring to the annual rate cap, the most the interest rate can be in the second year of the loan is **7.125%**.

Scenario 3: Points and premiums calculations are generally just a matter of multiplying the loan amount by the % specified. With points, you need to remember that 1 point = 1% of the loan amount. Also, take into consideration the LTV – the borrowers are putting down 10% so, while the property value is $272,225, the loan amount is approximately $245,000. In this scenario, a PMI premium of 1.35% would equal **$3,307.50** ($245,000 × .0135). The origination fee is **$3,675** ($245,000 × .0150).

Ethics

Page left intentionally blank.

ETHICS

Learning Objectives

This chapter was created based on the Ethics section of the NMLS National Test Content Outline. The topics found in this chapter could likely appear on the NMLS national test in multiple choice question format. In this chapter, students will:

- Review ethical goals of some of the federal mortgage lending laws including:
  - Real Estate Settlement Procedures Act (RESPA)
  - Truth-in-Lending Act (TILA)
  - Gramm-Leach-Bliley (GLB) Act
  - Equal Credit Opportunity Act (ECOA)
  - Fair Housing Act
- Examine the ethical conflicts that arise during the appraisal of property used to secure a home loan
- Consider ethical expectations of the mortgage industry through the Codes of Conduct published by several professional organizations
- Investigate the key elements of mortgage fraud and learn how to prevent it
- Explore ethical dilemmas faced by consumers, originators, brokers, lenders, appraisers, and settlement service providers during mortgage lending transactions
- Review case studies relevant to ethics, fraud, consumer protection and fair lending

Introduction

Federal mortgage lending laws are the result of Congressional recognition of the need to ensure that mortgage professionals conduct home loan transactions fairly and ethically. There are numerous lending practices that violate basic notions of what constitutes honest, fair, and ethical lending. These practices include, but are not limited to:

- Advertising loans that are not actually available
- Pressuring appraisers to provide inaccurate valuations of real estate
- Making loans based on the equity in a borrower's home and not on repayment ability
- Using discriminatory lending practices
- Mishandling borrower's funds
- Failing to maintain the confidentiality of a borrower's personal information

The use of these unethical practices contributed to the meltdown of the mortgage market, rising foreclosure rates, and a long period of decreasing real estate values. The Congressional response to the lending crisis was to pass additional laws which focus on particular abuses that occurred when loan funds were plentiful and mortgages were originated without strict compliance with appraisals and underwriting standards.

Ethical correctness is of particular concern when examining the role that mortgage professionals play in pairing borrowers with mortgage loans. During the last boom in the real estate market, mortgage professionals who were not affiliated with depository institutions became the primary originators of mortgage loans, and these originators faced fewer regulatory constraints than loan officers who carried out more traditional mortgage lending transactions in banks and in other depository institutions.

During this era when there were few restrictions to borrowing and lending, there were ongoing debates about the role that mortgage professionals should play in helping loan applicants to obtain a mortgage. These debates raised the following questions:

- Should a mortgage broker or originator work as the agent of a loan applicant?

- Should the doctrine "caveat emptor" (let the buyer beware) apply in the mortgage lending market?

At the beginning of the lending boom, consumers seemed to benefit from a broad range of product choices, and with the availability of options such as reduced documentation and no documentation loans, they had the opportunity to choose loan products with minimal intervention or oversight from originators or lenders. An issue that is beyond the scope of this course, but one that will always arise in a discussion of the lending crisis, is whether it was ethical for lenders to have made these risky products available to consumers.

In response to the widespread use of unethical lending practices during the lending boom, Congress passed laws to address abusive practices and to ensure that mortgage professionals conduct fair and ethical transactions.

PROMOTING ETHICAL VALUES THROUGH FEDERAL LENDING LAWS

Following is a description of some of the ethical issues addressed in federal lending laws and a description of the statutory and regulatory provisions that are intended to curb unethical practices.

Real Estate Settlement Procedures Act

Ethical Issues Regarding Referrals

One of the ethical problems that the Real Estate Settlement Procedures Act (RESPA) intends to address is the ability of mortgage professionals to pocket fees that they have not earned with work, but they have secured with the simple act of referring consumers to particular settlement service providers. Naturally, loan applicants rely on referrals to secure the services needed to complete the processing of a loan. Most consumers take part in very few real estate closings over the course of their lives and do not have contacts with the appraisers, insurers, inspectors, attorneys, and closing agents who can help them to close on a home. However, consumers should not have to pay for these referrals, which is exactly what happens when the cost of paying a referral fee is inevitably passed on to the consumer.

Violations of RESPA and Regulation X occur when a referral results in giving or accepting an unearned fee or any other thing of value. Things of value can include non-monetary compensation such as meals, sporting event tickets and other forms of entertainment as well as items such as office equipment or expense reimbursements. It has been a common misconception in the mortgage industry that a thing of value is acceptable as long as its value is nominal – such as less than $25. This is simply not the case.

The most certain way to avoid ethical and legal liability for referrals is to offer or receive nothing for a referral other than a thank you note. When referrals take place between affiliated businesses that have a legitimate arrangement, providing loan applicants with the Affiliated Business Disclosure Statement is mandatory and is an important aspect of RESPA compliance (12 C.F.R. §1024.14).

Regulation X also permits *"Normal promotional and educational activities that are not conditioned on the referral of business and that do not involve the defraying of expenses that otherwise would be incurred by persons in a position to refer settlement services or business incident thereto"* (12 C.F.R. §1024(g)(1)(vi)). For example, an insurance company can give a mortgage broker pens and notepads inscribed with its name, and the broker may then make these items available to customers.

> *Violations occur when a referral involves giving or receiving an unearned fee or other thing of value. The most certain way to avoid ethical and legal liability is to offer to receive nothing in return for a referral other than a thank-you note.*

Ethical Issues Regarding the Compensation of Mortgage Brokers

For many years, the ability of mortgage brokers to accept yield spread premiums (YSPs) from lenders was a very controversial practice. YSPs were commissions that mortgage brokers obtained from lenders for originating a loan with an interest rate higher than the rate for which a borrower qualified. Consumer interest groups led efforts to eliminate YSPs, claiming that they were unethical because they gave mortgage brokers the incentive to steer borrowers away from loans with lower interest rates to place them in more expensive loans.

On September 24, 2010, the Federal Reserve Board published a Final Rule in the Federal Register concerning payment of YSPs [99]. This Rule amended Regulation Z with the creation of special prohibitions and restrictions for the compensation of mortgage loan originators, including mortgage brokers. The rule addressed YSPs and other compensation practices that led to inflated costs for mortgage products.

Under the 2010 Rule, mortgage brokers may not earn compensation that is based on the terms or conditions of a loan. Any fee earned as a result of originating a loan at an interest rate that is higher than the rate for which the borrower qualifies must be used to subsidize closing costs and must be disclosed as a credit to the borrower.

Changes were made to the GFE in 2010 to reflect the new prohibition against YSPs. Page two of the GFE includes a block of information on "Understanding Your Estimated Settlement Charges." As shown below, this block of information contains three options for selecting an interest rate and covering settlement costs.

Understanding your estimated settlement charges

Your Adjusted Origination Charges

1. **Our origination charge**
   This charge is for getting this loan for you.

2. **Your credit or charge (points) for the specific interest rate chosen**
   ☐ The credit or charge for the interest rate of [   ] % is included in "Our origination charge." (See item 1 above.)
   ☐ You receive a credit of $ [   ] for this interest rate of [   ] %. This credit **reduces** your settlement charges.
   ☐ You pay a charge of $ [   ] for this interest rate of [   ] %. This charge (points) **increases** your total settlement charges. The tradeoff table on page 3 shows that you can change your total settlement charges by choosing a different interest rate for this loan.

| **A** | Your Adjusted Origination Charges | $ |

Referred to now as "borrower credits," YSPs are disclosed in this section. When a borrower credit is involved in a transaction, mortgage brokers must disclose to the borrower that he/she will *"...receive a credit of $_____ for this interest rate of _____%..."* stating that, *"This credit **reduces** your [out of pocket] settlement charges."* This disclosure is intended to ensure that borrowers understand that they have accepted a higher interest rate in order to finance their settlement charges.

Ethical Issues Regarding the Compensation of Loan Originators

Although the Federal Reserve Board addressed other issues related to loan originator compensation, the Consumer Financial Protection Bureau (CFPB) rewrote the rule in 2013, and its Loan Originator Compensation Rule became effective in January 2014. The CFPB's rule reflects many of the provisions of the Federal Reserve's rule, such as the prohibition against steering, and addresses many additional issues that relate to the compensation of loan originators. The Rule applies to *"...closed-end consumer credit transactions secured by a dwelling"* (12 C.F.R. §1026.36(b)). It is applicable even if the home securing a loan is not the borrower's principal residence, and applies to first and subordinate lien mortgages.

The CFPB's Loan Originator Compensation Rule applies to **"loan originators,"** and the Rule defines the term to include a person who earns compensation by performing any of the following activities:

- Taking an application
- Arranging a credit transaction
- Assisting a consumer in applying for credit
- Offering or negotiating credit terms
- Making an extension of credit
- Referring a consumer to a loan originator or creditor, or

- Advertising or communicating to the public an ability or intent to perform any loan origination services

(12 C.F.R. §1026.36(a)(i))

The term "loan originator" includes an employee, agent, or contractor of a creditor or mortgage company if the employee, agent, or contractor meets this definition. "Loan originator" also includes a creditor that table-funds loans.

The law defines **"compensation"** to include salaries, commissions, and any other financial or similar incentives such as bonuses, awards, services, trips, and similar prizes (12 C.F.R. §1026.36(a)(3)).

When the mortgage market was booming, many consumers were harmed when loan originators directed them towards expensive loan products in order to earn additional compensation. The CFPB's Loan Originator Compensation Rule attempts to eliminate the incentives that loan originators received for putting their earnings potential ahead of concerns such as loan suitability. The Rule attempts to achieve this goal by creating the following prohibitions:

Prohibition Against Compensation Based on the Terms of a Transaction: Under this prohibition, loan originators may not receive, and others may not pay them, compensation that is based on any of the transaction's terms or conditions (12 C.F.R. §1026.36(d)(1)). Examples of prohibited compensation include, but are not limited to:

- A loan originator receiving higher compensation based on the transaction's interest rate, such as receiving 2% of the loan amount if the interest rate is above 6%, and 1% of the loan amount if the interest rate is 6% or less

- A loan originator receiving higher compensation based on whether the loan contract contains a prepayment penalty

- A loan originator receiving higher compensation for closing more than ten transactions per month with an interest rate higher than 6%, and

- An individual loan originator receiving additional compensation if the consumer buys creditor-required title insurance from the originator's employer or its affiliate, rather than a third party [100]

Prohibition against Dual Compensation: Under this prohibition, loan originators may not receive direct compensation from a consumer and additional indirect compensation from a creditor that funds mortgage loans. A direct payment from a consumer is a payment to a loan originator that is made pursuant to an agreement between the consumer and a person other than the creditor or its affiliates (12 C.F.R. §1026.36(d)(2)).

Prohibition against Steering: Under this prohibition, loan originators may not *"...direct or 'steer' a consumer to consummate a transaction based on the fact that the originator will receive greater compensation from the creditor in that transaction than in other transactions the originator offered or could have offered to the consumer..."* (12 C.F.R. §1026.36(e)).

In order to be able to show that he/she is not violating the prohibition against steering, the loan originator must:

- Obtain loan options from a significant number of creditors with which he/she regularly does business, and

- For each type of transaction in which the consumer expresses an interest, present:
  - The loan with the lowest interest rate
  - The loan with the lowest interest rate that also does not have risky features, such as negative amortization, interest-only payments, prepayment penalties, or a balloon payment during the first seven years of the loan term, and
  - The loan with the lowest amount of discount points, origination points, or origination fees

(12 C.F.R. §1026.36(e)(3))

The Loan Originator Compensation Rule is a very complex rule with numerous provisions that address the fine points of what constitutes "compensation" and illegal compensation practices. Loan originators who have any doubts or questions about a specific compensation practice or arrangement should discuss these concerns with their managers or employers.

> *New rule changes by the CFPB attempt to eliminate the incentives that loan originators received for putting their earnings potential ahead of concerns for borrower protection, such as loan suitability.*

Markups and Up-Charges

Another controversial compensation practice used by mortgage brokers is the use of unilateral markups and up-charges. Markups and up-charges occur when one settlement service provider increases the charges of another settlement service provider and retains the additional fees.

HUD argues that markups and up-charges that are made by and for the benefit of a single party are in violation of RESPA's fee-splitting prohibition. Some members of the regulated community argue that the law only prohibits overcharges that are split or shared with another party because RESPA's fee-splitting prohibition does not apply to unilateral overcharges. The regulations also address a *"...portion, split, or percentage of any charge made or received for the rendering of a settlement service..."* (12 C.F.R. §1024.14(b)).

The conflicting arguments regarding markups were presented to the Supreme Court in February 2012, and the Court wrote a decision confirming that markups are prohibited under RESPA only if the marked-up fee is actually split. It is important to note, however, that markups are still subject to challenge under state laws that prohibit deceptive business acts and practices, and that under these laws, it may be illegal to charge borrowers more than the exact costs of services performed.

Discussion Scenario: Loan Originator Compensation

MortgagePro is a company that is licensed as a mortgage broker. MortgagePro works with three different lenders that fund the transactions that are originated by MortgagePro's loan originators. Each lender has a slightly different compensation agreement with MortgagePro. After MortgagePro receives its compensation from lenders, it pays its loan originators. MortgagePro calculates loan originator compensation as .5% of the fee earned from lenders, and it has provided its loan originators with information about the compensation arrangement with each of its lenders.

After reading that Regulation Z includes provisions on loan originator compensation that became effective in 2014, MortgagePro's manager contacts the company's attorney to request a review of the company's compensation program to ensure that it is in compliance with the law. The manager also asks the attorney whether MortgagePro can continue to help its customers by using cash earned from yield spread premiums to pay closing costs.

Discussion Questions

- *Does MortgagePro's method for calculating loan originator compensation violate the provisions of the CFPB's Loan Originator Compensation Rule?*
- *How can MortgagePro ensure that it is compensating its loan originators without violating the law?*
- *Can MortgagePro continue using yield spread premiums to help its customers to cover closing costs?*

Discussion Feedback

The Loan Originator Compensation Rule prohibits steering in transactions involving closed-end first or subordinate lien loans secured by a dwelling. MortgagePro's compensation program is a violation of this prohibition because it encourages loan originators to place a loan with one lender instead of another in order to earn a higher fee. The Rule expressly prohibits a loan originator from steering a consumer *"...to consummate a transaction based on the fact that the originator will receive greater compensation from the creditor in that transaction than in other transactions the originator offered or could have offered the consumer..."* (12 C.F.R. §1026.36(e)).

MortgagePro can avoid steering problems by paying its loan originators a set percentage of the amount of each loan instead of paying them a percentage of the amount that the company earns on each loan. Even if MortgagePro did not disclose its compensation arrangement with lenders to its loan originators, they would quickly learn that they earned more on loans placed with one lender than they earned on loans placed with others. Note that if MortgagePro had exactly the same compensation arrangement with each of its lenders, it could pay its loan originators a percentage of its earnings in each transaction because the loan originators would not have any incentive to steer borrowers to a particular loan. MortgagePro can also avoid steering by paying mortgage loan originators an hourly rate or a fixed salary.

Yield spread premiums are prohibited when used as a form of compensation for mortgage brokers. A mortgage broker may still originate a loan for an interest rate that is higher than the rate for which a borrower qualifies. However, the broker is not allowed to pocket any portion of the commission earned for originating a loan at a higher rate. Instead, fees that result from the borrower accepting a higher interest rate must be credited to the borrower to reduce settlement charges. These fees must be disclosed as a lender credit to the borrower.

Truth-In-Lending Act

Sales & Marketing and TILA (12 C.F.R. §1026.16 and §1026.24)

One of the principal ethical problems that the Truth-in-Lending Act (TILA) is intended to address is the use of deceptive and misleading advertising to solicit mortgage business. Typical violations of the law include an advertisement's use of **trigger terms**, such as "low monthly payments," without stating the less advantageous terms of repayment. The annual percentage rate (APR) is the most frequently required information when trigger terms are present.

Another common violation involves the advertisement of mortgage products that are not available. For example, the Federal Trade Commission (FTC) recently brought a lawsuit against one mortgage broker that used the Internet and direct mail to advertise a "3.5% fixed payment loan" that was not actually available to any loan applicants.

In 2008, the Federal Reserve tightened the advertising provisions of Regulation Z by creating additional trigger terms, new advertising requirements, and a list of prohibited practices. The CFPB now implements and enforces these regulations. The prohibitions included in these regulations address a number of the deceptive and unethical practices that lure consumers to mortgage products which do not live up to the promises made in advertisements. These practices, which are expressly prohibited in closed-end transactions secured by a dwelling, include:

- **Misleading advertising of "fixed" rates and payments**: Today, even after the lending crisis has led to the elimination of many risky mortgage products, mortgage products are complex, and there are many that combine fixed and variable rates, such as a stepped-rate mortgage with an initial lower rate that is subject to an increased fixed rate. The use of the word *"fixed"* in advertisements for these types of loans is prohibited unless there is conspicuous and equally prominent information about variable rates and increasing payments.

- **Misleading comparisons in advertisements**: Comparisons between an advertised mortgage for closed-end credit and a hypothetical loan that a consumer may have are prohibited unless the ad includes the requisite disclosures regarding APRs and payments. An advertisement to "save $300 per month on a $300,000 loan" is an implied and prohibited comparison between the payment due on the advertised loan and a consumer's current loan payments.

- **Misrepresentations about government endorsement**: Statements that lead consumers to the incorrect assumption that a mortgage product is endorsed or sponsored by the government are illegal.

- **Misleading use of the current lender's name**: Some lenders and mortgage brokers have made direct solicitations that lead consumers to the incorrect assumption that their own lender is contacting them with information on mortgage products.

- **Misleading claims of debt elimination**: This prohibition addresses the practice of suggesting, in an advertisement, that a borrower can obtain the elimination, forgiveness, or waiver of his/her obligations to another creditor. Examples of these types of misleading statements include, "Refinance today and wipe your debt clean!" and "Pre-payment penalty waiver."

- **Misleading use of the term counselor**: An advertisement cannot refer to a for-profit lender, mortgage broker, or its employees as a "counselor."

- **Misleading foreign-language advertisements**: Some advertisements target immigrants who lack fluency in English by advertising favorable lending terms, such as a low introductory rate, in their first language, while providing information on the additional and less favorable lending terms in English.

(12 C.F.R. §1026.24(i))

Regulation Z also prohibits the use of misleading terms in advertisements for open-end mortgages such as home equity loans. "Free Money!" is an example that the regulations provide of a misleading and, therefore, prohibited term (12 C.F.R. §1026.16(d)(5)). Another prohibition related to open-end credit is the use of misleading statements regarding tax deductions for interest paid on home equity loans (12 C.F.R. §1026.16(d)(4)).

Mortgage brokers, mortgage bankers, and loan originators that violate TILA's advertising restrictions and prohibitions are subject to enforcement actions by the FTC and the CFPB. The FTC demonstrated its focus on deceptive advertising in the fall of 2007 when it sent letters to over 200 advertisers, stating that their ads relating to mortgage products were deceptive and in violation of the law. The FTC has also set up a web page to help consumers understand mortgage ads. Entitled "Deceptive Mortgage Ads: What They Say; What They Leave Out," the web page advises that consumers ask the following when seeking mortgage financing:

- What are the monthly payment amounts and how often can they increase?

- Does the monthly payment include an amount that is set aside to cover taxes and insurance?

- What is the loan term and is a balloon payment due at the end of the term?

- Does the loan include prepayment penalties?

- If the loan has a teaser rate, is it possible to refinance the loan without paying a penalty before the rate resets?

The FTC consumer alert on deceptive mortgage ads is available online [101]. The page includes examples of deceptive loans. Mortgage professionals can avoid FTC enforcement actions by reviewing this page, as well as other information published by the FTC, to ensure that their marketing strategies are not deceptive or illegal.

In 2011, the FTC adopted its own set of prohibitions for unfair and deceptive acts and practices in the advertising of mortgages called the Mortgage Acts and Practices (MAP) Rule. The CFPB is now the agency that has primary authority to implement and enforce these rules.

The regulations issued pursuant to the MAP Rule are known as **Regulation N** (12 C.F.R. §1014 *et seq.*). The Rule prohibits *"...any material misrepresentation, expressly or by implication, in any commercial communication, regarding any term of any mortgage credit product..."* (12 C.F.R. §1014.3).

Specific misrepresentations prohibited by the MAP Rule include misrepresentations related to:
- Interest paid each month and whether interest payments may result in negative amortization
- The APR, simple rate, periodic rate, or any other rate
- Fees related to the mortgage product
- The cost of related products, such as credit insurance
- Costs for taxes and insurance, and whether they are included in the loan payment
- Prepayment penalties (these are allowed in very few transactions)
- Variable and fixed rates, particularly the mischaracterization of a rate as fixed
- Comparisons between actual and hypothetical rates and payments
- The type of mortgage and whether it is amortizing or will result in negative amortization
- Cash or credit that will be available as a result of the transaction
- The amount and timing of payments
- Potential for default
- The effectiveness of the mortgage in resolving existing debts
- Any affiliation between the creditor and a government endorsed or sponsored program
- Affiliations with the borrower's current lender
- How long a borrower with a reverse mortgage can stay in his/her dwelling
- The likelihood that a consumer can secure a mortgage product and whether he/she has been preapproved for a product
- The likelihood that a consumer can get a refinancing or a loan modification
- The availability and nature of mortgage counseling and the qualification of the counselor

(12 C.F.R. §1014.3)

Under the MAP Rule, persons that use commercial communications for mortgage products must keep copies of sales scripts and training and marketing materials for a period of **24 months** *"...from the last date the person made or disseminated the applicable commercial communication regarding any term of any mortgage credit product..."* (12 C.F.R. §1014.5). This recordkeeping requirement matches the general requirement under TILA to retain records for two years (12 C.F.R. §1026.25(a)).

TILA includes provisions addressing the use of deceptive and misleading advertising to solicit mortgage business. Typical violations include the use of "trigger terms" in advertising.

Equity-Based Lending

In 1994, Congress amended TILA with the adoption of the Home Ownership and Equity Protection Act (HOEPA). As the first federal anti-predatory lending law, HOEPA has been subject to numerous revisions since it was originally enacted, but one of its principal goals has always been to curb the unethical practice of equity-based mortgage lending.

Equity-based lending occurs when a lending decision is not based on the creditworthiness of the borrower and repayment ability but instead on the equity available in his/her home. When housing prices were high, unscrupulous loan originators made these types of loans to subprime borrowers who often lacked the experience or sophistication to understand the meaning of oppressive lending terms such as balloon payments, prepayment penalties, and payment schedules that would result in negative amortization.

Borrowers who accepted subprime high-cost loans often found themselves caught in an endless series of lending transactions as they refinanced one bad loan with another. Equity-based lending sometimes led to equity stripping, another predatory practice in which borrowers were encouraged to repeatedly refinance without a tangible net benefit. In order to discourage lenders from "loan flipping," HOEPA prohibits refinancing within 12 months of the original extension of credit unless the refinancing is in the borrower's interest.

The Dodd-Frank Act mandated many changes to HOEPA in order to extend the protections of the law to a broader range of lending transactions. Included are changes that:

- **Extend HOEPA protection to more mortgages**: HOEPA's coverage is no longer limited to closed-end transactions. It now covers open-end loans that are secured by the borrower's principal dwelling, as well as loans for the purchase of a principal dwelling (12 C.F.R. §1026.32(a)).

- **Add a prepayment penalty threshold**: Prepayment penalties were a common feature of high-cost subprime loans, and now, if a loan includes a prepayment penalty that is in force for more than 36 months or that exceeds more than 2% of the amount prepaid, the loan is subject to HOEPA (12 C.F.R. §1026.32(a)(1)(iii)).

- **Add more items to the points and fees calculation**: HOEPA has three types of thresholds: APR, points and fees, and prepayment penalty. By adding more items, such as loan originator compensation, to the calculation of points and fees, more transactions are likely to trigger this threshold and become subject to HOEPA (12 C.F.R. §1026.32(b)(1)).

Finally, by requiring a thorough assessment of borrower repayment ability that is based on "... *the consumer's current and reasonably expected income, employment, assets **other than the collateral, and current obligations including any mortgage-related obligations...*" creditors are required to look beyond the available equity in a home prior to making a high-cost mortgage (12 C.F.R. §1026.34(a)((4)).

Congress also addressed equity-based lending in the Dodd-Frank Act by amending TILA to prohibit the making of a residential mortgage loan *"...unless the creditor makes a reasonable and good faith determination based on verified and documented information that, at the time the loan is consummated, the consumer has a reasonable ability to repay the loan according to its terms, and all applicable taxes, insurance...and assessments"* (15 U.S.C. §1639c(a)(1)). The CFPB's rule that implements this requirement is known as the **Ability to Repay Rule (ATR Rule)**, and it applies to most mortgage lending transactions, including:

- Mortgages secured by second homes as well as those secured by a principal residence
- First-lien and subordinate-lien transactions, and
- Purchase money mortgages, refinances, and closed-end home equity loans

The only transactions that are exempt from the ATR Rule are:

- Open-end home equity plans
- Reverse mortgages
- Temporary or bridge loans of 12 months or less, and
- Timeshare plans

(12 C.F.R. §1026.43(a))

The Rule requires creditors to determine a borrower's ability to make monthly payments based on the fully indexed rate of the loan. The monthly payments must be fully amortizing and substantially equal. When evaluating a borrower's ability to make the fully amortizing monthly payments, the creditor must consider and verify the borrower's income, employment, assets, mortgage payment obligations, mortgage-related obligations such as taxes and insurance, other debt obligations, debt-to-income ratio, and credit history (12 C.F.R. §1026.43(c)(2)). Lending transactions based on the consideration of these factors are markedly different from the equity-based transactions that took place during the lending boom.

In addition to the ATR Rule, the CFPB adopted the **Qualified Mortgage Rule (QM Rule)**. This Rule creates a presumption that mortgages meeting particular product feature prerequisites satisfy ability to repay standards. The origination of qualified mortgages gives creditors protection from liability based on any alleged failure to assess repayment ability. Since qualified mortgages offer creditors a "safe harbor," the new focus for loan originations is likely to be on making qualified mortgages. This focus will move the industry even further from the unsafe and unethical past practices that were related to equity-based lending.

With the Ability to Repay Rule and the Qualified Mortgage Rule setting new standards for consideration of repayment ability and safer lending, the CFPB is helping to move the mortgage industry further from harmful practices used in the past.

Gramm-Leach-Bliley Act, Title V

One of the most important ethical considerations during transactions for home loans is the obligation to protect the privacy and confidentiality of the personal information that consumers provide to mortgage professionals in order to secure a mortgage. In the 1990s, it became apparent that personal information was not only unprotected, but also sold for considerable profit. For example, in June 1999, an action brought by Minnesota's Attorney General revealed that a bank had sold customers' personal information, including checking account numbers, credit card numbers, demographic data, summaries of checking account and credit card activity, credit scores, homeownership status, names, telephone numbers, and addresses, to a large telemarketing firm for $4,000,000. The sale of this information was made without the knowledge or permission of the bank's customers. The unauthorized sale and use of personal information, and other failures to protect personal information, are ethical challenges that the Gramm-Leach-Bliley Act (GLB Act) is intended to address.

The primary purpose of the GLB Act (also known as the Financial Modernization Act) was to eliminate barriers and restrictions between different sectors of the financial services industry, such as those that existed between depository institutions, investors, and insurers. However, some members of Congress were concerned that with fewer restrictions on information sharing between financial service providers, there would be little protection left for personal information. One of these congressmen was Representative Joe Barton who experienced the sale of his own personal information to a lingerie company. Testimony like his, and lawsuits such as the Attorney General's action in Minnesota, persuaded Congress of the need for legislation to protect the personal information of consumers.

Title V of the GLB Act has established that financial institutions have specific legal obligations to protect the privacy of consumers' personal financial information. The regulations for implementation and enforcement of the GLB Act are known as Regulation P, and the CFPB now has implementation and enforcement authority. The challenge of complying with this law is greatest for large banks and lending institutions which intend to maintain and profitably use personal information by sharing or selling it to nonaffiliated third parties. In an effort to balance the needs that consumers have for privacy protection and the interests of the marketplace in sharing information, the GLB Act does not absolutely prohibit the sharing of personal financial information; instead, it provides limitations and restrictions on the types of information that can be exchanged and the parties that can receive it. The law also requires financial institutions to give consumers the opportunity to "opt out" of the sharing of personal information.

Compliance with the GLB Act involves the filing of initial privacy notices, opt-out notices, annual privacy notices, adherence to the Act's prohibition on the sharing of account numbers, and the maintenance of an effective security system.

The obligation for non-depository institutions, such as mortgage bankers and mortgage brokers, to provide privacy notices is determined by the following factors:

- Whether the institution shares nonpublic personal information with nonaffiliated third parties, and
- Whether the individual involved in a transaction is a consumer or a customer

Consumers are individuals who have no continuing relationship with a mortgage banker or broker, and they will only receive a privacy notice if the institution shares nonpublic personal information with nonaffiliated third parties (12 C.F.R. §1016.4). Mortgage professionals have a greater ethical obligation to customers, who are defined to include individuals who enter an agreement or understanding for the brokering or arranging of a mortgage loan.

Customers must always receive an initial privacy notice, which is due as soon as the consumer provides any personally identifiable financial information to the mortgage professional in an effort to obtain a mortgage loan (12 C.F.R. §1016.4(c)(3)(ii)(E)).

The initial privacy notice must explain a mortgage banker or broker's practices regarding the collection of nonpublic personal information and the sharing of it with third parties (12 C.F.R. §1016.6). State-licensed mortgage bankers and brokers may use a simplified privacy notice if they:

- Do not share nonpublic personal information with nonaffiliated third parties, and
- Only share nonpublic personal information in order to process a transaction, such as a mortgage application, at the consumer's request

These simplified notices must include:

- A statement that the financial institution does not disclose nonpublic personal information to affiliated or nonaffiliated parties
- A description of the categories of nonpublic personal information that it collects
- A description of the financial institution's efforts to safeguard the confidentiality and security of nonpublic personal information, and
- A statement that the financial institution makes disclosures to nonaffiliated third parties as needed in order to conduct everyday business, such as the processing of loan applications

(12 C.F.R. §1016.6(c)(5))

If a mortgage banker or broker shares nonpublic personal information with nonaffiliated third parties, they must provide a more detailed initial privacy notice. They must also provide both consumers and customers with:

- An opt-out notice, and
- A reasonable opportunity to opt out of the sharing of their information with a nonaffiliated third party

(12 C.F.R. §1016.10(a))

Since non-depository mortgage bankers and mortgage brokers rarely retain the servicing rights to a loan, there are few circumstances in which they would be required to provide annual privacy notices. In fact, the regulations provide that for these individuals, the obligation to provide privacy notices ends when the customer has obtained a loan and no longer requires the services of a mortgage banker or broker (12 C.F.R. §1016.5(b)(3)(iv)).

The Safeguards Rule

In addition to protecting the privacy of nonpublic personal information by meeting requirements for offering privacy notices and opt-out opportunities to consumers and customers, mortgage professionals must safeguard personal information as long as they retain it.

As directed by the GLB Act, the FTC established standards for non-depository mortgage lenders and loan originators to follow when creating and implementing administrative, technical, and physical safeguards to:

- Protect the security and confidentiality of customer information
- Protect against unanticipated threats to the security and integrity of customer information, and
- Protect against unauthorized access or use of customer information

(15 U.S.C. §6801(b))

The FTC's rule is known as the **Safeguards Rule**, and it became effective in May 2003. While the CFPB is the agency that is primarily responsible for supervising and enforcing compliance with the GLB Act, the law has left authority for implementing the Rule and enforcing compliance for non-depository mortgage bankers and brokers in the hands of the FTC. The Rule generally requires mortgage professionals to:

> *"...develop, implement, and maintain a comprehensive information security program that is written in one or more readily-accessible parts and contains administrative, technical, and physical safeguards that are appropriate to [the] size and complexity, the nature and scope of activities, and the sensitivity of any customer information at issue."*

(16 C.F.R. §314.3(a))

The five basic elements of a security program are:

- Designation of an employee or employees to coordinate the security program
- Identification of reasonably-foreseeable internal and external risks to security
- Implementation of the program, including regular tests for its effectiveness
- Oversight of service providers, which includes an obligation for mortgage professionals to ensure that third-party settlement service providers adequately safeguard the security of nonpublic personal information
- Adjustment of the security program to respond to changes in business operations that may impact the security of nonpublic personal information

(16 C.F.R. §314.4)

The GLB Act includes a prohibition against the sharing of account numbers for marketing purposes. The law states that a financial institution may not disclose, for purposes other than to report to a consumer reporting agency, an account number or similar form of access number to any nonaffiliated third party to be used in telemarketing, direct mail marketing, or other marketing through electronic mail to the consumer (15 U.S.C. §6802(d)).

The GLB Act creates numerous compliance issues for mortgage professionals, and with the FTC and the CFPB having authority to enforce the provisions of the law, its requirements demand ongoing consideration. By reviewing privacy notices and security policies to determine if they comply with the requirements of the GLB Act, mortgage professionals can protect themselves from enforcement actions and can also assess the fulfillment of their ethical duty to protect the privacy of the personal information of their customers.

Equal Credit Opportunity Act

Discrimination in lending and credit transactions is the unfair and unethical practice that the Equal Credit Opportunity Act (ECOA) is intended to discourage. ECOA was the first law to directly address disparate treatment of borrowers based on their personal characteristics. ECOA is intended to promote the availability of credit to all creditworthy applicants regardless of race, color, religion, national origin, sex, marital status, or age, and regardless of the fact that the applicant has income from a public assistance program or that the applicant has exercised his/her rights under the Consumer Credit Protection Act.

More specifically, ECOA prohibits creditors from making inquiries about personal characteristics, such as gender, that are irrelevant to a borrower's creditworthiness. However, there are some exceptions to the law's prohibition on unlawful inquiries. These exceptions include, but are not limited to, the following:

- Inquiries regarding race, ethnicity, sex, marital status, and age are permitted for purposes of federal programs that monitor compliance with fair lending laws, including inquiries for the purpose of complying with the Home Mortgage Disclosure Act.

- Creditors may obtain information about an applicant's race, ethnicity, religion, sex, age, or other protected characteristics in order to determine the applicant's eligibility for special-purpose credit, such as a credit assistance program offered by a not-for-profit organization, or for a federal or state program to assist the economically disadvantaged.

(12 C.F.R. §1002.5(a))

There have been ongoing efforts by some federal legislators to create additional protections under ECOA by prohibiting discrimination based on sexual orientation and gender identity. For example, the "Housing Opportunities Made Equal Act of 2013" includes provisions that would amend ECOA by making it illegal to discriminate on the basis of sexual orientation and gender identity. Previous efforts to pass similar amendments have failed, but these are changes to the law that Congress has been considering for several years.

Redlining

Redlining is a particular discriminatory practice that violates ECOA. The term "redlining" came from the practice of using red lines on a map to designate areas that lenders regarded as an unsafe credit risk. Ironically, this method of controlling lending risk was devised by the Home Owner's Loan Corporation, which was established in 1933 as part of the New Deal's program to refinance mortgages that were in default in order to avoid foreclosure. Redlining had the unfortunate effect of restricting lending funds to entire communities, thereby contributing to the decay and demise of countless neighborhoods inhabited by families whose low-income, immigrant status, or race were regarded as indicators of a poor credit risk.

Reverse Redlining

During the mortgage lending boom, when funds for loans were easy to access and commissions for loan originations were high, many neighborhoods that had been marked as a poor credit risk were suddenly targeted by predatory lenders. Many unethical mortgage brokers and originators made loans in these neighborhoods to people who lacked the experience, knowledge, or adequate skill in the use of the English language to understand the terms and conditions of the loans they were signing. Although these practices were in violation of ECOA, Congress adopted the Home Ownership and Equity Protection Act (HOEPA) to take direct aim at the practice of making these types of predatory loans.

Fair Housing Act

Congress adopted the Fair Housing Act to achieve three goals:
- To provide fair housing throughout the United States
- To prohibit discrimination in the sale and renting of housing, and
- To prohibit discrimination in mortgage lending transactions

With regard to mortgage lending transactions, the scope of the Fair Housing Act is broad, and applies to transactions in the primary mortgage market, where loans are made, and to transactions in the secondary mortgage market, where loans are sold to investors.

Since the adoption of the Fair Housing Act in 1968, the Department of Housing and Urban Development has been the federal agency with authority to implement and enforce it. Despite the many changes in regulatory authority brought by the Dodd-Frank Act, HUD continues to be the agency that promulgates regulations under the Fair Housing Act and that oversees compliance with the law.

Under the Fair Housing Act, the protected classes include:
- Race or color
- National origin
- Religion
- Sex
- Familial status
- Handicap

Any lending or housing decisions that discriminate against persons based on a protected class are in violation of the law.

For the past several years, members of Congress have made efforts to revise the Fair Housing Act, as well as ECOA, to prohibit discriminatory practices based on gender identity, sexual orientation, marital status, and source of income. It is important for mortgage professionals to understand that the federal Fair Housing Act does not preempt state laws, which may have a broader scope and stricter requirements. Many state fair lending laws expand their scope by creating protected classes that are not included in the federal law. It is, therefore, important for loan originators to understand the fair lending laws of the states in which they practice and to be mindful of any actions that may be construed as discriminatory in states in which the protected classes include more categories.

Loan originators should be aware that the CFPB and the Department of Justice have made fair lending a top priority. The CFPB has an office devoted to fair lending that is known as the Office of Fair Lending and Equal Opportunity. Actions for violations of fair lending laws, such as ECOA and the Fair Housing Act, are handled by the Department of Justice in its Fair Lending Unit of the Civil Enforcement Division.

> *The CFPB and the Department of Justice have made fair lending a top priority, and mortgage professionals should note the standards for protected classes that are set by both federal and state law, as they may vary in scope.*

Ethics and Disclosure

There are many consumer disclosures required during the loan origination process. Each disclosure has different rules regarding timing and format, and providing each disclosure in the format and at the time required is the best means of ensuring that consumers have all the disclosures that they need to understand their rights and obligations as borrowers, and to ensure that mortgage professionals are in compliance with the law. Failure to provide borrowers with information that will help them to make a sound decision about lending products is unethical. Failing to provide disclosures is a common act of predatory lenders which has contributed to defaults on countless mortgages. Disclosures are intended to educate and inform borrowers so that they understand their rights as borrowers and can make informed decisions throughout the process.

There are a number of appropriate methods for providing disclosures. Handing disclosures to a loan applicant or borrower at a face-to-face interview is always a fail-safe method. In this case, consumers can ask questions, and the loan originator may ensure they receive the information requested and that they understand it. Because origination is often handled over the phone or Internet, the next best method for disclosure is via the U.S. Mail or a fax machine.

Email and secure electronic document handling are also becoming common methods for providing loan origination documents, including disclosures. One provision of Regulation X provides that RESPA disclosures *"...may be provided in electronic form, subject to compliance with the consumer consent and other applicable provisions of the Electronic Signatures in Global and National Commerce Act (E-Sign Act)"* (12 C.F.R. §1024.3). Regulation Z also allows lenders to provide disclosures in an electronic format if they are made in compliance with the E-Sign

Act. Specific provisions of Regulation Z that address the electronic delivery of disclosures include Section 1026.23(b), which allows rescission notices to be provided electronically, and Section 1026.19(c), which provides that consumers who access an application for an ARM electronically may also receive the related disclosures in electronic form.

The many disclosures required over the course of a transaction for a mortgage must be made within the timeframe mandated by the law. Mortgage professionals must make certain that they understand and comply with the deadlines for disclosures.

> *Failing to provide borrowers with information to help them make sound financial decisions is unethical. As electronic document handling become more common, customer consent may be required before receiving certain disclosures electronically.*

Appraisal

The appraisal of the real estate used as collateral in a mortgage lending transaction is one of the most critical components of loan origination since the loan amount is directly tied to the value of the property. Appraisals are also the component of mortgage lending transactions with which unethical actions are most commonly associated. Appraisers are often faced with pressure to return a specific property value to meet a borrower's financing needs. During the lending boom, originators as well as borrowers were tempted to pressure appraisers to deliver the numbers needed to close a transaction.

The unchecked overvaluation of real estate was a principal contributing factor to the collapse of the mortgage lending market and is also one of the reasons that so many mortgages are now "under water." Recognizing the contribution of overvaluation to these problems, Congress devoted Subtitle F of Title XIV of the Dodd Frank Act to "Appraisal Activities." The ultimate goal of these new laws is to encourage appraiser independence.

The Dodd-Frank Act's provisions on appraisals are found in 15 U.S.C. §1639e, and they are intended to protect appraiser independence by prohibiting:

- Coercion, bribery, and any other actions intended to influence the judgment of an appraiser
- Appraisers and appraisal management companies from having a financial or other interest in the property
- Extension of credit by a creditor that knows there has been a violation of the prohibition on coercion or of the prohibition against conflicts of interest

The law also mandates:

- Reporting appraiser misconduct to state appraiser licensing authorities (15 U.S.C. §1639e(e))
- Paying reasonable and customary fees to fee appraisers (appraisers that are not employees of creditors or of appraisal management companies hired by creditors) (15 U.S.C. §1639e(i))

In October 2010, the Federal Reserve Board issued an interim final rule to implement the provisions in the Dodd-Frank Act that address appraisal independence. These rules, now implemented and enforced by the CFPB, are known as the rules for "Valuation Independence" and they apply to the following persons and transactions:

- **Covered persons**: The term "covered person" is defined to include creditors and persons that provide settlement services in connection with a covered transaction (12 C.F.R. §1026.42(a)(1)). "Settlement services" is very broadly defined under 12 U.S.C. §2602(3) to include the origination of mortgages and all of the other services associated with loan origination, such as title searches, appraisals, obtaining credit reports, and inspection services. Therefore, a "covered person" includes a loan originator.

- **Covered transactions**: The term "covered transaction" is very broadly defined to include an extension of consumer credit that is or will be secured by the consumer's principal dwelling (12 C.F.R. §1026.42(a)(2)). Under such a broad definition, covered transactions include those for open-end and closed-end loans, purchase money mortgages, and reverse mortgages.

Instead of referring to "appraisals," the Valuation Independence Rule uses the term **"valuation,"** which is defined as *"...an estimate of the value of the consumer's principal dwelling in written or electronic form, other than one produced by an automated model or system"* (12 C.F.R. §1026.42(a)(3)). Another important term found in the Rule is **"valuation management functions,"** and it includes the functions of persons who:

- Are involved in selecting, contracting with, or employing a person to prepare a valuation

- Manage, oversee, or administer the receipt of orders for valuations, the processing and preparing of valuations, the submission of valuations to creditors, and the receipt of fees for the valuations, and

- Review or verify the work of those who prepare valuations

(12 C.F.R. §1026.42(a)(4))

Under this broad definition, valuation management functions are not limited to the actions of appraisers, but include the acts of creditors, mortgage brokers, or loan originators who order appraisals.

The appraisal rules prohibit:

- **Coercion**: The rule states that no creditor and no person who provides settlement services *"...shall or shall attempt to directly or indirectly cause the value assigned to the consumer's principal dwelling to be based on any factor other than the independent judgment of a person that prepares valuations..."* (12 C.F.R. §1026.42(c)(1)). The rules list the following examples of actions that would constitute coercion:

  ○ Influencing a person preparing a valuation to report a minimum or maximum value

  ○ Withholding or threatening to withhold timely payment unless the consumer's dwelling is valued at or above a certain amount

  ○ Suggesting that current or future use of the services of the person preparing the valuation will depend on the result of the valuation

- Excluding a person from consideration for future valuations if the value reported does not meet or exceed a predetermined threshold

- Conditioning compensation paid to the person preparing the valuation on the closing of the loan

- **Misrepresentation**: The rules state that *"...no person that prepares valuations shall materially misrepresent the value of the consumer's principal dwelling in a valuation." The rules also clarify that a misrepresentation is "material" if it is "...likely to significantly affect the value assigned to the consumer's principal dwelling"* (12 C.F.R. §1026.42(c)(2)).

- **Extension of Credit when a Knowing Violation Has Occurred**: If a creditor knows at or before consummation that a violation of the Valuation Independence Rule has occurred, then it must not extend credit based on the valuation unless i*t "...documents that it has acted with reasonable diligence to determine that the valuation does not materially misstate or misrepresent the value of the consumer's principal dwelling"* (12 C.F.R. §1026.42(e)).

- **Conflict of Interest**: The rules prohibit persons that prepare valuations from having *"...a direct or indirect interest, financial or otherwise, in the property or transaction for which the valuation is or will be performed"* (12 C.F.R. §1026.42(d)).

In order to understand the scope of the prohibition that addresses conflicts of interest, it is necessary to become familiar with the Official Interpretations of the Rule. Generally, the Rule does not prohibit a lender's use of staff appraisers as long as there are "firewalls" between its loan originators and its appraisers. The Official Interpretations state that whether the use of employees or affiliates in the preparation of a valuation is prohibited *"...depends on the facts and circumstances of a particular case, including the structure of the employment or affiliate relationship"* [102].

> *Recent legislation prohibits specific unethical activities in relation to appraisals, including coercion, misrepresentation, extension of credit when a violation has occurred, and conflict of interest.*

When the Federal Reserve Board adopted the Rule, it noted that a literal interpretation of the law would prohibit the use of appraiser affiliates and in-house appraisers, and that *"For many creditors and providers of valuations...complying with the statute under this interpretation would be impractical or impossible"* [103]. The Board, therefore, wrote the Rule to include the following two "safe harbors" for compliance:

- **Safe Harbor for Creditors with More than $250 Million**: If a creditor had assets of more than $250 million for the past two calendar years (as of December 31 for each year), then there is no conflict of interest based on employment by, or affiliation with, the creditor if:

- The compensation of the appraiser or other person performing valuation management functions is not based on that value produced by the appraisal

- The appraiser or other person performing valuation management functions reports to a person who is not involved in generating or approving mortgage loans

- The compensation of the appraiser or other person performing valuation management functions is not based on closing the transaction for which the appraisal is performed, and

- No employee, officer, or director who is involved in generating or approving mortgage loans is directly or indirectly involved in selecting, retaining, or influencing the selection of an appraiser or in preparing an approved list of appraisers

(12 C.F.R. §1026.42(d)(2))

- **Safe Harbor for Creditors with Less than $250 Million**: If a creditor had assets of less than $250 million for the past two calendar years (as of December 31 for each year), then there is no conflict of interest based on employment by, or affiliation with, the creditor if:

  - The compensation of the appraiser or other person performing valuation management functions is not based on the value produced by the appraisal, and

  - The creditor requires that any employee, officer, or director who orders, performs, or reviews a valuation to abstain from any decision to approve, not approve, or set the terms of the transaction

(12 C.F.R. §1026.42(d)(3))

Although the Valuation Independence Rule strictly forbids interference with the independent judgment of an appraiser or other person who is preparing a valuation, it is not illegal to:

- Ask the appraiser to consider additional and appropriate information, including information about comparables

- Request further substantiation or explanation for the conclusion that the appraiser reached regarding the value of the property

- Ask for the correction of errors in the valuation

- Obtain multiple valuations in order to secure the most reliable one

- Withhold compensation for the appraiser based on a breach of contract or substandard performance of services

(12 C.F.R. §1026.42(c)(3))

In addition to the prohibited practices found in the Valuation Independence Rule, this regulation also includes a mandatory reporting requirement that applies to *"…any covered person that reasonably believes an appraiser has not complied with the Uniform Standards of Professional Appraisal Practice or ethical or professional requirements for appraisers under applicable state or federal statutes or regulations…"* (12 C.F.R. §1026.42(g)(1)). The legal obligation to report misconduct arises when a failure to comply with appraisal standards and practices is "material." For purposes of determining if the mandatory reporting requirement applies, a compliance failure is material *"…if it is likely to significantly affect the value assigned to the consumer's principal dwelling…"* (12 C.F.R. §1026.42(g)(1)).

Discussion Scenario: Mandatory Reporting Requirement for Appraisal Misconduct

Mike is a mortgage broker who originates mortgages for home purchases and home equity lines of credit. Mike is trying to help a client who owns a luxury home to secure a home equity line of credit to cover college expenses for one of her children. The lender that Mike uses to fund the loans ordered an appraisal from one of its affiliate appraisal management companies.

When Mike read the appraisal report, he was surprised to find that the valuation was significantly lower than anticipated. Upon inquiry, he discovered that the appraiser who wrote the report was not from the geographic area where the client's principal dwelling was located. Furthermore, he discovered that the comparables that the appraiser used were for one home that was sold as a foreclosure and another that was a short sale. Mike wondered if the appraiser had even noted that these were not normal sales transactions reflecting the true value of two high-end properties.

Mike knows that the Valuation Independence Rule is intended to encourage accurate appraisals, and he wonders if there are any provisions that can help him challenge the valuation. At the same time, he is concerned that if he raises these challenges, he may be considered to have violated prohibitions against influencing the appraiser. He is also concerned that since the property was possibly undervalued and not overvalued, and that the new rules, which were written to address the rampant overvaluation of property, cannot offer him a legal basis for challenging a low appraisal.

Discussion Questions

- *Is the Valuation Independence Rule applicable in situations in which collateral is undervalued?*

- *Are there any provisions in the Valuation Independence Rule that Mike can rely on to challenge the accuracy and reliability of the appraisal and can he challenge the appraisal without violating rules against interfering with an appraiser's independent judgment?*

- *Based on the information presented in this scenario, if Mike finds that the appraisal was inaccurate and carelessly prepared, does he have a duty to report his findings?*

Discussion Feedback

Although overvaluation was a rampant problem and one that led to the lending crisis, the Appraisal Rule prohibits coercion and other acts to influence valuation, whether the objective is to deliver a value that is higher or lower than the actual value of the principal dwelling used to secure a home loan. However, if the valuation that Mike is concerned about is not designed to meet a threshold amount, whether it is above or below the true value of the property, the violation at issue in this scenario is not one that is related to coercion.

Although the Rule prohibits covered persons from interfering with the opinion expressed in an appraisal report, there are exceptions, and these include contacting the person preparing the valuation to request substantiation of the valuation, to request consideration of other comparables, and to ask for a correction of errors. The use of a foreclosure and a short sale as comparables may also indicate a violation of standards set in the Uniform Standards of Professional Appraisal Practices.

Mike is a covered person who has a duty to report compliance failures of appraisers. The compliance failure in this scenario is material since it affects the value assigned to the collateral. The Board cites the performance of an assignment in a grossly negligent manner as an example of a material failure to comply that should be reported to the appropriate state agency. The use of a foreclosure and a short sale as comparables in this transaction is certainly negligent, although it would be up to state licensing authorities to determine if this type of carelessness is grossly negligent.

Discussion Scenario: Prohibited Interest in a Transaction

David is a loan originator for a mortgage company, and one of his clients has requested his services in securing a home equity line of credit, using his primary residence as security for the loan. The client has indicated that he needs to secure as much credit as possible, and David has assured him that with the help of an appraiser that he has used in many of his HELOC transactions, the credit line should be generous.

Cindy, a co-worker, has overheard David's conversation with his client. Having just attended a conference on the Valuation Independence Rule, she believes that David may be violating the Rule by ordering the appraisal and that she may be required to report his actions. When Cindy approaches David to discuss his possible violations, he argues that the Rule does not apply to him for two reasons. First, he argues that the Rule does not apply to loan originators or to open-end transactions. Second, he states that even if the Rule were applicable, it does not create reporting requirements for actions of loan originators.

Discussion Questions

- *Is a loan originator a covered person under the Valuation Independence Rule, and is a home equity line of credit a covered transaction?*
- *Is David acting in violation of any provisions of the Valuation Independence Rule?*
- *Does Cindy have a legal obligation under the Valuation Independence Rule to report David's actions?*

Discussion Feedback
The Valuation Independence Rule applies to David as he negotiates his client's application for a HELOC. The Rule defines "covered persons" to include persons that perform any type of settlement services. This description is clearly broad enough to apply to loan originators.

The Rule also applies to the transaction in which David is engaged. David is incorrect in asserting that the Rule does not apply to open-end transactions. The Valuation Independence

Rule applies to open-end transactions, including HELOCS and all other transactions secured by the borrower's principal residence.

David has a prohibited conflict of interest in this transaction. By selecting the appraiser, he is performing a "valuation management function," and he is performing this valuation management function in the same transaction in which he has a financial interest. The Valuation Independence Rule prohibits persons who perform valuation management functions from having a direct or indirect financial interest in the transaction.

Cindy does not have any mandatory reporting requirements under the Valuation Independence Rule, but she may have a duty under other rules. The reporting requirement is limited to appraiser violations and misconduct and does not extend to the acts of other settlement service providers, such as loan originators.

Fraud Detection, Reporting, and Prevention

The moral and ethical incorrectness of mortgage fraud is never contested. The Federal Bureau of Investigations (FBI) defines mortgage fraud as *"the intentional perversion of the truth for the purpose of inducing another person or other entity in reliance upon it to part with something of value or to surrender a legal right"* [104]. Mortgage fraud takes many forms, including:

- **Liar Loans**: When lenders were willing to fund low-documentation and no-documentation loans, borrowers took advantage of these products by inflating their stated income and enhancing their other qualifications. These actions are illegal under state and federal lending laws and may result in criminal sanctions.

- **Predatory Lending**: When real estate agents and mortgage loan originators encourage a consumer to purchase a home based on an inflated appraisal or steer him/her towards high-cost mortgage products with unfavorable lending terms, they are committing fraudulent acts against consumers and are subject to criminal action.

- **Industry Insider Fraud**: This type of fraud involves the conspiratorial actions of members of the mortgage industry who use lending transactions as a means of securing funds from lenders. With their knowledge of the mortgage lending process, unscrupulous mortgage bankers, mortgage brokers, loan officers, underwriters, processors, real estate agents, appraisers, and lawyers have worked together to close fraudulent loans and pocket the loan funds.

The FBI takes mortgage fraud very seriously, and the focus of its efforts is on "Industry Insider Fraud." Following is a description of some of the tactics that are employed in fraudulent schemes carried out by industry insiders:

- **Inflated Appraisals**: Inflated appraisals are one of the most common elements of fraudulent lending transactions. In some cases, the values of properties used to secure mortgages are inflated by unscrupulous appraisers for as much as 100% of their true market values.

- **Property Flipping**: Property flipping occurs when a property is bought and resold within a very short period of time. Some property flips occur within the same week, and even on the same day. The resale usually involves the use of an inflated appraisal of the property's value.

- **Straw Buyers**: A straw buyer is an individual who accepts a fee, ranging from $500 to several thousand dollars, to provide his/her name, Social Security Number, and other personal information for use on a mortgage application. Although it appears that the straw buyer is applying for a purchase money mortgage and although the mortgage application may indicate that the buyer intends to reside in the home, the straw buyer does not intend to own or possess the property used to secure the loan. Straw buyers walk away from these transactions, often unaware that they are liable for fraud and for making false statements to the government. The parties to the scheme pocket most of the money obtained through the loan, the property used to secure the loan lies vacant, and the loan typically goes into foreclosure.

- **Straw Sellers**: A straw seller is an individual who accepts a fee to falsely claim ownership to a property. Falsified or fabricated title documents, including sham warranty deeds, are created to support the fraudulent claim that the straw seller is the owner and occupier of the property securing the loan. Straw sellers may appear at closings where the property, which they claim to own, is transferred to straw buyers.

- **Air Loans**: When a fictitious borrower obtains a mortgage loan and "secures" it with fictitious property, the loan is known as an air loan. Fraudsters may even use fictitious employers, appraisers, and credit agencies in order to obtain verifications necessary to process the loan application.

- **Identity Theft**: Identity theft occurs when a fraudster uses another individual's name, Social Security Number, driver's license number, and other personal information to secure credit or make purchases. The use of the information is made without the knowledge of the individual whose personal information is included in fraudulent loan applications or other documents.

- **Sale or Assignment of a Sales Contract**: Instead of flipping a property by reselling it, some fraudulent real estate investors may obtain a contract on a property with an inflated value and offer to sell the sales contract or assign it to an unwitting buyer for a fee. The "investor" walks away from the transaction with several thousand dollars in his/her pocket, and the new buyer closes on a property that has an inflated price and only a fraction of the value that the buyer anticipated.

- **Cursory Inspections**: Fraudulent real estate brokers or investors may try to unload property with an inflated value and questionable title history on an unsuspecting buyer. When these buyers ask to inspect the property, the seller may discourage an inspection or rush the potential buyer through the home. A hasty inspection is most likely to occur when a faulty appraisal has inflated and grossly misrepresented the value of the property.

The precipitous decline in home values and the distress of homeowners facing foreclosure has given rise to new fraudulent schemes, and one that is currently on the rise is a scheme known as **"flopping."** Unlike property flipping, which uses an inflated appraisal to secure a loan for more than a property is worth, property flopping is executed by forcing the sale of a home for less than it is worth and reselling it at its true value. Flopping schemes can be very elaborate and can involve a number of co-conspirators. It often involves the false promise of foreclosure relief to a beleaguered homeowner who signs over his/her rights of homeownership to a foreclosure specialist who resells the home after claiming that attempts to refinance the home or modify the loan were not workable.

In 2009, Congress took action to step up enforcement against those who commit mortgage fraud with the adoption of the **Fraud Enforcement and Recovery Act (FERA)**. This law is intended to facilitate the prosecution of those who commit mortgage fraud and to increase the financial resources that are available to investigate and prosecute fraud cases. FERA revised the federal criminal code by specifically providing that the law against defrauding a financial institution includes actions related to the "mortgage lending business."

FERA authorized needed resources to address mortgage fraud, allocating funds for the FBI, the United States Attorneys, and the Department of Justice for the investigation and prosecution of mortgage fraud and securities and commodities fraud. FERA also authorized the creation of the Financial Crisis Inquiry Commission, which was directed to examine the causes of the current financial crisis, including the role of fraud in the financial sector. The Commission released its report on January 27, 2011. Among its conclusions was one that *"...there was a systematic breakdown in accountability and ethics...."* and that *"...we witnessed an erosion of standards of responsibility and ethics that exacerbated the financial crisis"* [105].

> *The FBI has focused attention on industry insider fraud, in which industry professionals use the fraudulent practices listed above as a means of collecting loan funds from lenders.*

Actions for mortgage fraud may include allegations that the defendant has violated numerous federal laws, including laws that prohibit:

- Bank fraud
- Wire fraud
- Mail fraud
- Making false statements to the government or to a financial institution
- Money laundering, and
- Conspiracy

Convictions for these crimes may lead to penalties of up to $1,000,000, imprisonment for up to 30 years, or both. A conviction for mail fraud or wire fraud can result from the simple acts of using the U.S. mail or interstate wire communications such as the phone or Internet to carry out a fraudulent scheme. Providing a depository institution with false information in order to secure funding for a loan may lead to convictions for bank fraud or for making false statements to a financial institution. Money laundering can involve elaborate schemes to distance ill-gotten funds from their source, or may be as simple as depositing funds of $10,000 or more in a bank when the depositor knows that the funds were derived from an illegal activity (18 U.S.C. §1957).

In a description of recent money laundering investigations, the Internal Revenue Service (IRS) provided an example of a mortgage fraud scheme that led to a 17-month prison term for one defendant and a 30-month sentence for his co-conspirator. Both defendants falsified loan documents in their business as mortgage brokers. The defendant who earned the 30-month sentence had fabricated supporting documentation for loan applicants, including false down payments and numerous "cut and paste documents." Both defendants provided false information to the IRS regarding the income from their business as mortgage brokers. By mailing and transmitting false information to the government, they committed mail fraud and wire fraud.

Furthermore, by transferring $42,532.43 in mail fraud proceeds from one bank account to another, one of the defendants also earned a conviction for money laundering [106].

> *The Fraud Enforcement and Recovery Act (FERA) was enacted to facilitate the prosecution of those who commit mortgage fraud and to increase financial resources available to investigate and prosecute fraud cases.*

Techniques for Mortgage Professionals to Use in Detecting Fraud

Loan originators are the mortgage professionals who are in a position to detect the unethical behavior of borrowers, including the attempts of borrowers to complete fraudulent mortgage transactions. There are no foolproof methods for preventing mortgage fraud. A mortgage professional can often detect and address issues of mortgage fraud with a thorough analysis of the loan file. No specific factor "proves" that fraud or misrepresentation is present. However, there are clues that should alert the mortgage professional to the possibility of fraud and encourage a deeper investigation into anything questionable or inconsistent.

Fraud detection requires attention to detail and awareness of common fraudulent activities. A list of common items that might trigger a fraud investigation includes:

- **Verifying Identity**: Identity theft is difficult to catch. However, forensic auditors have found several consistent indicators that suggest identity theft. Several common examples include:
  - Social Security Numbers, which should be consistent with the number reported on the credit report, residence history, pay stubs, or W-2 forms, can be verified by contacting the Social Security Administration
  - Credit histories should be consistent with the applicant's age, stated work and residential history
  - Identification documents should be clear and readable. Any evidence of smeared inks or poor printer alignment should prompt further investigation.
  - Co-borrowers should not call each other by nicknames that do not relate to the names provided on the application
- **Detecting False Documentation**: Borrowers making false claims on a mortgage application may use false documents to support them.

An originator can use the following techniques to detect fraudulent documents:

- Compare the handwriting and signatures on the original application to all supporting documents and identification
- Verify business addresses and phone numbers using phone books and business directories
- Track the chain of custody of all verifications
- Check the back of pay stubs, bank statements, and W-2 forms to detect watermarks and printed fraud prevention patterns
- Compare earning claims to public salary databases for the industry and region
- Consider how reasonable the claims made on the documents are. For example, a common error on falsified W-2 forms is to report tax withholdings that do not match the income level.
- Identify discrepancies between summary pages and attached schedules on a tax return

The demise of programs such as "no documentation" loans should result in a significant decrease in borrowers lying outright about their income and assets. However, it is important to perform a comprehensive review of all documentation for the purposes of loan qualification. Borrowers with special income circumstances, such as business owners and self-employed individuals, may require additional due diligence.

Income qualification should always be performed using factual data and not assumptions or estimates. Borrowers should submit tax documents and bank statements for a detailed review. Lenders may also require IRS authorizations such as the 4506-T to obtain actual transcripts of tax returns.

- **Falsified Appraisals**: The primary focus of an appraisal review is to determine whether or not the comparables are valid. When loan-to-value ratios are high and the property value is the prominent element in approval of a loan application, it is important to carefully review an appraisal.

  Several warning signs of potential appraisal fraud that loan originators should investigate include:

  - A mismatch between ages of the subject property and comparables
  - A substantial increase in property value over a short period of time
  - Comparables that are not physically similar to the subject property in terms of room count, total square footage or type of construction
  - Sales prices of comparables that do not match market conditions
  - Use of comparable sales that are not in the same subdivision and that have closed more than six months earlier
  - Use of comparable properties outside of a one-mile radius
  - Unreasonable adjustments for lot size, topography, or land value
  - Total net adjustments of more than 15% of the value

- Photos that are blurry or appear to have been downloaded from a website
- Any evidence that values have been altered, such as blurred or misaligned print

- **The Sales Contract**: Sales contracts are often full of changes, scratch-outs, and revisions to the changes. They can be difficult to read, especially if all that is available is a faxed copy. Still, an originator can look for several clues that might indicate fraud. For example:
  - The purchase price should not be greater than the list price
  - Do preliminary title reports show that the seller is on the title or that the seller purchased the property within the past year?
  - Assignments of beneficial interest are often fraudulent
  - Does the sequence of signatures on amendments match?
  - Do the buyer, seller, or agent have similar names or otherwise appear to be related or affiliated in any way?

- **The Credit Report**: A thorough review of the credit report will provide a great deal of information about the borrower. All information provided on the application should be compared to the information reported by the credit bureau. A discrepancy is not always an indication of fraud or misrepresentation, but further investigation is advised if any material discrepancies arise. Loan originators should:
  - Verify credit for all names(s) listed on the loan application
  - Check credit for all states in which the borrower previously resided
  - Pay attention to name order; if documents identify a different name order, check credit under both
  - Crosscheck all addresses identified on the credit report and other file documentation
  - Review employment information on the credit report and compare to the application information and other file documentation
  - Review employment information, especially if "self-employed" is indicated, and compare to application information
  - Determine whether verification of employers and dates of employment match those provided by the borrower on the application and documentation

- **The Common Sense Test**: The best way to prevent mortgage fraud is to stop and think through the proposed transaction. If an originator feels uncomfortable, he/she should talk with a control person for the mortgage company with which the loan originator is affiliated. Evaluate the loan file as one picture that tells a story. Use common sense to assess file consistency:
  - Consider the borrower's level of income compared to current outgoings, savings patterns and accumulated assets
  - Consider the borrower's type of employment or profession compared to income level, job history and education
  - Closely review the structure of the transaction
  - Contact the borrower's corporate office (often shown on the W-2 or 1099) for verifications. This diminishes the possibility of a borrower coaching the verifier.

Discussion Scenario: Mortgage Fraud, Falsified Appraisals, and Fair Lending

Foreclosure and Short Sale Services (FSSS) is a business that solicits homeowners who are falling behind on their mortgage payments. It advertises online and in newspapers where there are high rates of foreclosure. In its advertisements, FSSS promises that, "A Foreclosure Doesn't Have to Leave You Homeless. Let Us Help!"

Margaret is a 65-year old resident of a neighborhood where FSSS is soliciting clients. She refinanced her home in early 2006 with a 5/1 adjustable-rate mortgage. In June 2013, her mortgage reset for the second time, making her monthly payments unaffordable. The mortgage broker who helped Margaret with her 2006 refinance is now out of business, so Margaret decides to meet with a loan officer at the bank where she has a checking account. Thirty days after she files her loan application, and a month after her payments on her mortgage become delinquent for the first time, Margaret receives an adverse action notice from her bank, stating that her income was below the bank's minimum requirement and that her application showed that her current obligations are excessive in relation to her income. The letter also included a notice stating:

> *The federal Equal Credit Opportunity Act prohibits creditors from discriminating against credit applicants on the basis of race, color, religion, national origin, sex, marital status, or age (provided the applicant has the capacity to enter into a binding contract); because all or part of the applicant's income derives from any public assistance program; or because the applicant has in good faith exercised any right under the Consumer Credit Protection Act.*

Margaret has only one credit card and carries a small balance on it, and after reading the notice, she wonders if the bank is discriminating against her due to her age. She calls to speak with a loan officer about resubmitting her loan application, but receives little encouragement about her prospects of success.

In desperation, Margaret responds to an advertisement that she had seen for FSSS, and the company immediately sends a representative to Margaret's house. The FSSS foreclosure specialist is named Bill, and he explains that he is licensed as a real estate agent and as a loan originator for the FSSS lending division, and that he resolves most of his clients' mortgage problems by arranging for FSSS to purchase their homes and to give them the opportunity to remain in the house as tenants. "I take care of everything," he says. "I set up the closing, arrange for funding of the loan, and can help you with the upkeep of the house while you are a tenant."

Bill is accompanied by an appraiser and a home inspector. The FSSS appraiser and home inspector are in Margaret's home for an hour, and when their inspection is complete, they consult with Bill, who agrees to offer Margaret $110,000 for her home and a rental agreement that would allow her to stay in the house by paying the same monthly sum that she owed on her mortgage before the rate reset. Margaret knows that the amount that FSSS offered is $40,000 less than the appraised value of other homes on her street.

When Margaret questions the amount offered, the appraiser and the home inspector point out numerous concerns regarding the condition of the house, which they say are contributing factors to its low value. They also say, "FSSS will have to put at least $45,000 into this house if we purchase it from you and resell it for $150,000. That doesn't give us much of a profit."

Margaret is hesitant, and asks if FSSS will give her time to think. "Don't think too long," Bill tells her. "We can only buy so many properties, and there's a huge need for our services in this area. We'll probably only offer two more contracts this month."

Two weeks later, after her other attempts to secure a loan have failed, and another mortgage payment is due, Margaret calls FSSS and asks if they will meet with her again. To make certain that she is making the right decisions, Margaret asks her daughter to be present to review the documents. Margaret's daughter prepares for the meeting by ordering an appraisal on her mother's home, which comes back at $148,000.

Bill returns to Margaret's house with a contract for the sale of the house and a rental agreement. When Margaret's daughter reviews the rental agreement, she finds that the lease is only a six-month lease and that, in addition to rent, the agreement requires her mother to pay monthly maintenance fees that would push the rent towards an amount that her mother cannot pay. Margaret does not sign the contract.

Discussion Questions

- *Does this case involve mortgage fraud, and does the fact that the value of the home is under-estimated rather than over-estimated make a difference?*
- *During its transaction with Margaret, did FSSS violate any provisions of the Valuation Independence Rule?*
- *What federal laws would provide a basis for an action against FSSS for its foreclosure rescue scam?*
- *Do the facts in this scenario point to any violations of the Equal Credit Opportunity Act by Margaret's bank?*
- *Did FSSS commit any violations of fair lending laws?*

Discussion Feedback

FSSS is most accurately described as a predatory lender since it preys on at-risk homeowners, but this case also involves mortgage fraud. The scenario suggests that FSSS has a line of credit that it uses to fund its loans. By using a falsified appraisal to secure access to funds for the loan, FSSS is making a false statement to a financial institution. While inflated appraisals were common during the lending boom, under-valuations are common in foreclosure rescue schemes and are also illegal. Furthermore, FSSS would be likely to submit another false appraisal that inflates the value of Margaret's home if it succeeded in getting her out of the house.

FSSS and Bill violated numerous provisions of the Valuation Independence Rule. By ordering an appraisal and planning to submit it to a creditor, Bill was performing valuation management functions, and the Rule prohibits those performing valuation management functions from having an interest in the transaction. If FSSS were obtaining legitimate appraisals, it would either use an outside appraisal company that does not communicate directly with its originators, or it would have a policy in place to ensure that Bill and other employees who order appraisals do not also participate in decisions to approve the loan. Clearly, the appraisal violates the prohibition in the Valuation Independence Rule against misrepresenting the value of a consumer's principal dwelling.

A number of laws could provide a legal basis for a claim against FSSS. Federal laws include the Fraud Enforcement and Recovery Act of 2009 (FERA), which was enacted to facilitate prosecutions against those who commit fraud in the mortgage lending business. The coordinated efforts of Bill and the appraiser and home inspector to defraud Margaret and to obtain a loan based on a fraudulent appraisal can subject all three to prosecution for conspiracy. By using the phone to communicate with consumers like Margaret, and advertising its services online, the fraudulent activities of FSSS involve wire fraud. If it also used the mail to contact customers, FSSS may have committed mail fraud. It has also committed fraud against the bank that provides FSSS with a credit line. Finally, if it succeeded in purchasing Margaret's home from her and deposited its illegal profits from the transaction into a depository institution, it could be prosecuted for money laundering.

The bank followed the correct procedure by providing Margaret with a notice of adverse action within 30 days of the receipt of her loan application. However, if Margaret believes that she may be the victim of age discrimination, she should investigate this possibility. She may want to begin by contacting a local nonprofit housing counselor. She can also contact the Office of Fair Lending and Equal Opportunity at the Consumer Financial Protection Bureau or the Fair Lending Unit of the Civil Enforcement Division at the Department of Justice. With the DOJ's focus on giving immediate and priority attention to fair lending claims, Margaret may be able to pursue this potential claim before she loses her home.

FSSS may also be liable for violations of fair lending laws. By targeting specific neighborhoods with its predatory services, it is engaging in reverse red-lining, which is illegal under ECOA and the Fair Housing Act.

Ethical Standards Established by Professional Organizations

Many professional organizations, such as the Maryland Association of Mortgage Brokers, the Florida Association of Mortgage Brokers, the Wisconsin Association of Mortgage Brokers, and the National Association of Professional Mortgage Women, require their members to agree to maintain ethical and professional standards. These standards are set forth in Codes of Ethics, Best Business Practices, or in Standards of Professional Practice.

Mortgage industry Codes of Ethics vary by organization, however the essence of each code is very similar. Although exact provisions will differ, general ethical requirements include:

- Conducting business with honesty and integrity
- Using advertisements and solicitations that contain accurate information
- Providing full disclosure of the costs associated with a lending transaction
- Charging reasonable fees
- Maintaining the confidentiality of personal information
- Acting in accordance with all applicable laws and regulations

A Code of Ethics does not have the force and effect of federal and state laws and regulations. However, mortgage lending laws provide a legal basis for the enforcement of the principles addressed in Ethics Codes and in Statements of Professional Standards.

Ethical Behavior of Industry Partners and Third Party Service Providers

No mortgage transaction may be completed without the participation of industry partners, including third party service providers such as credit reporting agencies, appraisers, title insurers, escrow agents, and attorneys. Mortgage professionals have a responsibility, not only to ensure their own ethical and legal compliance, but also to take steps to make certain that their industry partners are carrying out their duties related to a transaction in an ethical and legal manner.

Regulations adopted pursuant to the GLB Act create affirmative requirements for financial institutions to ensure that third party service providers are taking appropriate measures to protect the privacy of customer information. These regulations, known as "The Safeguard Rule," require financial institutions, including mortgage professionals, to oversee service providers by *"Taking reasonable steps to select and retain service providers that are capable of maintaining appropriate safeguards for the customer information at issue; and requiring… service providers by contract to implement and maintain such safeguards"* (16 C.F.R. §314.4(d)).

In 2012, the CFPB issued a bulletin addressing the supervision of service providers by banks and nonbanks, including mortgage bankers and brokers. The CFPB states in Bulletin 2012-03 that service providers that fail to comply with laws, including mortgage lending laws, may harm consumers and that *"…legal responsibility may lie with the supervised bank or nonbank as well as with the supervised service provider"* [107]. In the Bulletin, the CFPB outlines its expectations regarding the steps that banks and nonbanks should take for managing the risks of service provider relationships [108]. Risk management practices should include:

- Conducting due diligence to determine whether the service provider understands the laws with which it must comply, and determining whether the service provider is capable of compliance
- Reviewing the service provider's policies, procedures, and employee training to ensure that it adequately trains and oversees employees that have consumer contact or compliance responsibilities

- Entering a contract with service providers that includes *"...enforceable consequences for violating any compliance-related responsibilities, including engaging in unfair, deceptive, or abusive acts and practices..."*

- Creating a monitoring program to determine if the service provider is in compliance with the law, and

- Taking *"...prompt action to address fully any problems identified through the monitoring process..."* [109]

Regretfully, it is often settlement service providers and industry partners that act together to carry out fraudulent mortgage lending transactions. False appraisals and title reports are commonly linked to fraudulent transactions, and participants have frequently included attorneys who have closed on fraudulent loans and lenders who have falsely certified that loans meet the criteria for sale in the secondary market. The orchestrated efforts of service providers and industry partners made fraud against financial institutions a monumental problem when funds were readily available during the lending boom.

Following is a description of the roles that industry partners and service providers play in lending transactions and of the opportunities that these individuals and entities may have in identifying unethical and illegal activities that may take place during a mortgage lending transaction.

> *No mortgage transaction may be completed without the participation of industry partners, including third party service providers such as credit reporting agencies, appraisers, title insurers, escrow agents, and attorneys.*

Appraisers

As already discussed, property appraisal is an important component to successful loan origination. It cannot be stressed enough that ethical behavior with regard to appraiser relationships is critical for both legal and ethical compliance. Appraisers are well-trained and highly regulated professionals who must be permitted to make an independent, objective decision on the value of a property.

It is the responsibility of appraisers, prior to accepting an appraisal assignment, to review the assignment and determine if they have the knowledge and experience to complete it competently. Appraisers operate under a number of professional and ethical expectations including those of their state regulators and those of the Appraisal Standards Board at the national level.

The Financial Institutions Reform, Recovery and Enforcement Act of 1989 established the Uniform Standards of Professional Appraisal Practice (USPAP) as the generally accepted appraisal standards in the United States. USPAP is mandatory for appraisers in any kind of federal loan transaction. State level regulations for appraisers also require compliance with USPAP.

Included in the USPAP standards are requirements for appraisers to:

- Perform assignments with impartiality, objectivity, and independence
- Refrain from accepting an assignment or a compensation arrangement that is contingent on delivering a predetermined result
- Protect the confidential nature of the appraiser-client relationship by guarding against the disclosure of information to anyone other than those persons who are specifically authorized to receive it
- Keep records on each assignment for five years after the completion of the assignment

In addition to professional standards, state and federal laws also affect the appraisal practice. During the most recent housing boom, unethical appraisal methods came to light in many instances of mortgage fraud. Falsely inflated property values were used in fraudulent loan transactions which cost lenders billions.

Even when overvaluation is not used for the purposes of mortgage fraud, it is a problem. Many appraisers report that they have been pressured by loan originators, loan applicants and real estate professionals to arrive at a certain property value. While inaccurate appraisals often helped borrowers qualify for larger loans during the lending boom, the impact was devastating for the state of the housing and mortgage markets.

The overvaluation of the fair market value of real estate is considered a violation of the Financial Institutions Reform, Recovery, and Enforcement Act, as well as several other federal regulations. In response to the problems that industry pressure on appraisers has created, the amendments to Regulation Z regarding valuation independence attempt to create strict boundaries between appraisers and mortgage professionals who rely on their services to close mortgage loans.

> *The Uniform Standards of Professional Appraisal Practice (USPAP) is mandatory for appraisers in any kind of federal loan transaction. State-level regulations for appraisers also require compliance with USPAP.*

Underwriters

Underwriters are responsible for ensuring that loan applicants meet the requirements established by lenders and investors for loan programs. For example, if a borrower applies for a conventional conforming loan, the underwriter will determine if the loan amount meets GSE lending limits and if the loan-to-value ratio and the borrower's credit score, debt-to-income ratio, and down payment meet the conforming loan standards. The responsibilities of the underwriter provide a layer of checks and balances between loan origination and loan funding. Attention to detail prior to submitting a loan file to the lender for approval can dramatically increase successful loan approval.

In addition to ensuring potential borrowers meet loan program standards, underwriters are also taxed with spotting missing or questionable items in order to verify the accuracy of application materials. While performing these responsibilities, underwriters are in a position to be able to see any evidence of unethical or fraudulent activity that is related to a loan application. The following are some common "red flags" underwriters are trained to detect [110].

It is useful to be familiar with red flags and look for them during origination to ensure a smoother transition to underwriting.

- **Loan Application Red Flags**
  - Changes between the handwritten version of a loan application and the submitted version are significant or contradictory
  - Repeated or significant changes to applicant information throughout loan processing
  - Applicant information, including signatures and dates, that is incomplete or inconsistent
  - The address is a P.O. Box
  - Contact information for the applicant and employer is the same
  - Addresses, for commuting purposes, are unrealistic
  - Down payment is being made via a method other than cash
  - Assets compared to income do not make sense
  - Education is not consistent with profession

- **Credit Report Red Flags**
  - Credit history is missing entirely
  - Applicant's Social Security Number is invalid or was recently issued
  - Credit report lists significant debts or liabilities that the applicant did not report on the loan application
  - AKA (also known as) or DBA (doing business as) shows up

- **Employment and Income Red Flags**
  - Employer's address is a P.O. Box, the same as the borrower's residence, the same as another party to the loan transaction (seller, realtor, etc.) or the same as the subject property
  - Pay stubs, W-2s and other income documents are handwritten and/or do not include company name, logo or other business characteristics (particularly for larger employers)
  - Pay stub check numbers or sequence are inconsistent or do not correspond with payroll dates
  - Social Security Number on income documents does not match number on other application or verification documents
  - Year-to-date earnings on pay stubs are inconsistent with W-2s
  - Date of hire listed occurred on a weekend or a holiday
  - Employment or payroll documents show evidence of alteratio

- **Personal Identifying Information Red Flags**
  - Inconsistencies between the address provided in a loan application and the address that appears on a consumer report
  - An invalid Social Security Number, or one that is listed on the Death Master File by the Social Security Administration
  - Inconsistencies between different pieces of information provided by a loan applicant, such as a discrepancy between the applicant's SSN range and his or her date of birth
  - Social Security Numbers that begin with the number 9, or that have 000 or 666 as the first three digits or 0000 as the last four digits

- **Appraisal Red Flags**
  - Comparable properties are not located within a reasonable distance of the subject property
  - Significant appreciation in value over a short period of time
  - Large or inconsistent adjustments have been made to comparables
  - Information about the property is inconsistent with the loan transaction (i.e. appraisal lists refinance when the transaction is a purchase)
  - Appraisal is dated prior to the sales contract
  - Property owner and property seller are not the same

> *Underwriters are responsible for ensuring that loan applicants meet the requirements established for loan programs. The responsibilities of the underwriter provide a layer of checks and balances between loan origination and loan funding.*

Investors

Investors play a critical role in the strength of the mortgage market. The origination of loans takes place in the **primary mortgage market**. After closing on mortgage loans, lenders sell many of them in the **secondary mortgage market**. The overall soundness of the mortgage market depends on the interplay of primary lenders with mortgage insurers and secondary market investors.

The secondary mortgage market was born during the Great Depression. In the early twentieth century, depository institutions such as banks and thrifts originated virtually all mortgage loans, and the money that they used to fund them came solely from deposits. The number of mortgages that lenders could make was therefore limited by the amount of the institution's current deposits.

Government loan programs, which were originally conceived as a response to the Great Depression, created entities that bought mortgages and turned them into investments. The purchase of mortgages created a new source of funds for new loans. With the sale of mortgages to investors, depository institutions gained lending funds, and the amount of deposits no longer limited the number of mortgages that lenders could make.

Private investment banks participate in the secondary market, but **Government Sponsored Enterprises (GSEs)** have been the biggest buyers of home mortgages. GSEs include:

- **FNMA**: FNMA is an acronym for the Federal National Mortgage Association, also known as **Fannie Mae**. Fannie Mae has functioned as a private shareholder-owned company. Fannie Mae purchases FHA-insured loans and conforming conventional mortgages, securitizes them, and sells the mortgage-backed securities to investors. Fannie Mae was the first GSE and was established during the 1930s.

- **FHLMC**: FHLMC is an acronym for the Federal Home Loan Mortgage Corporation, also known as **Freddie Mac**. Like Fannie Mae, Freddie Mac has also functioned as a GSE that is stockholder-owned. Freddie Mac also purchases conforming mortgage loans, securitizes them, and sells them to investors. Congress created Freddie Mac in 1970 as a competitor for Fannie Mae.

- **GNMA**: GNMA is an acronym for the Government National Mortgage Association, also known as **Ginnie Mae**. Ginnie Mae is a GSE, but there are important distinctions between Ginnie Mae and Fannie Mae or Freddie Mac:
    - Ginnie Mae is government-owned, not stockholder-owned
    - Ginnie Mae's primary function is not to buy loans but to guarantee securities that are backed by FHA, VA, and Rural Housing Service loans
    - Ginnie Mae does not guarantee or deal in any other way with conventional mortgages

An unethical practice during the lending boom that unquestionably led to the losses suffered by GSEs was their purchase of subprime mortgages without conducting an adequate review of the safety of these products. In 2008, *"Fannie Mae and Freddie Mac lost a combined $3.1 billion between April and June. Half of their credit losses came from these types of risky loans with ballooning monthly payments"* [111].

The perceived need for the government's takeover is based on the fact that Fannie Mae and Freddie Mac hold and guarantee half of the country's mortgage debt. If these investors collapsed, the mortgage market and other credit markets could potentially become paralyzed. The Housing and Economic Recovery Act of 2008 transferred the oversight of Fannie Mae and Freddie Mac from HUD and the Office of Federal Housing Enterprise Oversight to the Federal Housing Finance Agency (FHFA). FHFA will have much more involvement with Fannie Mae and Freddie Mac than the former regulatory agencies had.

> *The overall soundness of the mortgage market depends on the interplay of primary lenders with mortgage insurers and secondary market investors.*

Warehouse Lenders

The availability of warehouse lines of credit has permitted mortgage bankers, brokers, and other non-depository financial institutions to fund loans. This practice is commonly known as table-funding.

In a table-funded loan transaction, a loan goes to closing with the mortgage broker or other originator listed as the lender. The loan is funded using the originator's warehouse line of credit that is made available by a wholesale lender. Within several days of closing, the loan is sold in the secondary market so that the warehouse lender can pay off the line of credit, or the loan is assigned to the creditor that provides the line of credit.

The practice of table-funding has contributed to the flexibility and agility of the mortgage industry over the past few years. However, it is important for mortgage professionals who participate in table-funding transactions to understand their responsibilities to warehouse lenders. Quite often, the fine print in table-funding agreements between originators and lenders includes buy-back provisions.

A buy-back provision means that, if there is any form of unethical conduct or fraud related to a particular loan, the originator may be responsible for buying the loan back. It can have devastating consequences for small originators if they are forced to shoulder the cost of such loans. Investors also include similar provisions in their agreements, requiring originators to repurchase loans that do not represent sound investment potential.

Real Estate Licensees

Mortgage professionals often have a close working relationship with real estate professionals. In fact, some states permit an individual to act or hold licenses as both a loan originator and a real estate agent. In cases in which an individual fills a dual role, it is always a legal requirement to appropriately advise consumers due to the potential conflict of interest.

In the absence of dual licensure, mortgage professionals must remain vigilant in their interactions with real estate agents. One primary area of concerns involves referrals and compliance with RESPA. Real estate agents are often in a position to refer business to loan originators and vice versa, and it is a violation of RESPA for there to be any compensation given or accepted in exchange.

Privacy is another area of concern when dealing with real estate professionals. In many cases, real estate licensees clearly establish an agency relationship with their customers. During the purchase or sale of a property, the real estate licensee is understandably concerned with the status of his/her customer's interest in the transaction. However, it is a violation of the customer's privacy to share personal protected information with the real estate agent. Such information may only be discussed with the borrower directly.

Some states permit individuals to act as both loan originators and real estate agents. In the absence of dual licensure, originators and real estate agents must be sure that their actions are compliant with RESPA.

<u>Employers</u>

Mortgage brokers often operate as small to mid-sized companies and employ one or more loan originators to provide lending services to loan applicants. Nearly all states that recognize the legal status of mortgage brokers as employers include provisions in their licensing laws which require them to provide careful employee oversight. Even without the inclusion of these provisions in licensing laws, other state laws that address the relationship of employer and employees create duties for mortgage brokers to provide adequate oversight of employees/ originators and to ensure that they are conducting business in full compliance with the law.

Comprehensive oversight of employees is important since, in many cases, an employer can be held responsible for the actions of its employees. The employer is expected to maintain policies and procedures, to communicate these expectations and to ensure staff members are following expectations. Civil and criminal liability can result if an employee commits violations of state or federal laws and the employer knew, or should have known, about the behavior.

Ethical Behavior of Consumers

The crash of the mortgage market in 2007 was followed by endless finger-pointing to lenders, mortgage brokers, loan originators, appraisers, credit rating agencies, Fannie Mae and Freddie Mac, mortgage investors, and Congress. American consumers are also responsible for the financial catastrophe. Countless consumers, including borrowers with sterling credit ratings, over-extended themselves and bought homes that were beyond their means and took out large home equity lines of credit to finance pursuits other than homeownership. Many were operating under the assumption that housing prices would continue to rise. Those who did not own homes jumped to get into the market before they were priced out of it, and others, in need of cash, assumed that they could pay off their credit lines with a future refinance when home prices were even higher. Later events proved that these were unsafe assumptions to make.

Some homebuyers engaged in unethical behavior and were able to do so since the lending standards were so lax. For example, many took advantage of no-doc financing and took out "liar loans" that were based on the misrepresentation of their income and other qualifications. Others represented that they would occupy homes that they were actually purchasing as investment properties. When the market crashed, some of the first loans to fail were often those held by consumers who had purchased "investment properties" that they never used or visited.

Lax lending standards facilitated these transactions. The concept of creative financing often meant that lenders were willing to offer nontraditional mortgages, such as interest-only loans and payment-option loans, to a broad range of borrowers. In the recent past, these types of products were only available to a few, very well-qualified borrowers who were seeking financing for a short term investment. For many of the consumers who used this type of financing to purchase a home or an investment property, the ultimate results of creative borrowing have been devastating. However, the fact that they sought these loans and accepted them cannot be overlooked.

When working with a borrower to originate a loan, it is extremely important to remind him/her that by providing inaccurate information or by making misrepresentations on a loan application, he/she is violating the law and may be subject to fines and even imprisonment. When providing income and employment information, listing assets and liabilities, and providing declarations of outstanding judgments, bankruptcies, or other financially significant facts, buyers are legally and ethically obligated to be truthful. Loan originators may save themselves hours of wasted effort and may save consumers from the risk of prosecution if they take the time to explain the repercussions of falsely stating that the information contained in a loan application is true. The loan applicant should be aware that his/her failure to truthfully complete the application could result in civil liability or criminal prosecution for mortgage fraud.

Ethical Issues Regarding the Role of Mortgage Brokers

The role that mortgage brokers play with respect to loan applicants has been a hotly contested issue. Ethical considerations have played a large role in this debate and are the basis for state laws and professional standards which hold that mortgage brokers owe special duties to consumers who are shopping for a mortgage.

In the debate over the duty that mortgage brokers owe to consumers, there are two primary arguments:

- When a consumer uses a mortgage broker to find a loan, a principal and agent relationship arises, and the mortgage broker owes fiduciary duties to the borrower.
- Mortgage brokers are intermediaries between consumers and lenders and owe no particular duty to borrowers who are ultimately responsible for understanding the terms of a lending agreement and deciding whether the loan is one that they can afford.

Regardless of where the broker's fiduciary duties lie, there is the question of what to tell the borrower. In those states which have adopted law that designates the broker as the agent of the borrower, there is no question. In those states in which the relationship is unclear, it becomes mandatory for an ethical broker to inform the borrower for whom he/she is working.

Mortgage Brokers as Agents and Fiduciaries

When the law of agency is applicable to relationships between mortgage brokers and borrowers, a mortgage broker serves as the agent for the borrower, who is the principal. In the role of an agent, a mortgage broker owes fiduciary duties to the borrower. Fiduciary duties include loyalty, good faith, and an obligation to put the interests of the principal (borrower) ahead of the agent (mortgage broker).

It benefits both mortgage brokers and borrowers to clarify the nature of the legal relationship between them. Borrowers often make the assumption that a mortgage broker is working as their agent, believing that brokers must represent their interests throughout the course of lending transactions. Of course, in many transactions that were made before the market crashed, borrowers learned that this assumption was untrue and that their mortgage brokers had no legal duty to serve as their agent or fiduciary.

There is no federal law that imposes the duties of an agent and a fiduciary on mortgage brokers or loan originators. Congress had the opportunity to address this issue in 2008 when it adopted the S.A.F.E. Act, but limited the "standards" for loan originators to licensing and registration requirements.

Although there are no federal standards that require mortgage brokers and/or loan originators to serve borrowers as fiduciaries, many state laws have addressed the issue directly by adding provisions to their licensing laws that expressly state that an agency or a fiduciary relationship exists between mortgage brokers and borrowers. These states include, but are not limited to, California, Illinois, Minnesota, Nevada, New Mexico, South Carolina, Washington, and Wisconsin. California and Washington are states with laws that expressly state that mortgage brokers have fiduciary duties as follows:

- In California, the law provides that licensed mortgage brokers owe fiduciary duties to borrowers. The California Association of Mortgage Professionals (CAMP) has adopted *Standards of Professional Practice* that reflect this legal standard stating *"CAMP members, whether by law or by professional commitment, have a fiduciary duty to their clients, and strive to maintain absolute fidelity to their borrower's best interest"* [112].

- In Washington, the law states that *"A mortgage broker has a fiduciary relationship with the borrower...."* (RCW 19.146.095 (1)) The law further states that having a fiduciary duty means that the mortgage broker must act in the borrower's best interests, carry out the borrower's lawful instructions, disclose all material facts to the borrower, use reasonable care in the performance of duties, and account for all money and property received from the borrower.

Illinois and Minnesota are states that refer to the relationship between mortgage brokers and borrowers as an agency relationship:

- In Illinois, *"A mortgage broker shall be considered to have created an agency relationship with the borrower in all cases..."* (205 ILCS 655/5-7 (a)) The law states that the duties that a mortgage broker owes a borrower as a result of this agency relationship include acting in the borrower's best interests, carrying out the borrower's lawful instructions, disclosing all facts to the borrower that may affect his/her rights, using reasonable care in performing all duties, and accounting for all money that the mortgage broker receives from the borrower.

- Minnesota is another state that has adopted a licensing law that provides that mortgage brokers are the agents of the borrowers that they represent. Using the same language found in the Illinois statute, Minnesota's Mortgage Originator and Servicer Licensing Act states *"A mortgage broker shall be considered to have created an agency relationship with the borrower in all cases...."* (Minn. Stat. §58.161, sub. 1. (2008)) Minnesota mortgage brokers have a duty to exercise "utmost good faith" towards borrowers and to make decisions that are in the best interests of borrowers without ever compromising their rights or interests.

Other states have laws that address the relationship between mortgage brokers and borrowers but without making an express declaration that an agency or fiduciary relationship exists. Colorado,

Maryland, North Carolina, and Virginia are examples of states that have taken this approach with the adoption of laws that require mortgage brokers to exercise good faith and fair dealing when working with borrowers in mortgage lending transactions.

Certainly there are many mortgage brokers that have conducted business with a commitment to pairing borrowers with suitable loan products. These mortgage brokers have not allowed the size of their commissions to be the determining factor in helping borrowers choose mortgages. Mortgage brokers must look at the statutes in the states where they do business to determine the full extent of their legal duties, and, regardless of whether the law specifically dictates that a relationship between broker and borrower exists, they must consider their ethical obligations to the borrower.

> *Many state laws provide that a mortgage broker owes fiduciary duties to the borrower. Fiduciary duties include loyalty, good faith, and an obligation to put the interests of the principal (borrower) ahead of the agent (mortgage broker).*

Discussion Scenario: Red Flags for Loan Originators

Review the following loan documentation and verification scenarios. Based on what you have learned about safe and compliant originations, select the best answer for each one.

The following are examples of loan documentation that you have received. Select the one that does not raise a red flag:

- A loan applicant submits a pay stub with a Social Security Number that does not match his credit report
- A loan applicant's pay stubs, W-2s and bank statements are crumpled and soiled, and many pages have been torn and taped back together
- A loan applicant submits pay stubs which have mismatched fonts and traces of correction fluid
- A loan applicant has multiple W-2s because she has had more than one job in the last two years

A loan applicant provides his Social Security Number. Select the option that is not questionable:

- The applicant lives in California but the first three digits are 224... which means the SSN was issued in Virginia
- His SSN is 000-00-3456
- He is in his 40s and mentioned that he was born in Delaware... but his SSN was issued last year
- Your credit reporting service notes the SSN appears on the SSA Death Master File

An applicant has told you she has been working on improving her credit and thinks she is ready to qualify for a loan. Which of the following credit report items make you think she has been the victim of identity theft?

- Several accounts are in charged off status - one as recently as nine months ago
- She has simultaneous credit with three new cell phone providers and has not made payments to any of them
- She had several 60-day and 90-day late payments last year and one 30-day late a few months ago
- She has not opened any new credit card accounts in over two years but obtained a new cell phone three months ago

You request a copy of your loan applicant's identification to meet Patriot Act regulations. Which of the following responses are suspicious and might constitute a red flag?

- "Sure thing! Isn't this picture awful? I've lost a little weight since then!"
- "Here you go. I left my driver's license at a pub the other day so I hope my passport works."
- "Ok, all I have is this photocopy. There was a mix-up at the DMV so I've been using this until that's resolved."
- "Of course. I need to get a license in this state! We moved here a month ago and I haven't made it to the DMV yet!"

Discussion Feedback
The following are examples of loan documentation that you have received. Select the one that does not raise a red flag.

A loan applicant has multiple W-2s because she has had more than one job in the last two years.
Multiple W-2s are not a cause for concern; many borrowers will have changed jobs and will present documentation from multiple employers. However, any income documentation which is not consistent with the credit report or loan application or that appears to have been tampered with should raise concerns.

A loan applicant provides his Social Security Number. Select the option that is not questionable.

The applicant lives in California but the first three digits are 224... which means the SSN was issued in Virginia.
A SSN issued in another state is not a red flag. However, one that was issued recently for an individual who logically should have had a number for some time, one that appears on the Death Master File or one that begins exclusively with 0s should raise concerns.

An applicant has told you she has been working on improving her credit and thinks she is ready to qualify for a loan. Which of the following credit report items make you think she has been the victim of identity theft?

She has simultaneous credit with three new cell phone providers and has not made payments to any of them.
Simultaneous and unpaid credit with multiple cell phone providers seems uncharacteristic for a borrower who has been working on improving her credit. When information such as this appears on a credit report, it could be a sign of identity theft.

You request a copy of your loan applicant's identification to meet Patriot Act regulations. Which of the following responses are suspicious and might constitute a red flag?

"Ok, all I have is this photocopy. There was a mix-up at the DMV so I've been using this until that's resolved."
Valid identification can include unexpired driver's licenses from any state and U.S. passports. It is also reasonable to expect that people do not always look exactly like their photo ID (although the resemblance should not be completely different!). However, a photocopy of identification is not acceptable.

Ethical Behavior of Loan Processors

The primary ethical obligation of a loan processor is to avoid overstepping the limitations of his/her role in a lending transaction. The term "loan processor" and the limitations of a loan processor's duties are defined by law. The S.A.F.E. Act defines a **loan processor** as *"...an individual who performs clerical or support duties at the direction of and subject to the supervision and instruction of a State-licensed loan originator; or a registered loan originator"* (12 U.S.C. §5102(5)(A)). State licensing laws have adopted a similar definition. The term "loan processor" is defined under federal and state law in order to distinguish the roles of loan processors from those of licensed and/or registered loan originators. The S.A.F.E. Act distinguishes between employees that serve as loan processors and those that serve as loan originators as described below:

- Loan processors are employees of nonbank entities (e.g. mortgage brokers) and depository institutions (e.g. banks) and are not required to obtain licenses. Since they are not trained or licensed, they may not perform the functions of employees who have become licensed as mortgage loan originators, and instead, they are limited to performing clerical or support duties.

- Loan originators are NMLS-registered employees of depository institutions and state-licensed/NMLS-registered employees of nonbank entities who are allowed to negotiate lending terms and rates with consumers.

The **"clerical or support duties"** which loan processors are allowed to perform are defined in the S.A.F.E. Act to include:

> *"The receipt, collection, distribution, and analysis of information common for the processing or underwriting of a residential mortgage loan; and communicating with a consumer to obtain the information necessary for the processing or underwriting of a loan, to the extent that such communication does not include offering or negotiating loan rates or terms, or counseling consumers about residential mortgage loan rates or terms."*

(12 U.S.C. §5102(5)(B))

It is the final clause in this definition of "clerical or support duties" that outlines the ethical responsibilities of loan processors. Unless they become licensed and/or registered as loan originators, they are legally and ethically required to refrain from:

- Offering or negotiating loan rates or terms, and
- Counseling consumers about suitable loan rates and terms

The ethical concern underlying these restrictions is one to ensure that consumers can distinguish between those individuals who are legally qualified to lead them through a lending transaction and those who are not. This ethical concern has become particularly important as the role of nonbank lenders has grown. During the lending boom, countless individuals served as loan originators, and many of them lacked the qualifications and licensing to negotiate mortgage loans. Unfortunately, the activities of many unlicensed loan originators were predatory, and they resulted in the placement of consumers in loan products that did not suit their needs due to the origination of loans without a consideration of the repayment ability of borrowers. Licensing requirements are intended to protect consumers from falling into these types of transactions.

> *Unless they become licensed and/or registered as loan originators, loan processors are legally and ethically required to refrain from offering or negotiating loan rates or terms and counseling consumers about suitable loan rates and terms.*

Both the S.A.F.E. Act and state licensing laws contain an express prohibition against individuals engaging in the business of a loan originator without first obtaining a unique identifier from the NMLS and:

- Securing employment with a depository institution, or
- Working for a nonbank entity as a state-licensed loan originator

Unless licensed, individual loan processors may not *"…represent to the public, through advertising or other means of communicating or providing information (including the use of business cards, stationery, brochures, signs, rate lists, or other promotional items), that such individual can or will perform any of the activities of a loan originator…"* (12 U.S.C. §5103(b)(1)).

These requirements and restrictions also extend to independent contractors. Loan processors must keep these distinctions in mind during the day-to-day practice of performing their clerical duties. Furthermore, licensed and registered loan originators must not delegate their responsibilities to loan processors, and if loan processors try to offer services that extend beyond the legal parameters of their jobs, their employers must remind them of the limitations that they are legally required to follow.

Sources

Page left intentionally blank.

SOURCES

[1] 76 Fed. Reg. 21 July 2011, 43570.

[2] CFPB. Sample Loan Estimate. http://files.consumerfinance.gov/f/201311_cfpb_kbyo_loan-estimate.pdf

[3] Department of Housing and Urban Development. "Buying Your Home: Settlement Costs and Information." http://portal.hud.gov:80/hudportal/HUD?src=/program_offices/housing/ramh/res/sfhrestc

[4] The Federal Reserve Board. "What You Should Know About Home Equity Lines of Credit." http://files.consumerfinance.gov/f/201204_CFPB_HELOC-brochure.pdf

[5] CFPB. Sample Closing Disclosure. http://files.consumerfinance.gov/f/201311_cfpb_kbyo_closing-disclosure.pdf

[6] Federal Register: June 7, 1996 (Volume 61, Number 111)

[7] CFPB. "Truth in Lending." http://files.consumerfinance.gov/f/201306_cfpb_laws-and-regulations_tila-combined-june-2013.pdf

[8] CFPB. "Finance Charge Chart." June 2013. http://files.consumerfinance.gov/f/201306_cfpb_laws-and-regulations_tila-combined-june-2013.pdf

[9] Official Interpretations to §1026.17(a)(1). (2) Segregation of Disclosures.

[10] In addition to showing the "amount financed" on the TIL Disclosure form, the creditor must provide an Amount Financed Itemization Form, which shows amounts given directly to the consumer, amounts paid on the consumer's account, and amounts paid to others on the consumer's behalf, such as other creditors who are paid off with the proceeds of a cash-out refinance. Appendix H-3 of Regulation Z provides a model itemization form.

[11] Appendix to Part 1026- H-6, Assumption Policy Model Clause.

[12] Appendix to Part 1026- H-4(k), No-Guarantee-to-Refinance Statement Model Clause.

[13] CFPB. "Consumer Handbook on Adjustable-Rate Mortgages." http://files.consumerfinance.gov/f/201204_CFPB_ARMs-brochure.pdf

[14] CFPB. "What You Should Know about Home Equity Lines of Credit." http://files.consumerfinance.gov/f/201204_CFPB_HELOC-brochure.pdf

[15] Ibid.

[16] Official Interpretations to §1026.20(c). Rate adjustments with a corresponding change in payment.

[17] 78 FR 10919 (Feb. 14, 2013)

[18] 78 FR 10924 (Feb. 14, 2013)

[19] Ibid.

[20] 78 FR 10925 (Feb. 14, 2013)

[21] 78 FR 10924 (Feb. 14, 2013)

[22] 78 FR 10926 (Feb. 14, 2013)

[23] 78 FR 10927 (Feb. 14, 2013)

[24] Ibid.

[25] Ibid.

[26] Official Interpretations to §1026.23(c). Delay of creditor's performance.

[27] Shim, Kim. "Right of Rescission in Times of Foreclosure." Federal Reserve Bank of New York, Consumer Compliance Outlook." Second Quarter 2010. http://www.philadelphiafed. org/bank-resources/publications/consumer-compliance-outlook/2010/second-quarter/right-of-rescission.cfm

[28] Ibid.

[29] CFPB, 13 Apr. 2012. Page 9. http://files.consumerfinance.gov/f/201204_CFPB_Sherzer-amicus-brief.pdf

[30] Official Interpretations to §1026.24(b). Clear and conspicuous standard.

[31] Official Interpretations to §1026.16(1). Clear and conspicuous standard.

[32] Official Interpretations to §1026.24(b). Clear and conspicuous standard.

[33] Official Interpretations to §1026.32(b)(1)(iii). (1) Other charges.

[34] Ibid.

[35] FFIEC. "Average Prime Offer Rates Tables." http://www.ffiec.gov/ratespread/aportables.htm

[36] "Appraisals for Higher-Priced Mortgage Loans; Final Rule." 78 Fed. Reg. (13 Feb. 2013), 10368-10447, Page 10370

[37] CFPB. "Final list of rural and underserved counties for use in 2014." July 2, 2013 http://www.consumerfinance.gov/blog/final-list-of-rural-and-underserved-counties-for-use-in-2014

[38] 78 FR 10444 (Feb. 13, 2013)

[39] 78 FR 10404 (Feb. 13, 2013)

[40] 78 FR 10405 (Feb. 13, 2013)

[41] 78 FR 10402 (Feb. 13, 2013)

[42] CFPB. "CFPB Takes Action against Nonbank and Bank for Inaccurate Mortgage Loan Reporting." 9 Oct. 2013. http://www.consumerfinance.gov/newsroom/cfpb-takes-action-against-nonbank-and-bank-for-inaccurate-mortgage-loan-reporting

[43] Federal Trade Commission. http://edocket.access.gpo.gov/cfr_2008/janqtrpdf/16cfr681.3.pdf

[44] American Bar Association. "Task Force on the Model Definition of the Practice of Law: State Action." http://www.americanbar.org/content/dam/aba/migrated/cpr/model-def/model_def_statutes.authcheckdam.pdf

[45] Department of Treasury. Final Rule. 77 Fed. Reg. 8150. 6 Feb. 2012

[46] Federal Bureau of Investigation. "Offense Definitions." http://www.fbi.gov/about-us/cjis/ucr/crime-in-the-u.s/2010/crime-in-the-u.s.-2010/offense-definitions

[47] Federal Bureau of Investigation. "Financial Crimes Report to the Public" May 2005. http://www.fbi.gov/publications/financial/fcs_report052005/fcs_report052005.htm

[48] Kolve, Ivo. Mortgage-Backed Securities. Financial Policy Forum, Derivatives Study Center. 29 July 2004. Page 2. http://www.financialpolicy.org/fpfprimermbs.htm

[49] "Understanding…Mortgage Securitization." Private-label Mortgage Backed Securities. http://securitization.weebly.com/private-label-mbs.html

[50] Bahena, Amanda. "What Role Did Credit Rating Agencies (CRAs) Play in the Financial Crisis?" University of Colorado. http://www.colorado.edu/AmStudies/lewis/ecology/rolecreditagencies.pdf

[51] San Jose State University Department of Economics. "The Nature and Origin of the Subprime Mortgage Crisis." http://www.sjsu.edu/faculty/watkins/subprime.htm

[52] McCoy Patricia, "Hearing on 'Securitization of Assets: Problems and Solutions.'" Presented to Subcommittee on Securities, Insurance, and Investment of the U.S. Committee on Banking, Housing, and Urban Affairs. 7 Oct. 2009. http://banking.senate.gov/public/index.cfm?FuseAction=Files.View&FileStore_id=02242b1f-27e9-4aa0-ae0f-3a1c0eacc7e6

[53] Ibid.

[54] Ibid.

[55] Ibid.

[56] Johnson, Barbara. "Role of the Credit Rating Agencies in the Subprime Mortgage Crisis," page 20. Alaska Pacific University. 9 Dec. 2008.

[57] O'Hara, Neil. "The Transparency Myth, page 22." American Securitization Forum. http://www.americansecuritization.com/uploadedFiles/Transparency%20(2).pdf

[58] Pressman, Aaron. "Fannie Mae and Freddie Mac Were Victims, Not Culprits." Bloomberg Businessweek. 28 Sept. 2008. http://www.businessweek.com/investing/insights/blog/archives/2008/09/fannie_mae_and.html

[59] Timiraos, Nick. "DeMarco: No Mortgage Limit Declines Before Spring 2014." The Wall Street Journal. 24 Oct. 2013. http://blogs.wsj.com/developments/2013/10/24/demarco-no-mortgage-limit-declines-before-spring-2014

[60] Hoak, Amy. "Lower 'Jumbo Limits' Coming." The Wall Street Journal. 17 July 2010. http://online.wsj.com/article/SB10001424052702304203304576450511770761504.html

[61] NCRC. "Challenging the Use of Discriminatory Credit Overlays." April 2012. http://www.ncrc.org/conference/wp-content/uploads/2012/04/NCRC_2012Conf_Program_Final_041212.pdf

[62] Taylor, John. "The FHA Reform Act of 2010: HUD's Proposals Strike Balance Between Access and Safety and Soundness." National Community Reinvestment Coalition. 11 March 2010. Page 4.

[63] Galante, Carol. "The Facts on FHA." The Huddle: U.S. Department of Housing and Urban Development's Official Blog. 27 March 2012.

[64] HUD Clips. "Mortgagee Letters from the FHA." http://portal.hud.gov/hudportal/HUD?src=/program_offices/administration/hudclips/letters/mortgagee

[65] HUD.Gov. "The Federal Housing Administration." http://www.hud.gov/offices/hsg/fhahistory.cfm

[66] HUD. "Potential Changes to FHA Single-Family Loan Limits Beginning October 1, 2011" 26 May 2011. Page 1. http://portal.hud.gov/hudportal/documents/huddoc?id=loanlimit1.pdf

[67] Taylor, John. "The FHA Reform Act of 2010: HUD's Proposals Strike Balance Between Access and Safety and Soundness, Testimony Before the U.S. House of Representatives." National Community Reinvestment Coalition." 11 March 2010. Page 3.

[68] Carpenter, Sean. "Good News from FHA." Ezine Articles. 12 March 2012. http://ezinearticles.com/?expert=Sean_M_Carpenter

[69] ElBoghdady, Dina. "FHA's Reserve Fund Hits 7-Year Low." The Washington Post. 10 Nov. 2009. http://www.washingtonpost.com/wp-dyn/content/article/2009/11/09/AR2009110903180.html

[70] Id., at 21.

[71] 75 Fed. Reg. 135. 15 July 2010. Page 41219

[72] Harney, Kenneth. "Seller Concession Rules for FHA Mortgages to be Changed." Los Angeles Times. 30 May 2010. http://articles.latimes.com/2010/may/30/business/la-fi-harney-20100530

[73] Cornett, Brandon. "FHA Mortgage Insurance in 2014: Upfront and Annual MIP Rates & Cancellation Policy." Home Buying Institute. 6 Dec. 2013. http://www.homebuyinginstitute.com/news/fha-mip-rates-and -rules-515?

[74] HUD. "Mortgagee Letter 13-04." 31 Jan. 2013.

[75] HUD. "Mortgagee Letter 13-04." 31 Jan. 2013.

[76] HUD. "Mortgagee Letter 13-05." 31 Jan. 2013.

[77] The Denver Post. "House votes to limit reverse mortgage initial draw." 12 June 2013. http://www.denverpost.com/business/ci_23443489/house-gives-fha-flexibility-reverse-mortgages

[78] HUD. Mortgagee Letter 2014-12. "Home Equity Conversion Mortgage (HECM) Program: New Principal Limit Factors." 27 June, 2014. Page 1. http://portal.hud.gov/hudportal/documents/huddoc?id=14-12ml.pdf

[79] VA. "Chapter 8: Borrower Fees and Charges and the VA Funding Fee." VA Pamphlet 26-7, Revised. Page 21. Accessed 8 July 2014. http://www.benefits.va.gov/WARMS/docs/admin26/handbook?ChapterLendersHandbookChapter8.pdf

[80] GAO. "Rural Housing: Changing the Definition of Rural Could Improve Eligibility Determinations: Report to Subcommittee on Housing and Community Opportunity." Dec. 2004. Page 10.

[81] State Guidance on Nontraditional Mortgage Product Risks, Page 5.

[82] CFPB. "High-Cost Mortgage and Homeownership Counseling Amendments." http://www. regulations.gov/#!documentDetail;D=CFPB-2012-0029-0016

[83] Asset Securitization, Comptroller's Handbook. Comptroller of the Currency Administrator of National Banks. Nov 1997. pg 2.

[84] Slack, Megan. "Consumer Financial Protection Bureau 101: Why We Need a Consumer Watchdog." The White House Blog. 4 Jan. 2012. http://www.whitehouse.gov/blog/2012/01/04/ consumer-financial-protection-bureau-101-why-we-need-consumer-watchdog

[85] Wisenberg, Solomon. "How to Avoid Going to Jail under 18 USC Section 1001 for Lying to Government Agents." FindLaw. Copyright 2004. http://library.findlaw.com/2004/ May/11/147945.html

[86] Mortgage Bankers Association. FBI Mortgage Fraud Warning." Copyright 2008.

[87] Freddie Mac. "Mortgage Fraud." http://www.freddiemac.com/singlefamily/preventfraud

[88] Black's Law Dictionary Free Online 2nd Edition. http://thelawdictionary.org/leasehold

[89] Id. http://thelawdictionary.org/fee-simple/

[90] Data Entry Instructions for Subordinate Financing in Desktop Underwriter. https://www. efanniemae.com/lc/technology/du/quicksteps/pdf/dusubfin.pdf

[91] Consumer Financial Protection Bureau. Consumer Handbook on Adjustable-Rate Mortgages. http://files.consumerfinance.gov/f/201401_cfpb_booklet_charm.pdf

[92] 78 FR 35438 (June 12, 2013)

[93] 78 FR 35439 (June 12, 2013)

[94] http://files.consumerfinance.gov/f/201308_cfpb_atr-qm-implementation-guide_final.pdf

[95] HUD. Mortgagee Letter 2013-04.

[96] HUD. Mortgagee Letter 2013-43.

[97] USDA. "Underwriting Guidelines (Applicant and Income Requirements)." http://www. rurdev.usda.gov/CA/pdf%20files%20and%20documents/GRH%20UNDERWRITING%20 GUIDEL.pdf

[98] HUD. "RESPA – Real Estate Settlement Procedures Act." March 2008. http://www.hud.gov/ offices/hsg/sfh/res/respa_hm.cfm

[99] Federal Register, Vol. 75, No. 185. September 24, 2010.

[100] CFPB. "2013 Loan Originator Rule." 7 June 2013, p. 27. http://files.consumerfinance. gov/f/201306_cfpb_compliance-guide_loan-originator-compensation-rule.pdf

[101] FTC Consumer Alert. "Deceptive Mortgage Ads: What They Say; What They Leave Out." September 2007. http://www.ftc.gov/bcp/edu/pubs/consumer/alerts/alt023.shtm

[102] Official Interpretations to 12 C.F.R. §1026.42(d)(1)(ii)(1))

[103] "Interim Final Rule; Request for Public Comment." Board of Governors of the Federal Reserve. 75 Fed. Reg. 208 (28 Oct. 2010): 66554-66587, Page 66564.

[104] Federal Bureau of Investigation. "Offense Definitions." http://www.fbi.gov/about-us/cjis/ucr/crime-in-the-u.s/2010/crime-in-the-u.s.-2010/offense-definitions

[105] "Conclusions of the Financial Crisis Inquiry Commission." 27 Jan. 2011. Page xxii. http://fcic-static.law.stanford.edu/cdn_media/fcic-reports/fcic_final_report_conclusions.pdf

[106] IRS. "Examples of Money Laundering Investigations-Fiscal Year 2013. 4 Nov. 2013. http://www.irs.gov/uac/Examples-of-Money-Laundering-Investigations-Fiscal-Year-2013 and Morse, Janice. "Mortgage Scheme Sends West Chester Woman to Prison." West Chester Buzz. 26 June 2013. http://westchesterbuzz.com/2013/06/26/mortgage-scheme-sends-west-chester-woman-to-prison

[107] CFPB. "CFPB Bulletin 2012-3." 13 Apr. 2012. Page 2. http://files.consumerfinance.gov/f/201204_cfpb_bulletin_service-providers.pdf

[108] Ibid.

[109] Id. at 3

[110] Mortgage Fraud Overview Presentation. Fannie Mae. May 2007.

[111] Zibel, Alan. "Government Plans Takeover of Fannie Mae, Freddie Mac." The Huffington Post. 26 March 2009. http://www.huffingtonpost.com/2008/09/05/government-nears-deal-to_n_124405.html

[112] CAMP Standards of Professional Practice. Article 1 Honesty and Integrity. 2010. http://www.ca-amp.org/about/standards-ethics.htm

Glossary

Page left intentionally blank.

A

ABANDONMENT

The voluntary surrender of property, owned or leased. Abandonment does not relieve obligations associated with ownership or lease.

ABATEMENT

A reduction in amount or intensity. Usually relates to a decrease in taxes or to a decrease in continuing payments such as rent.

ABSOLUTE TITLE

A title that is clear of any liens, judgments, or other encumbrances.

ABSTRACT

See **Title Abstract**.

ABSTRACT OF TITLE

See **Title Abstract**.

ABSTRACT UPDATE

Making current an existing Title Abstract.

ABSTRACTOR

A professional in the title industry (sometimes an attorney) who conducts a title search and produces an abstract

ACCELERATION CLAUSE

A clause in a mortgage or deed of trust that allows the lender to demand the immediate repayment of the balance of a loan under conditions such as default by the borrower.

ACKNOWLEDGEMENT

A declaration by a person who has signed a document that such signature is a voluntary act, made before a duly authorized person.

ACQUISITION COST

A term used in FHA loans meaning the total cost to close the loan.

ACT OF GOD

An unpreventable destructive occurrence of the natural world.

ADDENDUM

An addition or supplement to a contract.

ADJUSTABLE-RATE MORTGAGE (ARM)

A mortgage in which the interest rate is adjusted periodically based on a pre-selected margin, index and adjustment interval.
aka: Variable-Rate Mortgage

ADJUSTED BASIS

The cost of a property plus the value of any capital expenditures for improvements to the property, minus any depreciation taken.

ADJUSTMENT DATE

The date that the interest rate may change on an ARM.

ADJUSTMENT INTERVAL

The period elapsing between adjustment dates for an ARM. The interval can apply to interest or payment adjustments and is typically one, three or five years.
aka: Adjustment Period, Change Frequency

ADJUSTMENTS (IN APPRAISAL)

The dollar value added or subtracted from the sale price of a comparable property used to provide an indication of value of the subject property.

ADVANCE

A partial disbursement of funds under a note, usually made as part of a construction loan or a reverse mortgage.

AFFORDABILITY ANALYSIS

An analysis of a buyer's ability to afford the purchase of a home. Reviews income, liabilities, and available funds, and considers the type of mortgage planned, the area where a home is located, and the closing costs that are likely to be incurred.

AGENCY

A legal relationship created by law or contract in which the agent performs certain acts on behalf of the principal.

AMORTIZATION

Periodic payments on a loan requiring payment of enough principal and interest to ensure complete repayment of the loan by the end of the loan term.

AMORTIZATION SCHEDULE

A table that shows the portion of each payment that will be applied to interest and principal, and the balance remaining after the payment has been applied.

AMORTIZATION TERM

The length of time required to amortize the mortgage loan, expressed as a number of months.

ANNUAL PERCENTAGE RATE (APR)

A uniform measurement of the cost of a loan, including interest and financed costs of closing, expressed as a yearly percentage rate.

ANNUITY

Payments made at specified intervals, such as with insurance contracts or certain types of investments.

APPLICATION

The method by which a consumer formally applies to obtain a mortgage loan. The actual application form is the Uniform Residential Loan Application (URLA), or Form 1003.

APPLICATION FEE

Fee charged by a mortgage broker for processing a mortgage loan application. Might be a flat fee or a percentage of the loan amount.

APPRAISAL

An estimate of the fair market value of a real or personal property.

APPRAISED VALUE

An opinion of a property's fair market value based on an appraiser's knowledge, experience, and an analysis of the property utilizing recent comparable sales and market conditions.

APPRAISER

One qualified through state licensing procedures to estimate the value of real property.

APPRECIATION

The increase in the value of a property that has occurred over time.

ARM'S LENGTH TRANSACTION

A transaction among parties, each of whom acts in his or her best interest.

ASSESSMENT

A local tax levied against a property for a specific purpose, such as a sewer or street lights.

ASSET

Things that a person owns, that can be converted to cash such as property, investments, savings, etc.

ASSIGNMENT

The transfer of the rights and obligations under a mortgage from one person to another.

ASSUMABILITY CLAUSE

A provision in mortgage that allows transfer of the mortgage from one party to another.

ASSUMABLE MORTGAGE

A mortgage that a seller can transfer to a new buyer, with the buyer taking over the payments on the seller's existing mortgage. Lenders may require a credit review of the new borrower and payment of a fee for the assumption. If a mortgage contains a due-on-sale clause, the mortgage is not assumable by a new buyer.

ASSUMPTION FEE

The fee paid to a lender (usually by the purchaser of real property) when an assumption takes place.

ATTACHMENT

A legal seizure of property to force payment of a debt. An attachment creates a lien on real property.

ATTEST

To witness by observation and signature.

ATTORNEY'S OPINION OF TITLE

A written statement by an attorney made after examining public records and/or abstracts of title that, in his or her judgment, the title to a particular property is free of unsettled claims and liens.

B

BACK END RATIO
See **Debt Ratio**.

BAD TITLE
A condition where complete real estate ownership is impaired by unsettled claims and liens.
aka: Cloud on Title

BALANCE
The amount due, including principal, unpaid interest, and any fees or penalties owed.

BALLOON MORTGAGE
A mortgage with periodic payments including a final payment that is considerably larger than the preceding payments.

BALLOON PAYMENT
The final lump sum paid at the maturity date of a balloon mortgage.

BANKRUPTCY
The financial inability to pay one's debts when due and the debtor's application to the courts for relief through the restructuring or erasing of the debt.

BASIS POINT
One 100th of 1% of the loan amount (0.0001 x Loan Amount = 1 basis point)

BENEFICIARY
The person who receives or is to receive the benefits from a specific action or act.

BILL OF SALE
A written instrument given to pass Title of personal property from the seller to the buyer.

BIWEEKLY PAYMENT MORTGAGE
A plan to reduce the debt every two weeks instead of making monthly payments. The result is that the equivalent of one additional monthly payment is made each year.

BLANKET MORTGAGE
A mortgage that uses at least two pieces of real estate for security.

BONA FIDE
In good faith, without fraud.

BORROWER (MORTGAGOR)
One who applies for and receives a loan in the form of a mortgage.

BORROWER'S CREDITS
Credits at closing that are subtracted from the final closing costs. These might include fees or points paid by the seller, a portion of the yield spread premium, or fees paid by the borrower prior to closing, such as the appraisal fee.

BRIDGE LOAN
A short-term loan collateralized by the borrower's present home and used to close on a new house before the present home is sold.
aka: Swing Loan

BUY-DOWN
See **Permanent Buy-down** and **Temporary Buy-down**.

C

CAPS (FOR ARMS)
Consumer protections which limit the amount the interest rate or payment on an ARM may change. There are four caps in common use.

Initial Rate Cap
A limit on the amount that the interest rate can increase during the first adjustment period for an ARM.

Periodic Rate Cap
A limit on the amount that the interest rate can change during any adjustment periods.

Lifetime Rate Cap
A limit on the amount that an interest rate can change over the life of an ARM.
aka: Rate Ceiling

Payment Cap
A limit on the amount that the payment can change during one adjustment period on an ARM. Payment caps can result in negative amortization

CASH FLOW
The amount of cash derived from an income-producing property over a period of time.

CEILING
See **Caps**.

CERTIFICATE OF ELIGIBILITY
The document that qualified veterans must obtain from the VA in order to apply for a VA guaranteed home loan.

CERTIFICATE OF REASONABLE VALUE (CRV)
A statement issued by the VA showing the property's current market value based on a VA-approved appraisal.

CERTIFICATE OF TITLE
A statement provided by an abstract company, title company, or attorney stating that the title of real estate is legally held by the current owner.

CERTIFICATE OF VETERAN STATUS
A document available through the VA that veterans use to establish eligibility for certain FHA loans.

CHANGE FREQUENCY
See **Adjustment Interval**.

CHATTEL
Personal property. Anything owned that is not real property.

CLEAR TITLE

Defined with some differences under the Marketable Record Title laws of different states, a clear title is generally a title clear of liens, judgments, and other encumbrances.

CLOSING

A meeting between the buyer, seller and lender or their agents where real estate funds for its purchase legally change hands.
aka: Settlement

CLOSING COSTS

Expenses over and above the price of the property incurred by buyers and sellers when transferring ownership of a property. Closing costs normally include an origination fee, property taxes, charges for title insurance and escrow costs, appraisal fees, etc. Closing costs will vary according to the area of the country and the lenders used.

CLOUD ON TITLE

An outstanding claim or encumbrance on the title.

CODE OF ETHICS

A statement of principles concerning the behavior of those who subscribe to the code.

COFI

The 11th District Cost of Funds Index. One type of index used to determine interest rates for adjustable rate mortgages.

COLLATERAL

Property pledged as security for a debt.

COMBINED LOAN TO VALUE RATIO

A comparison, expressed as a percentage, of the combined cost of all mortgages on a home and the value of the home used to secure the loans.

COMMITMENT

A pledge or promise, a firm agreement.

CONDEMNATION

A non-judicial determination that a property is unfit to occupy made by a municipal building or health inspector.
or
An exercise of eminent domain to take ownership of a private property for public use.

CONSTRUCTION LOAN

An interim loan used to pay for the construction of buildings or homes. These are usually designed to provide periodic disbursements to the builder as he or she progresses.

CONFORMING LOAN

A loan that meets the lending limits and other criteria established by Fannie Mae or Freddie Mac.

CONSUMER REPORTING AGENCY (CRA)

An organization that prepares reports used by lenders to determine an applicant's credit history.

CONTRACT OF SALE OR CONTRACT FOR DEED

Contract between a purchaser and a seller of real estate to convey title after certain conditions have been met.

CONVENTIONAL LOAN

A mortgage not insured by the FHA or guaranteed by the VA.

CONVERSION CLAUSE

A provision in an ARM allowing the loan to be converted to a fixed-rate at some point during the loan term.

CONVEYANCE

The transfer of the Title of real estate from one to another.

COST OF FUNDS INDEX (COFI)

The rate charged to banks for borrowing money from a Federal Reserve Bank. Each district office sets its own rate. The 11th District COFI is the rate most often used as an index for an ARM.

COVENANT

Promise written into Deeds and other instruments agreeing to performance or non-performance of certain acts or preventing certain uses of the property.

CREDIT LIFE INSURANCE

A declining term life insurance policy used to insure repayment of a loan should the borrower die.

CREDIT RATING

See **Credit Risk Score**.

CREDIT REPORT

A report documenting the credit history and current status of a borrower's credit standing.

CREDIT REPOSITORY

An organization that gathers, records, updates, and stores financial and public records information about the payment records of individuals who are being considered for credit.

CREDIT RISK SCORE

A statistical summary of the information contained in a consumer's credit report. With this form of credit scoring, a numerical value is assigned to various pieces of information in the credit report, then a summary score is produced.

CREDITOR

A person or entity to whom an obligation is owed, such as a loan. See also **Lender**.

D

DEBT-TO-INCOME RATIO

The relationship, expressed as a percentage, between a borrower's monthly obligations on long-term debts and his or her gross monthly income.

DEBTOR

A person who owes a debt to a creditor or lender. See also **Borrower**.

DEED

A written instrument properly signed and delivered that conveys Title to real property.

DEED OF TRUST

In many states, a document used in place of a mortgage to secure the payment of a note.

DEFAULT

Failure to meet legal obligations in a contract, specifically, failure to make the monthly payments on a mortgage.

DEFERRED INTEREST

When a mortgage is written with a monthly payment that is less than required to satisfy the note rate, the unpaid interest is deferred by adding it to the loan balance.
See **Negative Amortization**.

DEFERRED PAYMENT LOAN (DPL)

A reverse mortgage that provides a lump sum used to repair or improve a house.

DELINQUENT

Past due.

DELINQUENCY

The state of having failed to make payments on time. This can lead to foreclosure.

DEPARTMENT OF HOUSING AND URBAN DEVELOPMENT (HUD)

The federal agency responsible for housing programs in the United States. Also has regulatory authority for a number of housing related federal statutes.

DEPARTMENT OF VETERANS AFFAIRS (VA)

An independent agency of the federal government which oversees programs and services for veterans. The VA guarantees long-term, low or no-down payment mortgages to eligible veterans.

DEPOSIT

Funds that are given in advance to show committed interest in the purchase of a property. (see also, **Earnest Money**)

DEPRECIATION

A decrease in the value of a property over time.

DISCOUNT POINT

Fee paid to a lender at closing and used to prepay a portion of the interest on the loan. Discount points are charged so that the note rate can be lower than the prevailing market rate.

DONOR

One who gives. In mortgage lending the term refers to those who make gifts of money for use in the purchase of a home, with no expectation of reimbursement.

DOWN PAYMENT

Money paid towards the purchase price of a home that is not financed.

DRY SETTLEMENT

A loan settlement in which loan funds are not made available on the same day as closing. Dry settlement is prohibited in many states unless the loan is subject to the right of rescission.

DUE-ON-DEMAND CLAUSE

A provision of a mortgage or deed of trust that allows a lender to demand immediate payment of the balance of the loan if very specific criteria relating to fraud and misrepresentation are met.

DUE-ON-SALE-CLAUSE

A provision in a mortgage or deed of trust that allows the lender to demand immediate payment of the balance of the mortgage if the mortgage holder sells the home.

E

EARNEST MONEY

Money paid by a buyer to a seller at the time of entering a contract to indicate intent and ability of the buyer to carry out the contract.

EASEMENT

The right to use part of another person's property. A common example would be a right of way (the right of one person to access their own property by traveling through someone else's property).

EMINENT DOMAIN

The right of a government or municipality to acquire private property for public use, even if the property owner objects.

ENCUMBRANCE

A claim against real property such as a lien, judgment, security interest, unpaid taxes, or an easement which may affect the ability to transfer ownership of the property.

ENTITLEMENT

The loan amount that the VA guarantees when extending a loan to a veteran

EQUAL CREDIT OPPORTUNITY ACT (ECOA)

A federal law that requires lenders to make credit available without discrimination on the basis of race, color, religion, national origin, age, sex, marital status or receipt of income from public assistance programs.

EQUITY

The difference between the fair market value of a property and the current balances of any liens against the property.
aka: Home Equity

ESCROW ACCOUNT

An account held by the lender into which the homebuyer deposits money for taxes and/or insurance payments. Escrow accounts may also hold other funds related to a real estate purchase such as earnest money.

ESCROW DISBURSEMENTS

The use of escrow funds to pay real estate taxes, hazard insurance, mortgage insurance, and other expenses as they become due.

ESCROW PAYMENT
The part of a mortgagor's monthly payment that is held by the loan servicer to pay for taxes, hazard insurance, mortgage insurance, and other expenses related to the loan.

EXECUTED CONTRACT
A contract whose terms have been completely fulfilled.

F

FAIR CREDIT REPORTING ACT (FCRA)
Federal legislation enacted in 1970 aimed at ensuring information used by lending institutions is accurate.

FAIR AND ACCURATE CREDIT TRANSACTIONS ACT (FACTA)
Federal legislation enacted in 2003 that amended FCRA. It affected the responsibilities of organizations that access and post information to consumer credit reports.

FANNIE MAE
See **Federal National Mortgage Association**.

FEDERAL HOME LOAN MORTGAGE CORPORATION (FREDDIE MAC)
A government sponsored enterprise created by Congress that purchases conforming mortgage loans and resells them in the secondary market.

FEDERAL HOUSING ADMINISTRATION (FHA)
A division of the Department of Housing and Urban Development. Its main activity is the insuring of residential mortgage loans made by private lenders.

FEDERAL NATIONAL MORTGAGE ASSOCIATION (FANNIE MAE)
A government sponsored enterprise created by Congress that purchases conforming mortgage loans as well as those insured by the FHA, and resells them in the secondary market.

FEDERAL TRADE COMMISSION (FTC)
Federal agency with responsibilities that include enforcing the compliance of mortgage brokers with federal lending laws.

FEE SIMPLE
The most basic form of real estate property rights. Means that a buyer acquires a property it includes the land and all improvements to the land.

FEE TRIGGERS
The threshold set for fees charged on a mortgage loan expressed either as a percentage of the loan amount or a set dollar amount. Exceeding the threshold triggers federal and state high-cost loan restrictions.

FEES
Any kind of money paid in conjunction with a mortgage loan, other than the actual loan amount and interest. Might include third party fees such as those for credit reports or appraisals, or origination/broker fees. Fees affect the total cost of credit when obtaining a loan.

FHA LOAN
A loan insured by the Federal Housing Administration.

FHA MORTGAGE INSURANCE
A fee paid at closing and/or with each monthly payment to insure an FHA loan.

FICO SCORE
The credit score obtained from the use of software developed by Fair, Isaac and Company. Although each major CRA ultimately developed its own formula for credit scoring, the term "FICO Score" is widely used today to refer to any credit score.

FINANCE CHARGE
Any kind of fees or charges associated with obtaining credit. Finance charges can include many items, including loan fees, miscellaneous fees, per diem interest, escrows for mortgage insurance, etc.

FIRM COMMITMENT
A promise by FHA to insure a mortgage loan for a specified property and borrower. A promise from a lender to make a mortgage loan.

FIRST MORTGAGE
The oldest lien against a property, or the lien with first priority.

FIXED INSTALLMENT
The monthly payment due on a mortgage loan, including payment of both principal and interest.

FIXED-RATE MORTGAGE
A mortgage with an interest rate that will remain the same for the entire term of the mortgage.

FLOAT
The opposite of locking an interest rate. Following formal application and identification of a loan program, a mortgage loan applicant may elect to wait to lock an interest rate (see Rate Lock) in anticipation of interest rates falling.

FLOOD INSURANCE
Insurance that compensates for physical property damage resulting from flooding. It is required for properties located in federally designated flood zones.

FORBEARANCE
When a lender delays foreclosure action in order to allow a borrower to make good on overdue payments.

FORECLOSURE
A legal process by which the lender forces a sale of a mortgaged property because the borrower has not met the repayment terms of the mortgage.

FRAUD
An intentional misrepresentation or concealment of a fact that deceives another, causing him/her to act upon the false representation or concealment to his/her detriment.

FREDDIE MAC
See **Federal Home Loan Mortgage Corporation**.

FSBO
> For **Sale By Owner**.

FULL DISCLOSURE
> A requirement to reveal all information pertinent to a transaction.

FULLY AMORTIZED ARM
> An ARM with a monthly payment that is sufficient to amortize the remaining balance, at the interest accrual rate, over the amortization term.

FULLY INDEXED RATE
> In an ARM, the interest rate indicated by adding the current index value and the margin.

FUNDING
> Funds provided by the lender at settlement. The act of disbursing the cash for a loan.

G

GEM
> See **Growing Equity Mortgage**.

GINNIE MAE
> See **Government National Mortgage Association**.

GOOD FAITH ESTIMATE
> An estimate of closing costs, made in compliance with RESPA requirements, that must be given to mortgage applicants within three days after loan application is complete.

GOVERNMENT NATIONAL MORTGAGE ASSOCIATION (GINNIE MAE)
> A government sponsored enterprise created by Congress to guarantee securities backed by FHA, VA, and RHS loans.

GRACE PERIOD
> The period during which one party may fail to perform without being considered in default.

GRADUATED PAYMENT MORTGAGE (GPM)
> A type of flexible-payment mortgage where the payments increase for a specified period of time and then level off.

GROSS INCOME
> For qualifying purposes, the income of the borrower before taxes and expenses are deducted.

GROWING-EQUITY MORTGAGE (GEM)
> A fixed-rate mortgage that provides scheduled payment increases over an established period of time. The increased amount of the monthly payment is applied directly toward reducing the remaining balance of the mortgage.

GUARANTY
> A promise by one party to pay a debt or perform an obligation contracted by another if the original party fails to pay or perform according to a contract.

GUARANTEE MORTGAGE
A mortgage guaranteed by a third party.

H

HAZARD INSURANCE
A form of insurance that indemnifies the insured from fire, burglary, and other specified losses.
aka: Homeowners Insurance

HOME EQUITY CONVERSION MORTGAGE (HECM)
A reverse mortgage insured by the FHA.
See **Reverse Mortgage**.

HOME EQUITY LINE OF CREDIT (HELOC)
A loan secured by a mortgage, a HELOC establishes a credit line that can be drawn upon as needed until the borrower reaches the maximum credit amount allowed.

HOUSING EXPENSES-TO-INCOME RATIO
The relationship, expressed as a percentage, between a borrower's housing expenses and their gross monthly income. aka: Housing Ratio, Front End Ratio

HUD
See **Department of Housing and Urban Development**.

HUD-1 STATEMENT
A document, due on the day of closing, that provides an itemized listing of all costs associated with a real estate transaction including the fees of the lender, mortgage broker, and other settlement service providers.
aka: Settlement Statement

I

IMPOUNDS
That portion of a borrower's monthly payments held by the lender or servicer to pay for taxes, hazard insurance, mortgage insurance, lease payments, and other items as they become due.
aka: Escrows, Reserves

INDEX
A published interest rate used, when combined with a margin, as the basis upon which the note rate of ARM will adjust.

INDEXED RATE
The sum of the published index plus the margin. For example if the index were 7% and the margin 2.75%, the indexed rate would be 9.75%.

INITIAL INTEREST RATE
The interest rate of an ARM at the time of closing. This rate changes for an adjustable-rate mortgage (ARM).
aka: Start Rate, Teaser Rate

INSTALLMENT

The regular periodic payment that a borrower agrees to make to a lender.

INSURED CLOSING LETTER

A legal document provided to a lender by a title company, promising to abide by closing instructions. It protects the lender from misuse of funds by the title company.

INSURED MORTGAGE

A mortgage that is protected by the Federal Housing Administration (FHA) or by private mortgage insurance.

INTEREST

The fee charged for borrowing money.

INTEREST ACCRUAL RATE

The percentage rate at which interest accrues on the mortgage. In most cases, it is also the rate used to calculate the monthly payments.

INTEREST ONLY (I-O)

A loan program where the borrower's payments are directed only at the interest due on the loan and not the principal.

INTEREST RATE BUYDOWN PLAN

An arrangement that allows a party to deposit money to an account. That money is then released each month to reduce the mortgagor's monthly payments during the early years of a mortgage.
See Temporary Buy-down

INTEREST RATE CEILING

See **CAPS**.

INTERIM FINANCING

Short-term financing made to cover costs while waiting for the requirements of a permanent loan to be met. A construction loan is a common form of interim loan.

J

JOINT TENANCY

Two or more people holding equal ownership of a property and providing for the automatic transfer to the surviving tenant of the interest of the deceased tenant.

JUDICIAL FORECLOSURE

A foreclosure process that is initiated by the lender filing a lawsuit in a court of law.

JUMBO LOAN

A nonconforming loan that exceeds the lending limits established by Fannie Mae and Freddie Mac for conforming loans.

JUNIOR MORTGAGE

A mortgage that is subordinate to the claims or lien positions of other mortgages recorded against a property.

L

LATE CHARGE

The penalty a borrower must pay when a payment is made a stated number of days after the due date.

LEASE-PURCHASE MORTGAGE LOAN

An alternative financing option that allows low and moderate-income home buyers to lease a home with an option to buy. Each month's rent payment consists of principal, interest, taxes and insurance (PITI) payments on the first mortgage plus an extra amount that accumulates in a savings account for a down payment.

LEASEHOLD

A form of real estate property rights. When a buyer acquires leasehold property, they purchase the improvements but lease the land for a certain term. At the end of the term they may or may not have the opportunity to purchase the land or renew the lease.

LENDER

An entity that makes funds available for others to borrow. See also **Creditor**.

LENDER'S TITLE INSURANCE

Insurance that protects against lender loss from title defects or liens that should have been cleared up prior to issuance of a title policy.

LIABILITIES

A person's financial obligations. Liabilities include long-term and short-term debt.

LIABILITY INSURANCE

Part of a homeowner's insurance policy that covers bodily injury or property damage occurring on the homeowner's property and that are a result of negligence.

LIBOR

The London Interbank Offered Rate. One type of index used to determine interest rates for adjustable rate mortgages.

LIEN

A claim upon a piece of property for the payment or satisfaction of a debt or obligation.

LIFETIME CAP

See **CAPS**.

LOAN

A sum of borrowed money (principal), generally repaid with interest.

LOAN OFFICER

Defined with specific differences under the mortgage lending laws of each state, a loan officer is generally an individual that arranges funding or negotiates mortgage loans for a potential borrower. A loan officer may work under the supervision of a mortgage broker, mortgage banker or lender.

LOAN ORIGINATOR

Defined with specific differences under the mortgage lending laws of each state, a loan originator is generally an individual that arranges funding or negotiates mortgage loans for a potential borrower. See also Loan Officer. The term may also be applied generally to any individual or entity that initiates the process for obtaining a mortgage loan.

LOAN-TO-VALUE RATIO (LTV)

The relationship between the amount of the mortgage loan and the appraised value of the property or purchase price, whichever is lower, expressed as a percentage.

LOCK

See **Rate Lock**.

LUMP SUM

A single disbursement of the total amount due.

M

MANDATORY ARBITRATION AGREEMENT

A provision in a contract that requires all parties to submit to arbitration to resolve disputes instead of seeking action in the courts.

MARGIN

The amount a lender adds to the index on an ARM to establish the adjusted interest rate.

MATURITY

The date on which the principal balance of a loan becomes due and payable.

MERGED CREDIT REPORT

A consumer credit report which contains information from two or more of the three credit repositories. A tri-merge report contains all three.

MORTGAGE INSURANCE (MI)

Insurance that indemnifies the lender against default by the borrower. MI is often required when the LTV exceeds 80%.

MORTGAGE INSURANCE PREMIUM (MIP)

The fee paid by borrowers for mortgage insurance on an FHA loan.

MONTHLY FIXED INSTALLMENT

That portion of the total monthly payment applied toward principal and interest.

MORTGAGE

A legal document that pledges a property to the lender as security for payment of a debt.

MORTGAGE BANKER

Defined with specific differences under the mortgage lending laws of each state, a mortgage banker is generally an individual or entity that makes and funds mortgages, services mortgages, and sells mortgages in the secondary market.

MORTGAGE BROKER

Defined with specific differences under the mortgage lending laws of each state, a mortgage broker is generally an individual or entity that arranges funding or negotiates mortgage loans for a potential borrower, and charges a fee for these services.

MORTGAGEE

The lender.

MORTGAGE LIFE INSURANCE

See **Credit Life Insurance**.

MORTGAGOR

The borrower.

N

NEGATIVE AMORTIZATION

An amortization method in which the monthly payments are not large enough to pay all the interest due on the loan. This unpaid interest is added to the balance of the loan.
Aka Deferred interest

NET EFFECTIVE INCOME

The borrower's gross income minus federal income tax.

NON-ASSUMPTION CLAUSE

A statement in a mortgage contract forbidding the assumption of the mortgage without approval of the lender.

NOTE

A legal document that obligates a borrower to repay a mortgage loan and which specifies the terms by which repayment will occur.

NOTE RATE

The stated interest rate on a mortgage or loan agreement.

O

OFFICE OF THRIFT SUPERVISION (OTS)

The regulatory and supervisory agency for federally chartered savings institutions. Formally known as Federal Home Loan Bank Board

ONE-YEAR ADJUSTABLE

ARM with an annual rate that changes yearly.

ORIGINATION

The process of taking and processing an application for a mortgage loan.

ORIGINATION FEE
The fee charged by a lender to make the loan; usually computed as a percentage of the face value of the loan.

OWNER FINANCING
See **Seller Carry-Back**.

OWNER'S TITLE INSURANCE
Voluntary insurance which protects a homeowner from third party rights affected on the property over the course of its past ownership, such as mechanic's liens, un-released mortgages, etc.

P

PAR RATE
The retail interest rate a borrower may receive without paying discount points.

PAYMENT CAP
See **CAPS**.

PAYMENT CHANGE DATE
The date when a new monthly payment amount takes effect on an ARM or a GPM. Generally, the payment change date occurs in the month immediately after the adjustment date.

PERMANENT BUY-DOWN
The payment of points to permanently lower the interest rate on a loan.

PERMANENT LOAN
A long term mortgage, usually of ten years or more, as opposed to a short term loan, such as a construction loan.
aka End Loan

PITI
Principal, Interest, Taxes and Insurance are the monthly housing expenses that a lender calculates in order to determine a borrower's housing expense ratio.

PLANNED UNIT DEVELOPMENT (PUD)
A type of residential development or subdivision that features areas owned in common by the residents and reserved for use by some or all of the residents.

PLEDGED ACCOUNT MORTGAGE (PAM)
Money placed in a pledged savings account, plus earned interest, is gradually used to reduce mortgage payments.

POINT
A fee equal to 1% of the loan amount.
(0.01 x Loan Amount = 1 point)

POWER OF ATTORNEY

A legal document authorizing one person to act on behalf of another.

PRE-APPROVAL

Lender's approval to make a loan based on verification of a loan applicant's income and examination of credit history. Pre-approval does not include a commitment by the lender to a particular interest rate or lending terms.

PRE-QUALIFICATION

Examination of information that a loan applicant has provided about his/her income and financial obligations to estimate how much money the loan applicant might be eligible to borrow.

PREPAID EXPENSES

Funds collected at closing that are necessary to create an escrow account or to adjust the seller's existing escrow account. Can include taxes, hazard insurance, private mortgage insurance and special assessments. aka: prepaids

PREPAYMENT

A payment that the borrower makes in advance of the due date. A prepayment may be a "partial prepayment" or a "prepayment in full."

PREPAYMENT PENALTY

Fees charged for an early repayment of debt. Prepayment penalties are subject to laws that restrict the amount of the penalty and that limit the imposition of prepayment penalties to the early years of a loan.

PRIME LOANS

Loans made to borrowers who have good credit scores, stable income histories, down payments, and low debt ratios.

PRIMARY MORTGAGE MARKET

Retail lenders, such as banks, savings and loan associations, credit unions, and mortgage companies, who make mortgage loans directly to qualified borrowers.

PRINCIPAL

The amount borrowed, and the portion of each monthly payment that reduces the remaining balance of a mortgage.

PRIVATE MORTGAGE INSURANCE (PMI)

Mortgage insurance purchased from a private (non-governmental) insurance company. PMI is often required by a lender when the LTV on a conventional loan exceeds 80%.

PROMISSORY NOTE

A legal agreement for a borrower to repay a loan.

PURCHASE AGREEMENT

See **Sales Contract**.

PURCHASE MONEY MORTGAGE

A mortgage loan obtained to a borrower for the purchase of a residential property in which the property is the collateral for the loan.

Q

QUALIFYING RATIOS
Investor specific calculations used to determine if a borrower can qualify for a mortgage. They consist of two separate calculations: a housing expense ratio and total debt ratio.
See **Debt Ratio** and **Housing Expense Ratio**.

QUITCLAIM DEED
A deed that transfers ownership without any guarantees or warranties. It is used to remove any clouds on a title (for instance, due to un-released mortgages). Quitclaims are also commonly used in cases of mortgage fraud such as property flipping.

R

RATE CAP
Safeguards which limit the amount the interest rate on an ARM may change each adjustment period or over the life of the loan. See **CAPS**
.

RATE LOCK
A lender's guarantee that the interest rate quoted will be good for a specific number of days from the day the lock is applied.

REAL ESTATE AGENT
A person licensed to negotiate and transact the sale of real estate on behalf of the property owner.

REAL ESTATE SETTLEMENT PROCEDURES ACT (RESPA)
A federal law that uses disclosure requirements to help consumers understand the cost of settlement services and which establishes prohibited practices to protect consumers from unearned fees.

RECASTING
A process used by lenders to adjust mortgage payments. Usually used in the case of Option ARMs and other nontraditional mortgage products when negative amortization has occurred.

RECONVEYANCE
A clause in a deed of trust that conveys title to a borrower once the loan is paid in full. Concept also applies to reconveyance contracts where homeowners have the option to repurchase their home pursuant to foreclosure assistance.

RESCISSION
The cancellation of a contract. With respect to mortgage refinancing, the Truth in Lending Law gives some homeowners three days after closing to exercise their right to rescind a refinance contract.

RECORDING FEES
Fees charged by a local recorder's office for recording a mortgage or deed of trust, thereby making it part of the public record.

REFINANCE

Obtaining a new mortgage loan on a property already owned.

REGULATION Z

The regulations issued under the Truth-in-Lending Act that set forth the specific requirements that a lender must follow in order to comply with the Truth-In-Lending law.

REVERSE MORTGAGE

A form of mortgage in which the lender makes scheduled periodic payments to the borrower using the borrower's equity in the home as security for the loan with repayment deferred until the occurrence of certain events such as death or the selling of the home.

REVOLVING DEBT

A type of credit arrangement in which a consumer is pre-approved for a line of credit and they may make purchases against that credit. Credit cards are a common form of revolving credit.

RIGHT OF FIRST REFUSAL

A clause in a property lease giving the tenant the opportunity, before anyone else, to purchase the property, in the event of a sale.

RULE OF 78

A method of determining an interest rate refund in the event a borrower pays off a fixed rate loan prior to its maturity.

S

SALES CONTRACT

A legally binding agreement between a buyer and seller detailing the terms and conditions of the sale of real estate.

SATISFACTION OF MORTGAGE

The document issued by the lender when the borrower pays the mortgage loan in full.
aka: Release of Mortgage

SECOND MORTGAGE

A mortgage recorded after, and is subordinate to, the first mortgage.

SECONDARY MORTGAGE MARKET

The financial market where private investors and government-sponsored enterprises such as Fannie Mae and Freddie Mac buy and securitize mortgages made by primary mortgage lenders. The secondary market provides primary lenders with a source of cash for making new loans.

SECURED LOAN

A loan that is secured by collateral such as property. The loan agreement contains a provision stating the lender has a claim against the property if the debt is not paid according to the terms of the agreement.

SECURITY

The real or personal property pledged as collateral for a loan.

SECURITIZATION

The process of pooling similar types of loans to create mortgage backed securities for sale in the financial markets.

SELLER CARRY-BACK

A purchase transaction, often involving an assumable mortgage, in which the party selling the property provides all or part of the financing.
aka: Owner Financing

SERVICER

An individual or entity that services a loan by performing responsibilities such as sending statements to borrowers, accepting payments, issuing late payment notices, and managing escrow accounts.

SETTLEMENT/SETTLEMENT COSTS

See **Closing** and **Closing Costs**.

STANDARD PAYMENT CALCULATION

The method used to determine the monthly payment required to repay the remaining balance of a mortgage in substantially equal installments over the remaining term of the mortgage at the current interest rate.

STATUTE

A law enacted by a legislative body. May include a law established by an Act or the rules or regulations which are used to promulgate the law.

SUBORDINATE LIEN

A lien on property that is junior, or subsequent, to another lien, or liens. In the event of foreclosure, subordinate financing does not receive priority until prior liens are paid. aka: subordinate financing, junior lien, junior financing.

SUBPRIME

Below the qualifications set for prime borrowers. Loans for borrowers who have either poor credit, an unstable income history, or high debt ratios.

SURVEY

A measurement of land, prepared by a registered land surveyor, showing the location of the land with reference to known points, its dimensions, and the location and dimensions of any structures or easements.

SWEAT EQUITY

Equity created by a purchaser performing work on a property being purchased.

T

TAX LIEN

A type of involuntary lien placed on a property title due to a homeowner's failure to pay property taxes.

TABLE FUNDING

A type of wholesale lending arrangement where mortgage brokers are permitted to originate, close and fund a loan. (See Warehouse Line of Credit).The loan is then immediately assigned to another entity. Table funding may also be used to describe the practice of funding a loan the same day it is settled (see Wet Settlement).

TEMPORARY BUY-DOWN

A financing tool used to temporarily reduce the interest rate and monthly payments on a mortgage. See **Interest Rate Buy-down**.

TENANCY BY THE ENTIRETY

An estate that exists between a husband and wife who have an equal right of possession and enjoyment during their lives, with the surviving spouse taking complete possession of the estate upon the death of the other.

TENANCY IN COMMON

An ownership of property by two or more persons each of whom has an undivided interest which passes, upon death, to his/her heirs.

THIRD-PARTY ORIGINATION

When a lender uses another party to completely or partially originate, process, underwrite, close, fund, or package the mortgages it plans to deliver to the secondary mortgage market.

TIME-PRICE DIFFERENTIAL

A method of expressing the cost of financing, it is the difference between the loan amount and the sum of the payments made over time.

TITLE

A document that gives evidence of an individual's ownership of property.

TITLE ABSTRACT

A report containing the history of the title associated with a particular property.

TITLE BINDER

Temporary title insurance expected to soon be replaced by a title insurance policy.

TITLE INSURANCE

A policy, usually issued by a title insurance company, which insures a against errors in the title search. A Buyer's Title Policy protects the homebuyer and a Lender's Title Policy protects the lender.

TITLE SEARCH

An examination of county and/or municipal records to determine the legal status of real property. Usually performed by a title company or an attorney.

TOTAL OBLIGATIONS RATIO

See **Debt Ratio**.

TREASURY RATE (T-RATE)

The current rate the U.S. Treasury is paying on securities it issues.

TRUTH-IN-LENDING ACT (TILA)

A federal law that protects consumers by requiring lenders to use uniform standards for disclosing the cost of credit and by requiring truthful advertising of credit.

U

UNDERWRITING
The process of evaluating a loan applicant's financial information and facts about the real estate used to secure a loan to determine whether a potential loan is an acceptable risk for a lender.

UNENCUMBERED PROPERTY
Real Estate with free and clear title.

UNIFORM SETTLEMENT STATEMENT
The form prescribed by RESPA for federally related mortgages that details all costs associated with the mortgage.
aka HUD-1 Uniform Settlement Statement

UNRECORDED DEED
An instrument that transfers Title from one party (grantor) to another party (grantee) without providing public notice of change in ownership.

UNSECURED LOAN
A debt that has no collateral or security.

URAR
Uniform Residential Appraisal Report

USURY
Interest charged in excess of the legal limit as established by state law.

V

VA LOAN
A long-term, low or no-down payment loan guaranteed by the Department of Veterans Affairs. Restricted to individuals qualified by military service.

VA MORTGAGE FUNDING FEE
A premium of up to 1.875% (depending on the size of the down payment) paid to the VA on a VA-backed loan.

VARIABLE-RATE MORTGAGE (VRM)
See **Adjustable-Rate Mortgage**.

VERIFICATION OF DEPOSIT (VOD)
A document signed by the borrower's financial institution verifying the status and balance of his/her financial accounts.

VERIFICATION OF EMPLOYMENT (VOE)
A document signed by the borrower's employer verifying his/her position and salary.

VOID

Having no legal force or effect; unenforceable.

W

WAIVER

The voluntary renunciation, abandonment, or surrender of some claim, right, or privilege. In mortgage refinance transactions, a borrower can waive the right of rescission in certain circumstances.

WAREHOUSE FEE

A fee charged by a lender used to offset the cost associated with holding a mortgage until it can be sold on the secondary market.

WAREHOUSE LINE OF CREDIT

A revolving line of credit used by mortgage brokers in order to fund loans.

WARRANTY DEED

A Deed that in which the grantor warrants that the title is clear and free of encumbrances.

WET SETTLEMENT

A loan settlement where the funds for the loan are disbursed the same. Wet settlement is generally required in most states for loan transactions not subject to the right of rescission.

XYZ

YIELD-SPREAD PREMIUM

The fee a lender pays to a mortgage broker for a loan with an interest rate higher than the par rate on the day the loan was locked or closed

ZONING

A legal mechanism for local governments to regulate the use of privately owned real property in order to prevent conflicting land use and promote orderly development